# British Social Attitudes
## the
## 9th report

**Social and Community Planning Research** (SCPR) is an independent, non-profit institute specialising in social surveys with its own research, interviewing, coding and computing resources. Some of SCPR's work - such as the survey reported in this book - is initiated by the institute itself and grant-funded by research councils or foundations. Other work is initiated by government departments, local authorities or quasi-government organisations to provide information on aspects of social or economic policy. SCPR also works frequently with other institutes and academics. Founded in 1969 and now one of the largest social research institutes in Britain, SCPR has a high reputation for the standard of its work in both qualitative and quantitative research. SCPR also houses the Joint Centre for Survey Methods and, with Nuffield College Oxford, the Joint Unit for the Study of Social Trends (JUSST), which is an ESRC Research Centre. SCPR is also a founding member of COMPASS (the European Consortium for Comparative Social Surveys) which carries out social research within the EC, and of the International Social Survey Programme (ISSP) which carries out cross-national studies in twenty-one countries worldwide.

## The contributors

**Steven Barnett**
Independent researcher; and Visiting Lecturer, Goldsmith's College, University of London

**Nick Bosanquet**
Professor of Health Policy, Royal Holloway and Bedford New College, University of London

**Lindsay Brook**
Research Director at SCPR and Co-director of the *British Social Attitudes* survey series

**Frances Cairncross**
Environment Editor, *The Economist*

**John Curtice**
Senior Lecturer in Politics and Director of the Social Statistics Laboratory, University of Strathclyde

**Tony Gallagher**
Lecturer in Educational Research in the School of Education, The Queen's University, Belfast

**Andrew Greeley**
Professor of Social Science, University of Chicago

**Anthony Heath**
Official Fellow at Nuffield College, Oxford

**Michael Johnston**
Professor and Chair, Department of Political Science, Colgate University, Hamilton, N.Y.

**Roger Jowell**
Director of SCPR and Co-director of the *British Social Attitudes* survey series; Visiting Professor at the London School of Economics and Political Science

**Kathleen Kiernan**
Research Director, Family Policy Studies Centre

**Dorren McMahon**
Research Officer at Nuffield College, Oxford

**Jean Martin**
Assistant Director of the Social Survey Division at Office of Population Censuses and Surveys

**Gillian Prior**
Researcher at SCPR and Co-director of the *British Social Attitudes* survey series

**Susan Saxon-Harrold**
Head of Research at the Charities Aid Foundation

**Bridget Taylor**
Formerly Researcher at SCPR and Co-director of the *British Social Attitudes* survey series; now Research Officer at Nuffield College, Oxford, with the British General Election Study

**Sharon Witherspoon**
Formerly Research Director at SCPR and Co-director of the *British Social Attitudes* survey series; now a postgraduate student at the State University of New York at Stony Brook

**Ken Young**
Professor of Politics and Vice-Principal, Queen Mary and Westfield College, University of London

# British Social Attitudes

## the
## 9th report

Edited by
Roger Jowell
Lindsay Brook
Gillian Prior
& Bridget Taylor

**Dartmouth**

SCPR
SOCIAL & COMMUNITY
PLANNING RESEARCH

Published by
Dartmouth Publishing Company Limited
Gower House
Croft Road
Aldershot
Hants GU11 3HR
England

Dartmouth Publishing Company
Old Post Road
Brookfield
Vermont 05036
USA

A CIP catalogue record for this book is available from the British Library and the US Library of Congress

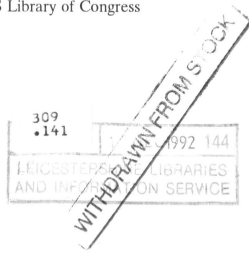

ISSN 0267 6869
ISBN 185521 328 1

Printed in Great Britain at the University Press, Cambridge

# Contents

## CHAPTER 8. COMMUNITY RELATIONS IN NORTHERN IRELAND

## CHAPTER 9. CLASS, RACE AND OPPORTUNITY

## CHAPTER 10. INTERIM REPORT: CHARITABLE GIVING

# Introduction

SCPR's *British Social Attitudes* (BSA) series is designed to monitor changing social values.  Now, with almost a decade of survey results to report, we can see some remarkable shifts in the way British people view the world and themselves.  In Chapter 6, Anthony Heath and Dorren McMahon present and discuss some of the largest changes - for instance, in attitudes to the EC, taxation and public spending, and nuclear power.  But, as they note, we must be cautious about interpreting such changes as shifts in values.  For instance, respondents these days have little enthusiasm for more privatisation.  But is this simply because there is so little left to privatise or because there has been some widespread ideological groundswell against privatisation?  We suspect the former.  Similarly, since our series began domestic rates have gone, the poll tax has come and is soon to go, the council tax looms.  We cannot, it seems, devise questions about local government finance that will survive a year, let alone five or ten.  And events abroad are even faster-moving.  Since our series began, the USSR has vanished out of all recognition, and the EC keeps on altering its shape, its structures and its role.  Questions we devised in 1983 and 1984 - which we confidently expected to survive the century - have already had to be revised or discarded.  We try to keep the camera steady, replicating most questions, but all too often our sense of control is illusory.

   That we have been able to refresh the series with new and pertinent questions, while retaining a long view, owes much to the steadfast support we have received since 1984 from the Sainsbury Family Charitable Trusts.  Their core-funding has not only enabled the series to survive, but - more important - to grow and maintain its independence.

We fiercely defend this independence, insisting on control of, and responsibility for, the contents of the questionnaires and annual books. In practice, however, we have never come to blows. All the funders of the series continue to respect and, we believe, value its autonomy, giving immensely useful advice on occasions, putting us right on others, but always from an appropriate distance.   In particular, we thank five government departments: the Employment Department and the Department of the Environment (early funders whose support was vital to the survival of the survey series); and the Home Office, the Department of Health and the Department of Social Security whose more recent support has enabled us both to continue fielding questions first asked in 1983, and to rejuvenate BSA with new ones on new topics. Funding in earlier years from the Departments of Trade and Industry and of Transport has been acknowledged elsewhere.   New government funding - from the Department of Education - is now secured from 1993 and will allow us to continue to track public attitudes towards schooling and higher education.

    In addition to its core-funding and government support, the series has always enjoyed stalwart support from the Economic and Social Research Council (ESRC), which helped to get the series off the ground and has continued to support it in a number of ways; and from the Nuffield Foundation (also seed-funders) who have not only helped to fund new modules of questions, such as on civil liberties, but support the extension of the series to Northern Ireland.  Funding has also come from Colgate University, New York, to part-fund a module on business ethics (Chapter 7); from the Charities Aid Foundation, to support a series of questions on charitable giving (see Chapter 10); and from the Health Education Authority for a questionnaire module on health and lifestyle.

    One of the series' earliest and most steadfast supporters is the Countryside Commission, whose contribution has been important in ways that neither SCPR nor they could have envisaged. In particular, the 1993 BSA survey will include the most comprehensive set of questions yet asked on environmental attitudes and awareness.   Not only will we continue tracking public concern about the changing countryside in Britain; in addition, *via* an award under the ESRC's Transport and the Environment Programme, we will look for the first time in depth at perceptions of the environmental impact of various transport policy options.   And there will also be two cross-national ventures on the environment in the 1993 questionnaire:  a module of questions carried as part of SCPR's participation in the *International Social Survey Programme* (ISSP), which will be asked in twenty-one countries during 1993.   In addition, as a result of an initiative between SCPR and social research institutes in four other EC countries (Germany, the Irish Republic, Italy and the Netherlands), a consortium (COMPASS) has been funded by the EC to extend the ISSP questionnaire module.  We will, of course, be closely involved in the design and interpretation of that study.

We are, as always, deeply indebted to the authors for their contributions, especially in view of the endless editing that their drafts often undergo. Almost fifty authors have over the years contributed chapters, and several have done so more than once. We thank all of them for their ideas and insights and for meeting unreasonable deadlines.

This report, like the last two, includes a chapter (by Tony Gallagher) which draws on data from the three *Northern Ireland Social Attitudes* (NISA) surveys carried out so far.* Already evidence is appearing of changing attitudes among people in the province, especially to some aspects of community relations there, although it is too soon to talk of firm trends. We are delighted that the NISA series is to continue, with support from all the Northern Ireland Departments, and we look forward to working again with colleagues at the Policy Planning and Research Unit (PPRU) and at The Queen's University, Belfast.

Formed in 1984 with just four members, the ISSP also continues to flourish. Representatives of research institutes in 18 countries gathered in Bergen in May 1992, for the ninth of the Programme's annual meetings, to finalise next year's questionnaire module (on environmental issues) and to discuss a future module on national identity. This report, like several of its predecessors, includes an intriguing analysis (Chapter 3) of cross-national comparisons, this time on religious beliefs and observance. We are very grateful to ISSP's archivists at the German ZentralArchiv in Cologne for their prompt and helpful responses to our queries, under the pressures of an expanding membership (next year it rises to 21).

Methodological research is still a core component of the BSA series. The Joint Unit for the Study of Social Trends (JUSST), an ESRC Research Centre linking SCPR and Nuffield College Oxford, continues to mount experiments and publish reports that will, we hope, provide social researchers with new and better tools for attitude measurement. For instance, in Chapter 1, Sharon Witherspoon and Jean Martin, building on earlier work carried out by JUSST, have now developed attitude scales which identify and measure a diversity of green attitudes and behaviours. JUSST funding also helps SCPR to continue its involvement in the ISSP. In addition, we are grateful to the Market Research Development Fund for a grant to part-finance an experiment examining the implications for the BSA time-series of changing sampling frame from the electoral register to the Postcode Address File (see Appendix I). A report is due soon.

As in 1988, there was no *British Social Attitudes* fieldwork round in 1992. Again, the core funds were used to supplement an award from the ESRC to carry out the latest in the series of *British General Election Studies* (BGES). Interviews with a freshly-drawn sample of around 2,800 electors

---

* A more detailed study of the NISA datasets will appear in Stringer, P. and Robinson, G. (eds.), *Social Attitudes in Northern Ireland: the 3rd Report*, (in press).

have duly been completed and we have also reinterviewed members of the 1987 election study sample, thus reintroducing a 'panel' element into the series. Around 1,200 'panellists' were interviewed by telephone both during and immediately after the election campaign, and 1,600 were interviewed face-to-face over the following ten weeks or so. An edited book on the 1992 election, successor to *How Britain Votes* and *Understanding Political Change*, will be published in early 1994.

With such a mass of accumulated data, BSA data users (not least the research team) welcome two new sources of material. First, as announced last year, the *British Social Attitudes Cumulative Sourcebook* was published (by Gower) in late 1991. Fully indexed and cross-referenced, it brings together the distributions of answers (numbers and percentages) to all the questions asked between 1983 and 1989. Our special thanks go to Gary Sebastian who helped us to compile the first edition and has already laid the groundwork for a second volume, planned but not yet scheduled for publication.

Since then, with ESRC support, we have (with colleagues at Strathclyde University) produced two fully-documented *combined* datasets (BSA, 1983-1991 and NISA 1989-1991) including in one computer file the data for all eleven surveys carried out so far. Its availability at the ESRC Data Archive at Essex University will, we hope, help considerably the study of trends, not only in national attitudes and values but also the particular movements of small sub-groups. BSA data for the years 1983-1990 (separately) are already available at the Archive on a CD-ROM disk.

In December 1991, Bridget Taylor left the research team on maternity leave; she is now based at Nuffield College and involved in BGES and some aspects of BSA and JUSST work. We welcome Lizanne Dowds who joined SCPR and the BSA research team in the autumn.

Each year approaching 3,000 members of the public agree to take part in the BSA survey, and another 900 or so in Northern Ireland are interviewed as part of NISA. Their co-operation is, of course, vital to the success of the series and we thank them all.

RMJ
LLB
GMP
BJT

# 1 What do we mean by green?

*Sharon Witherspoon and Jean Martin* *

Signs of public concern about environmental problems are nowadays so ubiquitous that it is hard to remember that the modern environmental movement has arisen largely within the last thirty years. Rachel Carson's *Silent Spring*, often cited as its genesis, was published in 1962. Eight years later, the first 'Earth Day' took place, signalling the presence in many Western nations of widespread public concern about the environment. Britain's Ecology Party - now the Green Party - was founded three years later, in 1973.

In those early days, pollution, whether chemical, industrial, nuclear, or in the form of pesticides, was the source of most public concern. During the 1970s and 1980s, issues of land-use gradually became prominent. In Britain, these were most often to do with preservation of the countryside and in particular the removal of hedgerows and other wildlife habitats; with forestry policies which favoured conifers over traditional deciduous forests, and with water pollution caused by fertilisers. Later, waste disposal and landfills became issues, with rather more immediate implications for individual behaviour. Elsewhere, these concerns broadened as tropical rainforests came under threat, and modern

* Sharon Witherspoon was formerly a Research Director at SCPR and a co-director of the *British Social Attitudes* survey series; she is now a postgraduate student at the State University of New York at Stony Brook. Jean Martin is an Assistant Director of Social Survey Division, Office of Population Censuses and Surveys; her work reported here was carried out in a private capacity and does not reflect the views of OPCS.

industrial and development policies seemed increasingly inimical to the preservation of ecological balance (McCormick, 1992).

Opposition to nuclear power also grew throughout the seventies, partly because of a number of serious accidents at nuclear power plants (notably at Three Mile Island in the United States and of course, at Chernobyl in 1986). Public fears were probably fuelled too by revelations that details of previous accidents (like those at the then Windscale nuclear power plant) had not been made public (Hall, 1986; Wynne, 1989a; Patterson, 1986). Although the anti-nuclear movement in the USA is often popularly credited with stopping any new nuclear power plant from opening there since the Three Mile Island accident, this is probably more due both to the economics of nuclear power generation and to the relatively decentralised and market-orientated electricity utilities in the USA (Patterson, 1986). In Britain the more centralised system has meant that pro-nuclear policies could more easily be implemented. Indeed, new nuclear power stations have been approved even since Chernobyl (Young, 1987). Even so, the British government did seem to recognise the political implications of fears over nuclear power when it altered its original plans to privatise nuclear electricity generation (McCormick, 1991). Though anti-nuclear sentiment has waxed and waned, nuclear waste has consistently registered as one of the greatest environmental concerns monitored by *British Social Attitudes* (Young, 1991). Chernobyl demonstrated that nuclear pollution has a global dimension, and that the public is deeply concerned about the potential world-wide implications of nuclear power.

There is some evidence of a fall in public concern about the environment in the early 1970s, as the energy crisis and economic recession seemed more pressing problems (Dunlap, 1992). But by the mid-1980s there was a rising public awareness in Western Europe and the United States of even more serious and complex environmental issues. The discovery of the seasonal 'hole' in the ozone layer over Antarctica in 1985, and the highly-publicised meetings in Montreal in 1987 and Helsinki in 1989, led to a decision to phase out the chemicals most responsible for the 'ozone hole' (carbonfluorochlorides - CFCs) by the end of the century (Young, 1990). It was acknowledged, however, that the CFCs already in use, and their continued use in applications for which no substitutes were available, would mean that the ozone layer would continue to thin for the foreseeable future. The announcement in February 1992 that a similar thinning might occur over the Arctic, and possibly over Northern Europe, caused further public disquiet (*Science,* 1992).

Also in the mid-1980s, the public was first exposed to the debate, argued in scientific circles since the early 1900s, over the so-called 'greenhouse effect'. The thesis that various gases, including carbon dioxide associated with the use of fossil fuels, were causing a gradual increase in the earth's temperature led to widespread and sometimes apocalyptic speculation about possible consequences: increasing volatility of weather systems, droughts, famines, flooding caused by rises in sea levels, and so on.

Although there is still disagreement about the level of warming that can be expected and the likely consequences (Mason, 1992), a scientific consensus that the threat is real does now seem to have emerged (Houghton, Jenkins and Ephraums, 1990). These new threats raise the stakes far beyond issues of chemical and industrial pollution and the need for cleaner consumption patterns. They call in effect for wholesale changes in consumption patterns and lifestyles in the industrialised countries.

That public awareness of the environment has grown is beyond doubt. Not only do surveys attest to it, but increasing numbers of books, consumer guides, newspapers, television programmes and so forth sell on the basis of their coverage of the environment. Goods from washing powders to cosmetics, water filters to batteries are marketed as being 'environmentally-safe' or 'environmentally-friendly', testifying that manufacturers see a market opportunity in the public's new environmentalism. Politicians from all parties claim that environmental protection is central to their policies. Indeed, in some sense we are all environmentalists these days.

Yet how, if at all, does this new-found public awareness of the environment translate itself into action? Except for the European Parliamentary elections in 1989 (when they won 15 per cent of the vote though no seats), the British Green Party has failed to make electoral progress. Moreover, Britain has so far seen relatively few US-style locally-based environmental movements which demand facilities such as door-step recycling from local authorities. Car sales may have fallen in recent years but nobody seriously believes this has been the result of a growing awareness of the environmental damage which cars produce. And although sales of organically-grown fruits and vegetables have been rising, they still account for a small fraction of the market, presumably because of their cost.

So sceptics may well ask whether the British public is really as green as it sometimes seems. We consider that issue in this chapter, asking both how *broad* environmental concern is, and how *deep* it is. In considering the *breadth* of concern we distinguish between two factors: whether it is felt by a majority or a minority, and to what degree; and among whom (whether it is confined largely to certain social groups or felt more generally). In examining the *depth* of people's views, we address questions such as how consistent people are in their environmental attitudes: for instance, are those who are concerned about the 'greenhouse effect' also more concerned about car and industrial pollution? And are those who are most concerned also those who are most likely to act in environmentally-responsible ways?

It is fitting that we examine evidence from the *British Social Attitudes* series in the year of the United Nations 'Earth Summit' in Rio de Janeiro. Hailed in advance as evidence that the world's governments finally accepted the need to act quickly to reach tough new agreements on what to do about global warming, deforestation and biological diversity, the Summit's results disappointed most environmentalists. It seemed that many Western governments (in particular the American) remained unconvinced that the proposals could be carried through in view of their heavy short-term political costs - in time, money and changes to lifestyles - particularly during a world recession.

## Dimensions of being green

Our first task is to define what we mean by 'green' and, in particular, to see if there is one underlying dimension of 'green-ness'. (We should note that when we use the word 'green' we refer to expressions of concern about a set of environmental issues, and to the propensity to translate that concern into action; we do not imply a judgment about the scientific 'environmental correctness' of those attitudes or actions.) Is someone who is concerned about the environment likely to be concerned about issues as diverse as, say, industrial pollution, nuclear power, the hole in the ozone layer and the loss of increasing numbers of plants and animal species? Many environmentalists would certainly argue that green-ness refers to a unifying underlying commitment to environmental protection. Our starting point, however, is that it is an empirical question as to whether or not there is a single, coherent and strongly-held core of beliefs and behaviours which can be labelled 'green'.

For instance, on the basis of existing evidence, we had grounds to believe that attitudes towards nuclear power would be somewhat different from other environmental attitudes (see, for example, Wynne, 1989b). In their analysis of the 1987 election, Heath *et al* found that attitudes to nuclear power are distinctly different from attitudes towards protection of the countryside; moreover, the sorts of people who are concerned about nuclear power are rather different from those who are concerned about the countryside (Heath *et al*, 1991, pp. 188-190). A methodological study of environmental attitudes carried out by the Joint Unit for the Study of Social Trends (Martin and Ashworth, 1991; Martin, 1991, p. 13) showed that attitudes to nuclear power were more stable over time than other environmental attitudes, and that a single scale of attitudes towards pollution would exclude attitudes towards nuclear power. Previous *British Social Attitudes* reports have also revealed that concern over nuclear power correlates more with views on nuclear defence than with other environmental worries (Young, 1985, 1986, 1987, 1990, 1991).

We might also expect that the sorts of people who are concerned about more abstract, less immediate global environmental issues, such as ozone depletion and the greenhouse effect, would be different from those who express concern over more visible issues such as industrial pollution. *A priori* we would expect the less educated to be less concerned about these abstract global environmental issues than about pollution. Moreover, insofar as industrial pollution may be seen as an indictment of business practices which put profit above concern for the environment, we might expect Labour Party supporters, who are more critical of business and its use of profits, to have distinctive views on pollution, though not necessarily to have such strong views on global environmental issues.

## The environmental attitude scales

After carrying out a preliminary factor analysis,[1] we were able to construct five environmental scales - three to do with different sorts of attitudes towards environmental issues, and two to do with people's willingness to take certain actions on behalf of the environment. The construction of scales enables us to 'cancel out' to some extent variations in responses to particular questions because of wording, context and so on (see Schumann and Presser, 1981; Tanur, 1991; de Vellis, 1991), and then to examine whether or not attitudes to different types of environmental problems are correlated with one another, and whether they draw their support from the same or different social groups.

All the questions about attitudes towards different environmental risks were asked with four response categories. Respondents were asked whether they were 'very', 'a bit', 'not very' or 'not at all concerned' about each one, or whether they felt the problem had a 'very', 'quite', 'not very' or 'not at all serious' effect on the environment. An immediate problem was that the distributions of answers to most items were very skewed: most British people nowadays express at least some concern about most of the items. This is largely a problem of question wording, since only one answer category is available to those who profess more than a low level of concern about any issue.[2]

After preliminary analyses, it was decided to treat each individual item as a trichotomy, combining the 'not very' and 'not at all' responses into one category, leaving the 'very' and 'a bit'/'quite' responses as the other two categories. These three categories were then scored either 2 ('very concerned') or 1 ('a bit concerned' or a 'quite serious risk'), or 0 for those expressing the least concern or seeing the least risk. So, the higher the level of concern about any issue, the higher the score the respondent will receive, with a maximum score of 2 and a minimum of 0.[3]

After examining several possible solutions, we concluded that the following three groups of items were both theoretically coherent and sufficiently highly correlated with one another to form reasonable scales. Below we show the individual items which make up each of the three attitude scales, and give the percentage of respondents who chose the *most* concerned answer category.

The first scale,[4] which we call the **global green scale**, includes items which measure levels of concern about:

- "the loss of plant and animal species" (54 per cent 'very concerned')
- "thinning of the ozone layer" (52 per cent 'very concerned')
- "insecticides, fertilisers and chemical sprays" (49 per cent 'very concerned')
- "the 'greenhouse effect'- a rise in the world's temperature" (41 per cent 'very concerned')
- "certain aerosol chemicals in the atmosphere" (42 per cent 'a very serious' effect on the environment)
- "using up the earth's remaining coal, oil and gas" (38 per cent 'very concerned')

The second scale,[5] which we call the **pollution scale**, includes attitudes towards environmental effects of:

- "industrial waste in rivers and seas" (70 per cent 'very serious' effect)
- "industrial fumes in the air" (52 per cent 'very serious' effect)
- "acid rain" (46 per cent 'very serious' effect)
- "lead from petrol" (39 per cent 'very serious' effect)

The third scale,[6] which we call the **nuclear power scale**, includes the following items:

- "the transport and disposal of dangerous chemicals" (66 per cent 'very concerned')
- "waste from nuclear electricity stations" (58 per cent 'a very serious' effect)
- "risks from nuclear power stations" (49 per cent 'very concerned')
- nuclear power stations "create very serious risks for the future" (endorsed by 40 per cent)

We should note that all three of these scales are still somewhat skewed towards the 'environmentally-correct' answer. For instance, 14 per cent of respondents gave the most concerned answer possible to *all* of the global issues, 25 per cent to *all* the pollution items, and 24 per cent to *all* the nuclear items.[7] Virtually no respondents received the lowest possible score on any of the three scales. Not only does this testify to high levels of public concern about all of these issues, but it also suggests that concern is so widespread that virtually everyone nowadays - regardless of education or income or political beliefs - expresses some disquiet about all the environmental issues we asked about.

However, it is not merely the case that more people in our sample are in the most extreme answer category on the pollution and nuclear power scales than on the global green scale. By looking at the *average* score on each scale we can assess whether respondents tend *consistently* to rate one set of issues as more serious than the others. The average score for the pollution scale is 1.44,* for the nuclear scale 1.36, and for the global green scale 1.33. This tells us something about the relative concern expressed about all three issues across the sample *as a whole:* pollution is much more a source of public concern than either nuclear power or global green issues. Our analysis[8] also shows that an average *individual* respondent assesses pollution as a more serious environmental problem than nuclear power, which is in turn rated as more serious than the global green issues. This is a finding of some interest. It suggests that respondents do not (yet) fear the potential consequences of the more gradual (and perhaps less soluble) environmental threats posed by current energy use and human interventions in the natural world as much as they fear current, more visible forms of damage to the environment.

So far we have shown only that respondents rate certain types of environmental threat as more serious than others. A separate question is whether respondents who express concern about any one environmental issue are also more likely to express concern about the other environmental issues. For instance, are people who worry about nuclear power also more likely to worry about global green issues? To find out we examined the correlations between the three attitude scales. We found that they are indeed relatively highly correlated with one another, and that each pair of scales is correlated to a similar extent:

### Correlations

| | |
|---|---|
| Pollution scale/global green scale | .569 |
| Nuclear power scale/pollution scale | .515 |
| Nuclear power scale/global green scale | .501 |

On the face of it, this might suggest that we could indeed construct one indicator of 'green attitudes', made up of items from all three scales (losing no information and simplifying our analysis somewhat), because there is likely to be a single underlying 'green dimension' to our respondents' attitudes. But this is *not* the case, as we shall show in due course. First, however, we consider the two further scales we constructed from the data - dealing respectively with consumer behaviour, and willingness to pay for environmental gains.

### *The environmental activism scales*

Attitudes towards the environment may be interesting in their own right, for instance, as evidence of the widespread permeation of new beliefs

---

* A respondent who gave the most concerned answer possible to all the items in any one scale would score the maximum of 2; someone who was unconcerned about all the items in any one scale would score the minimum of 0.

within a short period of time, or of the role of the media in promulgating such beliefs. But the true test of the strength of environmental attitudes must be the extent to which they lead people to behave in more environmentally-sensitive ways, or to support new policies which involve material sacrifices for the sake of the environment. We therefore devised two action-oriented scales from items in the survey.

The first is a scale of **green consumer behaviour**, in which each of the items is an action that can be undertaken by an individual or household without collective or political activity. Respondents were asked whether they carried out each of eleven 'green-related' activities 'regularly', 'sometimes', or 'not at all'. Maintaining consistency with the scoring for the attitude scales, we assigned a score of 2 for each item a respondent carried out regularly, a score of 1 for each item they did sometimes, and a score of 0 for each item they did not do at all. (As before, the final scale score is an average across all items.) The final scale[9] includes nine items (out of 11 asked about),[10] shown below with the proportion of respondents who said they did each 'regularly':

**Do you do any of the following *regularly, sometimes* or *not at all* nowadays?**

- buy environment-friendly aerosols? (55 per cent)
- buy free-range chicken or eggs? (39 per cent)
- buy toiletries or cosmetics not tested on animals? (33 per cent)
- return bottles, tins, newspapers and so on for recycling? (32 per cent)
- buy environment-friendly washing powders or detergents? (31 per cent)
- choose to eat less meat? (25 per cent)
- choose products made out of recycled materials? (23 per cent)
- refuse unnecessary packaging or wrapping? (17 per cent)
- buy organically-grown fruit and vegetables? ( 8 per cent)

This scale was much less skewed than the three attitude scales, with only a handful of respondents saying that they did all of the nine actions regularly, and an average (of a possible maximum of 2.00) of 0.93, just about in the middle of the range.[11] We were aware that a potential problem with this scale was that women might score higher than men only because some of the activities asked about are more likely to be done by women. But, to some extent, this problem bedevils any scale of consumerism, since women tend to do more of the regular household shopping than men (Witherspoon, 1988, p.182; see also Chapter 5).

Our second scale of green activism is more properly a scale of **willingness to pay** for the environment. It measures not so much behaviour as support for collective action to change pricing and tax policies. Although of course such support is an expression of respondents' attitudes, we include it as an activism measure because each item implies trading environmental protection for increased costs, unlike our attitude scales which were cost-free and unconstrained. The 'willingness to pay' items require of government and industry, as well as of ordinary people, that they are held responsible for the environment, thus coming closest to being a 'green manifesto'.

Each item in this scale had five answer categories, including a neutral midpoint. Thus the theoretical maximum score here is four, rather than two as before, and the minimum is zero. We give below the six items which make up this scale,[12] along with the proportion of respondents who gave the most 'environmentally-concerned' answer.

- "The government should do more to protect the environment, even if it leads to higher taxes." (13 per cent 'agree strongly')
- "Industry should do more to protect the environment, even if it leads to lower profits and fewer jobs." (13 per cent 'agree strongly')
- "Ordinary people should do more to protect the environment, even if it means paying higher prices." (13 per cent 'agree strongly')
- ...Much more "government spending on the environment" (even if "it might require a tax increase to pay for it") (endorsed by 12 per cent)
- "For the sake of the environment, car users should pay higher taxes." (4 per cent 'agree strongly')
- "For the sake of the environment, people should use less heating in their homes." (2 per cent 'agree strongly')

The willingness to pay scale is less skewed than the three 'cost-free' attitudinal scales or the consumer behaviour scale, again with almost no respondents giving the most 'pro-environment' answers to all six items. The scale mean is 2.33, out of a possible maximum score of 4 and a minimum of 0 - just above the half-way point of the range.[13]

## Who has green attitudes?

We have presented some evidence about the *breadth* of green attitudes and activism, having found that virtually everyone in our sample expressed at least some concern about the three issues we asked about in our attitude scales. We also saw that there was most concern about pollution, followed by concern about nuclear power and then by concern about global green issues; however, we also saw that green attitudes were much more widespread than green activism, whether in the form of individual consumer behaviour or of willingness to pay for green public policies. Now we turn to a different way of looking at the breadth of concern: are different groups of people differentially disposed to be green?

One hypothesis we wanted to examine is that people with more education are more predisposed to be concerned about the environment (see for example, Cotgrove and Duff, 1980; Inglehart, 1977; 1990; but see also Heath *et al*, 1991 for a different view). At its simplest, if people with degrees are more likely to be green than those with intermediate or no educational qualifications, we would expect their average scale scores to be higher. The scores are shown below:

**Mean scale scores by highest educational qualification**

|  | Degree | Intermediate qualification | No qualification |
|---|---|---|---|
| Global green scale | 1.37 | 1.35 | 1.26 |
| Pollution scale | 1.39 | 1.45 | 1.45 |
| Nuclear power scale | 1.24 | 1.32 | 1.45 |
| Consumer behaviour scale | 1.23 | 0.98 | 0.80 |
| Willingness to pay scale* | 2.76 | 2.33 | 2.34 |

* This scale has a maximum 'green score' of 4, while the others have a maximum score of 2.

The hypothesis that those with higher educational qualifications are more disposed to be green proves to be too simple. In respect of the **global green scale**, while it is true that those with no educational qualifications are the least concerned, it is also the case that graduates are hardly more concerned than those with intermediate qualifications. In the case of the **willingness to pay scale**, graduates score higher, but there is no distinction between those with intermediate educational qualifications and those with none. More directly contrary to the hypothesis about the effect of education, in the case of both the **pollution** and the **nuclear power scales**, those with degrees are actually *less* likely to express environmental concern than those without them. Indeed it is only the **consumer behaviour scale** which behaves according to the hypothesis, with green consumer behaviour increasing steadily with increasing educational levels. So, the relationship between education and being green seems to vary according to which dimension of green-ness is being examined. This is one reason why we have so far insisted on presenting each of the three attitude scales separately, rather than combining them into one composite scale.

Does an examination by social class present a simpler picture? Is being green related systematically to one's Socio-economic Group?[14] We present the evidence below, adding a final column consisting of respondents who are scientific, technical or medical professionals (a sub-group of the main professional, employer and managerial SEG category).

**Mean scale scores by Socio-economic Group**

|  | Professionals, employers & managers | Inter-mediate non-manual | Junior non-manual | Skilled manual | Other manual | Science, technical, and medical, professionals |
|---|---|---|---|---|---|---|
| Global green scale | 1.29 | 1.45 | 1.38 | 1.26 | 1.28 | 1.12 |
| Pollution scale | 1.36 | 1.53 | 1.51 | 1.42 | 1.45 | 1.13 |
| Nuclear power scale | 1.20 | 1.39 | 1.44 | 1.31 | 1.46 | 0.92 |
| Consumer behaviour scale | 1.00 | 1.14 | 1.05 | 0.83 | 0.82 | 0.97 |
| Willingness to pay scale | 2.42 | 2.60 | 2.40 | 2.19 | 2.22 | 2.51 |

Again our search for systematic differences is confounded. Most surprisingly perhaps, those in the professional, employer and managerial category are *less* green than the two other non-manual groups on every one of our measures of being green. And though intermediate and junior non-manual workers tend to be greener than manual workers on four out of the five scales, they are *less* concerned than unskilled manual workers in their attitudes towards nuclear power. We also find that our small group of scientific and medical professionals tend to be *less* concerned than professionals in general on all the environmental attitude scales, and less green in their consumption behaviour than all three non-manual SEGs. They are, however, more likely than most other groups, especially the professionals, to support environmentally-protective public policies. These scientific workers may be eschewing the new secular religion of environmentalism (Douglas, 1975; Douglas and Wildavsky, 1982), or displaying 'organised scepticism' (Merton, 1973), being more aware, perhaps, of the complexities of environmental risk; in any case, this group does not subscribe to any environmentalist party line.

Of course, the situation may be even more complicated than these tables show, since we may inadvertently be measuring the effect of variables other than education or social class, but which are correlated with them. For instance, professionals are more likely than other groups to have degrees, so the effects of education and social class may counteract one another to some extent. Social class is also correlated with income, so perhaps we are actually measuring some sort of income effect. Or perhaps the generally greater concern from the intermediate and junior non-manual groups arises from the fact that these sorts of jobs are held disproportionately by women, who we have found tend to be more environmentally-concerned than men (see Young, 1990, 1991).

To examine the effects of several background variables at the same time, we used regression analysis. This enables us to see whether or not there is a statistically significant relationship[15] between our scales and various individual background variables, controlling for other background variables.

The table below gives the results of such an analysis for our three attitudinal scales, showing only those variables which were statistically significant at the (conventional) five per cent level - that is, there is less than a five per cent possibility that we would have found that relationship by chance if there were none in fact.[16] A plus sign indicates that the variable is associated with being *more* environmentally-concerned; a minus sign indicates that it is associated with being *less* environmentally-concerned. Moreover, each number in the table shows the average number of points (out of the maximum of two in each attitude scale) that should be added to or subtracted from a person's score simply for having that characteristic, after controlling for other characteristics in the table.

**The effect of various background variables on green attitudinal scales**

| Background variables: | Global green scale | Pollution scale | Nuclear power scale |
|---|---|---|---|
| Men | -.12 | - | -.23 |
| Age 18-24 | - | - | - |
| Age 45-54 | +.10 | +.08 | - |
| Degree | +.13 | - | -.16 |
| Other educational qualification | +.11 | - | -.09 |
| Scotland | -.30 | -.18 | - |
| North | -.13 | - | - |
| Midlands | -.14 | - | - |
| Scientific, technical & medical professionals | - | -.23 | -.23 |
| Green Party | +.36 | +.49 | +.66 |
| Labour Party | +.12 | +.19 | +.28 |
| Liberal Democrats | +.13 | +.14 | +.24 |
| *Proportion of overall variance explained by the background variables (adjusted $R^2$)* | *7%* | *7%* | *14%* |

In interpreting this table, we should point out that we are comparing the background categories listed above with other omitted categories (called reference categories). Thus, the first row of figures shows that men are significantly less concerned than women (the reference category) on two of the three scales. On average, they lose over one-tenth of a point on the global green scale (compared to women) and nearly a quarter of a point on the nuclear power scale. They are not statistically different from women on the pollution scale.

The reference category for the regional variables is the South of England (including London) and Wales; people living in these areas are not significantly different from one another, and we show the extent to which people in other regions differ from them. In the case of the scientific, technical and medical professionals, we compare them with all those who do *not* do this kind of work. In the case of political parties, the reference category is made up of those who support the Conservative Party or who are non-aligned (who do not differ from each other significantly).

In addition, we should note that the proportion of variance explained gives us an idea of how much knowing a person's background helps us to predict how green he or she will be. If background matters a lot, we would expect this figure to be, say, 20 per cent or above; in other words we would be able to explain 20 per cent of the variance in answers by knowing about a person's background. As can be seen, in the case of two of our three attitudinal scales, the proportion of variance explained is fairly modest, though still statistically significant. In the case of the nuclear power scale, we do somewhat better.

Before we turn to the figures, we should note which variables are *not* included in the table. Social class is absent, since we found no evidence of any statistically significant class effect on these attitudes, once education and partisanship were controlled for.[17] Nor did we find that household income mattered independently of education. And religion is also missing, despite the relationship of religious attendance to attitudes to nuclear power mentioned last year (Young, 1991); we found no evidence of a relationship when age and education were controlled for.[18]

Referring to the figures themselves, as noted above we find that, after controlling for all the other variables in the table, men are less likely than women to express concern about the global green issues and about nuclear power. The age of respondents also matters, with middle-aged respondents (those between 45 and 54 years old) being more concerned than all other age groups about global green issues and pollution. The Scots are *less* concerned about these same issues than those living elsewhere, perhaps because concern over jobs and economic growth, which in current debate tend to be pitted against environmental protection, predominate outside the still relatively prosperous South of England. For whatever reason, Southerners are more inclined than those living in Scotland, the North or the Midlands to express concern about industrial pollution and the global issues of greenhouse warming, thinning of the ozone layer and so on, even *after* we take account of their different social and demographic make-up.

The table also reveals that the *same* background variable can affect the three attitude scales in wholly different ways. For instance, having a degree (or, to a lesser extent, an intermediate qualification) is *positively* associated with concern about global green issues, net of the other background factors; those with higher levels of education are more concerned about these abstract environmental threats. But education is *negatively* associated with concern about nuclear power. However, education *per se* does not seem to be associated with attitudes to pollution; here it is those who work as scientific, technical or medical professionals who display a distinctive pattern, being *less* likely than others to be concerned. Scientific professionals are also much less likely than others to express concern about nuclear power; since most will also possess degrees, their loss of .23 of a point for being a scientific professional should be added to the loss of .16 of a point for having a degree, giving a total loss averaging nearly four tenths of a point out of the possible maximum of two.

Finally, we see that party identification has an effect on scores on all three attitude scales.[19] As we have noted, in none of the three areas did we find that Conservative identifiers differed significantly from those with no party allegiance. As expected, respondents who identify with the Green Party are much more likely to express environmental concern about all three issues, adding between one-third and two-thirds of a point (out of the possible range of two points) compared with Conservatives and the non-aligned. Labour and Liberal Democrat identifiers are also more concerned about all three issues than Conservatives and the non-aligned, though less markedly so. Further, we can see that party identification has the strongest effect on just that issue which has been closest to politically partisan debate - nuclear power - and about which Labour and the Liberal Democrats have generally expressed more scepticism than have the Conservatives.[20]

The importance of political debate is further emphasised when we add a different sort of variable to our analysis - general interest in politics. Elsewhere in the questionnaire, respondents were asked:

> *How much interest do you generally have in what is going on in politics...*
>
> > *...a great deal,*
> > *quite a lot,*
> > *some,*
> > *not very much,*
> > *or, none at all?*

We collapsed these five categories for our analysis into three: those who said a 'great deal' were classified as having a high level of political interest; those who said 'quite a lot' or 'some' were classified as having a moderate level of political interest; and those who said 'not very much' or 'none at all' were classified as having a low level of political interest. We use the group with low levels of political interest as our reference (omitted) category, since we are interested in finding out how much more or less concerned about the environment the politically interested are, compared to everyone else. As the table below shows, political interest has a large and consistently positive impact on all three dimensions of environmental concern.

**The effect of political interest and background variables
on green attitudinal scales**

| | Global green scale | Pollution scale | Nuclear power scale |
|---|---|---|---|
| **Political interest variables:** | | | |
| High interest | +.29 | +.19 | +.18 |
| Moderate interest | +.19 | +.10 | - |
| **Background variables:** | | | |
| Men | -.16 | - | -.25 |
| Age 18-24 | - | - | - |
| Age 45-54 | +.08 | +.07 | - |
| Degree | +.05 | - | -.18 |
| Other educational qualification | +.08 | - | -.09 |
| Scotland | -.26 | -.16 | - |
| North | -.12 | - | - |
| Midlands | -.11 | - | - |
| Scientific, technical medical professionals | - | -.24 | -.22 |
| Green Party | +.34 | +.47 | +.65 |
| Labour Party | +.12 | +.19 | +.27 |
| Liberal Democrats | +.12 | +.13 | +.24 |
| *Proportion of overall variance explained by the background variables (adjusted $R^2$)* | *11%* | *8%* | *14%* |

Compared to their counterparts with low political interest, those with high interest gain just under a fifth of a point on their scores on the pollution and nuclear power scales, and nearly one-third of a point on their global green score. We should note that the addition of the political interest variable somewhat weakens the effect of having a degree on global green attitudes. In other words, some of the effect we were attributing to having a degree actually appears to arise because those with degrees tend to be more interested in politics and therefore perhaps to have followed more closely the extensive media coverage of environmental issues in recent years. In any event, political interest seems to be particularly important to the global green issues on which the mainstream political parties have yet to establish clearly differentiated positions. With the addition of the political interest variable, the amount of variation in the global green scale we now account for has risen from 7 per cent to 11 per cent; in contrast, the increase in the case of the other two scales is smaller.

**Who are the green activists?**

So far we have demonstrated that some background variables do make a statistically significant difference to our three dimensions of environmental attitudes, though the overall size of the effects is rather modest. We now turn to examine the social bases of our two scales of environmental activism.

**The effect of various background variables
on green activism scales**

| Background variables: | Consumer behaviour scale | Willingness to pay scale |
|---|---|---|
| Men | -.20 | +.09 |
| | | |
| Age 18-24 | - | -.14 |
| Age 45-54 | - | +.17 |
| | | |
| Degree | +.33 | +.42 |
| Other educational qualification | +.10 | - |
| | | |
| Scotland | -.24 | - |
| Wales | -.31 | - |
| | | |
| City | -.17 | -.15 |
| Suburb | -.12 | - |
| Small town | - | +.09 |
| | | |
| Socio-economic group: | | |
| Professionals, employers and managers | +.10 | - |
| Intermediate non-manual | +.16 | +.25 |
| Junior non-manual | +.14 | +.20 |
| | | |
| Green Party | +.44 | +.79 |
| Labour Party | - | +.06 |
| Liberal Democrats | +.12 | +.11 |
| | | |
| *Proportion of overall variance explained by the background variables (adjusted $R^2$)* | *23%* | *14%* |

The first thing to note about this table is that the background variables here are rather better at explaining or helping us to predict a person's score on the consumer behaviour scale than on any of the other scales. Looking at the last row of the table, we find that just over one-fifth of the variation in the consumer behaviour scores of our respondents is accounted for by the background variables we have included, compared to just over one-eighth of the variation in any of the other scales, including the willingness to pay scale (also shown above).[21]

Previously, when we looked at the average scores on the consumer behaviour scale, we saw large differences between those from different social classes and with differing levels of education. So it is not surprising that social class makes a difference to respondents' environmental activism, even though we found it did not matter for our three environmental attitude scales. Our reference category is made up of those in all manual occupations; respondents in skilled, semi-skilled, and unskilled occupations did not significantly differ from each other. Even after controlling for respondents' education, we find that those in non-manual occupations tend to score more highly on both these scales than do their counterparts in manual occupations. But, surprisingly perhaps, professionals, employers and managers score less highly on these two activism scales than do those in middle-level and junior white-collar jobs. It is possible that the only distinctively green members of this socio-economic group are professionals, while the managers and administrators within this category (who outnumber them) are not so environmentally-concerned. Further research on a larger sample would be needed to establish whether or not this is the case.

We also see that the region one lives in has an effect on the consumer behaviour scores, net of one's occupational level or education or party identity. The Scots and the Welsh lose between a quarter and a third of a point on the consumer behaviour scale compared to their English counterparts. But region makes no significant difference to respondents' scores on the willingness to pay scale. In addition, for both scales respondents who live in cities tend to get lower scores than those living in rural areas (the reference category).

Once again, it is hardly surprising that identifiers with the Green Party score more highly than others on both scales. But we were surprised to find that, whereas Labour identifiers and Liberal Democrats were more or less equally concerned on all the environmental attitude scales, Labour identifiers are *not* statistically different from Conservatives or the non-aligned on the consumer behaviour scale. Even in the case of the willingness to pay scale, they express less support than Liberal Democrats for tax and price increases for the sake of the environment. This is not because of their different socio-economic status, since we have controlled for this in our analysis. If the Labour Party wishes to establish itself as a 'green' party, it will have to persuade its supporters that the costs are worth it.

Perhaps most importantly we see from the table that education matters (again, net of class, age and so on) even more in the case of the two activism scales than it did for either the global green or the nuclear power scale.[22] This may be partly because of a link between education and a sense of personal efficacy - the sense that what one does may actually have an effect (Heath and Topf, 1987). To that extent, campaigns aimed at fostering environmental *awareness* alone may not in themselves promote environmentally-responsible *behaviour* (Ester *et al*, 1984).

Also linked to efficacy may be the important influence of political interest. Though for reasons of space we cannot show it here, we added the same political interest variables to our analysis of the two behaviourial scales; they had an even stronger effect than they did on the attitudinal scales. Once again, being politically interested is strongly correlated with environmentalism, with about one-third of a point added to the average scores of those with high levels of political interest for both activism scales. In addition, the proportion of variation in people's scores accounted for also increased. The introduction of the political interest variable lessened the additional points added for having a degree, as well as some of the other background variables. But most interestingly, once we had controlled for political interest, party identity more or less disappeared as a statistically significant factor in distinguishing people on the willingness to pay scale. Labour and Liberal Democratic identifiers were indistinguishable from Conservatives; only Green Party identifiers stood out. It may just be general political interest, rather than their party's policies, which makes Labour and Liberal identifiers support price and tax increases for the sake of the environment, perhaps because of the greater attentiveness to the media that high interest implies. Given the normally higher levels of support of both Labour and Liberal Democrat identifiers for government regulation in general (Heath *et al*, 1991), this must surely count as striking evidence of the weak environmental image of the mainstream parties.

### Are greens consistent?

We have concentrated so far on finding out who is likely to be green, and what kinds of people are differently disposed to be concerned about different kinds of environmental problems, or to take action about them. We have seen that environmental concern is widespread, especially in respect of pollution, though concern about global environmental issues is rather less in evidence. Environmentally-sensitive consumer behaviour, even with the relatively modest measures that make up our consumer behaviour scale, is much less widespread, and is influenced not only by education but by social class as well. The link to public policies is much less well-anchored, with a smaller proportion of our sample consistently favouring tax and pricing policies to protect the environment; the mainstream political parties have so far neither distinguished themselves clearly from each other on environmental policies, nor educated their supporters about the public policy consequences of environmentalism.

But we began this chapter by asking not just how widespread green attitudes and actions are, but also how *deep* they are. Do respondents who express higher levels of environmental concern put their beliefs into practice? How much of a difference do beliefs make to actions? If attitudes do matter, which ones matter most? Earlier, we saw that all three dimensions of green attitudes seemed to correlate about equally with each other, and we asked if that meant they would be interchangeable in their effects on other variables. In particular we need to find out whether the three environmental attitude scales are associated with our two activism scales; we investigate this first by looking at the extent to which the attitude and activism scales are correlated with each other.

|  | **Correlations** | |
|---|---|---|
|  | **Consumer behaviour scale** | **Willingness to pay scale** |
| **Global green scale** | .485 | .416 |
| **Pollution scale** | .286 | .408 |
| **Nuclear power scale** | .255 | .191 |

Here we get a clear indication that each of the three attitude scales has rather different social consequences. The global green scale is highly correlated with both the consumer behaviour scale and the willingness to pay scale; the pollution scale is highly correlated only with the willingness to pay scale. The nuclear power scale is rather weakly correlated with both behavioural scales. If we had conceived of green attitudes as comprising only a single dimension, these interesting and important patterns would have been obscured. To examine this further, we did create a single scale using the same items that make up our three attitudinal scales. This single green scale had a rather low reliability (a Cronbach's alpha of .52), and correlations of well under .10 with both the consumer behaviour scale and the willingness to pay scale. Thus, as far as the British public is concerned there is very little evidence of a single, coherent and generalised 'green world view' (see Young, 1991); rather there are clusters of attitudes, with more or less strong links between them.

Of course, the pattern revealed by these correlations occurs partly because social factors, like education and social class, are working independently on both the attitudes and the activism of our respondents. We cannot infer that the attitudes *lead* to green activism, since both may simply be expressions of the same underlying social factors. But we can investigate the relationship of attitudes to behaviour by introducing our environmental attitude scales as variables in the analyses of the consumer behaviour and the willingness to pay scales.[23] In this way we can discover the extent to which environmental attitudes influence environmental activism, net of social class, education and so on.

**The independent effects of green attitudes**
**on green activism scales**

|  | Consumer behaviour scale | Willingness to pay scale |
|---|---|---|
| **Green attitude scales:** | | |
| Global green scale | +.36 | +.25 |
| Pollution scale | - | +.31 |
| Nuclear power scale | - | - |
| **Political interest variables:** | | |
| High level interest | +.20 | +.19 |
| Middle level interest | - | +.05 |
| **Background variables:** | | |
| Men | -.18 | +.11 |
| Age 18-24 | - | -.12 |
| Age 45-54 | - | +.11 |
| Degree | +.29 | +.40 |
| Other educational qualification | +.09 | - |
| Scotland | -.13 | - |
| Wales | -.28 | - |
| City | -.14 | -.13 |
| Suburb | -.12 | - |
| Small town | - | +.08 |
| Socio-economic group: | | |
| Professionals, employers and managers | +.07 | - |
| Intermediate non-manual | +.11 | +.18 |
| Junior non-manual | +.10 | +.14 |
| Green Party | +.33 | +.55 |
| Labour Party | - | - |
| Liberal Democrats | +.09 | - |
| *Proportion of overall variance explained (adjusted R²)* | *40%* | *33%* |

The first point to emphasise about the table is that introducing the attitudinal variables changes the size of some of the effects that we had previously ascribed to social background variables. For instance, the effect of social class is now more muted once we take attitudes into account, as is the size of the effect we had previously ascribed as due to identifying with the Green Party. This pattern of intervening effects is what we might expect when chains of background factors, attitudes and behaviour are involved.

But the most important point about the table is the size of the effects we find for the different attitudinal variables. Respondents' attitudes towards global green issues strongly influence their consumer behaviour, adding on average about one-third of a point (out of a possible two points) to the expected score on this scale. Neither concern about pollution nor about nuclear power inclines people towards environmental consumerism.  It seems that an awareness of global environmental dangers does help to create a sense of personal commitment to 'responsible' behaviour.  In contrast, we find that concern about pollution influences respondents' willingness to pay for environmental protection. But so too does concern over global environmental change, with the size of the effect being roughly similar in each case.  Attitudes towards nuclear power again make no significant difference to the willingness to pay scale; to that extent they are an insecure basis for positive and committed environmentalism.

We also found that the addition of the attitudinal variables increases considerably the amount of variance we can explain (see the last row). Thus, if we know about a person's social background, and we know their scores on the global green and pollution scales, we can explain nearly 40 per cent of the variance in the consumer behaviour scale, and nearly a third of the variance in the willingness to pay scale.  Concern about some aspects of the environment, though not necessarily leading to environmentally-sensitive actions, is certainly influential.

## Conclusions

In last year's *British Social Attitudes* report, Ken Young wrote that the spread of green attitudes in Britain was a process of 'wider permeation rather than one of deepening commitment' (Young, 1991, pp. 124-125). Our analysis confirms that green attitudes are indeed widespread, especially when the environmental issue at stake is industrial pollution. Where the problem is more visible, where the environmental degradation takes effect with relative speed, where deep fears about dirt and danger are linked, and where there is felt to be a readily identifiable culprit, it seems that concern over environmental issues are at their highest.  They may even be linked to public support for policy remedies, as the correlation between views on pollution and the willingness to pay scale has shown.

But concern over the more insidious, more intractable environmental problems attributed to modern life in advanced industrial countries is not so widespread.  Issues like reliance on fossil fuels and the concomitant problems of global warming are not well-understood.  And although concern over these issues does correlate with individual consumer behaviour, it remains the case that most people are not prepared to make even the fairly modest changes to consumption patterns that our scale measures, much less the wholesale changes to 'appropriate consumption' (Young, 1991, p. 124) that are called for by environmental activists.  If the Green Party manifesto were taken as the standard by which we judged the greening of society, we would have to conclude that the penetration of green ideas and behaviour is both shallow and patchy.

It is unlikely moreover that merely raising public awareness or understanding of environmental problems will lead to more environmentally-sensitive behaviour. The solutions to many environmental problems would probably be too unpopular for the time being. For instance, we asked respondents whether "people should be allowed to use their cars as much as they like, even if it causes damage to the environment". Only eight per cent of them strongly disagreed with this proposition, and a further 35 per cent disagreed somewhat. Against this, nearly 40 per cent had no opinion either way, and 18 per cent agreed. There is thus no clear consensus about restricting car use. This ambivalence is symptomatic of the difficulty of constructing an environmentally-concerned majority, or at least one that is concerned enough to make sacrifices.

Once again we must draw attention to the role of education in buttressing environmental concern. Education matters partly no doubt because it is a means of understanding and putting into context the increasing amount of information available about the environment. But our analysis shows that education matters also because it is linked with greater efficacy and *political* interest, which in turn has a strong link with both environmental concern and activism. But note that it is interest in politics *per se* rather than support for a particular mainstream party which matters most, at least as far as environmental activism is concerned.

The weak role of party identification is, in a sense, an indication of the thinness of the political debate on the environment that has been conducted to date. Environmental issues were, for instance, conspicuously absent from the campaigns of the mainstream political parties in the 1992 general election. It is not so much that the main parties seem to agree on the issues. Rather it is that none of them seems anxious to engage in informed debate on environmental issues - and in the process, to create a better-informed public. Without this debate, understanding of the environmental implications of individual behaviour and support for public regulation of such behaviour for the sake of the environment is bound to remain weak. And the public will remain unable or unwilling to make choices about new environmental regulations or about changes in costing the earth (Cairncross, 1991).

We cannot, however, be too sure that a public debate would necessarily lead to consistently green policies. At the moment the most environmentally-aware and active members of the public are the educated members of the middle-class who might have most to lose from the likely mixture of tax, price and regulatory policies which an environmental policy might entail. Neither they nor the more disadvantaged social groups will escape the costs, whether financial or behavioural, of greater environmental regulation. If the political parties *do* take up the issue of environmentalism with greater vigour and attempt to distinguish themselves from one another, the question of who will pay for a greener Britain is bound to become a central part of the debate. In that case, we would expect political partisanship to have a greater influence on environmental attitudes, but we would also expect greater discord about the meaning of being green.

## Notes

1.  The factor analysis of selected variables suggested that a three-factor solution, accounting for nearly 61 per cent of the total variance, would be satisfactory. In general, the three identified factors contained the same items we included in each of the three attitudinal scales used in this chapter; that is, there was a clear pollution factor, a clear global green factor and a distinct nuclear power factor. However, we included the item on aerosol sprays in our global green factor, even though its factor loading was relatively modest, in order to improve the scaling properties of this indicator. The authors can provide further details upon request.
2.  This problem was explicitly taken into consideration in the design of the 1993 International Social Survey Programme (ISSP) module on attitudes to the environment. In that module, due to be reported in 1994, three (rather than one) answer categories will be offered to respondents who wish to show high to middling levels of concern. Preliminary pilot results from Britain suggest that this does reduce the skew to a considerable extent.
3.  Note that this means that some original scorings in the questionnaire were reversed; in all cases in this chapter, the higher the scale score, the 'greener' the respondent.
4.  The internal consistency of the scale - the extent to which the individual items are related to one another - can be measured by Cronbach's alpha, which can range from 0 (showing a low correlation) to 1.0 (perfect correlation). This scale has an alpha of 0.81, which is acceptably high.
5.  Cronbach's alpha is 0.80.
6.  Cronbach's alpha is 0.76.
7.  More technically, the amount of *skew* and *kurtosis* for each scale is given below:

|                    | Skew  | Kurtosis |
|--------------------|-------|----------|
| Global green scale | -.533 | -.540    |
| Pollution scale    | -.630 | -.448    |
| Nuclear scale      | -.640 | -.634    |

8.  We use a statistical test known as a 'paired t-test' to make this comparison.

| Difference between:                | T-statistic | Significance |
|------------------------------------|-------------|--------------|
| Pollution and nuclear scales       | 5.42        | .000         |
| Nuclear and global green scales    | 2.14        | .033         |

This tells us that the average respondent is statistically significantly more likely to rate pollution as the most serious environmental problem, nuclear power as the second most serious, and global green issues as the third most serious.
9.  Cronbach's alpha for this scale is 0.78.
10. We omitted two items: 'make a conscious effort to save electricity' and 'cut back on driving your car'. These were cut because analysis by Martin (1991) and Young (1991) showed that they did not relate well to the other items, and were related more to income, suggesting that financial, rather than environmental, considerations were motivating respondents. We particularly regretted losing the item about driving, given the environmentally-important effects of cars. The 1993 ISSP module on the environment, which will be analysed in a future *British Social Attitudes* report, has revised the question wording so that the inclusion of an item about driving may be possible in due course.
11. The more technical measures of skew for this scale are -.034 (skew) and -.602 (kurtosis).
12. Cronbach's alpha for this scale is 0.75.
13. The skew of this scale is .029, and the kurtosis is .009.
14. Socio-economic Group (SEG) is based on a classification of respondents' current or most recent occupation; it comprises 17 categories which we condensed to five for our

analyses. We would have preferred to use a version of the Goldthorpe class schema but, at the time of writing, it was not yet available for the 1991 data. In addition, our measure of SEG denotes the respondent's own social class, and thus does not take account of the class of others in the household.

15. To be more precise, regression analysis tests for the presence of a statistically significant *linear* relationship between our scales and the background variables. See Berry and Feldman, 1985.

16. In many cases, the results are significant at the .01 or .001 levels, or better. The authors can provide further details upon request.

17. This is true of social class as measured by Socio-economic Group. It is of course the case that social class is itself an important determinant of political partisanship, but other than its effects through party identification, we found no evidence of any additional effect.

18. But see Greeley, 1991 for some suggestions that this may not be the case in the United States. Our models suggested that only adherents of non-Christian religions - Muslims, Hindus, or Jews - were significantly different from others when education was controlled for, but we suspect that this results from other variables not included in our equations, rather than from religious affiliation *per se*. See also Witherspoon, 1991, for further discussion of this issue.

19. It is, of course, possible that the causal chain works the other way, with a respondent's environmental beliefs predisposing him or her to identify with a particular party. But whereas this *may* be the case with Green Party supporters, it is unlikely to be the case with the other parties; hence our decision to include party identification as, in essence, a 'cause' of environmental beliefs.

20. We can also see the overall strength of this increased role of partisanship by looking at the "adjusted $R^2$" presented at the bottom of the table. This shows the amount of variance in the sample's scale scores that can be 'explained' by the background variables in the model. In the case of the nuclear scale, we can account for nearly twice as much variance as we do in the case of the global green and pollution scales.

21. We should also note that while the consumer behaviour scale, like our previous scales, has a range of two points, the willingness to pay scale has a range of four points - a factor to bear in mind when examining the size of the relationships between background variables and scale scores.

22. Technically, to make this comparison we need to look at the standardised regression coefficients, since the willingness to pay scale ranges from 0 to 4, while the other scales range from 0 to 2. We find that the standardised coefficients for holding a degree was .07 to .08 in the case of the two attitudinal scales, but was more than twice as large, at .21, for both the activism scales.

23. This assumes that the environmental attitudes 'cause' environmental activism, though we note it is likely that there is some reciprocal causation, such that those who, for some reason, take up green behaviours become more concerned and aware about other environmental issues.

## References

Berry, W.D. and Feldman, S. (1985), *Multiple Regression in Practice*, Sage University Paper Series on Quantitative Applications in the Social Sciences, series no. 07-050, Newbury Park: Sage.

Cairncross, F. (1991), *Costing the Earth*, London: The Economist Books.

Cotgrove, S. and Duff, A. (1980), 'Environmentalism, Middle-class Radicalism and Politics', *Sociological Review*, (New Series) 28 (2), 333-351.

DeVellis, R. F. (1991), *Scale Development*, Sage University Paper series on Applied Social Research Methods, v. no. 26, Newbury Park: Sage.

Douglas, M. (1975), 'Environments at Risk', in Douglas, M., *Implicit Meanings: Essays in Anthropology*, London: Routledge.

Douglas, M. and Wildavsky, A. (1982), *Risk and Culture*, Berkeley: University of California Press.

Dunlap, R.E. (1992), 'Trends in Public Opinion Toward Environmental Issues: 1965-1990', in Dunlap, R.E. and Mertig, A.G. (eds.), *American Environmentalism: the U.S. Environmental Movement 1970-1990*, Philadelphia: Taylor & Francis.

Ester, P. *et al* (1984), *Consumer Behaviour and Energy Policy*, Amsterdam: Elsevier.

Greeley, A. (1991), *Religion and the Environment*, Working Paper, Chicago: NORC.

Hall, T. (1986), *Nuclear Politics*, Harmondsworth: Penguin.

Heath, A. *et al* (1991), *Understanding Political Change: the British Voter 1964-1987*, Oxford: Pergamon.

Heath, A. and Topf, R. (1987), 'Political Culture', in Jowell, R., Witherspoon, S. and Brook, L. (eds.), *British Social Attitudes: the 1987 Report*, Aldershot: Gower.

Houghton, J.T., Jenkins, G.J. and Ephraums, J.J. (eds.) (1990), *Climate Change - the IPCC Scientific Assessment*, Cambridge: Cambridge University Press.

Inglehart, R. (1977), *The Silent Revolution: Changing Values and Political Styles Among Western Publics*, Princeton: Princeton University Press.

Inglehart, R. (1990), *Culture Shift in Advanced Industrial Society*, Princeton: Princeton University Press.

Martin, J. (1991), 'Measuring Green Behaviour and Attitudes', in Joint Centre for Survey Methods Newsletter, *Measuring Social Values*, vol. 11, no. 2, London: JCSM.

Martin, J. and Ashworth, K. (1991), *Measuring Green Consumer Behaviour and Attitudes to Environmental Issues*, Draft working paper, Joint Centre for Survey Methods and Joint Unit for the Study of Social Trends.

Mason, J. (1992), 'The greenhouse effect and global warming', in Cartledge, B., *Monitoring the Environment: the Linacre Lectures, 1990-91*, Oxford: Oxford University Press.

McCormick, J. (1991), *British Politics and the Environment*, London: Earthscan Publications.

McCormick, J. (1992), *The Global Environmental Movement*, London: Belhaven Press.

Merton, R. (1973), 'Science and the Social Order', in Merton, R., *The Sociology of Science: Theoretical and Empirical Investigations*, Chicago: The University of Chicago Press.

Patterson, W.C. (1986), *Nuclear Power (second edition)*, Harmondsworth: Penguin.

Schuman, H. and Presser, S. (1981), *Questions and Answers in Attitude Surveys: Experiments on Question Form, Wording and Context*, New York: Academic Press.

*Science* (1992), Vol. 256, 8 May, p. 734.

Tanur, J.M. (ed.) (1991), *Questions about Questions: inquiries into the cognitive bases of surveys*, New York: Russell Sage Foundation.

Witherspoon, S. (1988), 'Interim Report: A Woman's Work', in Jowell, R., Witherspoon, S. and Brook. L. (eds.), *British Social Attitudes: the 5th Report*, Aldershot: Gower.

Witherspoon, S. (1991), 'A Proposal for an ISSP Module on Attitudes to the Environment', working paper prepared for the International Social Survey Programme.

Wynne, B. (1989a), 'Frameworks of Rationality in Risk Management: Towards the Testing of Naive Sociology', in Brown, J. (ed.), *Environmental Threats: Perception, Analysis and Management*, London: Belhaven Press.

Wynne, B. (1989b), 'Building Public Concern into Risk Management', in Brown, J. (ed.), *Environmental Threats: Perception, Analysis and Management*, London: Belhaven Press.

Young, K. (1985), 'Local Government and the Environment', in Jowell, R. and Witherspoon, S. (eds.), *British Social Attitudes: the 1985 Report*, Aldershot: Gower.

Young, K. (1986), 'A Green and Pleasant Land?', in Jowell, R., Witherspoon, S. and Brook, L. (eds.), *British Social Attitudes: the 1986 Report*, Aldershot: Gower.

Young, K. (1987), 'Interim Report: the Countryside', in Jowell, R., Witherspoon, S. and Brook, L. (eds.), *British Social Attitudes: the 1987 Report*, Aldershot: Gower.

Young, K. (1990), 'Living Under Threat', in Jowell, R., Witherspoon, S. and Brook, L., with Taylor B. (eds.), *British Social Attitudes: the 7th Report*, Aldershot: Gower.

Young, K. (1991), 'Shades of Green', in Jowell, R., Brook, L. and Taylor, B., with Prior, G. (eds.), *British Social Attitudes: the 8th Report*, Aldershot: Dartmouth.

**Acknowledgements**

The Countryside Commission has supported the *British Social Attitudes* survey series since 1985. Our thanks are due to the Commission, and to the Economic and Social Research Council who became a co-funder of the environment module in 1990. Their help and advice have been valuable and welcome.

# 2 The influence of the recession

*Frances Cairncross* *

In the spring of 1991, when the fieldwork for the eighth *British Social Attitudes* survey was under way, Britain was in the early stages of recession. Real gross domestic product had declined in the third quarter of 1990, and continued to fall throughout 1991. For the year as a whole, GDP was 2.2 per cent below that for 1990, the sharpest fall in any big industrial country. Real personal disposable incomes (RPDI) were still rising, but at a much more modest rate than in 1988-89. An increase in RPDI of over five per cent in two successive years had given way to a more modest one per cent growth between the second quarters of 1990 and 1991.

The pervasive message from responses to a range of questions about the economy is of an end to the fat years of the mid-1980s. An exploration of this darker mood is the theme of the first part of this chapter. Deepening pessimism colours replies to questions about inflation, unemployment and the general state of the economy. In particular, replies to questions on owner-occupation reflect the squeeze on the housing market. Encouragement of owner-occupation in the 1980s was part of a remarkable attempt to destroy the so-called 'dependency culture': the belief that the state would invariably step in to help those who could not succeed on their own. Home-ownership, so the theory ran, would give people a sense of self-reliance, and a stake in the country's prosperity, which would foster hard work and enterprise. Responses of home-owners suggest a rising (and understandable) disenchantment with

* Environment Editor, *The Economist*

owner-occupation - but not yet an end to Britain's enthusiasm for home-ownership.

The latter part of this chapter explores the fate of this attempt to detach the British from their alleged dependence on the state. It picks up a theme from *The 7th Report* in which John Rentoul suggested that what he described as 'Thatcherite individualism' had largely failed to alter the political values of the British people (Rentoul, 1990). The British assume that government has a duty to intervene, not just in the provision of social services (see, for instance, Rentoul, 1990; Taylor-Gooby, 1991), but in the management of the economy. Even after more than a decade of Thatcherism, most British people still feel that the main economic levers should be in the control of government.

Nor has a decade of Thatcherism made much impression on the British belief that equality of income matters more than equality of opportunity. The data reveal resentment of the reduction in top income-tax rates and a deep-rooted feeling that family background is the key to getting ahead. Training, touted by the government, industry and the Unions as a route to better pay and prospects, is seen mainly as a way to make work more interesting.

## Economic issues

Inevitably the answers to many of the survey questions bear the mark of the particular point in the economic cycle at which they were asked. The 1991 survey caught two overlapping tides of pessimism: inflation had only barely begun to abate, and the recession was promising to move into a downward stride. Responses reflect a growing mood of insecurity about economic prospects.

### Inflation and unemployment

Inflation had begun to decline from its peak of 10.9 per cent in autumn 1990, and all the forecasts were for a rapid fall throughout 1991. But this fall, although under way, was not clearly perceived. Forty-three per cent of those asked (barely fewer than the 46 per cent of 1990), still expected prices to have gone up by 'a lot' in a year's time. The relative optimism about inflation of 1986-87 (see Taylor, 1991) had receded. Not surprisingly, almost everybody expected *some* rise in prices; perhaps the few optimists who expected stability or even a fall in prices thought that they were being asked about the prospects for a deceleration in the rate of inflation, rather than the level of prices themselves.

Gloom about inflation was deepest among those on the fringes of the labour market, and among the poorest. Among part-time employees (overwhelmingly women), 55 per cent expected prices to rise by a lot over the year ahead, compared with 38 per cent of full-time employees and only 35 per cent of the self-employed.  As the table below shows, part-timers and those who described themselves as 'looking after the home' were the only two groups where the proportion expecting a large rise in inflation had actually *increased* since 1989.

**% saying prices will go up by a lot**

|  | 1989 | 1991 |
|---|---|---|
| **All** | 45 | 43 |
| **Economic status:** | | |
| Part-time employee | 50 | 55 |
| Looking after the home | 44 | 50 |
| Retired | 49 | 43 |
| Unemployed | 46 | 42 |
| Full-time employee | 42 | 38 |
| Self-employed | 34 | 35 |

Pessimism was also strikingly greater among those on low incomes (many of whom were part-timers) than among the better-off:  twice as many of those in the lowest income group (53 per cent) as in the highest (27 per cent) expected inflation to go up by a lot.  Indeed, those on the lowest incomes were, if anything, a little more pessimistic than in 1989.

Not surprisingly, more people were *personally* worried about inflation than about unemployment, although the gap had begun to close again since 1990, when almost three times as many people said inflation was a greater worry than unemployment.  As it turned out, of course, inflation in 1991 was not as high as most respondents seemed to expect.  By the end of the year, retail prices were only 4.5 per cent higher than at the beginning.  But in most other respects the survey proved a painfully accurate predictor of Britain's deepening economic adversity.

Gloom about prospects for unemployment was more widespread in 1991 than in any previous survey year.  Between 1989, the high-water mark of the Thatcher boom, and 1991, the proportion expecting unemployment to rise by 'a lot' in the coming year shot from 10 per cent to 42 per cent; the total expecting an increase of some sort rose from 25 per cent to 71 per cent.  Here, the differences in pessimism between those in part-time and in full-time work were less marked than in respect of inflation.  Indeed, pessimism had increased most sharply among those who had been most optimistic in 1989: employees and (especially) the self-employed:

**% saying unemployment will go up by a lot**

|                        | 1989 | 1991 |
|------------------------|------|------|
| **All**                | 10   | 42   |
| **Economic status:**   |      |      |
| Unemployed             | 17   | 47   |
| Part-time employee     | 15   | 47   |
| Full-time employee     | 8    | 45   |
| Looking after the home | 9    | 43   |
| Retired                | 9    | 37   |
| Self-employed          | 5    | 32   |

But as with inflation, the self-employed remained the most cheerful group. Why? Perhaps it requires irrepressible optimism (or blind conceit) to work for oneself.

More comprehensible is the finding that pessimism about the labour market has risen since 1989 among all income groups, but has increased almost fivefold among the highest earners (14 per cent of this group in 1989 expected unemployment to go up, compared with 71 per cent in 1991). After all, redundancies have risen by an unprecedented extent in the generally well-paid south-east, in financial services and in the middle ranks of management. Indeed, responses to a number of questions reveal a faster increase in economic insecurity among the best-off than among other income groups.

## Prospects for jobs and businesses

Pessimism about the labour market carried over into the view employees took of prospects in their own jobs: the proportion expecting their employer to shed labour in the coming year crept up from 20 per cent in 1989 (the low point in the survey series) to 26 per cent in 1991. The increase in pessimism was, not surprisingly, concentrated among private sector employees.

**% expecting workplace to reduce number of employees**

|                          | 1989 | 1991 |
|--------------------------|------|------|
| **All employees**        | 20   | 26   |
| **Employment sector:**   |      |      |
| Private non-manufacturing | 13   | 18   |
| Private manufacturing    | 17   | 32   |
| Public sector*           | 30   | 30   |

* Too few respondents were employed in public sector manufacturing industry to warrant showing their responses separately.

Most people, though, expected that the number of jobs at their workplace would (at the least) remain the same.  Of course, while unemployment had risen by some 540,000 from its low point in the spring of 1990 to spring 1991 (Employment Department, 1992), its sharpest acceleration since the early 1980s had only recently begun.

Hardly any employees reported that they expected to be made redundant or believed that the firm they worked for would close down. But those who *had* already lost their jobs were in a sombre mood. Confidence about finding a suitable job had actually built up between 1984, when only one in five unemployed people were confident of finding suitable new employment, and 1989 when 46 per cent expressed some confidence.  But it fell back sharply in 1990 - an interesting finding given that unemployment in April that year (when most of the fieldwork was carried out) was at its lowest point since 1980.

An even more dramatic decline, of 21 percentage points, had taken place between 1989 and 1990 in the proportion of unemployed people who thought there was a "real chance" of finding a job in their *local* area (from 62 per cent in 1989 to 41 per cent in 1990).  Between 1990 and 1991 pessimism showed no further advance.  Still, even in 1991, confidence in finding a new job was higher than it had been in 1986, accurately reflecting the fact perhaps, that national long-term unemployment was lower than it had been five years earlier (though the trends were now moving in the opposite direction).

Curiously, considering their relatively buoyant view of the labour market as a whole, the self-employed were every bit as morose about the future of their own businesses as were employees about their employer's prospects.  The proportion of self-employed reporting that their business was doing 'quite well' or 'very well' compared with a year earlier declined from 35 per cent in 1989 to 28 per cent in 1991, an all-time low for the survey series.  The proportion who said business was doing 'not very ' or 'not at all well' almost trebled, from 10 per cent in the balmy boom days of 1989 to 28 per cent - an all-time high - in 1991.  Looking ahead only 3 in 10 of the self-employed thought that their business would do better over the coming year.  This figure is particularly depressing since business confidence surveys, such as the CBI's, usually show confidence in the spring quarter (when our fieldwork took place) to be particularly high in contrast to other quarters.

| | 1989 | 1990 | 1991 |
|---|---|---|---|
| **% of self-employed predicting that their business will do ...** | % | % | % |
| ...     better than this year | 42 | 35 | 29 |
| ...     about the same | 43 | 44 | 44 |
| ...     worse than this year | 6 | 14 | 21 |

The gap between the proportion expecting to do better and the proportion feeling they would do worse was narrower than at any time since the survey series began.

The general sense of gathering storm clouds carries through into responses to a question about Britain's industrial performance over the coming year. The percentage predicting decline doubled between 1989 and 1991:

|                                                        | 1989 | 1990 | 1991 |
|--------------------------------------------------------|------|------|------|
| **Over the next year Britain's industrial performance will:** | %    | %    | %    |
| Improve a lot                                          | 5    | 3    | 4    |
| Improve a little                                       | 25   | 16   | 17   |
| Stay much the same                                     | 47   | 50   | 39   |
| Decline a little                                       | 12   | 19   | 23   |
| Decline a lot                                          | 4    | 7    | 12   |

Overall, 35 per cent of respondents in 1991 expected decline, only 21 per cent improvement. Here, too, the self-employed were little more sanguine than those who were working for somebody else; pessimism increased fairly evenly across all income groups.

**Living standards**

The first months of 1991 once again saw decelerating inflation and rising unemployment; they also saw a continuation of the diverging trends in real incomes, characteristic of the previous decade. Those in work were often still doing well: average earnings rose nearly nine per cent over the previous 12 months, easily outstripping inflation. But people on fixed incomes, and those living on social security benefits, had seen their living standards eroded: indeed, overall, real personal disposable incomes declined between 1990 and 1991.

These conflicting trends are reflected in the view respondents took of their own living standards. As the next table shows, through the middle years of the 1980s the proportion of respondents who thought of themselves as 'low income' steadily declined to a low of 43 per cent in 1990. By 1991, that trend seemed to be reversing.

|                                                      | 1983 | 1987 | 1990 | 1991 |
|------------------------------------------------------|------|------|------|------|
| **Among which group would you place yourself...**    | %    | %    | %    | %    |
| ...high income                                       | 3    | 3    | 3    | 3    |
| ...middle income                                     | 47   | 50   | 53   | 48   |
| ...low income                                        | 50   | 46   | 43   | 47   |

The counterpart was not a drop in the tiny proportion willing to admit that they had high incomes - that remained steady - but a decline in the percentage of those putting themselves in the 'middle income' group.

Compare answers to this question with actual income levels, and a striking but curious point emerges. The biggest proportionate rise between 1990 and 1991 in the percentage of people who classified themselves as in the 'low income' group was not among the poorest, but among those in the two highest household income quartiles.

| | % in each self-assessed income group | | | |
| | Middle | | Low | |
| | 1990 | 1991 | 1990 | 1991 |
|---|---|---|---|---|
| **All** | 53 | 48 | 43 | 47 |
| **Household income quartile:** | | | | |
| Lowest | 15 | 15 | 84 | 81 |
| Second lowest | 53 | 51 | 46 | 47 |
| Second highest | 76 | 68 | 22 | 29 |
| Highest | 81 | 75 | 8 | 12 |

Over one-third more people in these groups than a year earlier perversely described themselves as in the 'low-income' bracket. These are the groups most likely to have been squeezed by rising real interest rates and the deteriorating housing market. They may have thought of their overall financial position, rather than their income alone.

A similar conflict of perception is apparent when we asked about the extent to which household income had fallen behind prices. More than half (55 per cent) of all respondents thought their household income had *not* kept pace with prices over the previous year. This represents a rise of 23 per cent since 1987.

| | % saying household income has fallen behind prices | | % increase since 1987 |
| | 1987 | 1991 | |
|---|---|---|---|
| **All** | 45 | 55 | +23 |
| **Economic status:** | | | |
| Full-time employee | 33 | 42 | +27 |
| Part-time employee | 38 | 46 | +22 |
| Self-employed | 32 | 51 | +56 |
| Unemployed | 68 | 82 | +21 |
| Looking after the home | 52 | 60 | +15 |
| Retired | 60 | 67 | +12 |
| **Household income quartile:** | | | |
| Lowest | 70 | 76 | + 9 |
| Second lowest | 54 | 58 | + 7 |
| Second highest | 32 | 41 | +28 |
| Highest | 24 | 30 | +25 |

Strikingly, the proportion who thought their real income had declined rose by around a quarter among the better-off, and by more than a half among the self-employed. In fact, the majority would have enjoyed a real rise in living standards over this period.

At the same time, though, the proportion of employees who felt their pay was 'reasonable' continued to increase (rising from 54 per cent in 1987 to 63 per cent four years later); while the proportion who thought their pay was 'on the high side' was, although still modest at nine per cent, the highest in the survey series' history. On a rough and ready 'increase in relative prosperity' index, contentment increased between 1989 and 1991 most strikingly among employees in the public sector and among those with the highest earnings; it increased least among part-timers (who are mainly women), those in private services and the worst paid (three largely overlapping groups). But employees in every sector (private and public, manufacturing and services) felt more contented with their pay in 1991 than they had done two years previously.

A somewhat similar picture emerged when people were asked how well they were coping on their present income. As noted in *The 8th Report*, responses to this question have remained remarkably constant over the years (Taylor, 1991, p. 209). Overall, the proportion claiming to be living comfortably was slightly higher than in 1984 (when the question was first asked). Those in full-time work were particularly likely to feel better off than they had done seven years earlier. By contrast, the self-employed, unemployed and students were all feeling the pinch more. However, retired people appeared to be coping better than other economically inactive groups, a reply that matches answers to a specific question on the adequacy of the state retirement pension. Here, the proportion claiming that the pension was 'very low' had almost doubled (from 23 per cent to 45 per cent) between 1983 and 1990; but in 1991 it sharply declined to 1986 levels (35 per cent). In fact, since the mid 1980s, the real value of the state retirement pension has kept comfortably above that of the RPI index for pensioner households. While between 1983 and 1991 the state pension rose some 58 per cent in money terms, the pensioner RPI rose by only 47 per cent.[1]

The proportion of respondents who thought that their household income was unlikely to keep up with prices over the *coming* year was in 1991 much what it had been a year earlier, but higher than in 1989 (in turn higher than in 1987). By and large, pessimism increased most noticeably among those who had been most optimistic back in 1987, approaching the height of the boom (the self-employed and the better-off):

|  | % saying household income will fall behind prices | | % increase since 1987 |
|  | 1987 | 1991 |  |
|---|---|---|---|
| **All** | 39 | 47 | +21 |
| **Economic status:** | | | |
| Full-time employee | 29 | 38 | +29 |
| Part-time employee | 32 | 45 | +39 |
| Self-employed | 20 | 39 | +97 |
| Unemployed | 59 | 68 | +15 |
| Looking after the home | 47 | 54 | +14 |
| Retired | 57 | 61 | + 8 |
| **Household income quartile:** | | | |
| Lowest | 65 | 65 | - |
| Second lowest | 47 | 52 | +12 |
| Second highest | 29 | 37 | +28 |
| Highest | 19 | 24 | +27 |

Gloomiest of all in 1991, as they had been in 1987 but at lower levels, were the unemployed and the retired.

## The housing market

*Confidence in the market*

Although the weakening labour market probably contributed to the increase in pessimism we have noted, another important influence appears to have been the deteriorating housing market. In the early months of 1990 repossessions by building societies and banks had just begun to rise (Council of Mortgage Lenders, 1992, Table 11), as had the number of mortgages in arrear. But home-owners were already being squeezed from two directions.

First, from a trough of around 9.5 per cent in the spring of 1988 mortgage interest rates climbed to a peak of 15.4 per cent in February 1990. They began to fall only towards the end of 1990, and continued to decline throughout 1991. At the time of fieldwork, they stood at around 12.8 per cent (Council of Mortgage Lenders, 1992, Table 25). But the rate of increase of retail prices had fallen even more, so the real rate of interest on mortgage debt actually rose. Secondly, house-price inflation, running at an annual rate of 23 per cent in 1988, fell to seven per cent in 1990. In the first quarter of 1991, for the first time for a decade, house prices were actually static in money terms (Council of Mortgage Lenders, 1992, Table 16) and declined in real terms.

So home-owners with mortgages felt poorer in two separate ways. Their monthly repayments were taking a larger share of their incomes, and their main asset was worth less. Both their disposable income and their wealth declined. The experience of falling house prices was entirely new to most people. Thanks to the proliferation of 100 per cent mortgages in the late 1980s, a significant minority of home-owners found that they had debts that were larger than the asset against which they had borrowed. Among the worst affected were those who had scrambled to take out joint mortgages in the summer of 1988, before separate tax relief against multiple mortgages on a single property was withdrawn. Some building societies found that, by the end of 1991, almost half their repossessed properties had been owned by single people.

This searing experience for borrowers came at the end of a decade in which the government had worked hard to encourage the spread of home ownership. By spring 1991, almost one and a half million council tenants had bought their homes (CSO, 1992), taking advantage of large discounts, and more British households own their own homes than do households in the majority of EC countries (Tchernia, 1991). But the 1991 survey reflects, as did that of 1990 (Curtice, 1991), what appears to be a new and growing disenchantment with home ownership. We cannot yet tell, until the housing market recovers, whether this disenchantment represents a radical change in the British romance with home ownership, or whether it is a transient response to the fall in prices.

The recovery of the market will surely be slow, hindered in the early 1990s by the overhang of repossessed properties and frustrated sellers. In the latter part of the decade it will probably be restrained by demographic changes, as the number of people in their twenties, the main age of first-time home-buying, begins to decline. But as long as home-ownership is favoured by the taxation system, most British households are likely to continue to regard a home of their own as a good investment.

### Rewards and risks of home-ownership

When asked whether they would advise a newly married couple, both with steady jobs, to buy or to rent a home, hardly anyone suggested renting as a long-term answer. But the proportion who thought young-marrieds should buy a home as soon as possible dropped by 18 percentage points (from 78 per cent to 60 per cent) between 1989 and 1991, with a corresponding rise in the proportion who suggested waiting a bit and then buying. The proportion thinking that owning a home could be a risky investment, only 25 per cent in 1986, had risen by 1991 to 42 per cent. Indeed, most of the traditional arguments for home ownership appeared to have weakened since 1986, as the following table shows:

## Attitudes towards home ownership

### 'Positive' statements

| % strongly agreeing that: | 1986 | 1990 | 1991 |
|---|---|---|---|
| Buying a home works out cheaper than paying rent | 44 | 33 | 30 |
| Owning a home gives you freedom to alter it | 40 | 31 | 22 |
| Your own home will be something to leave to your family | 39 | 34 | 26 |
| Owning a home makes it easier to move | 27 | 19 | 16 |

### 'Negative' statements

| % agreeing that: | 1986 | 1990 | 1991 |
|---|---|---|---|
| Couples who buy their own home would be wise to wait before starting a family | 59 | 61 | 61 |
| Owning a home is too much of a risk for couples without secure jobs | 59 | 64 | 69 |
| Owning your home is just too much of a responsibility | 12 | 10 | 10 |
| Owning your home can be a risky investment | 25 | 34 | 43 |
| Owning your home ties up money you may need for other things | 35 | 37 | 35 |
| Owning your home is a big financial burden to repair and maintain | 50 | 55 | 57 |

For instance, fewer people than before agreed that buying a home is cheaper than renting, or that owning your home makes it easier to move when you want to. The proportion agreeing strongly with the proposition that 'owning a home gives you the freedom to do what you want to it' almost halved. More thought a home was a big financial burden to repair and maintain, and that it was too much of a risk for couples without secure jobs; fewer agreed that it was 'something to leave to your family'. Lack of confidence was especially pronounced among younger (18-34 year old) home-owners - presumably with mortgage burdens that were more difficult to bear.

The reasons for this disillusion are evident from responses to questions on how people were coping with their mortgages. Half of those buying a home on a mortgage admitted that they were having problems meeting the cost, and more than one in eight home-buyers said that coping with mortgage payments was 'very difficult'. Indeed, over a third (35 per cent) of those in the lowest income group claimed to be finding it 'very difficult' to cope.  Among those who expected to move home in the near future, there was a rise between 1990 and 1991 in the proportion who expected to rent from a local authority, and a fall in the proportion expecting to buy, a stark reversal of the trends apparent in the mid-to-late 1980s:

|                                    | 1985 | 1986 | 1989 | 1990 | 1991 |
|------------------------------------|------|------|------|------|------|
| % expecting to:                    | %    | %    | %    | %    | %    |
| Buy next home                      | 59   | 68   | 68   | 71   | 63   |
| Rent next home from local authority| 23   | 18   | 13   | 10   | 16   |
| Rent next home from other landlord | 11   | 9    | 11   | 14   | 15   |

Yet the answers to other questions strongly suggest that the British love affair with home ownership is not yet over.  True, there has been a small decline (five percentage points since 1987) in the proportion of tenants who would prefer to buy than rent their homes; but two-thirds of all tenants would still prefer to own their home (although three-quarters do not *expect* to be able to do so within the next two years).  The proportion of local authority tenants expecting to buy their current home (17 per cent) was also higher in 1991 than it had been in 1983 or 1987, although it was those in work, and especially in white-collar work, who were most confident of exercising their right-to-buy.  Surprisingly too, a substantial majority (64 per cent) of all respondents still thought that house prices in their area would rise over the year ahead; half of them thought they would go up by 'a little' and one in seven by 'a lot'.  In fact, nationally house prices declined by 3.8 per cent in money terms between March 1991 and March 1992 (although this overall fall disguises some quite marked regional variations).

No wonder that the British remain unenthusiastic about other investments.  Asked what they would do if their monthly payments were much lower, the most popular choices among owner-occupiers with mortgages were to spend more on themselves and their families, or to spend the extra money on home improvements.  One in five said they were 'very likely' to save any spare cash with a building society; one in ten said they would be 'very likely' to put the money in a pension or savings plan; and a mere two per cent said the same of shares or unit trusts.  Bricks and mortar remain, for the time being, the favourite investment of the British.

## The government's role in the economy

A theme explored in several of the *British Social Attitudes* reports is that of the role of the state *vis-à-vis* the role of the individual.  The remainder of this chapter takes up that theme.  This section explores the role that people expect the state to play in directing the economy and in tackling poverty.  The next section looks at self-betterment: how far do people see it as their own responsibility (rather than that of government) to improve their position in life?

In the *Special International Report*, Peter Taylor-Gooby drew attention to the fact that the British are second only to the Italians in their enthusiasm for government-financed job creation projects.  The British surpassed Americans, Australians, Austrians and West Germans in their belief that the government is responsible for providing a job for everyone who wants one and for keeping prices under control; they surpassed all these nations (even the interventionist Italians) in their belief that government should 'provide industry with the help it needs to grow' (Taylor-Gooby, 1989).

Given these views, it is perhaps not surprising that the 1991 survey should have found a rising tide of support for government intervention to tackle the deteriorating British economy.  The proportion supporting the control of wages by law, which had fallen from 48 per cent in 1983 to 28 per cent in 1989, rose over the following two years (to 33 per cent in 1991).  Clearly the memory of past failures of pay policy, legal and voluntary, has begun to dim.  So has the memory of the *débâcles* of price controls.  Support for the control of prices by law was still an astonishing 70 per cent in 1983, and had fallen only to 55 per cent by 1989.  The popularity of this expedient too has apparently begun to revive, gaining the support of 60 per cent of respondents in 1991.

Introducing import controls wins even more enthusiastic endorsement.  Indeed, there was no clear decline in support for protectionism (as there was for a prices and incomes policy) in the mid 1980s.  Since 1983 import controls have been consistently backed by around two-thirds of respondents.  Government action to cut interest rates had the backing of nine in ten respondents in 1991, while controls on hire purchase and credit, last used in the 1970s, were backed by four in five.

Interventionist industrial policy has consistently commanded majority support.  The proportion of respondents backing a rise in government subsidies for private industry had dwindled after 1983 (but to 53 per cent at the lowest) as industry climbed out of the early 1980s' recession.  But in 1990 enthusiasm began to revive, and in 1991 subsidies were advocated by 58 per cent of respondents.  The proportion in favour of government setting up construction projects to create more jobs has been between four-fifths and nine-tenths since the survey series began in 1983.  Moreover, three-fifths of those questioned in 1990 were in favour of support for declining industries to protect jobs.  Not surprisingly, there was a fall in support too for the Conservative government's general non-interventionist industrial philosophy.  In 1985, 52 per cent of respondents believed that there should be less government regulation of business: by 1991, that proportion had fallen to 42 per cent.

| % supporting: | All |
|---|---|
| Wage controls | 33 |
| Price controls | 60 |
| Reducing health and education spending | 7 |
| Increasing subsidies for private industry | 58 |
| Reducing defence spending | 55 |
| Government incentives for job-sharing | 70 |
| Government set up job-creating projects | 84 |
| Cutting interest rates | 90 |
| Controls on HP and credit | 81 |
| Cutting down on foreign goods | 67 |

On only three policies are there any party differences to speak of:

- price controls (71 per cent of Labour supporters as opposed to 49 per cent of Conservatives back them)
- defence spending (three in five Labour and Liberal Democrat identifiers support a reduction as opposed to just under half of Conservatives)
- subsidies for industry (27 per cent of Conservatives but 40 per cent of Labour identifiers *oppose* government subsidies).

The British enthusiasm for government intervention in industry is by no means unique, as the *International Social Survey Programme* shows. Looking just at Britain, Australia, West Germany, the United States and Italy, we are able to see trends over time since these questions were first asked in 1985 (see Taylor-Gooby, 1989).

Asked about most aspects of government intervention, whether it be price control or support for declining industries to protect jobs, the Italians leap to the head of the table (astonishingly, given that they have had the least effective and most short-lived governments by far of the countries surveyed). Britain, however, is typically the second- or third-most enthusiastic supporter of intervention.

Thus, asked in 1990 whether prices should be controlled by law, 54 per cent of British respondents were in favour, almost as many as in Australia (though well behind Italy's 87 per cent). Asked whether declining industries should be supported to protect jobs, 59 per cent of the British were in favour, much the same proportion as in West Germany - but well behind Italy's 76 per cent. Asked whether government should finance job-creation projects, 82 per cent of Britons were in favour - a proportion beaten only by the Italians, with 89 per cent. And asked whether government should help industry develop new projects and technologies, 88 per cent of Britons agreed - a proportion exceeded this time only by the Australians, with 91 per cent.

Only in one area are the British more wary of government intervention than other countries surveyed. Asked whether wages should be controlled by law, only 25 per cent of Britons were in favour, the same proportion as that of the strikingly non-interventionist Americans. On the other hand, asked whether government should cut its spending, the British leap to the opposite extreme: only 41 per cent were in favour, the smallest proportion in any of the five countries.

It seems, however, that hostility to industrial intervention has receded internationally. In every one of the five countries, the proportion of those favouring less regulation of business declined between 1985 and 1990 - even (although by the narrowest margin) in interventionist Italy. In Britain, the proportion who thought there should be less government regulation changed more than anywhere else, falling by 13 percentage points, from a majority of respondents in 1985 (55 per cent) to a minority in 1990 (42 per cent).

## Support for state welfare

Support for interventionist industrial policy goes hand-in-hand ideologically with enthusiasm for government spending on health and education. Taylor-Gooby (1989) found that in 1985, 88 per cent of Britons wanted more state spending on health and 75 per cent wanted more on education. Both these proportions were higher than in any of the five other countries surveyed. The story was much the same when these questions were repeated in 1990. Not surprisingly, the suggestion that government should reduce spending on health and education to help the economy was opposed by 91 per cent of respondents in 1991 - and by similarly massive majorities through the earlier years of the survey series. Such a consistent consensus is found in responses to only a very few other questions in the survey.

### Social spending and taxation

Not only do the British reject *cuts* in spending on health and education: a majority claims to support *tax increases* to finance more spending on welfare services. In 1983, just over half of respondents agreed that taxes and spending on health, education and social benefits should be kept at their present levels, while around a third wanted higher taxes to pay for more spending on these services. By 1990 these proportions had been roughly reversed:

| If the government had to choose, it should: | 1983 % | 1986 % | 1990 % | 1991 % |
|---|---|---|---|---|
| Reduce taxes and spend less | 9 | 5 | 3 | 3 |
| Keep taxes and spending at the same level as now | 54 | 44 | 37 | 29 |
| Increase taxes and spend more | 32 | 46 | 54 | 65 |

Indeed, 1991 saw the largest year-on-year rise in the survey series' history in the proportion of respondents claiming to be willing to see higher taxes to pay for more social spending - ironically, given the election defeat in 1992 of the two parties that proposed higher taxation for just such ends. The rise was more or less uniform across all social groups. As always with such questions, it is unclear whether respondents imagined paying the extra tax themselves - or benefiting from the improvement in services while others footed the bill. The election results suggest that the latter is more likely to be the case.

*Spending on welfare benefits*

Attitudes to spending on welfare *benefits* are more ambivalent. These questions are not all asked each year but the latest figures give a good picture. In 1991, 58 per cent of respondents agreed with the proposition that the government should spend more on welfare benefits for the poor, even if it meant higher taxes. In 1990, the proportion of respondents agreeing with the statement, 'large numbers of people these days falsely claim benefits', at 69 per cent had barely changed since 1983. A rather larger but equally constant proportion (84 per cent in 1990) agreed with the proposition that "large numbers of people who are eligible for benefits these days fail to claim them".

The favourite priority for more benefit spending has always been retirement pensions, followed at a long distance by benefits for disabled people. The most striking change in recent years has been an increase in support for more spending on child benefit: in 1990 it overtook unemployment benefit as the third most popular priority for additional social security spending. Of course, child benefit was pegged since 1987 at £7.25 a week for each child. During the following four years, its real value had declined and people seem to have been aware of this. The increase (by £1.00 a week, but for only the first child) at about the time of the 1991 fieldwork perhaps served as a reminder as to how much the value of child benefit had been eroded.

Support for more spending on unemployment benefit, stable for the first five years of the survey, declined steeply in 1989 as the number of people registered as unemployed fell below two million; but support failed to rise again as unemployment started to rise during 1990. Indeed several answers reveal a deep-rooted suspicion of the unemployed. Successive *British Social Attitudes* reports have shown that the British make distinctions between the 'deserving' and 'undeserving' poor, and that unemployed people tend to fall into the latter group (for instance, Taylor-Gooby, 1990, pp. 6-7). Thus, as many as two in five respondents in 1991 agreed that 'most unemployed people could find a job if they really wanted one', and three in ten believed that 'most people on the dole are fiddling in one way or another'.

Questions about the adequacy of benefits revealed even greater ambiguities. On balance, *British Social Attitudes* respondents have consistently thought that unemployment benefits were 'too low and cause hardship' rather than 'too high and discourage people from finding jobs'. Moreover, the gap between respondents who thought them too low and those who thought them too high widened from an average of 13 percentage points in 1983-86 to 23 points in 1987-91. The real value of unemployment benefit has kept pace with RPI but has lagged behind average earnings, and the public seems to be aware of this. Yet answers to subsequent questions reveal that many people do not know what unemployment benefit pays. We asked about the living standards of a married couple without children, living entirely on unemployment benefit. At first, 17 per cent of respondents described such a couple as 'really poor' while 20 per cent thought they 'had enough to live on'. Those proportions changed, to 41 per cent and eight per cent respectively, when respondents were asked about an identical couple living on £60 a week (the equivalent of unemployment benefit at that time, excluding any housing benefit).

## Social inequality

In the *Special International Report*, Tom Smith drew attention to the relative lack of support for welfare programmes in the capitalist democracies of the United States and Australia, compared with Europe's social democracies. One reason he advanced to explain this was their greater contentment with the current distribution of income and opportunities for the advancement of their citizens (Smith 1989). In sharp contrast, three-quarters of British respondents to the 1987 survey said that income differences were too large: a higher proportion than in any of the six other countries surveyed except Italy. And the proportion of Britons who felt they had a good chance of improving their living standard was only half as great as in the United States.

Questions asked on other *British Social Attitudes* fieldwork rounds in the mid-1980s brought out other aspects of this British sense of social injustice. In 1986, 70 per cent of respondents felt that a person whose parents were rich had a better chance of earning a lot than one whose parents were poor; almost as many (67 per cent) agreed that a person whose father was a professional person was more likely to earn 'a lot of money' than one whose parents were poor; and nearly half believed that 'what you achieve in life depends largely on your family background'.

These questions have not been asked recently. But others, put more regularly, suggest a rising belief in the persistence of social inequality in Britain. For instance, the proportion agreeing with the proposition that taxes on those with high incomes are too low increased by 13 percentage points between 1987 and 1989. It was in the intervening year that the top rate of income tax was cut from 60 per cent to 40 per cent. Subsequent years have continued to show that half of all respondents think the better-off are undertaxed:

**Taxation levels for different income groups**

|                                          | 1983 | 1987 | 1989 | 1991 |
|------------------------------------------|------|------|------|------|
| **For those with high incomes taxation is:** | %    | %    | %    | %    |
| Much too low/Too low                     | 32   | 39   | 52   | 49   |
| About right                              | 36   | 37   | 33   | 35   |
| Too high/Much too high                   | 29   | 21   | 12   | 13   |
| **For those with middle incomes taxation is:** | %    | %    | %    | %    |
| Much too low/Too low                     | 4    | 5    | 6    | 6    |
| About right                              | 50   | 56   | 64   | 66   |
| Too high/Much too high                   | 44   | 36   | 27   | 25   |

As this table shows, there was a steady fall until 1989 in the proportion believing that people on middle incomes were overtaxed. Since then it has remained fairly constant.

At the same time, the proportion who believe that the gap between those with high incomes and those with low incomes is excessive has gradually increased, from 72 per cent in 1983 to 79 per cent in 1991. Even among those on the highest incomes, this view gained ground markedly significantly between 1987 and 1991.

## Education and training

Education and training are important determinants of lifetime incomes. If the British had indeed developed a new self-reliance in the 1980s, one might perhaps expect to see an increased enthusiasm for training. There are some signs that this has occurred, but they are ambiguous.

Respondents have been asked in some years, but not in 1990 or 1991, whether they would be willing to retrain for a new job if they became unemployed. Four out of five expressed some willingness to retrain, but the proportion did not increase during the 1980s. Among those already unemployed, enthusiasm for retraining is *less* marked: three out of five were willing in 1989, but that proportion had fallen from four out of five in 1983.  Could this be a sign of disillusionment or despair, as greater numbers of long-term unemployed realise their chances of getting a job again are receding - whatever efforts they might make?

Questions in the most recent survey suggest an increase both in the amount of work-related training on offer, and in willingness to undertake it.  For instance, half of respondents in 1991 reported having some formal work-related training, compared with 40 per cent in 1987.  Half of all employees questioned said that, within the previous two years, they had been given special talks or lectures about their work or been asked to read things to help them learn about the job they were doing.  Some 43 per cent said they had had some on-the-job training, and 38 per cent had been placed with more experienced people to see how their job should be done.  A third of employees said they had been given practice assignments to learn their job, and been sent on courses to learn new methods.  In every case, these proportions were higher in 1991 than they had been in 1987.

Employees were also more likely to expect work-related training in the future: 45 per cent expected some in the coming two years, compared with 39 per cent in 1987.  Slightly over half of employees (52 per cent) expressed a wish for further training, a small increase on the figure for 1987.  Workplace training is clearly not seen as appropriate only for the young.

People nowadays are more likely to expect to be trained, and they increasingly see it as an employer's duty to provide training.  But many also feel it is to the employer's advantage.  For example, 51 per cent feel that "having well-trained staff benefits employers more than workers".  Eighty-five per cent agree with the statement that "employers would benefit if they spent more time and money on training their staff".  Three-quarters feel that "employers should be made to provide some sort of regular training for all staff".  And although 44 per cent also feel that "most employers are unwilling to pay for better training for their staff", this is fewer than the 51 per cent who agreed with that statement in 1987.

In this area, as in other areas of economic activity, the survey found a growing desire for government involvement.  In 1987, 51 per cent of respondents believed that the government ought to help employers pay for staff training; by 1991, that proportion had increased to 60 per cent.  In particular, people felt that the government should share the costs of training young people: seven out of ten supported that view.  Although 48 per cent took the view that government training programmes for school leavers benefited employers more than the young people taking part, this again is a slightly smaller proportion than those who took that view in 1987.

But why does training matter to people? From a national point of view, it may be important for economic competitiveness.  From an individual standpoint, it may be a means of self-advancement (or financial gain) and a way to make work more interesting and worthwhile.  Asked why they might like more training, hardly any employees (a mere three per cent) gave their main reason as "to earn more money" - and only a further eight per cent gave it even as a secondary reason. Easily the most popular responses were "to learn new sorts of skills" given by 35 per cent as their first or second reason, and "to make work more interesting" (23 per cent). (See also Brook, Prior and Taylor, 1992.)

It is interesting to compare these responses with some of those to questions on attitudes to work, which show that employees rank work interest as highly as job security, and significantly ahead of good opportunities for advancement or a high income.

## Party politics

Evidence from successive *British Social Attitudes* surveys suggests that the British psyche has emerged remarkably unscathed from a decade of Thatcherite rule. Traces of the 'enterprise culture' are rare (see, for instance, Blanchflower and Oswald, 1990; Jowell and Topf, 1988). Most people clearly believe that the state should guide the market economy with a heavy hand and look after those who cannot fend for themselves. Given that the survey was carried out only a year before a general election in which the Conservatives were returned for an unprecedented fourth term in succession, do the survey's findings say anything about the ideological differences among supporters of the three main political parties?

One striking finding is that although pessimism about the economy's prospects tended to be less widespread among Conservatives than among supporters of the other two parties, it had deepened more rapidly. For example, in 1989 only three per cent of Conservatives but 16 per cent of Labour identifiers had expected unemployment to rise 'a lot' over the coming year. In 1991, the Conservative proportion had risen tenfold, to 31 per cent, while the Labour proportion had roughly trebled, to 53 per cent. The increase in gloom among Liberal Democrat identifiers, from seven per cent to 41 per cent, was midway between the two.

This change of sentiment among Conservative identifiers seems to square with their experience at work. In 1989 they had been markedly more confident than supporters of the other two parties that staffing levels at their workplace were likely to rise over the year ahead. By 1991 that optimism had receded by 11 percentage points, and the rise in those expecting a reduction in the number of jobs at their workplace was more marked than for those of other political persuasions.

Similarly, in 1989 only 10 per cent of Conservative identifiers expected a decline in Britain's industrial performance over the year ahead, compared with 17 per cent of Liberal Democrats and 24 per cent of Labour Party identifiers. In 1991, those proportions had risen to 24 per cent, 46 per cent and 40 per cent respectively: again, the sharpest increase in pessimism was among Conservatives and Liberal Democrats. And the increase between 1987 and 1991, in the proportion of Conservatives who felt that their household income had not kept pace with prices over the past year was 30 per cent, a higher increase than among Liberal Democrats or Labour identifiers.

Nor do Conservative identifiers seem any more comfortable than they ever have done, according to our findings, with some of the main tenets of their party's philosophy. One-third in 1991 thought that taxes were too low for people with high incomes, an increase from the quarter who took that view in 1988. Half of Conservative identifiers believe in price control (although 71 per cent of Labour identifiers take that view). And Conservatives are more likely than those of other political persuasions to believe in subsidies for private industry: two-thirds of Conservatives back them, compared with 54 per cent of Labour identifiers.

## Conclusions

It is difficult to read through the results of the survey without wondering at the outcome of the 1992 general election. A year before that contest was held, the British were feeling a sense of deepening unease about the security of their jobs and the value of their favourite investment, their home. A growing number expected unemployment to rise; but few yet perceived clearly that the rate of inflation was slowing down.

More extraordinary, the survey reveals an acute contrast between the main economic aims of the Conservative government (still propounded, though in less strident tone, by John Major) and the beliefs of many electors, Conservative identifiers included. Protectionism and subsidies are seen as highly desirable instruments of economic policy. The concept of price control is popular. Social spending, especially on health and education, is seen as highly desirable. Tax cuts for the rich are resented. Training is not widely seen as a route to better pay and prospects. In all these ways, the British retain the attitudes that coloured the policies of both the main political parties through the postwar period up to the arrival of Mrs Thatcher.

This raises two intriguing but unanswerable questions. First, why was Mr Major returned to Downing Street? Part of the answer may be that the British thought that, while the economy was in a mess, that mess would be worse under Labour; part, that people feared the impact of Labour's tax plans on their incomes more than they cared about differences in dogma. But an alternative explanation may be that people have only a hazy idea of the economic policies for which the main parties stand, and cast their votes for other, less cerebral reasons.

The other question is the implication of this divergence between rulers and ruled over the longer term. British governments have long been interventionist. Mrs Thatcher's policies represented a radical break with a trend, and some of her supporters have argued that this was the reason for her extraordinary election successes. In fact, the survey's results suggest that her success was in spite of, rather than because of, her economic philosophy. If a future British government slipped back into industrial intervention, price controls and heavy taxes on the genuinely rich, the British might heave a sigh of comfortable familiarity.

## Note

1. Indices of retail prices for pensioner households are derived from Table 6.6 of the July 1992 issue of the *Employment Gazette* (Employment Department); and figures for state retirement pension rates since 1983 are taken from Table B1.01 of *Social Security Statistics 1991* (Department of Social Security).

## References

Blanchflower, D. and Oswald, J. (1990), 'Self-employment and the Enterprise Culture', in Jowell, R., Witherspoon, S. and Brook, L. with Taylor, B. (eds.) *British Social Attitudes: the 7th Report,* Aldershot: Gower.
Brook, L., Prior, G. and Taylor, B. (1992), *British Social Attitudes, 1991 Survey: A Report for the Employment Department,* London: SCPR.
Central Statistical Office (CSO) (1992), *Social Trends 22,* London: HMSO.
Council of Mortgage Lenders (CML) (1992), *Housing Finance,* No.14, May 1992, London: CML.
Curtice, J. (1991), 'House and Home', in Jowell, R., Brook, L. and Taylor, B. with Prior, G. (eds.), *British Social Attitudes: the 8th Report,* Aldershot: Dartmouth.
Department of Social Security (1992), *Social Security Statistics, 1991,* London: HMSO.
Employment Department (1992), *Employment Gazette,* July 1992, London: HMSO.
Jowell, R. and Topf, R. (1988), 'Trust in the Establishment', in Jowell, R., Witherspoon, S. and Brook, L. (eds.), *British Social Attitudes: the 5th Report,* Aldershot, Gower.
Rentoul, J. (1990), 'Individualism', in Jowell, R., Witherspoon, S. and Brook, L. with Taylor, B. (eds.), *British Social Attitudes: the 7th Report,* Aldershot: Gower.
Smith, T. (1989), 'Inequality and Welfare', in Jowell, R., Witherspoon, S. and Brook, L. (eds.), *British Social Attitudes: Special International Report,* Aldershot: Gower.
Taylor, B. (1991), 'Interim Report: Economic Outlook', in Jowell, R., Brook, L. and Taylor, B., with Prior, G. (eds.), *British Social Attitudes: the 8th Report,* Aldershot: Dartmouth.
Taylor-Gooby, P. (1989), 'The Role of the State', in Jowell, R., Witherspoon, S. and Brook, L. (eds.), *British Social Attitudes: special international report,* Aldershot: Gower.
Taylor-Gooby, P. (1990), 'Social Welfare: The Unkindest Cuts', in Jowell, R., Witherspoon, S. and Brook, L. with Taylor, B. (eds.), *British Social Attitudes: the 7th Report,* Aldershot: Gower.
Taylor-Gooby, P. (1991), 'Attachment to the Welfare State', in Jowell, R., Brook, L. and Taylor, B. with Prior, G. (eds.), *British Social Attitudes: the 8th Report,* Aldershot: Dartmouth
Tcherina, J-F., (1991), 'The Factual Data Obtained from the Eurobarometer Surveys: How They Help in Describing the Member States', in Reif, K. and Inglehart, R. (eds.) *Eurobarometer: the Dynamics of European Public Opinion,* Basingstoke: Macmillan.

**Acknowledgments**

SCPR is grateful to the Employment Department whose financial support for the survey series since 1984 has enabled us to continue to ask questions on labour market and workplace issues, including those on training that are reported here.

We also thank the Department of the Environment, who have provided funding since 1985 to enable us to field questions on housing issues.

# 3 Religion in Britain, Ireland and the USA

*Andrew Greeley* *

In the debate about the sociology of religion in Britain it has been pretty clearly established that religious belief, and religious practice in any but the ceremonial sense, are not at the high levels one might expect in a country where religion was once an important part of life (Wilson, 1969, 1976; Martin, 1967, 1969, 1978), and where the Church is established - in every sense of the word. The issue remains, however, as to whether the British are devout in comparison to people elsewhere. In this chapter, comparisons will be made with people in three other societies - the United States, the Irish Republic and the six counties of Northern Ireland - where levels of religious devotion have traditionally been high (even very high).

The data analysed in this chapter are taken from the questionnaire module on religion, fielded in 1991 as part of the International Social Survey Programme (ISSP). For fuller details of the Programme, see the Introduction to this report. The exact wording of questions is given in Appendix III.

As we shall see, the British are not on the whole devout, and indeed are not as religious as the three comparison groups available for this analysis. Yet they are certainly not an irreligious people.[1] Seven out of ten believe in God, more than half believe in life after death and in heaven; more than two out of five believe in religious miracles and some kind of biblical inspiration; almost two thirds belong to a religious denomination. Moreover, 16 per cent attend services at least two or three times a month,

---

* Professor of Social Science, University of Chicago.

more than one out of four pray at least once a week and 28 per cent have had an intense 'mystical' experience.* The picture in Britain is indeed more complicated than that in the three comparative groups, and so for the sociologist of religion more interesting. Britain is not a country where religion is especially vigorous, but neither is it a country where religion is dying. There is reason to believe that this condition is not new and indeed may be several centuries old.

## The 'decline of religion'

Much of the discussion of 'secularisation' presumes an earlier era (often not precisely designated) characterised by high levels of religious faith and devotion, a kind of golden age since when there has been an obvious and indisputable decline. However, the existence of this golden age is usually assumed rather than proven, and the most recent historical research casts doubt on the assumption. Instead, some scholars are beginning to question whether there was all that much devotion in western Europe even in the high middle ages. Finke and Stark (1992) note that most medieval rural churches were far too small to provide room for all the people in their parishes, and cite evidence that in 1738 thirty Oxfordshire parishes reported only a combined average total of 911 communicants on the four great festivals of Christmas, Easter, Whitsun, and Ascension. They calculate church membership in England as 11.5 per cent of the population in 1800, 16.7 per cent in 1850 and 18.6 per cent in 1900. As we shall see, the monthly attendance at religious services reported by British respondents in the present analysis is in fact higher even than this last figure.

The histories of the British churches in the 19th century are filled with quotes deploring the lack of devotion among the people. Earlier still, Wickham's (1957) study of Sheffield shows that there is little evidence of religious devotion at the beginning of the 18th century. Even allowing for the clerical propensity for alarmist views, it seems clear that the industrial urban working class was not devout. The portrait of the Church of England painted by the 19th century's most perceptive sociological novelist, Anthony Trollope, would hardly lead one to believe that congregants were elbowing each other to obtain admission to churches and chapels on Sunday morning.

Was England 'burned out' religiously following the civil war? Or was there, even when the Puritans were fighting the King's men, just beneath the surface of events little propensity to religious devotion? Butler (1990), in perhaps the best account of religion in Britain and the USA in

---

* Throughout this chapter, unlike the rest of the chapters in this report, and for reasons of comparability, respondents answering 'Can't choose' or 'Don't know' or not answering are excluded from the base when calculating percentages. Figures in Appendix III show the full distribution of responses in Britain and Northern Ireland to each question.

the 17th century, notes that Dissent (Congregationalism) declined rapidly after the end of the Cromwellian years, from a high of no more than five per cent in 1670 to less than two per cent of the population in 1700.[2] The real religion of Britain at the time (and of the USA too) was, it may be argued, magic. Indeed, there is some doubt as to whether the peasant populations of Europe were ever converted to orthodox and devout Christianity. They may have gone to church services when they were constrained to do so. But in the absence of this constraint, they participated irregularly (if at all) and mixed Christian practices with survivals of pagan superstition and magic that have by no means disappeared even today (Carroll, 1992). It is not suggested that these peasants - the overwhelming majority of Europeans outside Britain *were* peasants until the present century - were not Christian. However, it now seems probable that they were Christian in their fashion and according to their own norms - a style of Christianity acceptable neither to the religious authorities of their time (though the authorities were able to do relatively little about it) nor to the sociologists of religious faith and religious devotion of the present time.

Clearly the starting point of the evolutionary 'secularisation' model needs to be re-examined. Moreover further work on the popular religious beliefs and practices of the so-called Ages of Faith has yet to be done (Greeley, 1992). In any event, the notion that the British were more religious at some time in the past than they are now is certainly not proven, may not be provable, and may in fact be untrue. Perhaps Britain was never all that religious; instead, an explanation is needed not for the low level of devotion in Britain but for the high level in Ireland and the United States.

Studies by scholars such as Larkin (1972, 1984)[*] trace current levels of devotion in Ireland to the time after the Great Famine of the 1840s when the Irish-speaking 'bog Irish' who had only loose ties to Catholicism were either wiped out by hunger and disease or left the country. One way for a country to become more devout is for it to lose people who are not devout, either to migration or death.

Moreover, religious affiliation in the United States at the time of the American Revolution was low and religious devotion hardly fervent. The Congregationalist zeal of Puritan New England was being replaced either by Unitarianism or a genteel Congregationalism which the Pilgrim Fathers would not have recognised. It was only after the so-called 'Second Great Awakening' in the early years of the last century that the United States began its path towards high levels of affiliation and devotion, a pilgrimage which Finke and Stark (1992) have called 'The Churching of America'.

Hatch (1989) attributes the remarkable flowering of religion after 1800 more to the 'democratisation' of the USA in the wake of the Revolution

---

[*] See also Connolly (1982) and Greeley (1988)

than to the techniques of religious revival. For three decades, he argues, the USA was swept by 'religious populism', led by lay leaders and preachers and supported by a popular press and popular hymnody. The ordinary people, he suggests, took religion away from the clergy and directed it themselves towards their own purposes and their own goals.

At about the same time as the Second Great Awakening in the USA, and shortly before the development of devotional Catholicism in Ireland under Cardinal Paul Cullen, Britain was experiencing an intense Methodist movement. The first two developments shaped the religious histories of their respective countries; the last petered out. Why was American Methodism able to generate enormous popular support, while British Methodism gradually lost whatever ability it might have had to attract the working class? According to Hatch (1989), it was because Thomas Coke, the British Methodist leader, insisted on social respectability; while the American Frances Asbury, with his camp meetings, appealed both to the immigrants pouring into the east and to the pioneers moving out to the west. So religion perhaps provided a community function that it did not in Britain (save perhaps for the Irish immigrants). Religion also became an essential part of the social location and self-definition of Americans; as Herberg (1955) argued several decades ago, most Americans identify themselves as either Protestant or Catholic or Jew, a kind of self-definition which is not nearly so powerful (to the extent that it exists at all) in Britain.

In Ireland, torn by religious and political conflict, religion was and is also a critically important component of identity. Although Catholicism was and is the religion of the majority in the island, Ireland also was and is a pluralistic society in which the majority religion was not an established church. Moreover the Catholic Church in the Republic is not an established church today, at least not in the way the Church of England is in Britain. The United States is *de jure* pluralistic, Ireland *de facto* pluralistic, and Britain in theory and in practice is not pluralistic.

Stark, Melton and Iannaccone (1992) have suggested that religion is more likely to flourish when various denominations are forced to compete in an open marketplace. According to this model, the USA has the most open market and Britain the least, with Ireland (north and south) somewhere in between. Little wonder then that the established Church in Britain fares relatively badly, while serious competition against it is discouraged.

## Cross-national comparisons

In the next section, we compare our findings in Britain with those in the United States, the Irish Republic and Northern Ireland. We look first at religious beliefs and religious observance, then at the place of God in people's lives, and lastly at the place of religion in public life.

*Beliefs*

Seven out of ten people in Britain believe in God, as opposed to more than nine out of ten in the other three societies; though as we shall see there are some ambiguities in the stance of British 'unbelievers'.  Just over 60 per cent of British respondents have 'always' believed in God as opposed to approximately 90 per cent in the other three societies.  Sixteen per cent of Britons once believed but no longer do and eight per cent once did not but do now - a net 'loss' to believers of eight percentage points.  In Northern Ireland, in contrast, there is a net 'gain' to believers of three percentage points.  In the USA and the Irish Republic, the figures balance out.

  The God in whom Britons believe is notably less likely than the God of the Irish and the Americans to be depicted as personally involved with the people.  Only 37 per cent of British respondents picture God as concerned "with every human being personally", as opposed to more than three quarters of respondents in the other societies.  As the table below shows, Britain stands out in other ways too.

**Religious beliefs (percentages)**

|  | **Britain** | **USA** | **Irish Republic** | **Northern Ireland** |
|---|---|---|---|---|
| Believe in God | 69 | 94 | 95 | 95 |
| God concerned personally* | 37 | 77 | 77 | 80 |
| **% believing in:** | | | | |
| Life after death | 55 | 78 | 80 | 78 |
| Heaven | 54 | 86 | 87 | 90 |
| Religious miracles | 45 | 73 | 73 | 77 |
| Hell | 28 | 71 | 53 | 74 |
| The Devil | 28 | 47 | 49 | 69 |
| The Bible is the 'actual' or 'inspired word of God' | 44 | 83 | 78 | 81 |

* The percentages combine 'strong agreement' with 'agreement' to the appropriate item.  This pattern will be followed in all tables in this chapter unless otherwise noted
** The percentages combine 'definitely' and 'probably' believing in each item

For instance, just over half of Britons believe in life after death, while approximately four out of five respondents in the other countries do so. The same proportion of the British also believe in heaven, but approaching nine out of ten do in the USA and Ireland.

  In summary, a little less than half of the British give reasonably 'orthodox' answers to most questions, compared with approximately three quarters of people in the other three societies.  The detailed figures for belief in God and God's personal concern provide a useful thumbnail sketch of religion in Britain: about a quarter to a third are not religious at all, a little less than two-fifths are 'seriously religious' and the rest are somewhere in between - conventionally but not seriously religious.

*Observance*

Some two-thirds of Britons profess an affiliation to a religious denomination - again as opposed to more than nine out of ten in the other three societies. Although only six per cent of British respondents were raised with no affiliation, 35 per cent now say they have no affiliation. Almost 40 per cent of Britons are affiliated to the Church of England, 10 per cent are Roman Catholics, five per cent are Presbyterians (Church of Scotland), four per cent belong to the 'Free Churches' (Baptist and Methodist) and seven per cent have other denominations or faiths. 'Retention rates' (the proportion still belonging to the denomination in which they were brought up) are highest (68 per cent) among Roman Catholics followed by 62 per cent for the Church of England and the same for the Presbyterians. But higher still are retention rates (nine in ten) among the small number of people who were raised with no religious affiliation (and continue to have none). The steepest decline in affiliation is to the Church of England: 58 per cent of respondents were raised in the Established Church but only 39 per cent identify with it today.[3] Later we will search for an explanation of this apparent decline.

There are yet more differences between the British on the one hand and the Irish (whether Green or Orange) and the Americans on the other, as the next table shows. In religious attendance, frequency of prayer and participation in 'church activities' (other than attending services) the British stand out as conspicuously less devout.

**Religious observance and experience (percentages)**

|                                                          | Britain | USA | Irish Republic | Northern Ireland |
|----------------------------------------------------------|---------|-----|----------------|------------------|
| Affiliated with a denomination                           | 64      | 93  | 98             | 92               |
| Attend service two or three times a month                | 16      | 43  | 78             | 58               |
| Pray weekly                                              | 27      | 58  | 75             | 65               |
| 'Church activity' monthly                                | 11      | 31  | 17             | 28               |
| Intense experience*                                      | 28      | 33  | 22             | 24               |
| 'Conversion' experience**                                | 17      | 46  | 16             | 29               |
| Feel close to God (*extremely/ somewhat*)                | 46      | 85  | 79             | 76               |
| Describe themselves as religious (*extremely/very/somewhat*) | 43      | 73  | 77             | 68               |

\* Ever felt "Close to a powerful spiritual force that seemed to lift you out of yourself"
\*\* Ever been "A turning point in your life when you made a new and personal commitment to religion"

Although considerably less devout on all the measures, the British are about as likely as anyone else to report that they have had an 'ecstatic' religious experience - indeed, more likely than those in either sample of

Irish respondents. If religion is ultimately founded on such experiences, then Britain seems to present an environment no more (or less) hostile to them than any other country. Some religious responses, it would seem, are more sensitive to social contexts than others (Greeley 1989): thus, respondents in Britain and in the Irish Republic who report an intense religious experience outnumber those who report a conversion experience. As far as self-description is concerned, however, the British self-image is once again more secular. A little less than half describe themselves as 'close to God' or as 'religious', compared to between about 70 per cent and 85 per cent of people in the three other societies.

So the patterns for religious observance, practice and experience supplement those in respect of religious belief. More than two-fifths of the British are seriously religious and approximately a quarter could be considered devout. However none of the four societies seems to have a monopoly on intense religious experiences.

## The meaning of life

There is somewhat more fatalism in the British Isles than there is in the United States. Only 13 per cent of Americans say "there is little people can do to change the course of their lives" but (as the next table shows) around a quarter or more of Britons and Irish (from north and south) take that grim view. The British alone are also more likely to think that life has no purpose. But the absence of religious devotion, it would seem, does not necessarily lead to *massive* fatalism and nihilism. Even in Britain, as many as one in five think that life is decided by God and that it is God who makes life meaningful, and only around one in seven believe that life is without purpose.

**Attitudes towards the meaning of life**

| % saying: | Britain | USA | Irish Republic | Northern Ireland |
|---|---|---|---|---|
| There is little that people can do to change the course of their lives *(strongly agree/agree)* | 22 | 13 | 24 | 27 |
| Life is meaningful only because God exists *(strongly agree/agree)* | 21 | 49 | 50 | 54 |
| Life does not serve any purpose *(strongly agree/agree/neither agree nor disagree)* | 14 | 8 | 9 | 11 |
| The course of our lives is decided by God *(strongly agree/agree)* | 20 | 40 | 58 | 54 |
| We each make our own fate *(strongly agree/agree)* | 61 | 62 | 66 | 51 |
| "Very happy these days" | 33 | 37 | 41 | 37 |

The British are also a little less likely than other respondents to report that they are 'very happy', but compared with some of the differences we have found so far, these variations are small. In summary, the British seem to view life from a somewhat grimmer perspective than do the other three societies, and are less likely to see God as giving meaning to life. But who knows whether this pessimism is associated with a less vigorous religious faith, or whether it merely reflects a greater realism about the human condition?

*Religion and public life*

We also asked a series of questions to investigate the extent to which people believe that religion has a place in public life, and to try to gauge attitudes to churches and religious organisations. We found that the British have much less confidence in churches than do the Irish or the Americans, although (as the next table shows) the latter were far from unanimous in *their* vote of confidence. But criticism of churches for having too much power is most widespread in Ireland (north and south), though even there the critics are clearly in a minority.

**Religion and public life - 1 (percentages)**

|                                                        | Britain | USA | Irish Republic | Northern Ireland |
|--------------------------------------------------------|---------|-----|----------------|------------------|
| Confidence in churches*                                | 18      | 41  | 46             | 43               |
| Churches have 'far too much' or 'too much power'       | 28      | 23  | 37             | 37               |
| Religious leaders should not try to influence how people vote | 74 | 65 | 76            | 72               |
| Religious leaders should not try to influence government | 59    | 63  | 70             | 62               |

* 'Complete confidence' or 'a great deal of confidence'

However, solid majorities in all four societies think that church leaders ought not to try to influence voters or government decisions, the Irish (both north and south) being both united and especially emphatic about church leaders' relations with government.

When we move to questions of religious tolerance and the place of religion in society, the British and the Irish in the south are less likely than the Northern Irish and the Americans to think that atheists are unfit for public office. Again the British, but this time alongside the Americans, are less likely than the Irish (south and north) to be in favour of banning anti-religious books. The Americans are the most likely, and the British the least, to believe that their country would be better off "if more people with strong religious beliefs held public office". However, support for daily school prayers is widespread in all countries - even among the more secular British.

**Religion and public life - 2 (percentages)**

|  | Britain | USA | Irish Republic | Northern Ireland |
|---|---|---|---|---|
| Politicians who do not believe in God are unfit for public office *(strongly agree/agree/neither agree nor disagree)* | 31 | 59 | 35 | 52 |
| Books and films that attack religions should be prohibited by law *(definitely /probably)* | 30 | 34 | 49 | 54 |
| It would be better for [Britain] if more people with strong religious beliefs held public office *(strongly agree/agree)* | 17 | 39 | 28 | 24 |
| There should be daily prayers in all state schools *(definitely/probably)* | 70 | 73 | 83 | 87 |

With the exception of school prayers then, the British are clearly the most secularist in their approach to the relationship between religion and public life. They are also less likely than their counterparts across the Irish Sea to view their churches as a political threat, almost certainly because in fact the British churches *are* less of a threat. But it is worth noting that large majorities in Northern Ireland and the Republic - both allegedly priest-dominated societies - also disapprove of church involvement in politics, an apparent indictment of a situation in which religious leaders both south and north of the border *do* seem to have considerable political influence.

## The British perspective

We now turn from cross-national comparisons to an analysis of religion in Britain. We look at responses to a battery of eleven questions (eight about belief, observance and experience, and three about the relationship between religion and public life) which serve as a quick summary of Christian religious (or quasi-religious) attitudes and behaviour, and discuss interdenominational, demographic and other differences.

### Denomination

As noted previously, 36 per cent of British respondents identify with the Church of England, 10 per cent with Roman Catholicism, four per cent each with Presbyterianism and with the Free Churches, three per cent with other Protestant denominations and three per cent with other

religions. In addition, four per cent call themselves 'Christian' but give
no denomination, and the remaining 35 per cent have no religion. Since
most sub-sample sizes are small, only fairly large differences between
groups are likely to be statistically significant. It is for this reason that we
limit the analyses below to Christian denominations.

Catholics are consistently more devout and more believing than the
other denominations and Anglicans generally the least devout (save, of
course, for those with 'no religion').

**Religious beliefs and observance in Britain**

|  | All | Church of England | Roman Catho- lic | Presby- terian | Free Churches | Other Protest- ant | No relig- ion |
|---|---|---|---|---|---|---|---|
| % believing in: | | | | | | | |
| God | 69 | 84 | 92 | 88 | 91 | 89 | 28 |
| Life after death | 55 | 57 | 78 | 67 | 77 | 66 | 35 |
| Religious miracles | 45 | 49 | 80 | 46 | 78 | 61 | 22 |
| Pray weekly | 27 | 30 | 52 | 30 | 38 | 52 | 8 |
| Attend service two or three times a month | 16 | 14 | 36 | 25 | 31 | 49 | 1 |
| Intense experience | 28 | 27 | 32 | 29 | 51 | 42 | 19 |
| Feel close to God | 46 | 51 | 72 | 60 | 71 | 69 | 18 |

As can be seen, those who profess no religion are by no means
completely irreligious. Twenty-eight per cent of them believe in God, 35
per cent in life after death; about one in six say they are close to God.
However, as the table below shows, only a third have any confidence in
churches, and they are much more likely than all the professed Christian
groups to believe that the churches have too much power and much less
likely to approve of prayer in schools. Even so, sizeable minorities of the
non-religious are clearly ambivalent about religion. And from other
analyses (not reported here for lack of space) it seems possible that part
of the reason for some of these people's rejection of religion is that they
have both more liberal moral and sexual attitudes and a greater suspicion
of churches than their counterparts do.

**Religion and public life in Britain (percentages)**

|  | All | Church of England | Roman Catho- lic | Presby- terian | Free Churches | Other Protest- ant | No relig- ion |
|---|---|---|---|---|---|---|---|
| Confidence in churches* | 58 | 66 | 77 | 76 | 78 | 81 | 34 |
| Churches have too much power | 28 | 24 | 20 | 18 | 12 | 6 | 45 |
| In favour of school prayers | 70 | 82 | 87 | 77 | 95 | 90 | 45 |

* 'Complete', 'a great deal of' or 'some' confidence.

Almost five out of six Christian Britons are either Anglicans or Roman Catholics with the former four times as numerous as the latter. As noted, Catholics are more likely to be devout than Anglicans, and they are also more likely to have confidence in churches.[4]

## Region

An examination of the eleven regions of Britain[*] reveals a common religious culture - as measured by our eleven-item battery - in eight of the regions, but differences from this common culture in three: Wales, Scotland, and the North-West.[**] Since these three regions were similar to each other in religious culture, we group them together for purposes of analysis and dub them (not altogether inaccurately as will be seen) 'the Celtic Fringe'.

As shown in the next table the 'Fringe' differs significantly from the rest of Britain on nine of the eleven items, proving to be consistently more devout and more religious on these items.

|  | All | 'Celtic Fringe' | Rest of Britain |
|---|---|---|---|
| % believing in: |  |  |  |
| God | 69 | 75 | 66 |
| Life after death | 55 | 62 | 52 |
| Religious miracles | 45 | 51 | 43 |
| Affiliated with a denomination | 64 | 67 | 63 |
| Pray weekly | 27 | 32 | 25 |
| Attend service two or three times a month | 16 | 19 | 14 |
| Intense experience | 28 | 28 | 28* |
| Feel close to God | 46 | 52 | 43 |
| Confidence in churches | 58 | 62 | 56 |
| Churches have too much power | 28 | 28 | 29* |
| In favour of school prayers | 70 | 75 | 69 |

\* Not significantly different from the 'Celtic Fringe'

---

\*  Registrar-General's Standard Regions of Scotland, Northern, North-West, Yorkshire and Humberside, West Midlands, East Midlands, East Anglia, South-West, South-East, Greater London and Wales.

\*\* Comprising Cheshire, Lancashire, Greater Manchester and Merseyside.

But the explanation for this difference is not, as it turns out, surprising when one looks at the different religious composition of the 'Fringe'. In the rest of Britain, Anglicans make up 40 per cent of the population and Catholics and Presbyterians 10 per cent between them. However, in the 'Fringe' the combination of Catholics (15 per cent) and Presbyterians (14 per cent) exceeds the Anglican proportion (22 per cent). When this is taken into account, *all* the differences between the 'Fringe' and the rest of Britain decline not only to statistical insignificance but virtually to zero. So the 'Fringe' may be legitimately called Celtic because of the Scottish and Irish influences (for example, of the large Irish Catholic communities in Liverpool and Manchester). In sum, the only difference in regional religious culture we can detect is actually a difference in denominational composition.

*Gender*

Women have traditionally been thought to be more devout and more religious than men. Not so long ago this difference was generally attributed (though sometimes only implicitly) to the chauvinistic view that women were neither as logical nor as realistic as men. A more plausible explanation, and one which fits at least some of the data, is that the difference has arisen out of women's role in the family, which involves more 'socio-emotional' (caring) responsibilities than men's more 'instrumental' (doing) responsibilities. Indeed, women's devoutness and religiosity are more like those of men (though by no means the same) *before* they acquire a spouse and children. Once you start 'taking care' of people, perhaps, you begin implicitly to assume greater responsibility for their 'ultimate' welfare.[5]

There has, however, been a suggestion that as women become more involved in the workforce and assume greater 'instrumental' responsibilities in life, gender differences on religious issues will diminish. We tested this assumption.

First of all, as the next table shows, women *are* clearly much more likely than men to be devout and religious. On only one item out of the eleven are women much the same as men; on all the rest, women are more orthodox.

|  | All | Men | Women | Women Working full-time | Not working full-time |
|---|---|---|---|---|---|
| **% believing in:** | | | | | |
| God | 69 | 60 | 76 | 69 | 79** |
| Life after death | 55 | 47 | 61 | 65 | 60** |
| Religious miracles | 45 | 40 | 50 | 49 | 51** |
| Affiliated with a denomination | 64 | 58 | 69 | 57 | 73 |
| Pray weekly | 27 | 21 | 33 | 25 | 36 |
| Attend service two or three times a month | 16 | 12 | 19 | 17 | 20** |
| Intense experience | 28 | 30 | 26* | 27 | 25** |
| Feel close to God | 46 | 38 | 52 | 47 | 54 |
| Confidence in churches | 58 | 53 | 62 | 57 | 65** |
| Churches have too much power | 28 | 33 | 24 | 26 | 24** |
| In favour of school prayers | 70 | 66 | 74 | 64 | 78 |

\* Difference from men not statistically significant
\*\* Difference between women working full-time and women not working full-time is not statistically significant.

To what extent can these differences be explained by the supposedly less 'instrumental' role of women? Might the differences already be diminishing as women assume greater participation in the workforce? First of all, as the table above shows, non-working women are *not* significantly more religious than working women in respect of seven out of the eleven items in our battery. The other four differences are statistically significant - but not when one takes age into account. In other words it is the younger women who tend to be less religious regardless of whether they are in paid work or not.

Does this finding suggest that, as young working women grow older, they will continue to be different from older non-working women? Or will younger women grow more religious as they age, and hence sustain the similarities in respect of religious attitudes and behaviour between those women who work and those who do not? To answer this question we need to know how devout were young working women in the recent past. In the absence of such data, we must suspend judgment. The propensity of some sociologists to see an age correlation as a social trend ignores the possibility that an age correlation may be merely a life-cycle phenomenon. In the absence of data enabling us to follow a specific birth cohort through the life-cycle, we cannot reject the explanation that as men and women grow older they become more religious, and that there is thus no long-term trend in Britain towards a decline in devotion.[6]

Moreover, further analysis has shown that (when age is not taken into account) women in full-time jobs are still significantly more religious than are full-time working men. So whether or not workforce participation leads people to have less religious attitudes, it does not prevent women from being more religious than their male counterparts. However one looks at it, therefore, women in Britain are likely to continue to be more religious than men.[7]

## Education

If religion, as it is often alleged, is a remnant of a 'pre-scientific' mentality, it might be expected to lose its importance as educational attainment increases. Are the better-educated more likely to be sceptics? The data in the next table address that question. First of all, educational attainment (as measured by age at school leaving) does not correlate significantly with six out of our battery of eleven items. The negative, significant correlation between education and belief in God does not persist once age is taken into account. In fact, the only difference that remains statistically significant after controlling for age is support for daily prayer in schools, where the less educated are the more in favour.

|  | | Age at school leaving | | |
| --- | --- | --- | --- | --- |
|  | All | 15 or less | 16-18 | 19 or more |
| % believing in: | | | | |
| God | 69 | 75 | 66 | 43** |
| Life after death | 55 | 55 | 58 | 48* |
| Religious miracles | 45 | 51 | 43 | 41** |
| Affiliated with a denomination | 64 | 72 | 57 | 36** |
| Pray weekly | 27 | 31 | 24 | 26* |
| Attend service two or or three times a month | 16 | 14 | 13 | 26* |
| Intense experience | 28 | 27 | 29 | 30* |
| Feel close to God | 46 | 55 | 42 | 35** |
| Confidence in churches | 58 | 60 | 56 | 60* |
| Churches have too much power | 28 | 30 | 27 | 27* |
| In favour of school prayers | 70 | 84 | 65 | 53 |

* Correlation with school leaving is not statistically significant
** Correlation with school leaving becomes statistically significant when age is taken into account

Belief in religious miracles, perhaps a classic indicator of a 'pre-scientific' mentality, persists even among two in five of those who left school aged 19 or older (and hence were likely to have had some tertiary education). Education does not seem to be threatening religion in Britain.

*Age and gender*

Research on religion and life-cycle carried out in the USA offers persuasive evidence that religious faith and observance begin to decline in the middle teens, reach bottom in the middle twenties and then slowly climb up, until they level off in the middle forties.    Thus a simple correlation between religion and age cannot be seen to prove that there is any long-term decline in faith.   However the data in the figure below show an interesting pattern of difference in belief in God for men and women.   The curve showing the relationship between age and faith for women fits exactly the pattern that our cohort research in the USA would lead us to expect; by the time they are in their thirties women are as likely as older women are to believe in God.

**Belief in God by age and gender**

Age of respondent

However, the pattern for men leads us to expect that cohort analysis might prove that men who are presently under fifty (born after 1942) will be less likely to believe in God all their lives than those who are over fifty.   Future replications of the present survey will also enable that possibility to be explored.

We found a somewhat similar pattern for the proportion of men and women who have no religious affiliation.   Only 10 per cent of women aged 70 and over and twenty per cent of men of the same age have no affiliation.   For men this proportion increases almost linearly to 60 per cent of those under thirty with no religious affiliation, and for women the increase levels off to 45 per cent for those in their thirties.

**No religious affiliation by age and gender**

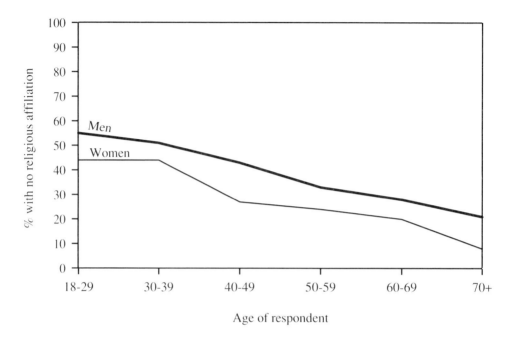

Age of respondent

Subsequent replications of this question will be necessary to confirm whether or not these correlations indicate a long-term trend.

Three points must be re-emphasised about the decline in belief in God. First, the phenomenon under analysis may well just be a life-cycle phenomenon, and it may be that men born since 1942 will turn out to grow more religious as they become older. Secondly, the decline is confined largely, if not entirely, to men. And thirdly, the level of unbelief does not rise among those born after 1952 (at present aged under 40). It looks very much like a one-shot phenomenon - a sharp decline which has since levelled off.

There is one more curious twist to the question of British belief in God which the next section will explain.

## The God of the unbelievers

We asked three different questions about the existence of God. In the first, respondents were asked to endorse one of six statements, ranging from "I don't believe in God" to "I know God really exists and I have no doubts about it". Ten per cent of Britons opted for the first statement; and a further 14 per cent gave the agnostic response that they did not know whether there is a God and knew of no way to find out. So it seems that around a quarter of Britons do not, or cannot, believe in God. Yet that figure is somewhat unstable, since in response to *the very next question* - "How close do you feel to God most of the time" - only 13 per cent of respondents chose the option "I do not believe in God"; seemingly the wording in this context implied too strong a rejection of God for many agnostics.  To complicate the matter further, some 31 per cent of respondents chose one of the two options in a third question ("I don't believe in God now and I never have" or "I don't believe in God now, but I used to").  So we might think that somewhere under a third of the British are atheistic or agnostic.

But of those who say that they do not believe in God ("now" or "never have"), nearly three in 10 nonetheless profess to being *neither* atheist nor agnostic.  Moreover, 15 per cent of non-believers report having had an intense religious experience, and three per cent say they pray at least once a week (to whom it may concern?).  Two out of five of them support daily prayers in schools.  And while unbelievers are twice as likely as believers to say that life has no purpose, still only one in five admit to such nihilism.

However, our data give little support to those theologians and clerics who think that the churches can reclaim 'relevance' by taking a strong stand on social issues: there is no difference between believers and unbelievers on the questions of equalisation of income or government provision of jobs.

In Britain, therefore, there seems to be considerable uncertainty about God, some inclined perhaps to believe despite themselves.

What about Ireland and the USA?  Do the 'unbelievers' there have the same ambivalence?[*]  The table below suggests that in the other societies 'unbelievers' are around half as likely as they are in Britain to choose the atheist response.  The remaining 80 per cent of unbelievers in the USA and Ireland do not exclude the possibility of God (compared with 60 per cent in Britain).  So not only are there considerably fewer 'unbelievers' in Ireland and the USA, those Irish and Americans who categorise themselves as 'unbelievers' are more inclined to give God the benefit of the doubt.  Moreover, in Britain even the 'believers' are more likely to have doubts:  only 44 per cent of them are 'theists' as opposed to 70 per cent in the other societies.

|  | Believe in God | | Don't believe in God | |
|  | **Britain** | **Other societies** | **Britain** | **Other societies** |
|  | % | % | % | % |
| Atheist | * | 1 | 41 | 22 |
| Agnostic | 1 | 1 | 31 | 44 |
| Uncertain | 11 | 5 | 19 | 29 |
| Doubter | 37 | 21 | 4 | 3 |
| Theist | 44 | 70 | - | 2 |

---

[*] Our analyses are somewhat hampered by the very small number of non-believers in Ireland (south and north) and the United States. Ninety-four per cent of respondents in these three societies believe in God. So we have combined all their responses.

While there are considerable ambiguities in both Britain and the other three societies, in the former they 'tilt' against God, but in the latter in favour.

Perhaps the social context affecting responses to questions about God is somewhat different in Britain than in other countries. It may be that to the British a confident acknowledgement of the existence of God is somehow perceived of as a limitation on their personal choice or intelligence. When asked about God, Britons certainly are inclined to hesitate and say "Yes, but ...," or to shift their responses from question to question. Perhaps the God in which one is asked to believe may also differ from society to society. Or are the British simply exhibiting the diffidence and lack of fervour that is supposedly (and stereotypically) a national trait? A comparison between Britain and other European societies more secular than Ireland (say Germany or the Netherlands or Norway) will become possible later and should yield very interesting results.


## Conclusions

Britain is clearly a less religious society than the other three in this analysis, though by no means an irreligious society. How can one account for the differences? Why are the British less religious than the Americans or the Irish? The difference does not seem to be of recent origin. Church attendance in the USA and Ireland has long been higher. And even among Britons in the oldest age group, fewer believe in God and fewer are affiliated to a denomination.

We have already noted too that in the late medieval and early modern eras (as far as scholars can reconstruct them) Europeans were not particularly devout. High levels of religious observance in Europe are the result of rather recent historical developments. For instance, social and political structures seem to have aided and abetted the early to middle 19th century religious revival in Ireland (as they did in the USA), and to have impeded a parallel revival in England. Perhaps the worst thing for religion in England was the establishment of the Church of England. Or to put it differently, religion and religious devotion were unlucky in Britain and lucky in Ireland and the USA.

At least such an explanation may point in the right direction if we are trying to understand why religion seems so much more vigorous in Ireland and the USA, and to discover why they are the exceptions (along with Canada) within the North Atlantic world. The question can be reversed, however; we might just as well ask why religion is relatively weak in western and central Europe, and relatively strong in much of the rest of the world. According to this perspective, the exceptions are Britain and most countries of the European continent west of Poland, while Ireland and the United States are more typical of the human condition.

In any event, religion certainly manifests itself differently in the three (or four) English-speaking cultures under consideration. None of the cultures is totally irreligious. None is without its ambiguities and inconsistencies. Perhaps all four societies can be accused of some measure of religious (or irreligious) hypocrisy. But the differences need to be taken seriously by anyone interested in the impact of political and social history, and existing social structures, on human culture and behaviour.

To end this chapter with - as is perhaps appropriate for its American-Irish author - an Irish 'bull': the British are more religious than they think they are. Indeed, as Rodney Stark has commented on an earlier draft of this paper, they are also possibly more religious than they used to be.

## Notes

1. Brierley (1991a and 1991b) has provided a considerable amount of data from the English Church Census of 1989. The census however was essentially a census of churches and therefore of people who were affiliated with the churches. While it presents enormous amounts of data, it tells us very little about that vast majority of English men and women who are not affiliated with churches.
2. Butler (1990) adds that in Yorkshire in 1743 only 20 per cent of adults attended worship regularly and only 31 per cent attended at Easter.
3. But the picture is not quite as simple as that - it rarely is in religious matters in Britain as we shall see. When asked what their spouse's (or partner's) religious affiliation was, only 12 per cent - 15 per cent of men and 10 per cent of women - said that he or she had no religious affiliation. Since the spouses (or partners) of a random sample of people are themselves a random sample, it is clear that almost a quarter of respondents are willing to attribute to their wife, husband or partner a religious affiliation the spouse does not claim (34 per cent of currently married or cohabiting Britons report no religious affiliation). Perhaps respondents have stricter criteria for their own religious affiliation than they apply to their partners. Perhaps married respondents remember how the issue of religion was negotiated at the time of marriage. Or perhaps in a country where there is a single established Church dominating the religious landscape, 'affiliation' is not a matter of great saliency to many Britons. If pushed, they might claim some vague affiliation with the 'C of E', but it is not a relationship of which they are sufficiently conscious spontaneously to claim it in response to a survey question.
4. In another paper the author will compare British Catholics and their counterparts in Ireland and the USA to determine whether living in a society which is less avowedly devout and religious has an effect on Roman Catholics.
5. Personal observation convinces the writer that the amount of prayer required of a woman (in her own mind) tends to increase with the number of children and grandchildren for whom she has assumed responsibility. If one adds to a woman's spouse the number of children and grandchildren under her 'jurisdiction', one might find a variable that goes a long way towards accounting for the greater religious devotion of women.
6. In cohort analysis the writer has done in the United States with Michael Hout of the University of California, the preponderance of the data supports the life-cycle explanation.

7. On the other hand, if intense religious experiences are the ultimate measure of receptiveness to religion, then women and men do not differ on this most fundamental religious dimension. A 'gender-linked' culture may create in women a greater disposition to religious participation and acceptance of cognitive religious propositions, but it does not make them any more likely to have experienced religious 'ecstasy'.

## References

Brierley, P. (1991a), *Christian England: What the Church Census Reveals*, London: MARC Europe.

Brierley, P. (1992b), *Prospects for the Nineties: Trends and Tables from the 1989 English Church Census*, London: MARC Europe.

Butler, J. (1990), *Awash in a Sea of Faith*, Cambridge Massachusetts: Harvard University Press.

Carroll, M. (1992), *Madonnas that Maim*, Baltimore: John Hopkins University Press.

Connolly, S.J. (1982), *Priest and People in Prefamine Ireland*, Dublin: Gill and Macmillan.

Finke, R. and Stark, R. (1992), *The Churching of America*, (in press).

Greeley, A. (1988), 'The Success and Assimilation of Irish Protestants and Irish Catholics in the United States', *Sociology and Social Research*, 4: 229-236.

Greeley, A. (1989), 'Protestant and Catholic: Is the Analogical Imagination Extinct?', *American Sociological Review*, 54: 485-502.

Greeley, A. (1991), *The Pragmatics of Prayer*, Unpublished Paper, Chicago: NORC.

Greeley, A. (1992), *The Two Catholic Traditions*, Unpublished Paper, Chicago: NORC.

Hatch, N. (1989), *The Democratization of American Christianity*, New Haven: Yale University Press.

Herberg, W. (1955), *Protestant, Catholic, Jew*, London/New York: Doubleday.

Larkin, E. (1972), 'The Devotional Revolution in Ireland', *The American Historical Review*, 7: 623-652.

Larkin, E. (1984), *The Historical Dimensions of Irish Catholicism*, Washington D.C.: The Catholic University of America Press.

Martin, D. (1967), *A Sociology of English Religion*, London: SCM Press.

Martin, D. (1969), *The Religious and the Secular: Studies in Secularization*, London: Routledge & K. Paul.

Martin, D. (1978), *A General Theory of Secularization*, Oxford: Blackwell.

Stark, R., Melton, G. and Iannaccone, L. (1992), *The Secularization of Europe Reconsidered*, forthcoming.

Wickham, R. (1957), *Church and People in an Industrial City*, London: Lutterworth Press.

Wilson, B. (1969), *Religion in Secular Society*, Harmondsworth: Penguin.

Wilson, B. (1976), *Contemporary Transformations of Religion*, Oxford/New York: Oxford University Press.

## Acknowledgement

Since 1989, the ESRC has (through its funding of the Joint Centre for the Study of Social Trends) helped ensure SCPR's continuing participation in the International Social Survey Programme. We thank the Council for its financial support.

# 4 The North-South divide

*John Curtice* *

In *The Fifth Report* in this series we examined how far there were regional differences in social attitudes in Britain in the 1980s (Curtice, 1988). Using data from the 1983-87 surveys, we identified some important differences in attitudes between those living in the north of Britain - that is the North of England, Scotland and Wales - and those in the south - that is the Midlands, London and the South of England.[1] In particular, we found that people living in the south were more likely than people living in the north to take an optimistic view of the state of the economy. Thus they were, for example, more likely to believe that unemployment would fall in the next twelve months and that their household income would move ahead of prices. At the same time people living in the south were less likely to be in favour of government intervention to secure greater economic equality. They were more likely to be opposed to government action to reduce income differences or even to the raising of unemployment benefit. In short, greater economic optimism was matched by greater ideological commitment to the operation of a market economy.

This difference in economic attitudes between the two halves of Britain could not be accounted for by differences in their social composition. Even when we took into account differences between the regions in social class, housing tenure and levels of unemployment, the south still appeared more optimistic and more pro-market than the north. It seemed that how

---

* Senior Lecturer in Politics and Director of the Social Statistics Laboratory, University of Strathclyde.

people thought was influenced not only by who they were but also by where they lived. Britain was not 'one nation'; it exhibited clear signs of a regional cleavage. Further, the economic issues which divided the regions were also amongst those that most sharply separated Conservative identifiers from Labour ones; so this ideological divide seemed likely, at least in part, to account for the increasing geographical polarisation of Conservative and Labour support in the two halves of Britain.

These findings were perhaps none too surprising. After all, the market economy *was* more successful in the mid-1980s in much of the south than in the north - as it had been for most of the post-war period. The recession of the early 1980s *did* affect the north more adversely than the south, while the subsequent boom of the mid-1980s benefited the south more than the north. These trends indeed resulted in a considerable *widening* of the gap in the economic prosperity between the two halves of Britain.

**The regional impact of recession**

In the late 1980s the regional economic polarisation of Britain was thrown into sharp reverse (Spencer, Beange and Curtice, 1992). First of all, the north began finally to reap some of the benefits of the boom. And then, as the economy began to slow down in 1989, it was the south - and London and the South-East in particular - which suffered first and most heavily. One way in which this manifested itself was in unemployment levels. Although the level of unemployment was everywhere lower in the second quarter of 1991 than four years earlier, the fall had been faster than the national average throughout the northern half of the country and slower than average in most of the south. And although this still left the level of unemployment in London and the South-East one percentage point below the UK average, just four years earlier the gap had been three points (Spencer, Beange and Curtice, 1992).

Equally striking were the trends in house prices. Over the four-year period between 1987 and 1991 house prices rose by more than twice as much in the North of England as in the south. Only Scotland continued to lag somewhat. This trend was more than sufficient to reverse the widening of the house price gap which had occurred between 1983 and 1987. Indeed, house prices actually fell in London and the South of England as the recession tightened its grip at the beginning of the 1990s. Elsewhere they continued to hold steady, or even moved slowly ahead (Spencer, Beange and Curtice, 1992).

So while the *level* of economic activity remains higher in the south than in the north, the *trend* of most of the 1980s has been put sharply into reverse. This experience gives us good reason to re-examine the variations in attitudes towards economic issues of people living in different parts of Britain. Perhaps the most likely consequence of the reversal, we anticipated, would be a change in the geography of economic optimism. In the mid-1980s, the north was more pessimistic than the south about future trends in unemployment and in the ability of household incomes to keep ahead of prices. This might no longer be true.

But perhaps more intriguing and more important is the impact, if any, of the new economic geography on the *ideological* divide between the regions. Has the recent relative weakness of the economy in the south shown any signs of undermining commitment among southerners to the operation of the market economy? While we might anticipate that subjective evaluations would be responsive to short-term fluctuations in the economy, ideological beliefs in the relative merits of government intervention and the free market would, we suspect, be more deeply rooted. Certainly, Britain's recent economic experience provides an excellent testbed in which to examine whether or not this is the case. It is to such an examination that this chapter is devoted.

## The data

Each year approximately 3,000 respondents are interviewed on the *British Social Attitudes* survey. But not all the questions are asked of all respondents; approximately one-third of the questionnaire is split into two parts with each part only being asked of half the sample. So in many cases we have answers from only 1,500 people. Once we have broken these respondents down according to where they live, there are commonly too few in any particular region for us to be sure whether any differences between the regions are real, or whether they could simply be a consequence of sampling variation. However, many of the survey questions have been asked in more than one year. So we can combine the results from more than one survey to give us an estimate of the pattern of attitudes in a region based on a more satisfactory sample size.

This is the strategy adopted here. In most of the chapter, our figures are based on the combined results of the three surveys conducted between 1989 and 1991. And we compare these figures with the combined results of the 1983-1987 surveys.[2] (A survey was not conducted in 1988.) This enables us to pursue our substantive interest in comparing the regional pattern of opinion at the turn of the decade with that in the mid-1980s. The assumption we make in doing this is that while the *overall* levels of support for any particular attitudinal position may change from one year to the next, the *size* of any difference between the regions is broadly stable within each of our two time periods.[3]

## Interpreting regional differences

We also have to bear one other point in mind. Britain's regions vary not only in respect of their economic fortunes but also in their social composition. For example, as the following table shows, not only are household incomes higher on average in the South of England and in London than elsewhere, but also a higher proportion of residents of these regions are members of the salariat than elsewhere.

**Social composition of regions, 1989-91 combined**

|  | Scotland | North | Wales | Midlands | London | South |
|---|---|---|---|---|---|---|
| **Social class:** | % | % | % | % | % | % |
| Salariat | 29 | 23 | 18 | 22 | 31 | 33 |
| Working class | 35 | 41 | 42 | 41 | 28 | 26 |
| **Tenure:** | % | % | % | % | % | % |
| Owner-occupier | 55 | 70 | 69 | 72 | 60 | 76 |
| **Economic position:** | % | % | % | % | % | % |
| Respondent or spouse unemployed | 8 | 9 | 11 | 8 | 7 | 5 |
| **Income:** | % | % | % | % | % | % |
| Top quintile | 19 | 15 | 11 | 15 | 32 | 27 |

Further, social position is itself commonly correlated with attitudes towards economic issues. Members of the salariat, for example, are generally more optimistic about the economy and are less in favour of government intervention to promote greater equality than is the population in general (see also Chapter 2). So if we find that people in the South of England and London are more optimistic about the economy than people living elsewhere, that does not in itself demonstrate that where people live influences what they think. It may be no more than a reflection of the kind of people who live in the different regions.

We need therefore to look not just at whether or not there *are* attitudinal differences between the regions. In addition we have to undertake multivariate analysis in order to estimate the strength of the association between region and attitudes, net of differences in social class, housing tenure and economic position.

Reassuringly, the differences in social composition we report above are not dissimilar to those we found for the 1983-87 period which were presented in *The Fifth Report* (see Curtice, 1988, p. 154). True, the working class has shrunk more in London and the South of England than elsewhere but, to counterbalance this, owner-occupation has increased most rapidly in Scotland and the North of England, and unemployment has fallen most there. It therefore seems unlikely that any differences we find between the 1989-91 and the 1983-87 periods can simply be accounted for by changes in the social composition of the regions. Further, given that the north/south divide could not be accounted for by differences in regional composition in the 1983-87 period, it is just as unlikely to be the case in the 1989-91 period. So looking at simple differences between the regions in the balance of attitudes is unlikely to mislead us seriously.

## Economic evaluations

### *Optimism and pessimism*

We concentrate first on economic evaluations - respondents' views both of their own economic situation, and of how well or badly they think the country is doing.

**Economic evaluations by region, 1989-91 combined**

| | Scotland | North | Wales | Midlands | London | South |
|---|---|---|---|---|---|---|
| **% of respondents saying:** | | | | | | |
| Expect prices to go up a lot in next year | 45 | 49 | 53 | 43 | 41 | 41 |
| Expect unemployment to go up a lot in next year | 24 | 20 | 24 | 18 | 18 | 17 |
| Unemployment of greater concern than inflation to me and my family | 33 | 34 | 31 | 27 | 28 | 26 |
| Income has fallen behind prices in last year | 47 | 53 | 58 | 51 | 50 | 50 |
| Expect income to fall behind prices in next year | 45 | 50 | 54 | 48 | 42 | 46 |
| Living on household income difficult | 24 | 26 | 30 | 24 | 27 | 21 |
| Britain's industrial performance will decline over next year | 29 | 24 | 22 | 21 | 26 | 23 |

These figures suggest that there is still a slightly greater measure of economic pessimism in the north than in the south - but the differences are not large. Those living in the northern half of Britain are on average around five percentage points more likely to be pessimistic about future trends in inflation and unemployment (the first two rows of the table above) than those in the south. But on other issues the pattern begins to break down. Scots are as optimistic about their household incomes as those living in London and the South of England. And as far as evaluations of "Britain's industrial performance" are concerned (the last row of the table), there appears to be no systematic difference between north and south.

The limited size of the regional divide on economic evaluations is confirmed by multivariate analyses. In the following table we report for three of the items in the previous table the *independent* effect of region on evaluations, net of social class, tenure and work status. (The table gives the parameter estimates, from a logit analysis.) A plus sign indicates that people in that region are *more* likely to agree with the proposition indicated and are thus more *pessimistic*; a minus sign indicates that they are less pessimistic.

**The independent impact of region, 1989-91 combined**

|                                                    | Scotland | North | Wales | Midlands | London | South |
|----------------------------------------------------|----------|-------|-------|----------|--------|-------|
| Expect unemployment to go up a lot in next year    | +.11*    | -.01  | +.00  | -.03     | -.01   | -.05* |
| Income has fallen behind prices in last year       | -.13*    | +.03  | +.08  | -.01     | -.03   | +.04  |
| Expect income to fall behind prices in next year   | -.11*    | +.06* | +.09* | +.03     | -.11*  | +.03  |

* indicates statistically significant at the five per cent level, that is there is less than a one in 20 chance that sampling error could be responsible for the positive or negative estimate we have obtained.

According to our previous table, unemployment was one of those items on which there appeared to be something of a north/south divide. Yet our multivariate analysis reveals that the only statistically significant differences are that Scots are more pessimistic about unemployment and those in the South of England less so. Further the sizes of the differences are not large, and the rest of England and Wales reveal themselves to be more or less uniform in their evaluations.

Equally our analysis confirms that evaluations of household incomes do not fit a neat north/south pattern. True, those in the North of England and in Wales are somewhat less optimistic about the future purchasing power of their income. But Scots reveal themselves to be relatively optimistic, indeed just as optimistic as Londoners. And when it comes to incomes over the past year, Scots are unique in their positive evaluation, while the English regions show no real differences between them.

*Trends since the mid-1980s*

Just how different is this from the mid-1980s?  The following table shows
the difference between the periods 1989-91 and 1983-87 in the proportion
of respondents endorsing each of our propositions.  It reveals that on
many of the items the gap between north and south has clearly narrowed.

| Economic evaluation by region, combined data for 1983-87 vs. 1989-91 | | | | | | |
|---|---|---|---|---|---|---|
| | Scotland | North | Wales | Midlands | London | South |
| **% point difference\*** **between the two periods:** | | | | | | |
| Expect prices to go up a lot in next year | +14 | +16 | +20 | +18 | +13 | +16 |
| Expect unemployment to go up a lot in next year | -9 | -11 | -6 | -4 | -9 | -4 |
| Unemployment of greater concern than inflation to me and my family | -17 | -16 | -11 | -14 | -11 | -13 |
| Income has fallen behind prices in last year | -3 | -2 | +4 | +4 | +8 | +8 |
| Expect income to fall behind prices in next year | -4 | +1 | +3 | +4 | +9 | +6 |
| Living on household income difficult | -4 | -3 | - | -3 | - | +1 |
| Britain's industrial performance will decline over next year | +2 | +1 | +5 | +5 | +8 | +7 |

\* A minus sign indicates that respondents are *less* pessimistic or less negative than they
were in the mid-1980s; a plus sign that they are *more* pessimistic.

The picture is clearest in respondents' evaluations of the purchasing
power of their household incomes in the past year.  Here those living in
Scotland and the North of England actually became a little more cheerful,
while those living in London and the South of England became
considerably more gloomy.   The same broad picture is true of
expectations of future household incomes.
   On other items the direction of change is the same throughout the
country - but its rate differs.  Those living in Scotland and the North of
England have become slightly more pessimistic about Britain's industrial
performance while those in London and the South of England have
become much more pessimistic.   On unemployment the decline in

concern about its threat to one's family is more marked in Scotland and the North of England than elsewhere. Only on inflation is there no sign of any narrowing of the north/south gap.[4]

So the new economic geography of Britain at the turn of the decade had a clear impact on the regional distribution of economic optimism and pessimism. The relative optimism of the south which we found in the mid-1980s had all but disappeared in the wake of the severity of the recession. So, as expected, people's economic evaluations do seem sensitive to changes in the relative economic prosperity of the region in which they live.

**The housing market**

An area of the economy which we identified earlier as one in which there had been a sharp reversal of fortune in the south was the housing market. We might anticipate then that the market's relative weakness in London and the South of England at the end of the 1980s would have resulted in a sharper decline in the perceived attractiveness of owner-occupation there than elsewhere.

The *British Social Attitudes* survey has included a number of questions in recent years which tap people's attitudes towards owner-occupation. Unfortunately, however, they were first asked only in 1986 and were not repeated until 1989. So we cannot, as before, aggregate responses across more than one year for our earlier time period to provide a robust estimate of the pattern of attitudes in the six regions (or combinations of regions) we looked at before.

Instead we simply compare the results for two years, 1986 and 1991, separately for Scotland and the North of England and for London and the South of England (we exclude Wales and the Midlands from this analysis).[*] On this evidence it does seem that the weakness of the housing market in London and the South of England has had a particular influence on attitudes there. We find that on three of the items in the table below there is now no difference in attitudes between these two parts of the country, and that people in London and the South of England are actually *more* likely to believe that owner-occupation ties up money you need - a reflection perhaps of the relatively high ratio of house prices to incomes there.

---

[*] House prices have been much more buoyant in the Midlands than in the rest of the south of Britain in recent years. So, to investigate the effects of the changing housing market this analysis focuses on London and the South of England, compared with Scotland and the North of England, the geographically polar areas.

**Confidence in the housing market. 1986 and 1991***

| | 1986 | | 1991 | |
| --- | --- | --- | --- | --- |
| | Scotland & North | London & South | Scotland & North | London & South |
| **% strongly disagreeing that:** | | | | |
| Owning your home can be a risky investment | 33 | 38 | 12 | 13 |
| **% strongly agreeing that:** | | | | |
| Buying a home works out cheaper than paying rent | 43 | 47 | 29 | 30 |
| Owning a home makes it easier to move | 24 | 31 | 15 | 16 |
| **% agreeing that:** | | | | |
| Owning your home ties up money you may need for other things | 34 | 35 | 31 | 40 |

* Wales and the Midlands are not included in this analysis

In contrast, five years ago owner-occupation was more popular in London and the South of England than in Scotland and the North of England. True, the differences in the strength of the move away from owner-occupation between the two parts of the country are not large,[5] but such evidence as there is confirms the fact that economic evaluations are sensitive to regional circumstances.

## Economic ideology

If the severity of the recession in the south has influenced the level of economic optimism there, what effect has it had on economic ideology? Has the south lost not only its optimism but also its confidence in the market economy?  Or are attitudes towards greater economic equality and the value of government intervention in the economy more deeply rooted, and thus less responsive to short-term changes in relative economic advantage?

The next table looks at the distribution of responses in respect of six items on which there were some of the largest regional differences in attitudes in the mid-1980s (see Curtice, 1988).  In each case we show the proportion of respondents favouring the more 'left-wing' view, that is, scepticism about the operation of the market economy and support for greater equality.  A north/south divide still seems to be apparent.  With just two slight exceptions * the three regions in the northern half of the country are more 'left-wing' on all the items than the three in the south.

**Ideological differences by region, 1989-91 combined**

| % agreeing that: | Scotland | North | Wales | Midlands | London | South |
|---|---|---|---|---|---|---|
| Unemployment benefit is too low and causes hardship | 67 | 57 | 62 | 50 | 51 | 41 |
| Government should redistribute income from the better off to the less well-off | 58 | 54 | 55 | 47 | 51 | 43 |
| Ordinary people do not get their fair share of the nation's wealth | 69 | 71 | 65 | 67 | 66 | 59 |
| Big business benefits owners at the expense of the workers | 56 | 56 | 61 | 53 | 53 | 47 |
| There is one law for the rich and one for the poor | 65 | 71 | 71 | 67 | 63 | 63 |
| Unemployment should be a higher priority than inflation | 58 | 56 | 58 | 53 | 55 | 46 |

As in 1983-87, attitudes towards benefits for the unemployed (the first item in the table above) are particularly divergent - despite the narrowing of the regional gap in expectations about future trends in unemployment.

Multivariate analysis confirms this picture. In the next table we show the independent effect of region on economic ideology, again net of social class, housing tenure and economic position. A plus sign indicates that attitudes in a particular region are more likely to be 'left-wing', a minus sign that they are more likely to be 'right-wing'. As we can see, most of the signs for the three northern regions are positive and those for the three southern ones negative. And on all of the items there is at least one northern region where the positive estimate is statistically significant and one southern region where the same is true of a negative estimate.

---

* The exceptions are that agreement that "ordinary people do not get their fair share of the nation's wealth" is lower in Wales, and agreement that "there is one law for the rich and one for the poor" is lower in Scotland.

**The independent impact of region, 1989-91 combined**

|  | Scotland | North | Wales | Midlands | London | South |
|---|---|---|---|---|---|---|
| Unemployment benefit is too low and causes hardship | +.22* | +.05* | +.14* | -.11* | -.07* | -.23* |
| Government should redistribute income from the better off to the less well-off | +.08* | +.05 | +.10* | -.08* | -.01 | -.13* |
| Ordinary people do not get their fair share of the nation's wealth | -.00 | +.06* | +.15* | -.03 | -.04 | -.14* |
| Big business benefits owners at the expense of workers | -.01 | +.04 | +.15* | -.03 | -.04 | -.11* |
| There is one law for the rich and one for the poor | -.10* | +.11* | +.09 | -.00 | -.08* | -.02 |
| Unemployment should be higher priority than inflation | +.08* | +.04 | +.01 | -.05 | +.05 | -.13* |

\* = statistically significant at the five per cent level

Whereas the north/south gap on economic evaluations appears almost to have disappeared, the ideological gap still seems to be clearly in evidence. However, we need to exercise a little caution. If we compare these estimates with equivalent ones for 1983-87 (see, for example, Curtice, 1988, p. 136) they are on average a little lower. Equally there are one or two cases where the sign (+ or -) for a region is not in the expected direction; in the 1983-87 period there were no such cases. Has the ideological gap at least narrowed a little?

We can examine that question directly by comparing the proportion of respondents giving a 'left-wing' response in each region in 1989-91 with the equivalent proportion in 1983-87. And, as the table below shows, there are indeed some signs of a narrowing of the divide. For example, the proportion saying that "there is one law for the rich and one for the poor" rose by five percentage points in the Midlands and the South of England while it fell by three points in Scotland and Wales and rose by just three points in the North of England. More generally, on all of the five items where the South of England moved leftwards in 1989-91, Scotland did not move as rapidly leftwards; indeed in three cases it switched to the right.

**Economic ideology by region, combined data for 1983-87 vs. 1989-91**

| percentage point difference* between the two periods: | Scotland | North | Wales | Midlands | London | South |
|---|---|---|---|---|---|---|
| Unemployment benefit is too low and causes hardship | +2 | +2 | +12 | +7 | +6 | +5 |
| Government should redistribute income from the better off to less the well-off | +4 | +5 | -1 | +5 | +10 | +6 |
| Ordinary people do not get their fair share of the nation's wealth | -4 | +1 | -7 | +3 | +1 | +1 |
| Big business benefits the owners at expense of workers | -3 | +1 | +10 | +2 | -2 | +2 |
| There is one law for the rich and one for the poor | -3 | +3 | -3 | +5 | - | +5 |
| Unemployment should be higher priority than inflation | -20 | -21 | -17 | -16 | -17 | -22 |

\*   A plus sign indicates that responses are *more* 'left-wing' than in the mid-1980s; a minus sign that they are *less* so.

The items we have examined so far mostly tap attitudes towards the desirability or otherwise of greater equality within the market economy. We turn now to attitudes towards government intervention, using as evidence the answers to a set of questions asking specifically about the role and responsibility of government. These answers clearly confirm the existence of a regional divide. All of the northern regions (including Wales) are consistently more in favour of government intervention than are the three southern ones (including the Midlands).

**Attitudes towards government intervention, 1989-91 combined**

|  | Scotland | North | Wales | Midlands | London | South |
|---|---|---|---|---|---|---|
| **% agreeing that it is definitely the government's responsibility to:** | | | | | | |
| provide a job for every- one who wants one | 35 | 36 | 33 | 30 | 27 | 23 |
| provide a decent standard of living for the unemployed | 51 | 42 | 44 | 35 | 35 | 30 |
| reduce income differences between the rich and the poor | 44 | 46 | 45 | 36 | 41 | 30 |

And there are no consistent signs on these items that the regional gap has narrowed since 1983-87.

**Attitudes towards government intervention, combined data for 1983-87 vs. 1989-91**

|  | Scotland | North | Wales | Midlands | London | South |
|---|---|---|---|---|---|---|
| **percentage point difference\* between the two periods:** | | | | | | |
| **It is the government's responsibility to:** | | | | | | |
| provide a job for everyone who wants one | - | -3 | -17 | -3 | - | -4 |
| provide a decent standard of living for the unemployed | +2 | -6 | -16 | - | -5 | -2 |
| reduce income differences between the rich and the poor | -8 | -6 | -12 | -9 | +2 | -7 |

\* A minus sign indicates that respondents are *less* in favour of government intervention than in the mid-1980s; a plus sign that they are *more* in favour.

Interestingly, we also find that the biggest difference between the various regions on these items is in respect of the living standards of the unemployed, which mirrors our earlier finding of a sharp divide on the adequacy of the level of unemployment benefit.  This particularly deep regional divide on attitudes towards unemployment is also found in responses to a set of questions designed to tap attitudes towards the role of welfare and the welfare state.  (These items were first asked only in 1987 and so there is insufficient data to make a comparison with the earlier period.)  A number of the items show southerners to be a little less sympathetic than northerners towards the welfare state - but the clearest division is on attitudes towards unemployed people:

**Attitudes towards the welfare state, 1989-91 combined**

| % agreeing that: | Scotland | North | Wales | Midlands | London | South |
|---|---|---|---|---|---|---|
| Around here most unemployed people could find job if they really wanted one | 28 | 37 | 35 | 49 | 52 | 56 |
| Many people who get social security don't really deserve any help | 24 | 24 | 24 | 27 | 31 | 29 |
| If welfare benefits weren't so generous people would stand on their own two feet | 24 | 26 | 22 | 31 | 26 | 31 |

So, while the north/south divide in economic optimism has come close to disappearing in the wake of the recession, the ideological divide identified in our earlier analysis of data from the mid-1980s is still apparent.  In particular, despite the considerable narrowing of the north/south gap in unemployment levels, *attitudes* towards unemployment are still those which most sharply distinguish the two halves of Britain.  But there are some - albeit inconsistent - signs that the divide may have narrowed somewhat.  Attitudes towards equality and the operation of the market may not change dramatically as a result of short-term changes in the performance of the economy, but it seems we cannot assume that they are wholly impervious to changes in local economic context.


## Conclusions

What then have we discovered about the reasons for the ideological divide between north and south? And what conclusions can we draw about the regional variation in party performance at the 1992 general election?

On the first question, it is now clear that ideological differences (as opposed to differences in optimism or pessimism) between the north and south are based on something more than short-term trends in economic fortune.  While recent experience of rising unemployment and falling house prices has meant that much of the north/south gap in economic evaluations has disappeared, the ideological differences between north and south are still apparent if somewhat narrowed. The south still has relatively more faith than the north in the market economy.

This difference is probably rooted in two things. One is that although the recent trend in unemployment and economic growth has been more adverse in the south than in the north, the south still enjoys relatively higher levels of prosperity. The other is that the longer-term experience of the south is of course one of relative affluence; the impact of such an experience will not necessarily be wiped out by two or three years' relative misery.

The 1992 election also saw a modest reversal of the north/south political divide. Conservative support rose a little in the North of England and Scotland but fell in the rest of the country. Our findings on the closing of the gap in economic evaluations are consistent with the thesis that the electorate does indeed tend to blame the government for bad times and reward it for good ones (Fiorina, 1981). In particular, the growth of economic optimism in Scotland suggests that the Conservatives' relative success there cannot simply be explained by their defence of the constitutional *status quo*.

At the same time the extent of this political reversal was less than might have been anticipated, given the objective differences in regional economic trends and the strength of the association between short-term economic experience and geographical variation in party performance displayed at previous elections (Curtice & Steed, 1992; Spencer, Beange & Curtice, 1992). An explanation may lie in the ideological foundations of the Conservative party's strength in the south, which have by no means been destroyed. Thus some voters whom the Conservative party might otherwise have lost in the south because of the state of the local economy may well have retained their loyalty because of their deepseated ideological affinity with the Conservatives.[6] It is thus premature to assume that 1992 heralds the beginning of a long-term Conservative recovery in the North of England or Scotland.[7] That would require more than a short period of relative prosperity to achieve. On the other hand, our findings do suggest that a *long-term* recovery in the economy of the north could well result in the gradual disappearance of Britain's regional divide. That prospect, however, cannot be confidently predicted.

## Notes

1. In this chapter, the division of England into regions is based on the standard regions as defined by the Office of Population and Censuses and Surveys (OPCS). The North of England comprises the Northern region, the North-West and Yorkshire & Humberside. The Midlands comprises the East and West Midlands while the South of England includes the South-East (excluding London), the South-West and East Anglia. London is the area of the former Greater London Council.
2. Not all of the questions analysed here have been asked in all of the surveys. But unless otherwise indicated, all have been asked at least twice in each of the two time-periods; and the significance tests which have been applied take cognizance of the

actual number of respondents on which the analysis is based. However, the varying incidence of questions is a further reason why our assumption (see below) about the stability of inter-regional differences over time is important. For in our analysis we assume that our results are representative of the regional variation in attitudes in a time-period, irrespective of the *particular* two years in which a question was asked.

3.   Empirical examination of the data suggests that this assumption is not an unreasonable one. The two largest of our six regions are the North of England and the South of England and thus the difference in attitudes between these two regions is the least affected by sampling variation. In the following table we show for each year separately (a) the difference between the percentage of respondents in the North of England saying that their household income in the last twelve months had fallen behind prices and the equivalent percentage in the South of England, and (b) the same difference for those agreeing that "unemployment benefit is too low and causes hardship". Both questions feature prominently in the analysis in this chapter.

|         |      | (a) | (b) |
|---------|------|-----|-----|
| **1983-7** | 1983 | n/a | + 12 |
|         | 1984 | +9  | + 17 |
|         | 1985 | + 17 | + 24 |
|         | 1986 | + 12 | + 18 |
|         | 1987 | + 13 | + 21 |
| **1989-91** | 1989 | + 1 | + 14 |
|         | 1990 | + 7 | + 22 |
|         | 1991 | -   | + 12 |

4.   This informal analysis is broadly confirmed by comparing parameter estimates from a logit analysis for the two periods. For example there was a statistically significant negative parameter estimate for the South of England in the 1983-87 period on all three of the items analysed earlier, compared with just the one we have reported for 1989-91. So as suggested earlier, the changes are not an artefact of differential changes in social composition.

5.   Loglinear analysis does however indicate that the difference in the trend in the two halves of the country on one item (home ownership tying up one's money) is statistically significant at the 5 per cent level. A model which excludes a term which measures the interaction between region, survey year and attitude towards this item fails to give an adequate fit to the data.

6.   We should note here that the surveys find only small and generally reduced regional differences on taxation, an issue which featured prominently in the general election campaign. It was suggested that Labour's proposals for increased taxation for those on higher incomes would particularly affect its support in London and the South-East. The percentage of respondents in each region who agreed between 1989 and 1991 (together with the change since 1983-87) that taxes for those with high incomes were too low was as follows:- Scotland 57 (+12); North 52 (+11); Wales 52 (+11); Midlands 49 (+14); London 47 (+12); South 49 (+18). Thus the obstacles towards Labour increasing its support appear, as suggested here, to lie beyond those particular proposals.

7.   It is worth noting here also that the *British Social Attitudes* surveys do not show any narrowing of the north/south divide in the distribution of party identification - a longer term measure of party loyalty than vote. The level of Conservative identification in the 1989-91 surveys (compared with 1983-87) was Scotland 26 (+3); North 30 (unchanged); Wales 21 (-1); Midlands 39 (-3); London 38 (+2); South 46 (+1). So identification with the Conservative Party rose (slightly) in Scotland; it also did so in London and the South of England. The equivalent figures for Labour are Scotland 35(-6); North 46 (+4); Wales 54 (+6); Midlands 35(+5); London 37 (+2);

South 24 (+2). Note that the surveys anticipated quite clearly Labour's election difficulties in Scotland, and at the same time do not indicate any particular growth in Labour Party support in London or the South of England.

## References

Curtice, J. (1988), 'One Nation?', in Jowell, R., Witherspoon, S. and Brook, L. (eds.), *British Social Attitudes: the 5th Report*, Aldershot: Gower.
Curtice, J. and Steed, M. (1992), 'The Results Analysed', in Butler, D. and Kavanagh, D., *The British General Election of 1992*, Basingstoke: Macmillan.
Fiorina, M. (1981), *Retrospective Voting in American National Elections*, New Haven: Yale University Press.
Spencer, P., Beange, R. and Curtice, J. (1992), *The 1992 Election and the North-South Divide*, London: Lehman Bros.

## Acknowledgements

This chapter has been prepared using the *British Social Attitudes* Combined Dataset 1983-91 deposited at the ESRC Data Archive, University of Essex. Financial support for the creation of this dataset from the Economic and Social Research Council (under grant no. R000 23 3230) is gratefully acknowledged.

Miss Ann Mair of the Social Statistics Laboratory, University of Strathclyde was the Computing Officer on that project and also generously assisted in the production of the statistical analyses required for the preparation for this chapter.

The questions on attitudes to home ownership are part of a questionnaire module on housing issues included since the survey began. We are grateful for the steadfast financial support of the Department of the Environment that has enabled us not only to maintain the time-series (and the unique set of data that emerges each year), but to refresh the module with new items.

# 5 Men and women at work and at home

*Kathleen Kiernan* *

One of the major debates of the 1970s was on the changing role of women in society. In the 1980s the focus shifted on to the changing roles of men as well as women. Now it looks as if it will shift yet again, on to the nature of the relationship between work and family life. This chapter examines what men and women think about a range of issues to do with employment and family life, comparing their respective reasons for working, the extent to which job opportunities are seen to be becoming more equal, and the way in which the public views issues such as job segregation and stereotyping of occupations. We re-examine the level of support for the 'traditional' model of breadwinner husband and homemaker wife, looking at the domestic division of labour within British households. We also re-explore attitudes to sexual relationships, and to divorce and its ramifications.

## The labour market

The single long-term trend that is probably most responsible for changing the roles of men and women is the marked increase in the level of women's participation in the labour market. Data from the annual *Labour Force Surveys* show that during the 1980s women's share of total employment rose, primarily as result of the growth of part-time jobs in the service sector. Even so, men are more likely than women to be

---

* Research Director, Family Policy Studies Centre.

employed, employed full-time and to be in permanent employment. In 1991, according to the *Labour Force Survey*, 75 per cent of men were economically active, compared with 53 per cent of women. Seventy-six per cent of people in employment were working full-time: the proportion being much higher for men (93 per cent) than for women (55 per cent). Over two-thirds of non-married women worked full-time compared with one half of married women. Two out of three people who work part-time said that they did so through choice; only 8 per cent said they were working part-time because they could not get a full-time job. (Employment Department, 1992a). Women are more likely than men to have a temporary job; for example, in 1991, 7.3 per cent of all employed women were in temporary jobs compared with 4.6 per cent of men.

Another significant change to the labour market during the 1980s was the marked increase in the numbers of self-employed persons, up from 2.2 million or 9 per cent of all employed persons in 1981, to 3.3 million or 13 per cent of employed persons in 1991 (Employment Department, 1992b). Self-employment may be a particularly attractive option for women because it provides greater flexibility for combining work and family commitments. There is evidence from the *Labour Force Survey* that self-employment rates are greater among women with dependent children than those without (Employment Department, 1992b).


*Reasons for working*

On the *British Social Attitudes* survey, we asked a range of questions about why people work. Are there any differences between men and women in their motives for working and does it vary according to whether they are employees or self-employed? Is work "just a means of earning a living or does it mean much more ... than that"? As we have found consistently in this series, most people in work (68 per cent of men and 70 per cent of women) say that work contributes more to their lives than money alone. Respondents were shown a list of statements and asked to select the ones that best described their reasons for working. As we see below there are some noticeable differences in the reasons given by male and female employees. As respondents were free to give as many reasons as they wished, the answers add up to more than 100 per cent.

| | Employees | |
|---|---|---|
| | **Men** | **Women** |
| **Reasons for working:** | *%* | *%* |
| Need money for basic essentials | 80 | 59 |
| To earn money to buy extras | 36 | 43 |
| To earn money of my own | 24 | 34 |
| Enjoy working | 52 | 60 |
| Working is the normal thing to do | 32 | 18 |
| To follow my career | 42 | 28 |
| For the company of other people | 19 | 41 |
| For a change from children/housework | 2 | 17 |

Naturally, the great majority of men say they work to make money for basics such as food and housing. A (much smaller) majority of women also say they work to earn money for basic requirements. Among women, however, enjoying work is as popular a reason. Other social reasons, such as for company or for relief from domestic duties, are also much more frequently expressed by women than by men. While women are more likely than men to work in order to earn money of 'their own', men are more likely than women to regard working as the 'normal' thing to do. Comparisons with responses given in the 1984 survey (Witherspoon, 1985, p. 68) show that there has been little change in the responses of men and women over the time period.

Given the growth in self-employment in recent years, we examined whether self-employed men and women differ from employees in their motives for working.

| | Self-employed | |
|---|---|---|
| | **Men** | **Women** |
| **Reasons for working:** | *%* | *%* |
| Need money for basic essentials | 79 | 55 |
| To earn money to buy extras | 37 | 48 |
| To earn money of my own | 23 | 19 |
| Enjoy working | 69 | 77 |
| Working is the normal thing to do | 36 | 21 |
| To follow my career | 23 | 30 |
| For the company of other people | 15 | 25 |
| For a change from children/housework | 2 | 20 |

As we see, however, responses of employees and the self-employed are, with a few exceptions, broadly similar. The notable differences are that the self-employed (men and women) seem to derive greater enjoyment from their work than employees; self-employed men also seem less career orientated than employees, while self-employed women are less likely than employees to work for social reasons. One might expect such differences given that self-employed people tend to have less clearly

defined career paths and often work on their own. The differences
between men and women in reasons for working that we saw among
employees are also largely apparent among the self-employed.


*Equal opportunities*

We asked a range of questions to assess respondents' attitudes towards
the principle of equal opportunity, and to specific legislative measures, as
well as their perceptions of the actual extent of discrimination in the
workplace.

Respondents overwhelmingly believe that opportunities *should* be
equal; there is almost universal agreement that "in a fair society, every
person should have an equal opportunity to get ahead" (97 per cent of
men and 95 per cent of women agree or agree strongly). Moreover, 85
per cent of respondents support laws against sex discrimination. As we
see below, support seems to have increased in recent years.

*There is a law in Britain against sex discrimination; that is against giving*
*unfair preference to men - or to women - in employment, pay and so on.*
*Do you generally support or oppose the idea of a law for this purpose?*

|             | 1983 | 1984 | 1987 | 1991 |
|-------------|------|------|------|------|
|             | %    | %    | %    | %    |
| Support     | 76   | 80   | 75   | 85   |
| Oppose      | 22   | 17   | 22   | 13   |

Given the fluctuations in responses over time, we should perhaps be
cautious about interpreting the recent increase as a robust change.

Although the public overwhelmingly (and increasingly) seems to oppose
sex discrimination, there is little indication from our surveys that people
perceive any improvement in recent years in employment opportunities,
incomes and promotion prospects for women.

|                                    | 1984 | 1987 | 1991 |
|------------------------------------|------|------|------|
| **Job opportunities are:**         | %    | %    | %    |
| Better for women                   | 7    | 6    | 7    |
| No different for men and women     | 37   | 34   | 23   |
| Worse for women                    | 51   | 54   | 62   |
|                                    |      |      |      |
| **Income and wages are:**          | %    | %    | %    |
| Better for women                   | 2    | 1    | 2    |
| No different for men and women     | 31   | 27   | 23   |
| Worse for women                    | 61   | 66   | 65   |

Nowadays only one in four respondents believe there is no difference in
the job opportunities of men and women "with similar education and
experience", down from 37 per cent in 1984. The responses of men and

women are very similar. Moreover, a higher proportion of respondents now than in 1984 believes that job opportunities are worse for women.

Two out of three respondents believe that the earnings of women are worse than those of men with similar education and jobs. Women are more likely than men to believe this, but the difference is perhaps surprisingly small: 67 per cent of women compared with 63 per cent of men.

Responses to questions on promotion prospects for women have shown little change during the 1980s. Around 80 per cent of people persistently believe that "women are generally less likely than men to be promoted at work even when their qualifications and experience are the same". Around half of these men and women think this happens a lot, the other half only a little, but the belief that it happens at all is remarkably stable. Overall, it seems, the public perception of inequality between men and women in the workplace is somewhat higher nowadays than it was in the early 1980s - an indictment perhaps on the success of measures to ensure equal opportunity. On the other hand, the recession has probably taken its toll on perceptions too.

So, perhaps the safest interpretation is that people's perceptions of equal opportunities have changed very little over the last decade. This highlights the need for such initiatives as the recently-launched 'Opportunity 2000' - a national drive to promote equal opportunities for women at work. Under this scheme, employers go through a three-stage process of auditing existing policies, setting measurable goals, and making a public commitment to achieving them.

## Occupational segregation

A striking feature of labour markets in advanced societies is the dissimilarity in the occupations of men and women. Women are clustered in fields such as health, education and welfare, and clerical work. Even in more progressive societies like Sweden where, since the 1930s, women have been deemed to be workers first and mothers second, and where creative and aggressive measures have been devised to steer women out of traditional female occupations, the picture has changed very little over the last 20 years (Ruggie, 1988).

The extent of occupational segregation among men and women in our sample is shown below. It is clear that women are less likely than men to be in the higher managerial and administrative grades. The proportions of full-time working men and women in professional occupations are broadly similar but the type of professional activity varies markedly: three out of 10 of the men are in the health and education sectors compared with more than six out of 10 of the women. Similarly, women in the associate professional and technical fields are mainly to be found in these traditional sectors. Part-time working women are especially concentrated into personal services such as hairdressing and sales, and 'other occupations', a category which includes catering assistants, cleaners and shelf-fillers - jobs which tend to be poorly paid and offer little job security.

|  | Full-time male employees | Full-time female employees | Part-time female employees |
|---|---|---|---|
| Occupational order* | % | % | % |
| Managers and administrators | 20 | 10 | 2 |
| Professional occupations | 11 | 13 | 3 |
| Associate professional and technical | 10 | 13 | 9 |
| Clerical and secretarial | 9 | 30 | 19 |
| Craft and related occupations | 16 | 5 | 3 |
| Personal and protective services | 5 | 11 | 17 |
| Sales occupations | 4 | 6 | 14 |
| Plant and machine operators | 16 | 7 | 2 |
| Other occupations | 9 | 4 | 29 |

* This table shows occupation broken down by SOC major groups. See Appendix I for further information.

As another indicator of the degree of occupational segregation we ask all men and women employees whether there are members of the opposite sex doing the same sort of work as themselves at their workplace. Although the majority of both men and women report working in segregated occupations, men are somewhat more likely than women to do so. But there does appear to have been some easing of occupational segregation amongst men since 1984:

|  | All employees | | | |
|---|---|---|---|---|
|  | 1984 | | 1991 | |
|  | Men | Women | Men | Women |
|  | % | % | % | % |
| Works with own sex only | 72 | 51 | 58 | 54 |
| Works with both sexes | 27 | 47 | 41 | 42 |
| Works alone/only person doing that job | * | 2 | * | 2 |

* = less than 0.5 per cent

Around a quarter of men in 1984 said there were women doing the same sort of work as them at their workplace; this has risen to 41 per cent in 1991. Men are now as likely as women to be working with members of the opposite sex. There has been little corresponding change among female employees, and as a result the proportions of men and women working with both sexes are broadly similar. This development is more likely to be related to changes in the occupational structure than to any overt policies to desegregate the work place. The proportion of non-manual jobs has been increasing at the expense of manual jobs: in 1981, 49 per cent of economically active persons were in non-manual occupations compared with 56 per cent in 1991 (OPCS, 1982, 1992). Non-manual occupations tend to be less sex-segregated than manual ones.

Traditionally women's work, particularly part-time work, has shown no similar trend, as the table below shows.

|  | Women employees | | | |
| --- | --- | --- | --- | --- |
|  | 1984 | | 1991 | |
|  | **Full-time** | **Part-time** | **Full-time** | **Part-time** |
|  | % | % | % | % |
| Works with own sex only | 45 | 64 | 50 | 59 |
| Works with both sexes | 54 | 33 | 46 | 36 |
| Works alone/only person doing that job | * | 2 | 2 | 2 |

Part-time women employees tend to be considerably more occupationally segregated than their full-time counterparts. Six in 10 of them work with other women only, whereas full-timers are almost as likely to work with men as to work exclusively with women. Overall, there is little sign that traditionally women's occupations are becoming less segregated: the extent of sex-exclusivity among part-timers has hardly changed since 1984, while among full-timers the proportion working with both sexes has, if anything, decreased.

The question on occupational segregation was followed by one on job stereotyping. Employees were asked whether they thought of their work as mainly men's work, mainly women's work, or work that either men or women do. Unsurprisingly, men are more likely to describe their work as mainly men's work than women are to describe theirs as mainly women's work:

|  | All employees | | | |
| --- | --- | --- | --- | --- |
|  | 1984 | | 1991 | |
|  | **Men** | **Women** | **Men** | **Women** |
|  | % | % | % | % |
| **Work is:** | | | | |
| Mainly men's work | 49 | 1 | 35 | 1 |
| Mainly women's work | - | 36 | * | 26 |
| Work that either men or women do | 50 | 63 | 64 | 72 |

However, between 1984 and 1991 there has been an increase in the proportion of employees who think that their work is suitable for either sex, possibly because the nature of work and of workplaces has changed in the intervening period. We have seen that women in part-time employment are more likely to be working with their own sex than are their full-time counterparts. Women in part-time employment are also more likely than those in full-time employment to view their work as women's work, but less so in 1991 than in 1984.

Employees who thought of their work as being mainly for their own sex were also asked two further questions: whether they thought that men or women *could* do the same sort of work; and, if so, whether they thought they would be willing to do so. Fifty-nine per cent of these men employees thought that women *could* do the same work as they do, and of these a half thought that women would be willing to do so. In contrast nearly all the women, 93 per cent, thought that men could do the same work as they do, and of these, around a half thought that men would be willing to do so.

## *Occupational stereotypes*

As in the 1984 and 1987 surveys respondents were asked to look at a list of occupations and to categorise them as being particularly suitable for men, particularly suitable for women, or suitable for both equally. Here we compare the proportions giving egalitarian responses.

|  | % saying each job is "suitable for both men and women equally" | | |
|---|---|---|---|
|  | **1984** | **1987** | **1991** |
| **Traditionally male jobs** | | | |
| Car mechanic | 25 | 31 | 37 |
| Police officer | 49 | 62 | 61 |
| Bank manager | 58 | 70 | 75 |
| Director of an international company | n/a | n/a | 72 |
| **Traditionally female jobs** | | | |
| Secretary | 38 | 44 | 43 |
| Nurse | 57 | 67 | 64 |
| **Other occupations** | | | |
| Member of Parliament | 82 | 89 | 85 |
| Family doctor/GP | 87 | 93 | 88 |
| Social worker | 87 | 83 | 81 |

Over time the general tendency has been for the more traditionally male and female jobs to be regarded as less sex-exclusive, albeit from different starting points. However, much of the change was between 1984 and 1987, since when there has been little further movement. A majority of the public still views traditionally gender-exclusive jobs such as car mechanic or secretary as gender-exclusive, but rather less so than in 1984.

In contrast, only one in three views police work or nursing in this way. An MP's job, or that of a family doctor or a social worker is seen as almost gender-neutral. Not quite as gender-neutral are the jobs of bank managers and directors of international companies, though over 70 per cent in each case think that these positions are equally suitable for men and women.

Responses of men and women are very similar across five of the occupations. Exceptions are the more stereotypical occupations (police officer, secretary, car mechanic and nurse) which women are more likely than men to believe are suitable for both sexes equally. This pattern was similar to that found in the 1984 survey (Witherspoon, 1985). Generally, the evidence from our time series points to a weakening of the traditional occupational stereotypes, but also to a slowing of the pace of change.

## Gender roles

Most men and women under retirement age are in the labour market and contribute to family incomes. Yet the belief that men should be the breadwinner persists, on balance, among both men and women.

### The homemaker-breadwinner model

Respondents were asked how much they agreed or disagreed with the following statement:

*A husband's job is to earn the money; a wife's job is to look after the home and family.*

|  | All % | Men % | Women % |
|---|---|---|---|
| **Strongly agree/ Agree** | 33 | 35 | 31 |
| **Neither agree nor disagree** | 21 | 23 | 20 |
| **Strongly disagree/ Disagree** | 44 | 41 | 47 |

Women are more likely than men to disagree with the statement, but not by much. Around a third of both men and women support the traditional homemaker-breadwinner model, and around one in four or five are uncertain or neutral: or are they ambivalent, or even indifferent? Moreover, there is no strong evidence that men and women are increasingly likely nowadays to reject the traditional model. The proportions disagreeing are not far different from those in 1987 or, for that matter, 1984.

The overall picture does, however, disguise very large sub-group differences. Broadly, as the table below shows, the younger one is, and the higher one's level of education, the more likely one is to reject the traditional roles of men and women.

*A husband's job is to earn the money; a wife's job is to look after the home and family.*

| | % disagreeing or strongly disagreeing | |
| --- | --- | --- |
| | **Men** | **Women** |
| **Total** | 41 | 47 |
| **Age group:** | | |
| 18-34 | 65 | 68 |
| 35-44 | 54 | 54 |
| 45-54 | 30 | 53 |
| 55-59 | 29 | 31 |
| 60 or older | 13 | 19 |
| **Highest educational qualification:** | | |
| Degree/Professional | 53 | 63 |
| A' level | 57 | 61 |
| O' level/CSE | 34 | 54 |
| Other/None | 28 | 32 |

Although, as noted, women overall are more likely to disagree with the statement than are men, the responses of men and women of different ages are broadly similar. But women are more 'traditionalist' at a slightly later age than are men.

Looking at the attitudes of women in the labour market, we find, not surprisingly, that women who work full-time are the most likely to disagree with the homemaker-breadwinner division of labour - three-quarters do so. In contrast, women without paid work are the least likely to challenge this model.

We also examined the responses of men and women in 'couple house-holds'* in which the man works and the women either works full- or part-time or is not in paid work, and found that men's attitudes do vary noticeably according to the employment status of their partner:

---

* These are households in which the man and woman (one of which is our respondent) are either married or living as married.

*A husband's job is to earn the money; a wife's job is to look after the home and family.*

|  | % disagreeing or strongly disagreeing | |
| --- | --- | --- |
|  | Men | Women |
| Man works and ... |  |  |
| Woman works full-time | 58 | 72 |
| Woman works part-time | 49 | 45 |
| Woman not in paid work | 33 | 40 |

As might be expected, men with partners who are *not* in paid work are the least likely to reject the traditional division of labour. What is perhaps surprising, however, is the discrepancy we find between the attitudes of men and women in households where both partners work full-time. Seventy-two per cent of women in such households reject the traditional division of labour, compared with only 58 per cent of men. A substantial proportion of men with partners who work full-time thus seem to be somewhat uncomfortable about it.

*Attitudes to women working and the family life-cycle*

Women's employment patterns are largely explained by their responsibility for young children. Mothers of children aged under five are far less likely to be in paid work than women without young children. And when mothers of young children *are* in paid work they are far more likely than other women to work part-time. *General Household Survey* data for the period 1987-89 show that four out of 10 mothers whose youngest child is under five are in employment compared with seven out of 10 mothers of older children. Additionally, while one half of women without dependent children work full-time, only one in five women with dependent children work full-time (OPCS, 1991).

So the presence of a child aged under five in the household is perhaps the main determinant of whether mothers are in the labour market and whether they work full-time. During recent periods the general trend has been for each new cohort of mothers to return to the labour market sooner than the preceding cohort, and for more and more women with young children to take full-time jobs. Thus, in 1981, 25 per cent of mothers with a child aged under five years were working, around three-quarters part-time and one-quarter full-time. By 1989, however, 41 per cent of such mothers were in the labour market, with around two in three working part-time (OPCS, 1991).

Here we consider men's and women's *attitudes* to women working at different stages of their life-cycle namely: between marrying and having children; when there is a child under school age; after the youngest child starts school; and after the children leave home. Respondents were asked whether they thought the women should work outside the home full-time, part-time or not at all at each of these stages.

| % saying women should work .... | | | |
|---|---|---|---|
| | Full-time | Part-time | Not at all |
| After marrying and before there are children | 82 | 7 | 1 |
| When there is a child under school age | 5 | 33 | 52 |
| After the youngest child starts school | 21 | 63 | 6 |
| After the children leave home | 72 | 14 | 1 |

Clear majorities of both men and women agree that women should go out to work full-time before the advent of parenthood and after their children are grown up. But when there are children at home, attitudes change. Only a minority (around one in five) thinks that mothers with school-age children should work full-time, and there is near universal agreement that women should *not* work full-time when they have pre-school age children.

These bald and contrasting attitudes need further examination. In particular, let us consider the two phases where young children are present in the household and see what men and women think mothers should do. As we have noted, when there are children under school age, only five per cent feel that the mother should work full-time; a further one in three (33 per cent) feel she should work part-time; but the majority (52 per cent) think the mother should not work outside the home at all. The responses of men and women are similar. As for families with school age children, however, only a very small minority (six per cent) think the mother should stay at home. Men are more likely to believe this than women (eight per cent compared with four per cent). The most popular response was that women should work part-time, with rather more women (67 per cent) than men (60 per cent) choosing this option.

There are also some differences according to the respondent's age. Younger women are less likely than older women to say that women should stay at home when they have pre-school age children. Only around one in three women under age 35, compared with the over two in three women aged 60 and over, think that mothers of pre-school age children should stay at home. There is a broadly similar but less consistent age gradient in the responses of men. In contrast, however, women in the prime child rearing age groups, 25-44 years, are *less* likely than their male counterparts to say that women with school age children should work full-time (one in four women compared with one in three men). This difference probably reflects the lessons of women's experience in combining family and work responsibilities (see Witherspoon and Prior, 1991).

## The domestic domain

In Britain, as in most other European countries over the last decade or so, there has been a clear change in sex role attitudes: both men and women have increasingly espoused more egalitarian views (Kiernan, 1992). Is there, however, any evidence that in the domestic domain, where it is seemingly a simple matter of private negotiation between men and women, that couples nowadays are sharing more domestic responsibilities and tasks? In 'couple households' where the man works and the woman is not employed, or works part-time, it would seem logical in terms of maximising household efficiency that the woman take on more of the domestic tasks. By the same logic, we would expect full-time homemakers to perform more domestic tasks than women who work part-time. Similarly, in households where both partners work full-time we might expect the division of labour to be more or less equal, unless one partner works much longer hours than the other. So let us examine the extent to which the division of labour within couple households varies according to the employment status of the woman.

Respondents in couple households were asked which partner is "mainly responsible for general domestic duties". In the great majority of cases (75 per cent) the woman is responsible and in 16 per cent the duties are reported to be shared equally between the man and the woman. Men are more likely than women to say that duties are shared equally (20 per cent, compared with 12 per cent of women), perhaps because they (or their partners) are unfamiliar with how much work is actually done, or more likely because perceptions are coloured by stereotypes or even by guilt. The responses according to employment status are shown below.

| | | **Respondents living in households where...** | | | |
| | **All** | **...man works, woman works full-time** | **...man works, woman works part-time** | **...man works, woman not in work** | **Other house-holds** |
|---|---|---|---|---|---|
| **Who is responsible for general domestic duties?** | % | % | % | % | % |
| Mainly woman | 75 | 67 | 83 | 89 | 66 |
| Shared equally | 16 | 24 | 13 | 6 | 21 |

Couples in households where both partners work full-time are more likely than other couples to share responsibility for domestic tasks. Even so, in two out of three of these households, the arrangements are unequal, with the woman taking the brunt of the work. There are indications, however, that egalitarian arrangements may be becoming more common: in 1987, women were mainly responsible for domestic duties in 72 per cent of these households (Witherspoon, 1988), compared with 67 per cent in 1991.

As expected, women who work part-time are more likely to be mainly responsible for domestic duties than their full-time counterparts, and a bit less likely than those who do not work. More surprisingly, perhaps, in 'other households', two out of three of which contain a partner aged 60 or more, sharing is as common as in full-time working households.

*Who performs household tasks?*

Once again, as in 1983, 1984 and 1987, we asked about the division of household tasks between men and women in couple households. As we see from the table below, men still tend to be exclusively responsible for the household repairs and for more or less nothing else. Women are still primarily responsible for the laundry, cleaning and cooking (in that order). Shopping, dishwashing and financial matters are more likely to be shared. Changes over time in the sharing of individual household tasks, as judged by responses to the earlier surveys, are barely perceptible.

|  |  | Households where man works and ... | | |
|---|---|---|---|---|
| **Who:** | **All households** % | **... woman works full-time** % | **... woman works part-time** % | **... woman is not in paid work** % |
| **does household shopping?** |  |  |  |  |
| mainly man | 8 | 4 | 5 | 5 |
| mainly woman | 45 | 42 | 51 | 57 |
| shared equally | 47 | 53 | 44 | 37 |
| **makes evening meal?** | % | % | % | % |
| mainly man | 9 | 7 | 5 | 3 |
| mainly woman | 70 | 60 | 75 | 81 |
| shared equally | 20 | 32 | 20 | 16 |
| **does evening dishes?** | % | % | % | % |
| mainly man | 28 | 28 | 20 | 18 |
| mainly woman | 33 | 24 | 41 | 37 |
| shared equally | 37 | 46 | 38 | 42 |
| **does household cleaning?** | % | % | % | % |
| mainly man | 4 | 5 | - | - |
| mainly woman | 68 | 63 | 82 | 82 |
| shared equally | 27 | 30 | 18 | 17 |
| **does washing and ironing?** | % | % | % | % |
| mainly man | 3 | 3 | - | 1 |
| mainly woman | 84 | 78 | 91 | 91 |
| shared equally | 12 | 17 | 9 | 8 |
| **repairs household equipment?** | % | % | % | % |
| mainly man | 82 | 84 | 85 | 81 |
| mainly woman | 6 | 3 | 7 | 8 |
| shared equally | 10 | 10 | 8 | 10 |
| **organises household money and bills?** | % | % | % | % |
| mainly man | 31 | 27 | 29 | 40 |
| mainly woman | 40 | 44 | 41 | 36 |
| shared equally | 28 | 28 | 30 | 23 |

Men are more likely to share and participate in virtually all the household tasks if their partners work full-time. Although we might have expected women who work part-time to fall midway between women in full-time work and the homemakers, it turns out that they are much closer to the homemakers. This may be partly because 'part-time' work can refer to a wide range of hours worked per week. For example, 29 per cent of part-time working women in our sample worked less than 15 hours a week and a further 50 per cent less than 24 hours a week. Considerations of equity and efficiency may demand that women who work far fewer hours than their male partners should do more of the domestic duties. However, in one important feature of domestic life, the organisation of household finances, women in part-time and full-time employment are equally likely to play a part (in contrast to women who do not have a paid job, who are much less likely to play a part in financial matters). This seems to suggest that it is not so much the *level* of earnings that affects the control of financial resources as much as whether or not the woman earns at all.

Among the routine domestic tasks we asked about, the one in which men are most likely to participate (apart from repairs) is doing the evening dishes. This is seemingly an idiosyncrasy of the British male, or a success story for the British female. Across the 12 member states of the European Community, British men were the most likely to participate in dishwashing by a large margin - seven out of 10 compared with a European average of four out of 10 (Kempeneers and Lelievre, 1992).

Other survey data from a range of countries also suggest that looking after children is frequently a more popular activity among fathers than the more routine housekeeping tasks (Kiernan, 1992). Indeed, our survey provides evidence in support of this, in that a third of fathers claim to share equally in the care of sick children, rising to a half among families where both parents work. "Teaching the child(ren) discipline" is a task that is also shared in the majority of families. Moreover, there has been a sharp increase in the extent to which fathers share (or at least claim to share) in looking after sick children; in 1987, only 18 per cent of fathers did so, but by 1991 that proportion had doubled to 39 per cent.

|                                | All house- holds | Households where man works and ... | | |
|                                |     | ... woman works full-time | ... woman works part-time | ... woman is not in paid work |
| --- | --- | --- | --- | --- |
| **Who:**                       |     |     |     |     |
| **looks after sick children?** | %   | %   | %   | %   |
| mainly man                     | 1   | 3   | 2   | -   |
| mainly woman                   | 60  | 44  | 51  | 80  |
| shared equally                 | 39  | 52  | 48  | 20  |
| **teaches children discipline?** | % | % | %   | %   |
| mainly man                     | 9   | 13  | 9   | 9   |
| mainly woman                   | 17  | 13  | 15  | 22  |
| shared equally                 | 73  | 74  | 76  | 70  |

*Attitudes and household tasks*

We might expect that respondents with more egalitarian attitudes would be more likely than non-egalitarians to share domestic tasks, although this is not entirely predictable, as attitudes and behaviour frequently conflict. To examine this issue we looked at the behaviour of the 45 per cent of respondents who disagreed with the non-egalitarian statement "A husband's job is to earn money; a wife's job is to look after the home and family", and contrasted it with the behaviour of the 33 per cent who agreed with it. We confined our attention to couple households in which the man was in work. Reassuringly, as the next table shows, men with more egalitarian attitudes are indeed much more likely to perform most of the household tasks than are the non-egalitarians.

**% of men who share household tasks in couple households where the man is in work**

|                            | | Men | |
|                            | All | 'Egalitarian' | 'Non-egalitarian' |
| --- | --- | --- | --- |
| Household shopping         | 46  | 52  | 35  |
| Evening meal               | 25  | 32  | 15  |
| Evening dishes             | 44  | 48  | 44  |
| Household cleaning         | 23  | 31  | 15  |
| Washing and ironing        | 11  | 16  | 2   |
| Household repairs          | 8   | 13  | 3   |
| Organising household money | 25  | 31  | 19  |

Egalitarian attitudes in a man increase his chances of sharing domestic tasks. On the other hand, similar attitudes in a woman do not have the same effect on her partner (see table below). Partners of egalitarian women are no more likely, with the exception of preparing the evening meal, to share domestic tasks. So, since women's attitudes appear to have less of an impact on the equitable division of labour in the home, it is primarily men's attitudes that need to change if progress towards equality is to be achieved (see also Witherspoon and Prior, 1991, p. 152).

**% of women who share household tasks in couple households where the man is in work**

| | **Women** | | |
| | **All** | **'Egalitarian'** | **'Non-egalitarian'** |
| --- | --- | --- | --- |
| Household shopping | 40 | 47 | 41 |
| Evening meal | 21 | 29 | 13 |
| Evening dishes | 42 | 47 | 39 |
| Household cleaning | 19 | 23 | 20 |
| Washing and ironing | 10 | 14 | 8 |
| Household repairs | 11 | 13 | 5 |
| Organising household money | 29 | 29 | 27 |

Possible clues as to the direction of change in the domestic division of labour may be derived from respondents' answers as to how household tasks *should* be divided up.   Among couple households there is a noticeable gap between the proportions saying that tasks *should*  be shared equally and those who say they *are* shared equally: for most of the tasks the ratio is at least two to one.  Since responses of men and women are again broadly in accord, the gender breakdown is not reproduced here.

**% of respondents in couple households saying...**

| | **...should share equally** | **...do share equally** |
| --- | --- | --- |
| Household shopping | 74 | 47 |
| Evening meal | 54 | 20 |
| Evening dishes | 75 | 37 |
| Household cleaning | 60 | 27 |
| Washing and ironing | 36 | 12 |
| Household repairs | 29 | 10 |
| Organising household money | 64 | 28 |

Similar questions were asked in the 1984 and 1987 surveys (Witherspoon, 1985, 1988).  As can be seen below, since the proportions saying that tasks *should* be shared have risen, but *practice* has not changed much, the gap between attitudes and practice on the domestic front has thus tended to widen over the years.  Moreover, for tasks such as household repairs and laundry, both men *and* women appear to be so resistant to change in either attitudes or practice that they are likely to remain overwhelmingly gender-specific tasks for the foreseeable future.

|                              | Gap between 'should' share equally and 'do' share equally (percentage points) | | |
|------------------------------|------|------|------|
|                              | 1984 | 1987 | 1991 |
| Household shopping           | 23   | 22   | 27   |
| Evening meal                 | 19   | 25   | 34   |
| Evening dishes               | 23   | 33   | 38   |
| Household cleaning           | 22   | 29   | 33   |
| Washing and ironing          | 12   | 18   | 24   |
| Household repairs            | 9    | 15   | 19   |
| Organising household money   | 30   | 32   | 36   |

The gap between attitudes and practice, in addition to the wide variation between types of household and types of chore, make the phenomenon of gender-specific divisions of labour very difficult to explain, and changes very difficult to predict. As Thompson and Walker (1989, p.857) note with apparent frustration: "Women's employment, time availability, resources, conscious ideology, and power do not account for why wives still do the bulk of family work".


## Partnership issues

We now turn to other sorts of partnership issues - in particular, attitudes to pre-marital and extra-marital sexual relationships, and to partnership breakdown and its aftermath.

   The predominant form of male-female partnership is the married couple and it is still the case that most men and women do marry. However, since about the beginning of the 1970s people have been marrying later, divorcing more and cohabiting to a greater extent, either as prelude to marriage, or instead of marrying or between marriages. Cohabitation has risen dramatically since the early 1980s; for example, the proportions of single women cohabiting has increased from eight per cent in 1981 to 16 per cent in 1988/89 (OPCS, 1991). In addition, divorce has become more prevalent: indeed, if present trends were to continue, more that one in three marriages would end in divorce and one in four children would experience the break-up of their parent's marriage by the time they were 16 years old (Haskey, 1988, 1990). Partnerships have thus become more varied and more fragile in recent times.


### Sexual relations

Alongside the trend towards increased cohabitation, and probably an important pre-condition for it, has been a growing acceptability of pre-marital sex, which had already begun to assert itself well before the 1980s.

The 1983 *British Social Attitudes* survey showed that by then only a minority (28 per cent) thought that pre-marital sex was 'always' or 'almost always wrong'. By 1991 that proportion was still lower at 19 per cent. As one might expect, younger people are much more likely than older people to regard sex before marriage as acceptable. The table below shows one of the steepest age gradients in the survey. As the younger generation ages, however, they may well take their attitudes with them, thus in time reducing the age gradient on this issue.

| Age group: | % saying sex before marriage is 'Not wrong at all' |
|---|---|
| 18-24 | 87 |
| 25-34 | 85 |
| 35-44 | 76 |
| 45-54 | 59 |
| 55-59 | 47 |
| 60-64 | 29 |
| 65 or older | 29 |

As far as behaviour is concerned, the available evidence suggests that pre-marital sex has long been commonplace (Dunnell, 1979; Bone, 1985). Attitudes and behaviour in respect of pre-marital sex have thus proceeded in the same direction. This does not seem to be the case in respect of extra-marital sexual relations. Using the same scale, we ask respondents whether it is wrong or not wrong for "a *married* person to have sexual relations with someone other than his or her husband or wife", and the great majority of respondents (83 per cent) say that extra-marital relations are 'always' or 'almost always wrong'. Moreover, attitudes to extra-marital sex do not appear to have become more permissive over time. In 1983, for instance, an almost identical proportion responded in the same way (Airey, 1984). Not surprisingly, it is the youngest respondents again who hold the most permissive attitudes, and the older respondents who are the least permissive: 78 per cent of 18-24 year olds think extra-marital relations are wrong (always or mostly), compared to 90 per cent of those aged 65 years and over. Although separated and divorced persons are the least censorious on this issue, even so a clear majority of them (seven out of 10) also regard such behaviour as wrong. Respondents who are married, living as married or widowed are all equally strict on this issue - nearly nine out of 10 of them disapprove.

Thus, there is an interesting contrast between attitudes to pre-marital and extra-marital sex. The former is increasingly accepted, the latter not. Moreover, our data suggest that the principle of fidelity within 'marriage' applies just as strongly to cohabiting relationships as it does to legal marriages.

*Attitudes to divorce*

The *British Social Attitudes* survey regularly asks whether divorce should be "easier to obtain than it is now, more difficult, or should things remain as they are?"  Around a half (48 per cent) of respondents think that the laws should remain as they are, just over one-third (35 per cent) think divorce should be made more difficult, and only one in 10 think it should be made easier.  These figures have remained largely unchanged since 1983 when the question was first asked (see Scott, 1990).  More women (38 per cent) than men (31 per cent) think divorce should be made more difficult.  Interestingly, however, couples with children living at home are no more likely than couples without to want divorce to be made more difficult.  In 1989 we also asked a more direct question on whether the law should differentiate between couples with and without young children, and found that 46 per cent would support easy divorce for couples without children, compared to only 17 per cent who would support easy divorce for couples with young children (Scott, 1990, p. 66).

*Divorce and child support*

Issues surrounding the financial support of children when parents live apart have been high on the political agenda over the last year or so.  "No father should be able to escape from his responsibilities", said Mrs Thatcher in 1990 (Thatcher, 1990), a view that was manifested in the Child Support Act of 1991 which includes the establishment of a Child Support Agency to trace defaulting parents and enforce payment.

Our latest survey included a set of questions relating to child support and its implications.  Respondents were asked to imagine a married couple with a child at primary school who decide to divorce, the child remaining with the mother.  Then we asked whether the father should be made to make maintenance payments to support the child, and whether or not  the amount should depend on his income, or on the mother's income.  Not surprisingly, there is almost unanimous agreement that a father *should* be made to support his child: 90 per cent of men and 95 per cent of women are in favour.  In addition, nine out of 10 men and women believe that the level of payment should depend on the father's income.  But there is less unanimity about whether the level of support should depend on the *mother's* income.  Overall, 67 per cent (73 per cent of men and 63 per cent of women) think that it should.  Separated and divorced *men* are more likely to agree that the amount of maintenance should depend on the mother's income, whilst separated and divorced *women* are more likely to disagree.  More highly educated respondents, and the better-off financially are also more likely to believe that financial circumstances alter cases.

**% agreeing that amount of maintenance should depend on the mother's income**

|  | All | Men | Women |
|---|---|---|---|
| **All** | 67 | 73 | 63 |
| **Marital status** | | | |
| Married/living as | 69 | 72 | 67 |
| Separated/divorced | 65 | 79 | 55 |
| Widowed | 52 | 60 | 49 |
| Not married | 70 | 76 | 63 |
| **Highest educational qualification:** | | | |
| Degree/Professional | 75 | 78 | 71 |
| A' level | 80 | 81 | 79 |
| O' level/CSE | 66 | 67 | 66 |
| Other/None | 60 | 69 | 55 |

Since a substantial proportion of divorced people remarry, we also asked whether remarriage should affect the payment of child maintenance. The question was as follows: "Suppose the mother remarries. Should the father go on paying maintenance for the child, should he stop, or should it depend on the new husband's income?" Only 16 per cent said that the father should stop paying child maintenance altogether, while a further 38 per cent believe it should depend on the income of the new step-father. As the table below shows, women are more likely than men to say that maintenance should continue.

| On mother's remarriage, child maintenance from the father should: | All | Men | Women |
|---|---|---|---|
| | % | % | % |
| Continue | 42 | 32 | 51 |
| Stop | 16 | 20 | 13 |
| Depend on the new husband's income | 38 | 44 | 33 |

With the rise in cohabitation, more children are of course being born to, and reared by, cohabiting couples. Do people discriminate between married and cohabiting parents when it comes to providing child support following separation? The answers show that there is an almost universal view that fathers, regardless of their legal tie, should maintain support for their children: 91 per cent of respondents said they would have given the same responses about a cohabiting father as about one who was legally married.

In sum, people do not want divorce to be made easier, but equally they do not want it to be made more difficult. There is general agreement that fathers should continue to support their children following separation, regardless of whether couples were legally married. However, attitudes to the continuation of maintenance payments on remarriage of the mother suggest that people are less positive about support from the father when the mother forms a new partnership. This implies, perhaps, that the role of biological father is not seen by everyone as entailing a life-time commitment to the financial maintenance of children. Rather, step-fathers are also expected to contribute to the maintenance of their step-children. Yet under existing legislation, it is the biological parents only who are liable for the maintenance of their dependent children until they are 19 years old or leave full-time education (whichever comes first), regardless of changes in family circumstances.

**Conclusion**

At the end of 1992, when the Single European Market comes into being, more impetus will be given to the progress towards equality between the sexes. The EC already has a programme for Equal Opportunities for Women and Men, three aims of which are "to increase the participation of women in the labour market", "to improve the quality of women's employment by maximising their potential" and "to reduce barriers to women's access to, and participation in, employment, also through measures designed to reconcile the family and occupational responsibilities of both women and men" (Commission of the European Communities, 1991). Such programmes may in time help to reduce the division of labour and specialisation between the sexes that we have observed.

On the other hand, changes in legislation, commitments to equal opportunity, exhortations, and increased female participation in the labour market all give the impression that considerable progress has been made in the pursuit of independence and equality for women. Undoubtedly, of course, the trend *is* towards greater equality and independence between men and women, and away from relationships of asymmetry and dependence. But our data suggest that a gap between attitudes and reality persists. Behaviour still seems to be lagging behind attitudes and ideals. More worryingly, the overall impression from our analyses is that, particularly since the late 1980s, there has been a flattening of the trend towards equality between the sexes both in the workplace and in the home. This may be a function of changing economic circumstances, or it may reflect the tenacity of longstanding habits and attitudes. Still, the greater participation of women in the labour force is likely to continue to chip away at the bastions of an unequal society. Perhaps it is just that the growth in more egalitarian attitudes and behaviour which characterised the early 1980s has been cast into a temporary recession, coinciding as it would with the economic recession. It is very unlikely that the division of labour and specialisation between the sexes that persists will disappear quickly. But it is equally unlikely that the long- term trend towards equality will actually be reversed.

## References

Airey, C. (1984), 'Social and Moral Values', in Jowell, R. and Airey, C. (eds.) *British Social Attitudes: the 1984 Report*, Aldershot: Gower.
Bone, M. (1985), *Family Planning in Scotland in 1982*, London: HMSO.
Commission of the European Communities (1991), 'Equal Opportunities for Women and Men: the Third Medium-Term Community Action Programme - 1991-1995'; *Women of Europe*, Supplement, no 34, Brussels: CEC.
Dunnell, K. (1979), *Family Formation, 1976*, London: HMSO.
Employment Department (1992a), 'Results of the 1991 Labour Force Survey', *Employment Gazette*, April, 1992, London: HMSO.
Employment Department (1992b), 'Self-employment: into the 1990s', *Employment Gazette*, June, 1992, London: HMSO.
Haskey, J. (1988), 'Current Prospects for the Proportions of Marriages Ending in Divorce', *Population Trends*, 55.
Haskey, J. (1990), 'The Children of Families Broken by Divorce', *Population Trends*, 61.
Kempeneers, M. and Lelievre, E. (1992), 'Employment and Family in the European Community', *Eurobarometer*, No. 34.
Kiernan, K.E. (1992), 'The Respective Roles of Men and Women in Tomorrow's Europe', in *Human Resources in Europe at the Dawn of the 21st Century*, Luxembourg: Eurostat.
Office of Population Censuses and Surveys (OPCS) (1982), *Labour Force Survey 1981*, London: HMSO.
Office of Population Censuses and Surveys (OPCS) (1991), *General Household Survey 1989*, London: HMSO.
Office of Population Censuses and Surveys (OPCS) (1992), *Labour Force Survey 1990 and 1991*, London: HMSO.
Ruggie, M. (1988), 'Gender, Work and Social Progress', in Jenson, J., Hagen, E. and Reddy, C. (eds.), *Feminization of the Labour Force: Paradoxes and Promises*, Polity Press: Cambridge.
Scott, J. (1990), 'Women and the Family', in Jowell, R., Witherspoon, S. and Brook, L., with Taylor, B. (eds.), *British Social Attitudes: the 7th Report*, Aldershot: Gower.
Thatcher, M. (1990), 'Inaugural lecture of the George Thomas Society', London: National Children's Home.
Thompson, L. and Walker, A.J. (1989), 'Gender in Families: Women and Men in Marriage, Work and Parenthood', *Journal of Marriage and the Family*, 51.
Witherspoon, S. (1985), 'Sex Roles and Gender Issues', in Jowell, R. and Witherspoon, S. (eds.), *British Social Attitudes: the 1985 Report*, Aldershot: Gower.
Witherspoon, S. (1988), 'Interim Report: A Woman's Work', in Jowell, R., Witherspoon, S. and Brook, L. (eds.), *British Social Attitudes: the 5th Report*, Aldershot: Gower.
Witherspoon, S. and Prior, G. (1991), 'Working Mothers: Free to Choose?', in Jowell, R., Brook, L. and Taylor, B., with Prior, G. (eds.), *British Social Attitudes: the 8th Report*, Aldershot: Dartmouth.

**Acknowlegdement**

We are grateful to the Department of Social Security for its financial support (beginning in 1991) for the survey series; this enabled us to ask a series of questions, reported here, on attitudes towards child maintenance.

# 6 Changes in values

*Anthony Heath and Dorren McMahon* *

Since they started in 1983, the annual series of *British Social Attitudes* surveys have demonstrated that the social and political attitudes of the British public have changed in a number of respects. The evidence for these changes has been reported in separate chapters of the annual books. The aim of this chapter is to bring these separate analyses together in a more comparative way. It is not an exhaustive survey - which would fill a book. (Indeed the recently published *British Social Attitudes Cumulative Sourcebook* largely does that job.) Rather this chapter is intended to explore and classify some of the more general trends that seem to lie behind changes that have been reported over the years.

Broadly speaking, it may be useful to distinguish on the one hand between attitude changes that are responses to 'big events' in the external world (as perceived by our respondents) and on the other hand those changes that are the product of people's immediate experiences. By 'big events' since 1983 we mean, for example, the gradual thawing of the cold war under Mr. Gorbachev, followed by the collapse of the communist system, or the rolling back in Britain of the frontiers of socialism and the extensive privatisation of industry under Mrs. Thatcher's Conservative administrations.

Some of these big events are ones that many people experience only indirectly *via* the mass media. Other changes are not perhaps newsworthy

---

* Anthony Heath is Official Fellow at Nuffield College, Oxford; Dorren McMahon is a Research Officer at Nuffield College.

in the same way but have more direct effects on people's lives: for example more women have gone out to work, living standards have gone up generally, young people have stayed on at school longer, and unemployment - or the threat of it - has risen sharply.

It would be surprising if both sorts of changes were not associated in some ways with attitude changes. But in what ways?

We start by reviewing the evidence of attitude change within a number of categories - the end of the cold war, the rolling back of socialism in Britain, the environment and disasters such as the nuclear accident at Chernobyl, the spread of AIDS and its implications, and the domestic division of labour. Then we shall look for any common processes that seem to underlie these changes.

### The fall of communism and the rise of the EC

The end of the cold war may not have made the world a more peaceful place, but it has changed the nature of the threats we face. The spectre of confrontation between the superpowers has receded and there has been an acknowledged decline in the need for spending on armaments. Certainly, there has at various times been talk of a 'peace dividend', enabling government spending to be redirected from defence to other uses. The first reference to it came as early as 1989, and the debate quickly gathered momentum, although it was interrupted during the Gulf War in the autumn and winter of 1990/1991.[1] It is of interest to see what impact these events abroad have had on the attitudes of the British public towards national defence.

The beginning of the end of the cold war probably dates from Mr Gorbachev's accession to power in the USSR in 1985. In 1989 came the year of revolutions in east-central Europe as communist regimes were toppled in Poland, Hungary, East Germany, Czechoslovakia, Bulgaria and Romania; the Berlin Wall came down, and later Germany was reunified. (The break-up of the former USSR came after the last *British Social Attitudes* fieldwork round). To the extent that these events have changed attitudes in Britain, we might expect to find early changes after 1985 and greater change after 1989.

We have regularly asked respondents a series of questions about defence and international affairs which help to inform this exploration (see for instance, Whiteley, 1985).

Among the questions asked since 1984 is one which addresses attitudes to the cold war, in particular whether:

> *Russia is a greater threat to world peace than America,*
> *Russia and America are equally great threats to world peace,*
> *or neither is a threat to world peace.*

In most years in which we have asked this question, a majority has said that Russia and America are equally great threats. But, as the first row of the table below shows, the proportion saying that *neither* is a threat to world peace has risen sharply from five per cent in 1984 before Mr Gorbachev came to power to 28 per cent in 1990, suggesting that the British people have, if nothing else, certainly noticed the ending of the cold war.

| % agreeing that ... | 1983 | 1984 | 1985 | 1986 | 1987 | 1989 | 1990 |
|---|---|---|---|---|---|---|---|
| Neither America nor Russia is a threat to world peace | n/a | 5 | 6 | 9 | 8 | 20 | 28 |
| Having our own nuclear missiles makes Britain a safer place to live in | 61 | 56 | 54 | 52 | 58 | 55 | 54 |
| Britain should keep its nuclear weapons until we persuade others to reduce theirs | 78 | 73 | 68 | 69 | 72 | 72 | 69 |
| Britain should continue to be a member of NATO | 79 | 79 | 74 | 76 | 79 | 79 | 81 |
| Britain should continue to be a member of the EC | 53 | 48 | 56 | 61 | 63 | 68 | 76 |

n/a = not asked

However, as the next three rows in the table above show, there is little evidence that these changed perceptions have led to any major shift in attitudes towards Britain's own defence arrangements. For example, we have also regularly asked respondents about their attitudes towards Britain's nuclear weapons:

> *Which, if either, of these two statements comes closest to your opinion on British nuclear weapons?*
>
> *Britain should **rid** itself of nuclear weapons, while persuading others to do the same.*
>
> *Britain should **keep** its nuclear weapons until we persuade others to reduce theirs.*

As we can see, from the second and third rows of the table above, public attitudes on this subject are generally rather hawkish, a majority consistently preferring to retain Britain's nuclear weapons. This majority was at its largest in 1983; it declined somewhat in 1984, and again in 1985. Since then, however, there has been no further decline. In many ways it is the high figure for 1983 which is in need of explanation: perhaps it was a reflection of the Falklands War, which had just concluded and which may have made people more aware of Britain's need for defence. Perhaps it was just because it was the election year in which Mr. Foot, then leader of the Labour Party, was steadfastly supporting a unilateralist position for his party. At any rate, the data give no support to the view that events in the communist bloc in the years after 1985 have encouraged the British public to change its attitudes towards Britain's 'independent' nuclear defences. On the other hand, there has been little serious political debate on this subject since around 1984, when the Labour Party began to ditch 'unilateralism' as a plank in its defence policy. Until then some strong Labour Party identifiers may have been sympathetic to the cause of unilateralism purely or mainly on the grounds that their party supported it (see Heath, Jowell and Curtice, 1985; Heath *et al*, 1991).

Attitudes towards Britain's defence arrangements have also been tapped by our question on NATO. Since the *raison d'être* of NATO was the existence of the threat posed by the then USSR and its allies in the Warsaw Pact, this is the topic on which attitude change was perhaps most likely. However, what we find in the fourth row of the table above is a remarkably stable series, with very little year-to-year fluctuation. Indeed, in four of the seven surveys precisely the same proportion of respondents (79 per cent) felt that Britain should continue to be a member of NATO.

From this set of questions, then, there is little sign that events abroad have had any major impact on attitudes at home, except for perceptions of the superpowers. People seem to be aware enough of the changes in eastern Europe but they have not been inclined to favour any change in direction for British defence policy as a result.[2]

A rather sharp contrast to the stable support for NATO is provided by answers on the European Community, shown in the fifth row of the table above.

Here, despite the many public disagreements over the nature and extent of Britain's political and economic integration into the EC, we see a more or less steady increase in support for continued British membership. At the beginning of our series in 1983 and 1984, opinion was rather evenly split between staying in and moving out. By 1990 there was overwhelming support for staying in. Indeed, the net increase between 1983 and 1990 of 23 points is one of the largest we shall see in this chapter.

We must be careful not to over-interpret this result. As on the nuclear defence issue, it almost certainly reflects the fact that political debates in Britain have themselves changed. From the time of Mr. Kinnock's accession to the leadership of the Labour Party, the arguments switched from the question of continued membership of the EC, which all the main political parties then accepted, to ones about the extent of integration into the Community. In time the Labour and Liberal Democrat Parties were to become greater champions of integration than the Conservatives. In any event, the British may well have been reluctant Europeans initially, but they now appear to be content with a European future.

So if we look at public attitudes over time in support for unilateralism, membership of NATO and of the EC, it seems that on 'external' issues like these the public takes its cues from the political parties. Thus none of the political parties has ever advocated withdrawal from NATO, and public attitudes have been stable. Conversely, in the case of unilateralism and the European Community, the Labour Party has changed its stance on both issues, and trends in public attitudes mirror these movements.

## The retreat of socialism at home

The failure of socialism in the former communist countries, even if it does not seem to have led to any change in attitudes towards Britain's defence policy, may perhaps have affected the popularity of socialist solutions to economic problems at home. After all, all recent rhetoric from the former communist bloc has been to vindicate capitalism. However, any effect of this kind in Britain would be difficult to disentangle from the institutional changes here that have been going on quite independently.

There are several key elements to the institutional changes introduced by Mrs Thatcher's three Conservative administrations: the privatisation of industry; the attempts to free the market from government controls; and the reduction of government expenditure. A fourth element of Mrs Thatcher's reforms was her trade union legislation, but we do not have questions which are entirely suitable for tackling this theme. These have been among the most dramatic attempts at economic restructuring ever undertaken by a peacetime government in the West, and have already been the focus of a great deal of academic investigation.[3]

On the role of government intervention in the *market*, questions have regularly been asked on the control of wages and of prices by law. Control of wages and prices had of course been key elements of the Social Contract of Mr Callaghan's Labour government that was defeated in 1979.

As the first two rows of the table below show, on both these possible means of impeding free market forces we see fairly clear trends: support for wage and price controls declined sharply between 1983 and 1989, (though from different starting points) and has since stabilised or, if anything, begun to return. The net changes over the period as a whole have been 15 points (on wage controls) and 10 points (on price controls).

|                                                                      | 1983 | 1984 | 1985 | 1986 | 1987 | 1989 | 1990 | 1991 |
|----------------------------------------------------------------------|------|------|------|------|------|------|------|------|
| **% favouring ...**                                                  |      |      |      |      |      |      |      |      |
| Control of wages by law                                              | 48   | 42   | 39   | 40   | 34   | 28   | 30   | 33   |
| Control of prices by law                                             | 70   | 66   | 64   | 61   | 58   | 56   | 56   | 60   |
| Less state ownership of industry                                     | 49   | 36   | 31   | 30   | 30   | 24   | 24   | n/a  |
| **% saying ...**                                                     |      |      |      |      |      |      |      |      |
| Government's role in the electricity industry should be to own it    | n/a  | n/a  | 25   | 28   | 26   | 32   | 28   | n/a  |
| Government should increase taxes and spend more on health, education and social benefits | 32 | 39 | 45 | 46 | 50 | 56 | 54 | 65 |
| It should definitely be the government's responsibility to provide health care for the sick | n/a | n/a | 85 | 84 | n/a | n/a | 84 | n/a |

Here, then, there has been increased acceptance of the free market, yet support for free market principles is still less than whole-hearted. For example, a majority of people continue to support price control by law. The taste for interventionism may have abated somewhat, but it has not entirely disappeared.

A second key element of the period has been *privatisation*. And here we see what looks like a shift in the opposite direction, with sharply declining public support for further privatisation. Thus the proportion saying there should be less state ownership of industry halved from 49 per cent in 1983 to 24 per cent in 1990.

However, responses to this particular question on state ownership raise a major problem of interpretation. Unlike most of our other questions it asks respondents whether they would like to see changes from *current* arrangements, and of course current arrangements changed from year to year. Between 1983 and 1991 British Telecom, British Gas, the electricity industry and several others had moved from public into private ownership. So in 1991, the question about state ownership would probably have been taken to refer largely to British Coal and British Rail, the only major industries remaining in the public sector.[*]

It is therefore a tenable hypothesis that attitudes have not actually changed at all. The person who wanted 'less state ownership' in 1983 may have wanted exactly the same number of industries to be in state

---

[*]   The government's plans for further privatisation, at least according to the Conservative Party's 1992 manifesto, are: to privatise British Coal, local authority bus companies and local authority airports; to end the British Rail monopoly; under the terms of the Ports Act 1991 to privatise the trust ports; and to privatise Northern Ireland electricity.

ownership as the person who says in 1990 that 'enough is enough'. We can look for clues in the answers to another question we introduced in 1985 on the government's role in the electricity industry: we ask whether the government's role should be to:

*Own it*

*Control prices and profits but not own it*

*Neither own it nor control its prices and profits*

Since this question is not time-specific, answers give us a better guide to whether attitudes have actually changed over time. And the answers do *not* show the same pattern of change as the question on state ownership. As the fourth row in the table above shows, there is much less variation over time in attitudes. Opposition to privatisation of the electricity industry peaked in 1989 (at the time when the measures were being debated in Parliament and had perhaps rather more media coverage than usual), but it fell back again almost immediately. The safest interpretation is that, in the period covered by our surveys, attitudes towards state ownership of industry have moved neither to left nor right.[4]

Similar problems to those on state ownership arise with the answers on taxation and government, shown in the penultimate row of the table above. We asked respondents:

*Suppose the government had to choose between the three options on this card. Which do you think it should choose?*

> *Reduce taxes and spend **less** on health, education and social benefits*
>
> *Keep taxes and spending on these services at the same level as now*
>
> *Increase taxes and spend **more** on health, education and social benefits?*

In answer to this question we find that the proportion saying the government should increase taxes and spending has increased by a massive 33 points from 32 per cent in 1983 to 65 per cent in 1991. But we cannot tell whether this represents a shift in attitudes or whether it is just a consequence of people's perceptions of a shift in the actual levels of taxes and spending. As with the state ownership question, respondents were effectively being asked whether they want some change from *present* levels of taxes and spending, and their perceptions of the level in 1983 were almost certainly different from their perceptions of the level in 1991.[5] The doubling of support for more taxes and spending may be more a sign of disapproval of changes that have happened rather than a change in public values over the period. Certainly, if we take responses to the question which asks people whether it should be the government's responsibility to provide health care for the sick, we see from the final row of the table above that the high proportion who say it should *definitely* be the government's responsibility has been remarkably steady over time.  It fails to show the increase we might have expected if people had become more left-wing in their attitudes towards the welfare state. On the other hand, there is a 'ceiling effect' in operation here: the public is nearly unanimous on health care already.

Still, neither on state ownership nor on government spending can we confidently say that attitudes have shifted in a left-wing direction.  Nor is there any evidence that they have moved to the right, as they clearly seem to have done on the issues of wage and price controls.  Our interpretation is that while the public has become more accepting than it used to be of the free market in determining wages and prices, it is no more accepting of free market arrangements in health care. As Taylor-Gooby (1991) put it:

> The 1980s have been a decade of rapid and profound welfare reform.  The forty-year tradition of the state as the dominant agency in welfare provision has been challenged by cuts ... (p. 41).

But:

> there is still no evidence that a rolling back of the welfare state would be in accord with popular opinion (p. 25).

Again, it is possible that people have accepted the cues provided for them by the political parties.  The Labour Party has abandoned any semblance of its Social Contract, and all the main parties now accept free market principles of competition in industry.   Conversely, not even the Conservative Party, whatever its critics may suspect, is in favour of the privatisation of the National Health Service.   True, it has introduced reforms to establish an internal market in which GPs purchase services from hospitals, but that is not remotely the same thing as an external market in which patients purchase services from GPs.

On these issues, however, the direction of influence between public and parties may be the other way around.  It may well be the parties here which are taking their cue from the public, not - as in the case of foreign affairs - the public taking their cue from the parties.   Otherwise the government *may* have conceived of privatising the NHS or parts of it.

## The environment

While free market reforms, privatisation of industry and the reduction of taxation and government expenditure have been brought on to the political agenda by recent Conservative administrations, issues to do with the environment have had a more complex history.  On the one hand there have been disasters like the release of radioactivity from the nuclear power station at Chernobyl in the Ukraine in 1986, and the oil spill from the *Exxon Valdez* along the shores of Alaska in 1989;  on the other there have been the pressure group activities of Friends of the Earth, Greenpeace and similar organisations to publicise global environmental problems.    There have also been people's direct experiences of environmental problems in their own 'back yards', for example as the result of motorway building or new housing developments.

   The immediate impact of the Chernobyl disaster on public attitudes can be seen clearly from our question on the risks of nuclear power.  We regularly ask respondents:

> *As far as nuclear power stations are concerned, which of these statements comes closest to your own feelings?*
>
>> *They create very serious risks for the future*
>> *They create quite serious risks for the future*
>> *They create only slight risks for the future*
>> *They create hardly any risks for the future*

As the table below shows, the proportion who thought that nuclear power stations created 'very serious risks' soared from 30 per cent in 1985 to 49 per cent in 1986 after the Chernobyl accident.[6]  Attitudes slipped back thereafter, although not quite to their immediate pre-Chernobyl level.  As with political events in the (former) Soviet Union, the public seems to be aware of what is happening but attitudes do not appear to be greatly influenced by events over there, at least not enduringly.

| % saying that ... | 1983 | 1984 | 1985 | 1986 | 1987 | 1989 | 1990 | 1991 |
|---|---|---|---|---|---|---|---|---|
| Nuclear power stations create very serious risks for the future | 35 | 37 | 30 | 49 | 37 | 40 | 43 | 40 |
| Lead from petrol has a very serious effect on our environment | 48 | 45 | 39 | 42 | 34 | 45 | 38 | 39 |
| Industrial waste in the rivers and sea has a very serious effect | 62 | 67 | 56 | 65 | 60 | 75 | 75 | 70 |
| Waste from nuclear electricity stations has a very serious effect | 63 | 69 | 58 | 72 | 60 | 67 | 64 | 58 |
| Noise and dirt from traffic has a very serious effect | 23 | 20 | 21 | 25 | 25 | 31 | 28 | 29 |
| Acid rain has a very serious effect | n/a | n/a | n/a | 54 | 50 | 58 | 53 | 46 |
| Industry should be prevented from causing damage to the countryside, even if this sometimes leads to higher prices | n/a | 77 | 78 | 82 | 83 | 88 | 89 | 88 |
| If farmers have to choose between producing more food and looking after the countryside, they should produce more food | n/a | n/a | 53 | 45 | 36 | 36 | n/a | 37 |

In addition to this specific question on the risks of nuclear power, we have regularly asked a battery of questions on the environment (see Chapter 1), which includes risks to the environment from lead in petrol, industrial waste, nuclear waste, noise and dirt from traffic, and acid rain. Respondents are asked how serious they think the risks (or the effects) are.

As can be seen from the table above (rows two to six) perceptions of these various sources of pollution are in general rather volatile, showing no uniform trends over time. Thus we see a net fall during the period of nine points in the percentage who felt that lead from petrol has a very serious effect on the environment, a net fall of eight points on acid rain, a net fall of five points on waste from nuclear power, but increases of eight points on industrial waste in the rivers and sea, and six points on noise and dirt from traffic.

This does not suggest that there has been a major change in environmental awareness, at least not in the period covered by our surveys. There does seem to have been a general increase in environmental concern in 1986, at the time of the Chernobyl accident, and another one in 1989 (the year in which the British Green Party did particularly well in the European Parliament elections). But these increases in concern seem to have been short-lived, leaving no lasting impact on public attitudes. Moreover, the year-to-year volatility of the answers suggests that public perceptions of these issues may be rather superficial.

However, when we move from rather remote issues such as acid rain and nuclear waste to ones that are closer to home, a clearer pattern becomes evident. We have asked a number of questions on the British countryside, shown in the last two rows of the table above, in which respondents are asked in effect to choose between protecting the countryside as against economic gains.

On these questions we find a much more stable pattern of response over time, rather than the volatility of the more remote issues. The year-to-year fluctuations are small, and they cumulate into a consistent trend: an unspectacular but steady shift of attitudes in favour of protecting the countryside against incursions of one sort or another.

### AIDS and the moral climate

As a number of previous reports in this series have shown, attitudes towards homosexuals became more censorious in the 1980s as public concern about AIDS mounted. As Brook has suggested "Our data cannot, of course, prove the link but they certainly imply a clear connection. Either that, or we are witnessing a selective return to more puritanical values, coincidentally on just those issues that are connected strongly in the public mind with AIDS" (Brook, 1988, p. 72).

We do not as yet have a long enough series of questions on AIDS to explore attitude change, but a question on homosexuality has been asked regularly since the inception of the *British Social Attitudes* series. It forms part of the following set of questions on sexual relations:

> *If a man and a woman have sexual relations before marriage, what would your general opinion be?*

> *What about a married person having sexual relations with someone other than his or her partner?*

> *What about sexual relations between two adults of the same sex?*

As the table below shows, increased censoriousness towards homosexuality (and incidentally towards adultery and premarital sex) peaked in 1987, having risen from 50 per cent in 1983 to 64 per cent during the four year period when the initial impact of the arrival of AIDS was at its greatest. Since then attitudes have partially swung back, although not to their 1983 level.

|                                                                                                      | 1983 | 1984 | 1985 | 1986 | 1987 | 1989 | 1990 |
|------------------------------------------------------------------------------------------------------|------|------|------|------|------|------|------|
| **% agreeing that ...**                                                                              |      |      |      |      |      |      |      |
| Sexual relations before marriage are always wrong                                                    | 17   | 15   | 14   | n/a  | 13   | 12   | 13   |
| A married person having sexual relations with someone other than his or her partner is always wrong  | 59   | 59   | 57   | n/a  | 63   | 55   | 56   |
| Sexual relations between two adults of the same sex are always wrong                                 | 50   | 54   | 59   | n/a  | 64   | 56   | 58   |
| The law should allow an abortion if the couple agree they do not wish to have the child              | 46   | n/a  | 55   | 56   | 59   | 59   | 62   |
| The law should allow an abortion if the woman decides on her own she does not wish to have the child | 38   | n/a  | 49   | 44   | 54   | 49   | 56   |

In contrast, not only was the 1987 increase in censoriousness towards heterosexual sex outside marriage smaller in magnitude than that towards homosexuality, but the subsequent fall was also steeper. The net change, then, in sexual attitudes over the period was in a more permissive direction. As Wellings and Wadsworth reported in 1990:

> In *The 5th Report*, Harding (1988) predicted that the trend towards more liberal attitudes to sexual morality over the past few decades was unlikely to suffer more than a temporary setback. This most recent round of data seems to prove him right so far (Wellings and Wadsworth, 1990, p. 123).

Even more striking trends in a liberal direction are apparent in attitudes towards abortion. As with AIDS there has been considerable publicity, particularly over The Human Fertilisation and Embryology Bill 1990 which specified time limits for the stage of a pregnancy at which abortions could legally be performed.

The *British Social Attitudes* surveys have regularly asked questions about seven different circumstances in which abortion might or might not be allowed, ranging from circumstances such as "the woman became pregnant as a result of rape", and "the woman's health is seriously endangered by the pregnancy", to reasons of preference such as "the couple agree they do not wish to have the child", and "the woman decides on her own she does not wish to have the child". Almost identical trends over time are revealed on all the items, and so we illustrate the pattern only with the last two items in the table above.

Here we see net increases of 16 and 18 points in the proportions saying that abortion *should* be allowed by law. In this respect at least society certainly seems to have become more permissive.[7]

## Women's roles

Finally we come to a topic which has had perhaps the fewest news headlines but is of course intimately connected with people's daily lives, namely the domestic division of labour (see also Chapter 5). We regularly ask respondents how they think "family jobs should generally be shared between men and women". We ask, for example, who they think "should do the household shopping: mainly the man, mainly the woman or should the task be shared equally?" And then we ask similar questions about a range of other household tasks. Again, since the trends are consistent, we illustrate the pattern with a selection of items. We focus on doing the household shopping, preparing the evening meal, and doing the washing and ironing, as shown in the first three rows of the table below. Very small proportions believe these three tasks should be mainly the *man's* responsibility (and these proportions have not changed substantially); we show only the proportions who say that the tasks should be shared equally between the man and the woman.

|  | 1984 | 1987 | 1991 |
|---|---|---|---|
| **% agreeing that...** | | | |
| Household shopping *should* be shared equally | 63 | 68 | 76 |
| Washing and ironing *should* be shared equally | 22 | 30 | 40 |
| Making the evening meal *should* be shared equally | 39 | 45 | 58 |
| Household shopping *is* shared equally | 39 | 43 | 47 |
| Washing and ironing *is* shared equally | 9 | 9 | 12 |
| Making the evening meal *is* shared equally | 16 | 17 | 20 |

There has been a consistent pattern of increase in the proportion who believe the tasks should be shared equally: 13 points up in the case of the household shopping; 18 points up for doing the washing and ironing; 19 points up for making the evening meal.

But this tells us only what people feel the division of labour in the home *should* be. We must never assume that a shift in attitudes will automatically be reflected in a shift in behaviour. However, when we look at respondents' reports of what actually happens in the home, we do find modest changes in the same direction. For example, while only 39 per cent of respondents said in 1984 that the household shopping actually *is* shared equally, compared with the 63 per cent who said it *should be* shared equally, now the figures are 47 per cent and 76 per cent respectively. The gap has widened somewhat, but the direction of movement is consistent.

## The sources of attitude change

So we have seen a number of different patterns. We have seen temporary shifts in attitudes towards homosexuality and nuclear power; we have seen rather stable attitudes towards Britain's defence arrangements, and rather volatile attitudes towards the environment; we have seen consistent and major changes in attitudes towards Europe, towards aspects of the free market, and towards the current levels of government spending and state ownership; and we have seen somewhat more modest changes towards the domestic division of labour and towards women's 'right to choose'. But these changes have not been all in the same 'political' direction. Over the period covered by our surveys people seem generally to have moved to the right on the free market but to have stayed still or perhaps even moved to the left on government spending and state ownership; they have become more permissive on abortion, but not on homosexuality.

How are we to make sense of these complex patterns? The temporary shifts following events such as the Chernobyl accident and the intense publicly-funded AIDS campaign of 1987 are perhaps the easiest to understand. In these two cases there were highly publicised events that brought home to people, for a short while at least, the dangers of nuclear power or of some sexual practices. On the other hand, not all highly publicised events lead to attitude change, even temporary change. Thus we saw that the events in eastern Europe did not have even a temporary effect on attitudes towards Britain's defence arrangements. It may of course be that people did not make the connection between these events in eastern Europe and Britain's defence. The link between the two, if there is a link, is made by the notion of the 'peace dividend', and this did not have anything like the same amount of publicity as the revolutions of 1989. Or it may be that the existence of countervailing events, such as the Falklands or Gulf Wars, cancelled the effects out.

There is, however, a link between the revolutions of 1989, Chernobyl, and AIDS in that they are all 'remote' events of which most people do not have (or have not yet had in this country) any direct, easily interpreted experience. They are all events whose implications are not self-evident and whose significance has to be interpreted through scientific, political or social theory. Thus the concept of a 'peace dividend' can be regarded as a kind of political theory analogous to the scientific theories of the transmission of AIDS. Social and political attitudes will thus be mediated by people's awareness of the relevant theories, their ability to comprehend them, and their belief in them; and this in turn will depend on the social authority of the theorists or commentators and the publicity given to their views. We have elsewhere termed this a 'top-down' theory of attitude change (Heath *et al*, 1990): attitude change (or stability) among the public on issues like these derives mainly from the interpretations of the authorities whom they respect.

At the other extreme from the 'big events' of Chernobyl and eastern Europe we have the humdrum matters of daily life in the family. Inglehart's phrase of the 'silent revolution' applies particularly well to this sphere of attitude change (Inglehart, 1977). The increased participation of married women in the labour force has not been newsworthy, but virtually everyone will have experience of it either through their own immediate families or those of their friends and relatives. This 'revolution' has a direct influence on issues such as the sharing of household tasks. We should note that the attitude change we have described in respect of the domestic division of labour is not restricted to working women (see also Chapter 5). Nor is it simply a matter of changed attitudes deriving from changed behaviour: on the contrary the behavioural changes have been slower to come about than the attitudinal ones. The social processes involved are not ones that we fully understand, but it is likely that they have more of a 'bottom-up' than a 'top-down' character.

In addition to the directness of people's experience of change, a second important factor is the strength of their previous attitudes towards the issues in question. Thus some attitudes may be more superficial than others, and we suggested that this may well be the case with attitudes towards the environment (see also Chapter 1). As we saw, attitudes towards environmental issues were more volatile from year-to-year (even excluding Chernobyl) than on any of the others we have examined. And it is noticeable that the nuclear power 'blip' in our trends in 1986 as a result of the Chernobyl accident was a much sharper blip than, for example, the blip in attitudes towards homosexuality as a result of the initial publicity connecting AIDS with homosexuality.

So we suggest that the less entrenched the attitudes the more subject they will be to change, especially from highly publicised events. Green issues in particular are relatively new issues which do not yet have strong institutional support - for instance, relatively few people belong to green organisations or know of any authority figures whom they recognise and respect on the subject. In other words, most people have not yet been socialised into distinctively green (or ungreen) attitudes through their families or through the organisations they belong to, or through their politics.

In direct contrast are attitudes towards the NHS and the welfare state, which seem to be deeply entrenched.[8] They are the old issues, on which attitudes have long been formed and which are supported by a network of institutional, political and personal loyalties.

Finally, we should relate the cautionary note we referred to earlier about the measurement of change. Our measurement methods assume (and have to assume) that the objects of measurement will remain relatively stable. Thus, when we measure attitudes to say, abortion, we have to assume that the meaning of abortion will not change substantially over the period of our measurement. Similarly, when we decide to measure attitudes to the Soviet Union, or to privatisation, we make the assumption that the goalposts will not move. But they do move, and in the process they damage our time-series. This has been more true of some of our measures than of others. It always bedevils interpretation but it always needs to be noted.


## Notes

1.  A possible 'peace dividend' came up as early as May 1989 when the defence White Paper was presented to the House of Commons. Various questions on the 'peace dividend' were later put to government Ministers during 1990. In the Commons debate on defence spending, June 18-19 1990, Labour members criticised the government for failure to 'undertake an assessment of the impact of change on defence-related industries and on HM forces and the possible savings and alternative uses of money allocated to the defence budget'.
2.  There has also been a regular question on attitudes to possible public expenditure cuts. Again, there has been little change in the proportion saying that they supported a policy of reducing government expenditure on defence. The proportion rose from 44 per cent in 1983 to 54 per cent in 1985, and has since remained around that figure, although rising to 64 per cent in 1990 before falling back to 55 per cent in 1991. There are however difficulties in interpreting trends in these answers because they depend (a) on perceptions of the extent of Britain's economic problems and (b) on the popularity or lack of it of the other options presented to respondents.
3.  See for example Vickers and Yarrow (1988) on privatisation. There has also been a lot of work on Mrs Thatcher's crusade to change values - see, for instance, Curtice (1986), Crewe (1988), and Gershuny (1991).
4.  However, according to the *British Election Studies,* there had been an earlier large shift to the right in public attitudes (in the late 1970s). See Sarlvik and Crewe (1983) and Heath *et al* (1991).
5.  Whether the actual levels of taxation and government spending, in real terms, have changed can be disputed. However, the crucial point is whether people *perceived* any changes. Heath *et al* (1991) show from the *British Election Studies* that, between 1983 and 1987, people did perceive major reductions in taxation and also in the standards of health and education. Questions on perceptions of government *spending* on health and education were not asked.
6.  See Young (1987) for an analysis of the 'Chernobyl effect'. The disaster occurred during the fieldwork period of the 1986 *British Social Attitudes* survey, but to a large extent the increased concern about the risks of nuclear power seemed to predate Chernobyl.
7.  We should note that Harding (1988) has suggested that the issue of abortion tends to be judged not so much on a 'personal-moral dimension', but rather as a matter of women's rights. This may help to explain why the extent of changes in attitudes to this issue is especially striking in relation to other 'moral' issues.
8.  In saying that attitudes towards the NHS are deeply entrenched, we run the risk of redescribing our survey findings rather than explaining them. However, we should note that aggregate stability is compatible with a high level of individual instability. Our hypothesis is that the attitudes towards the NHS will prove to be more stable at the individual level than will, say, attitudes towards the environment.

# References

*British Social Attitudes Cumulative Sourcebook: the first six surveys* (1991), compiled by Social and Community Planning Research, Aldershot: Gower.

Brook, L. (1988), 'The Public's Response to AIDS', in Jowell, R., Witherspoon, S. and Brook, L. (eds.), *British Social Attitudes: the 5th Report*, Aldershot: Gower.

Crewe, I. (1988), 'Has the Electorate Become Thatcherite?' in Skidelsky, R. (ed.), *Thatcherism*, London: Chatto and Windus.

Curtice, J. (1986), 'Political Partisanship', in Jowell, R., Witherspoon, S. and Brook, L. (eds.) *British Social Attitudes: the 1986 Report*, Aldershot: Gower.

Gershuny, J. (1992), 'British Economic Values in Mrs. Thatcher's Laboratory', in Gottlieb, A., Strumel, B. and Yuchtman-Yaar, E. (eds.), *Structural Economic Change in the East and in the West, Greenwich*, CN: JAI Press (forthcoming).

Harding, S. (1988), 'Trends in Permissiveness', in Jowell, R., Witherspoon, S. and Brook, L. (eds.), *British Social Attitudes: the 5th Report*, Aldershot: Gower.

Heath, A. F., Jowell, R. and Curtice. J. (1985), *How Britain Votes*, Oxford: Pergamon.

Heath, A. F., Jowell, R., Curtice, J. and Evans, G. (1990), 'The Rise of the New Political Agenda?' *European Sociological Review 6* , 31-48.

Heath, A. F. *et al* (1991), *Understanding Political Change: The British Voter 1964-1987*, Oxford: Pergamon.

Inglehart, R. (1977), *The Silent Revolution: Changing Values and Political Styles Among Western Publics*, Princeton: Princeton University Press.

Sarlvik, B. and Crewe, I. (1983), *Decade of Dealignment*, Cambridge: Cambridge University Press.

Taylor-Gooby, P. (1991), 'Attachment to the Welfare State', in Jowell, R., Brook, L. and Taylor, B. with Prior, G. (eds.), *British Social Attitudes: the 8th Report*, Aldershot: Dartmouth.

Vickers, J. and Yarrow, G. (1988), *Privatization: An Economic Analysis*, Cambridge, Mass: MIT Press.

Wellings, K. and Wadsworth, J. (1990), 'AIDS and the Moral Climate', in Jowell, R., Witherspoon, S. and Brook, L. with Taylor, B. (eds.), *British Social Attitudes: the 7th Report*, Aldershot: Gower.

Young, K. (1987), 'Nuclear Reactions', in Jowell, R., Witherspoon, S. and Brook, L. (eds.) *British Social Attitudes: the 1987 Report*, Aldershot: Gower.

# 7 What price profits?

*Michael Johnston* [*]

The role of the market economy, and the legitimacy and limits of private self-interest, have been among the most widely discussed social issues of the past decade. In Britain, successive Conservative governments advocated entrepreneurship and private provision over state planning, regulation, and the welfare state. Accompanying this policy revolution were two severe recessions, interspersed by a period of strong economic growth. American policy over the same period pursued similar goals with similar results. In the former USSR and eastern Europe, the long-declining centrally-planned economies, once deprived of their political underpinnings, abruptly collapsed. Almost worldwide nowadays, then, current popular orthodoxy espouses reliance upon private self-interest and the workings of the marketplace as the driving forces of the economy.

How do the British public judge this marketplace? What purposes (if any) do they believe business activity should serve, over and above the pursuit of profit for shareholders? What rules should govern business activity? This chapter is about social conceptions of right and wrong in this marketplace. It reports findings based mainly upon a group of questions in the 1991 *British Social Attitudes* survey, asking respondents to judge the degree of "wrongness" they see in a variety of hypothetical business-related actions, and to say how they think businesses should and would put their profits to use.

[*] Professor and Chair, Department of Political Science, Colgate University, Hamilton, New York.

We also draw upon some of the results of the 1984 and 1987 *British Social Attitudes* surveys. Then we asked people to make similar judgements of conduct in everyday dealings, some of them involving business transactions or encounters with government officials. The results showed that while people generally recognise and condemn actions that break the law, those actions are surrounded by a larger penumbra of activities which, while not in themselves illegal, are still seen as wrong (in varying degrees) by *social* standards. Actions that give a person an unfair reward or advantage, or in which the 'loser' is an ordinary citizen, or in which self-interest is cloaked in secrecy or deception, tend to be judged quite harshly. So too are actions - such as knowingly pocketing the wrong change - which break standards of 'respectability' or personal honour. Some *illegal* actions, by contrast, were judged relatively leniently - often when an ordinary individual was seen to benefit at the expense of a distant, impersonal organisation (Johnston and Wood, 1985; Johnston, 1988).

In Britain, we concluded, social standards of right and wrong were not strikingly at odds with the law; but they were by no means simple, or free of contradictions. Indeed, in certain instances, they seemed to override material self-interest. When asked what they would do if they found various sums of money lying in a deserted street - leave the money, hand it in to the police, or pocket it - the greater the sum of money that was involved the *fewer* people said they would pocket it. 'Honesty rules' can apparently become *more* salient the higher the stakes involved. To examine these standards more closely, we asked a further set of questions in 1991, this time focusing upon questions of right and wrong in business and economic dealings.

This chapter is not a study of business ethics in the sense of a formal analysis of the competing legal, organisational or professional standards applying to particular business roles. Nor is it a study of the ethical views of business decision-makers themselves. It is, instead, a study of people's judgements of a variety of types of 'market behaviour' after a decade in which such concerns have been the focus of political debate, government policy, and (sometimes) front-page news.

### Self-interest, or something more complicated?

It is tempting to view the past decade as one in which, for better or worse, the mixed economy and post-war consensus have given way to a policy of *enrichissez-vous* (for a variety of judgements on the 'Thatcher decade' and the abandonment of 'consensus politics', see Kavanagh, 1987, especially Chapters 3-5; Kavanagh and Seldon, 1989; Riddell, 1991; and Young, 1990, especially Chapters 9-11 and 22). But a look behind the facade reveals a more complex picture. The green movement, for example, has begun to affect public attitudes and government policy towards economic activity: while growth probably enjoys more legitimacy now than in, say, the mid-1970s, people are also more aware of its costs. The recent collapse of communism served to sharpen this awareness, as we learned more about the environmental consequences of state-run monopolistic development. Women's movements and consumer groups, among others, have also begun to place new constraints upon the ways businesses make and market their products and deal with their customers.*

All these disparate pressures may well lead to, or reflect, long-term changes in values. Inglehart (1977, 1990), for instance, argues that we are witnessing not a general turn (or return) to old-fashioned unfettered markets, but rather a much more complex and ambivalent reaction to the unprecedented affluence of the period following the Second World War. This reaction shows itself in what Inglehart (1990, pp. 66-103) refers to as the rise of 'post-materialist' values.[1]

If indeed values are changing, attitudes towards government may be changing too. For instance, the welfare state, once the protector of the many against the ravages of the market and the powers of the few, may in a sense yet become a victim of its own successes - having succoured a generation that will feel the need for its services less than it will resent its tax burden and fear (as we shall see) its institutional power (Inglehart, 1990, pp. 8-14).** Such a transition would mean that a preference for markets over government might be less a blanket endorsement of *laissez-faire* than a reflection of concern over institutionalised power in general.

Our data lend some support to this last argument. Between 1985 and 1990, respondents were asked to rate the power of trade unions, of business and of government on a five-point scale ranging from 'far too little power' to 'far too much power'. The table below shows the totals for each year saying that each had 'too much' or 'far too much power':

**Power of trade unions, business and government**

| % saying that each has 'too much' or 'far too much' power: | 1985 | 1986 | 1987 | 1989 | 1990 |
|---|---|---|---|---|---|
| Trade unions | 54 | 53 | 48 | 40 | 35 |
| Business and industry | 21 | 27 | 26 | 36 | 28 |
| Government | 48 | 50 | 44 | 54 | 47 |

N.B. No survey was carried out in 1988.

---

*   The 1990 *European Value Systems Study Group* survey found widespread support for a number of movements aimed at protecting individuals or the public against the power of dominant institutions (see Timms, 1992, pp. 24-25).

**   For evidence of changes in attitude to the welfare state, see Kavanagh, 1987, Chapters 2-6; Riddell, 1991, Chapter 7; and Dunleavy *et al*, 1990, Chapters 2 and 9. The term 'welfare state' itself encompasses a range of meanings and functions - see Esping-Anderson (1990).

Apprehension about trade union power - while seemingly a factor in Conservative victories under Mrs Thatcher - was ebbing away during the late 1980s, while concerns over the power of business and industry tended to rise. Of course this reflected the reality of the power shift that had taken place during the 1980s. But a reflection of another sort of power shift, perhaps, is the fact that in 1989 and 1990, concerns about both trade union and business power lagged well behind concerns about the power of government. Indeed, respondents seem to be suspicious of concentrations of power in general. Thus, we might expect them to be concerned too about the power and behaviour of those who run Britain's institutions - business and industry among them.

### Private profits, public interests

An important aspect of the resurgence of market-orientated policies, particularly in the more mature industrial nations, has been a growing consensus that profitable businesses are important to a society's overall well-being. But this does not necessarily imply a *carte blanche* for business. For example, respondents were asked, on the self-completion questionnaire, to say how much they agreed or disagreed with two statements, one on free enterprise and the other on government intervention:

> *Private enterprise is the best way to solve economic problems.*
>
> *The less government intervenes, the better it is for the economy.*

|  | Private enterprise best | Less government intervention |
|---|---|---|
|  | % | % |
| Agree strongly | 4 | 3 |
| Agree | 31 | 26 |
| Neither agree nor disagree | 36 | 40 |
| Disagree | 24 | 26 |
| Disagree strongly | 3 | 2 |

Only around a quarter of respondents took issue with the idea that private enterprise is the best economic strategy, while around a third agreed at least to some extent. But only a handful agreed strongly, and the largest single group was neutral - a less than ringing declaration of *laissez-faire* values. On the question of government intervention, equal proportions agreed and disagreed, and again the largest percentage of respondents had no view either way.

These responses are worth considering according to respondents' political allegiances. A decisive fissure along party lines might suggest that the overall result is merely a reflection of the divisions between supporters of the Conservatives and Labour, and not really ambivalence at all. But such is not the case. Some 55 per cent of Conservative Party identifiers agreed, or agreed strongly, with the statement that "Private enterprise is the best way to solve economic problems", compared with 36 per cent of Liberal Democrats and only 16 per cent of Labour identifiers. So there *are* divisions along party lines, though perhaps not as striking as might be expected after more than a decade of pro-market Conservative governments; and it is noteworthy that only eight per cent even of Conservative identifiers agreed *strongly*. And in respect of government intervention, only 37 per cent of Conservative identifiers agreed or agreed strongly that there should be less, compared to one in four Labour and Liberal Democrat identifiers. So support for private enterprise in Britain is strong, but even among Conservatives enthusiasm seems to be qualified. (For a similarly mixed assessment, see Riddell, 1991, Chapter 4.) We go on to explore some of the possible reasons.

## Who benefits from profits?

Successful businesses are preferable to unsuccessful ones; but who benefits from their success? We asked respondents to consider the hypothetical case of a big British company which had achieved "a large profit in a particular year". Which things, from a list of possible options, would the firm be *most likely* to do? And then which, from the same list of options, did respondents feel *should* be its first priority?

|  | Where *would* the profits go % | Where *should* the profits go % |
|---|---|---|
| **Investment:** |  |  |
| New machinery or technology | 20 | 26 |
| Training the workforce | 2 } 28 | 11 } 42 |
| Researching new products | 6 | 5 |
| **Workforce benefits:** |  |  |
| Pay rise | 6 } 8 | 27 } 39 |
| Improved conditions | 2 | 12 |
| **Customer benefit:** |  |  |
| Lower prices | 4 | 14 |
| **Shareholders/managers:** |  |  |
| Increased dividends | 34 } 54 | 3 } 3 |
| Bonus to top management | 20 | * |

\* = less than 0.5 per cent

The most striking aspect of these results is that expectations of what the firm *would* do, and of what it *should* do, diverge so widely. While only three per cent said that increasing shareholders' dividends should be the first priority, around a third believed it would come first. In contrast, just over a quarter of respondents proposed pay rises for employees as first priority, but only six per cent thought that this would actually happen. Cutting prices, improving conditions, and investing in training all attracted significantly more support as desirable goals than as likely courses of action. Meanwhile, using the profits to give a bonus to top management - seen by one in five respondents as the most likely use of the profits - was favoured by virtually no-one. This must cast some doubt on any argument that Britain has become an 'opportunity society' or an 'enterprise culture' in the sense of supporting large differentials in income as a fair reward (or incentive) for economic success. (See also Jowell & Topf, 1988, p. 121). In the end, only nine per cent of respondents believed that the hypothetical firm would take what they thought would be the 'right' decision.

These findings are reinforced by the results for two other questions:

*Who do you think benefits most from the profits made by British firms?*

*And who do you think* **should** *benefit most from the profits made by British firms?*

|  | Do benefit | Should benefit |
|---|---|---|
|  | % | % |
| Mainly their owners or shareholders | 65 | 18 |
| Mainly their directors and managers | 25 | 3 |
| Mainly their employees | 4 | 44 |
| The public generally | 4 | 32 |

Once again, while people believe a firm's employees and the public at large should be the main beneficiaries of business success, they expect the profits will in fact benefit mostly the shareholders and top managers. Even though these questions offered a much more limited range of possible responses, still only one in five respondents felt the profits *would* benefit most those they thought *should* benefit most. While private enterprise enjoys considerable general support among the British public, it seems that there are significant misgivings about the way its benefits are distributed in practice.

### The limits of self-interest: corporate and individual wrongdoing

Public attitudes towards markets also involve questions of what firms and people should *not* do - questions concerning the rules and limitations that apply to the pursuit and protection of self-interest.

We asked respondents to consider a series of seventeen situations in which some degree of wrongdoing might be taking place. These were as diverse as expense-account fiddling, nepotism, company price-fixing, 'insider dealing', and the abuse of company car privileges. Respondents were asked to judge them on a five-point scale ranging from 'nothing wrong' to 'very seriously wrong'. In addition, for three kinds of minor to moderate misconduct, we asked people whether they themselves might engage in the practice if the opportunity arose. Several of these items have been asked before in the 1984 and 1987 surveys, allowing us to consider stability and change in social standards during the past decade.

  Social and legal standards of right and wrong are relatively congruent in Britain (Johnston, 1991), not only in comparison with the developing world, where basic relationships between state and society are still being worked out, but also with standards in the United States, where a moralising culture coexists uneasily with entrepreneurialism and materialism (Eisenstadt, 1978). Not surprisingly, however, the social and the legal sometimes diverge in Britain too. Some actions are judged relatively leniently even though they may contravene widely recognised ethical standards, company regulations, or even the law.

## Lenient judgements

The following three items, which were least likely to be judged wrong by our respondents, illustrate this point:

*An employee uses his influence to get a relative a job at his workplace.*

*A company manager accepts a Christmas present worth £75 from a firm from which he buys products.*

*A householder is having a repair job done by a local plumber. He is told that if he pays cash he will not be charged VAT. So he pays cash.*

|  | Nepotism | Accepting gift | Evading VAT |
|---|---|---|---|
|  | % | % | % |
| Nothing wrong | 44 | 33 | 27 |
| A bit wrong | 22 | 20 | 28 |
| Wrong | 24 | 31 | 36 |
| Seriously wrong | 5 | 10 | 5 |
| Very seriously wrong | 3 | 4 | 3 |

Nepotism and 'treating' would violate the internal policies of most business firms* and VAT-dodging clearly breaks the tax laws. Still, a majority of respondents in each case said either that they saw 'nothing wrong' in such actions or that they were only 'a bit wrong'. The judgement on nepotism is broadly consistent with the results of a similar American survey (Johnston, 1986).[2] As for the Christmas gift for a company manager, the value we specified was not large, nor was it an explicit *quid pro quo* for past business or in anticipation of future orders; hence perhaps the leniency of the judgement.

Evading VAT *is* seen to be a more serious matter: only a quarter of respondents were willing to excuse it altogether while 44 per cent saw it (at the least) as 'wrong'. Even so, VAT-dodging by a householder is an impersonal crime and its effects are distant: the immediate costs accrue to the government, and anyway VAT, like taxes in general, may well be unpopular with many people.

None of these three actions is regarded as completely acceptable. But as in years past, it seems that there are certain types of misconduct - most often those involving private dealings, familiar people and situations, fairly small stakes, and no immediate victims - which are viewed in relatively tolerant terms.

*Severe judgements*

At the other end of the scale, several hypothetical actions were seen as very serious wrongdoing indeed. These involved both corporate and individual business conduct:

*A factory discovers that it is polluting a nearby river and does nothing about it.*

*A drug company delays supplies of an important new drug in order to keep its price high.*

*A lawyer is told by a client that the client's firm is about to announce big profits. The lawyer buys shares in that firm before the announcement is made.*

*A milkman slightly overcharges customers over a period and makes £300.*

*A company director makes a habit of taking time off as sick leave when he is not ill.*

---

*    In fairness we should note that the questions themselves did not specify whether there were applicable rules.

| | Factory polluting river | Delaying drug supplies | Insider dealing | Milkman over-charging | Malingering company director |
|---|---|---|---|---|---|
| | % | % | % | % | % |
| Nothing wrong | - | 1 | 5 | * | 1 |
| A bit wrong | * | 2 | 6 | 2 | 4 |
| Wrong | 9 | 26 | 29 | 26 | 34 |
| Seriously wrong | 30 | 33 | 29 | 43 | 37 |
| Very seriously wrong | 60 | 38 | 29 | 28 | 24 |

* = Less than 0.5 per cent

These five items collectively provide a fascinating view of what people apparently regard as the furthest limits to the legitimate pursuit of self-interest. The strength of the condemnation of the polluting factory is impressive indeed: not a single respondent was willing to label this as 'nothing wrong', and nine in ten saw it as 'seriously' or 'very seriously' wrong. Even more remarkable is the fact that this strong negative judgement extended across virtually all sub-sections of the sample.

It is also worth noting that the two 'worst' scenarios involved corporations, not individuals, and that the worst three have their principal impact upon society at large - the environment, health services, and the orderly functioning of markets - rather than upon individuals. As our discussion of attitudes to the uses of business profits suggested, people are apparently quite concerned about the wider consequences of business activity over and above their own material interests.

But individuals who take unfair advantage of their position are also of concern. Judgements on the 'fiddling' milkman and the malingering company director are quite strict - the former all the more so, given that the direct cost of this fiddle to any one customer would be small.

Another kind of difference between legal and social standards emerges. All five of these actions would contravene either the law or, at the very least, rules and regulations. All clearly violate more general ethical codes. Yet in practice the motives of the drug company and of the company director, and the circumstances leading to the lawyer's share purchase, might be very difficult to establish in the law courts. Nonetheless, in the judgement of public opinion, these actions and situations are viewed generally as unambiguously wrong.

Just *how* wrong an action is, however, can depend upon many things: the sorts of perpetrators and victims involved, the motives attributed to them, and more general considerations of honour and respectability. Consider, for example, the following pair of items:

*A company employee exaggerates his claims for travel expenses over a period and makes £75.*

*A company manager accepts a Christmas present worth £75 from a firm from which he buys products.*

|                     | Fiddling expenses | Accepting gift |
|---------------------|:-----------------:|:--------------:|
|                     | %                 | %              |
| Nothing wrong       | 3                 | 33             |
| A bit wrong         | 15                | 20             |
| Wrong               | 50                | 31             |
| Seriously wrong     | 21                | 10             |
| Very seriously wrong| 10                | 4              |

Here, two people who pocket a comparable 'profit' over and above their regular salary are judged in quite different ways, and the key to the contrast is probably the attributed motives. 'Christmas presents' are routine business and, even though some might see them as the acceptable face of petty bribery, most respondents seem to regard the transaction as innocuous. The deliberate 'fiddling' of travel records, however, is another matter: secrecy and deception are involved, and fewer than one in five people are willing to say there is 'nothing wrong' in it, or describe it as only 'a bit wrong'.

Is our hypothetical company manager being let off easily because his status is higher than that of our hypothetical 'employee'? Probably not, as two more items suggest:

*A junior employee makes a habit of taking time off as sick leave when he is not ill.*

*A company director makes a habit of taking time off as sick leave when he is not ill.*

|                     | Malingering junior employee | Malingering company director |
|---------------------|:---------------------------:|:----------------------------:|
|                     | %                           | %                            |
| Nothing wrong       | 1                           | 1                            |
| A bit wrong         | 5                           | 4                            |
| Wrong               | 45                          | 34                           |
| Seriously wrong     | 33                          | 37                           |
| Very seriously wrong| 15                          | 24                           |

Neither the junior employee nor the company director can count on much support from respondents; very few people see their actions as less than 'wrong'. Such behaviour does, once again, involve deliberate and repeated dishonesty. But the director's wrongdoing is evidently taken more seriously, perhaps because of his perceived importance to the company, or because of the large salaries and extensive benefits which many directors receive, or perhaps because he has abused a position of responsibility and failed to set an example.

We might have thought that this contrast reflects a 'people-like-me' factor, the public passing lighter judgements upon those with whom they have more in common (and who tend to act as *they* might?). However, although professionals, employers and managers (52 per cent) were more censorious than were semi-skilled manual workers (43 per cent) of a junior employee's abuses, they were also more censorious of a *director's* abuses (67 per cent compared to 54 per cent). In fact, the director was judged more strictly by *all* occupational groups; and when we compared the results from differing occupational groups within similar age ranges, the contrasts, while weaker, maintained this general pattern.

Thus, while these sorts of contrasting judgements arise to some extent from the respondent's own role in the workplace, they seem to involve more general attitudes towards duty and responsibility as well. Just how complex these 'intangibles' of personal conduct can be is shown by a further comparison:

*In making an insurance claim, a man whose home has been burgled exaggerates the value of what was stolen by £150.*

*A man gives a £5 note for goods he is buying in a big store. By mistake, he is given change for a £10 note. He notices, but keeps the change.*

|  | Overclaiming on insurance | Pocketing change |
|---|---|---|
|  | % | % |
| Nothing wrong | 6 | 8 |
| A bit wrong | 20 | 15 |
| Wrong | 55 | 59 |
| Seriously wrong | 13 | 11 |
| Very seriously wrong | 5 | 6 |

The point to note here is the *similarity* of judgements, rather than any sharp contrast. There is a significant difference in the amounts of money involved, and filing a false insurance claim is explicitly illegal and entails deliberate deception. Even so, the judgements are nearly identical. Why is this? Could it be that the insurance company is seen as a distant and impersonal victim, like the government in the VAT-dodging scenario? Might some people believe that the insurance company would have reduced the payout anyway? In contrast, pocketing or not pocketing extra change raises questions of personal honour and respectability - values few are apparently willing to disregard for the sake of only £5. Responses to our questions asked in 1987 on money found in a deserted street suggest that these sorts of 'honesty rules', and other intangible considerations, do sometimes override material interests (Johnston, 1988).

   Supporting evidence came when we asked people, for the VAT-dodging, insurance overclaiming and pocketing change items, "might you do this if the situation came up?" (see also p. 145 below).  A large proportion (71 per cent) admitted that they might be tempted to pay the plumber in cash to avoid VAT, but only a quarter said they might keep the extra change or inflate a burglary insurance claim.  Again, the similarity between these last two figures is noteworthy.  But the important point here is the gap between disapproval of an action and a propensity to indulge in it oneself. Most of us indulge in actions we judge to be wrong (especially perhaps in others?).


**Corporate conduct in the 'grey zone'**

There is also a range of corporate actions at or beyond the fringes of legality which are viewed with concern by many people, even if they are not judged as seriously as wilfully polluting a stream or delaying drug supplies for higher profits.  Many of these do not so much involve the effects of business activity upon society as a whole as they do the *ways* businesses promote their interests and reward their top executives.  Here, too, we see some interesting responses:

   *A British firm competing for a contract in a foreign country offers large gifts of money to officials.*

   *A tobacco manufacturer sponsors a national event popular with young people to get publicity.*

   *Two large breweries get together and agree to raise their prices at the same time.*

   *A company provides its directors with expensive company cars even though they are hardly ever used for work.*

   *A private taxi firm puts up its fares during a public transport strike.*

|  | Firm bribing officials | Tobacco manufacturer's sponsorship | Brewery cartel | Misuse of company cars | Taxi firm exploiting strike |
|---|---|---|---|---|---|
|  | % | % | % | % | % |
| Nothing wrong | 7 | 16 | 17 | 13 | 7 |
| A bit wrong | 10 | 11 | 10 | 11 | 13 |
| Wrong | 33 | 33 | 36 | 40 | 42 |
| Seriously wrong | 28 | 19 | 20 | 21 | 25 |
| Very seriously wrong | 20 | 19 | 14 | 13 | 12 |

These hypothetical cases lie within the 'grey zone' not because of any ambiguity in public response - they are all regarded as at least 'wrong' by 70 per cent or more of respondents - but rather because here public perceptions of wrongdoing seem to reach well beyond the formal standards laid down by the law.  To be sure, price collusion between two breweries would almost certainly violate British law; the company cars case raises touchy tax questions; and the offer of large amounts of money to foreign officials would contravene the laws of most nations, even those where bribery is customary and connived at.  The other two actions - sponsorship and raising prices opportunistically - break no laws at all.  All five actions are, however, viewed as undesirable business practices, and to a surprisingly similar (but by no means identical) extent.

   Censoriousness of some of these actions does vary across sub-groups. Price-fixing by brewers is expectedly (and self-interestedly) more strongly condemned by men, particularly young men, than by women; the taxi fare rises and company car 'perks' are judged more strictly by Labour Party identifiers than by Conservatives or Liberal Democrats; women are particularly critical of the 'misuse' of company cars and of the tobacco company's sponsorship of an event that attracts young people.  On the other hand, younger people tend to be less critical of the tobacco company's conduct; and professionals, employers and managers are less critical of the hypothetical abuses of company cars.

   Even stronger and more consistent associations are, however, to be found in respect of respondents' attitudes to private enterprise and government intervention generally.  Respondents agreeing that "private enterprise is the best way to solve economic problems" - and in particular, those *strongly* agreeing - tended to be much less censorious of the range of actions.   It seems that when confronted with somewhat more ambiguous examples of business conduct - the kinds that make up much of the controversy over the legitimate extent and limits of enterprise - many people draw upon their basic values in order to form coherent judgements.  This seems to be true even when the players and situations are distant, or when the legalities are unclear, and it is particularly true for those with strongly-held values.  It is also partly the explanation, perhaps, as to why - after a decade of free-market thinking and practice and exhortation - public support of private enterprise and profits is still qualified and selective.


## Complex - but enduring - standards

Judgements of others' behaviour, then, encompass a range of qualifications, equivocations and questions of context (Held, 1984).  If such judgements were to vary markedly from one year to the next, we might conclude that people's social standards of right and wrong were at least partly arbitrary, and thus difficult or impossible to interpret. However, our results suggest that these judgements remain broadly consistent over time, and thus may render complex but important verdicts upon the relationships between individual self-interest, the marketplace, and society.

Several of the questions in the latest *British Social Attitudes* survey had been asked in earlier years. (At times, adjustments have been made to the amounts of money involved, in order to take account of inflation.) These give us a perspective on change and continuity in social values during the 'decade of the market'. As the examples below make clear, the consistency of judgements of right and wrong over the past several years is impressive indeed:

*A company employee exaggerates his claims for travel expenses over a period and makes £75 (1984 and 1987: £50).*

*A householder is having a repair job done by a local plumber. He is told that if he pays cash he will not be charged VAT. So he pays cash.*

*A man gives a £5 note for goods he is buying in a big store. By mistake he is given change for a £10 note. He notices, but keeps the change.*

|                     | Fiddling expenses | | | Evading VAT | | | Pocketing change | | |
|---------------------|-----|-----|-----|-----|-----|-----|-----|-----|-----|
|                     | '84 | '87 | '91 | '84 | '87 | '91 | '84 | '87 | '91 |
|                     | %   | %   | %   | %   | %   | %   | %   | %   | %   |
| Nothing wrong       | 4   | 5   | 3   | 31  | 26  | 27  | 6   | 8   | 8   |
| A bit wrong         | 17  | 20  | 15  | 31  | 29  | 28  | 15  | 20  | 15  |
| Wrong               | 54  | 52  | 50  | 32  | 36  | 36  | 61  | 58  | 59  |
| Seriously wrong     | 23  | 15  | 21  | 3   | 6   | 5   | 16  | 10  | 11  |
| Very seriously wrong| n/a | 8   | 10  | n/a | 2   | 3   | n/a | 5   | 6   |

Several notes of caution are in order here. First, we are comparing separate samples from each year; this is not a 'panel study' of the same respondents interviewed several years apart. Secondly, a fifth response option, 'very seriously wrong', was added after 1984. Thirdly, the changes in money amounts are necessarily only approximate adjustments for the effects of inflation; moreover, changes in the economic climate (between 1987 and 1991 in particular) may well affect the *subjective* significance of a given sum, quite apart from its changing purchasing power. Even so, the very strong consistency over time in all three items since 1984 argue against the notion that there have been major shifts in social perceptions of right and wrong during the period.

At the very least, these figures and others lend no support to the argument that the past decade's changes have turned Britain into a greedier society. If anything, there has been a gradual increase, between 1984 and 1991, in the percentages voicing *strict* judgements. For instance, the 23 per cent who judged fiddling travel expenses as 'seriously wrong' in 1984 increased to a total of 31 per cent saying 'seriously' or 'very seriously' wrong in 1991; and for the overcharging milkman, the comparable change since 1987 was from 57 to 71 per cent. As noted, changes in the amounts of money involved make these comparisons less than exact. But as we shall see below, there are other reasons to think that the British are becoming marginally less tolerant of both corner-cutting and outright dishonesty in business dealings.

On the other hand, when we examine the responses obtained over the years to the questions which ask people whether they themselves might engage in different types of wrongdoing "if the situation came up", the story is a little more complex. Of course answers to a hypothetical question do not necessarily tell us what people would do in real situations. But they do provide clues as to how respondents see themselves, or would like others to see them.

|  | % answering 'yes' | | |
|---|---|---|---|
|  | 1984 | 1987 | 1991 |
| **Might you ...** | | | |
| ... exaggerate an insurance claim?* | n/a | 26 | 24 |
| ... pay a plumber in cash to avoid VAT? | 66 | 67 | 71 |
| ... keep £5 extra change? | 18 | 24 | 25 |

* 'By £100' in 1987; 'by £150' in 1991

The proportion saying that they might inflate an insurance claim has remained fairly stable; but there has been a small and recent rise (since 1987) in the proportion saying they might dodge VAT. This might reflect many things, such as the increase in VAT to 17½ per cent, the impact of the recession upon hard-pressed householders, or the unpopularity of taxes (or the government) in general at the time. What is clear is that the already large majority who might be willing to engage in some small-scale tax dodging seems to have grown larger still.

There has also been a gradual but clear growth in the proportions saying they might keep the extra change, despite the fact that the proportion judging it to be 'wrong' has held steady in recent years.[3] There are sharp contrasts by age, and to a lesser extent by gender:

|  | % saying they might keep extra change, 1991 | | | | | |
|---|---|---|---|---|---|---|
|  | 18-24 | 25-34 | 35-44 | 45-54 | 55-64 | 65+ |
| Male | 62 | 47 | 35 | 21 | 18 | 7 |
| Female | 35 | 38 | 23 | 12 | 6 | 6 |

While we do not wish to make too much of responses to one hypothetical question, these and other results suggest possible changes in some of the social standards defining the limits of material self-interest, either in the same individuals as they pass through the various stages of the life-cycle, or in society as one generation replaces another, or perhaps in both. They also bring us full circle to one of the questions raised at the outset:

whether values in Britain are altering in respect of the rules of the marketplace.

## Social continuity, inter-generational change

Our 'right and wrong' questions hardly encompass the whole range of attitudes towards markets and business dealings. But they do suggest that such judgements are often ambivalent and depend upon the perceived results of economic dealings for particular sorts of people in particular circumstances. We have also seen evidence of sharply diverging attitudes according to age.

This leads us to ask whether people who belong to a younger generation tend to value a wider range of social considerations above the pursuit of wealth than do their older counterparts. If they do, then as they replace their elders we might see a fundamental transition in attitudes towards enterprise. Or is it just that as people move through the life-cycles they change their values?

The evidence is mixed. The only true test is to question the same people at intervals, and this series is not of that kind. We have, however, used the technique employed by Heath and McMahon (1991) to find clues. And such evidence as we do have (we do not have space to present it all in detail) suggests that individuals' judgements do change notably as they age; they do not, it seems, carry their values with them into successive generations. The differences *within* age groups over time are almost always at least as great as those *between* adjacent generational groups within the same sample; so, for instance, people seem to become less tolerant of VAT-dodging as they age, as the table below shows:[4]

% saying 'nothing wrong'

Evading VAT

|       | 1984 | 1991 |       |
|-------|------|------|-------|
|       |      | 40   | 18-24 |
| 18-24 | 46   | 33   | 25-31 |
| 25-31 | 42   | 25   | 32-38 |
| 32-38 | 34   | 25   | 39-45 |
| 39-45 | 26   | 22   | 46-52 |
| 46-52 | 28   | 23   | 53-59 |
| 53-59 | 27   | 16   | 60-66 |
| 60-66 | 22   | 24   | 67+   |
| 67+   | 22   |      |       |

As we can see, the notable exception to this generalisation is the oldest age group in 1991 (people aged over 67), who did not join in the decreasing tolerance of other age groups. Indeed this group remained more or less as tolerant in 1991 as it had been in 1984.

Our results tentatively indicate that young people will continue to challenge the overall framework of values while they are young. They will, however, gradually adopt or become socialised into the normative framework, changing the social consensus somewhat, but at the same time being changed themselves in the direction of the consensus.

## Categories of wrongdoing

Perhaps the major contrasts in judgements of right and wrong in business are qualitative, with different sorts of people reacting to different *kinds* of wrongdoing. To examine this possibility, we can use factor analysis to examine the judgements of all items by all respondents, searching for clusters of items for which judgements vary in similar ways. Not only can we consider what the items making up such clusters might have in common; we can also calculate, for each respondent, a 'factor score', measuring (in this case) the strength with which she or he tends to judge those clusters of items as wrong (see **Tables 7.1** and **7.2**).

This technique generated four clusters of items, each of which is listed below under a summary heading suggesting what they might have in common:

- *Abuse of position*

  Director takes time off as sick leave when he is not ill
  Junior employee takes time off as sick leave when he is not ill
  Milkman overcharges customers

- *Opportunism*

  Directors receive company cars seldom used for business
  Tobacco manufacturer sponsors event popular with young people
  Taxi firm raises fares during transport strike
  Employee uses influence to get a job for a relative
  Company offers money to foreign officials

- *Personal taking*

  Inflating a burglary insurance claim
  Keeping extra change in a big store
  Exaggerating travel claims
  Manager accepts Christmas gift
  Paying plumber in cash to avoid VAT

- *Corporate/professional misconduct*

  Drug company delays supplies to keep price high
  Lawyer uses client's information to make money out of shares
  Breweries get together and agree to raise prices
  Factory pollutes river

A comparison of factor scores shows that different kinds of people do indeed react differently to these categories of misconduct. Conservative identifiers, for example, judge the abuse of position factor significantly more strictly than do Labour supporters, while the latter come down much more sharply on 'opportunism'. Professionals, employers and managers are relatively tolerant of 'opportunism', perhaps seeing these practices more as aggressive entrepreneurship than as wrongdoing, while manual workers judge these sorts of practices rather more severely.

There are age differences too: corporate misconduct is most strongly condemned by people in the 'middle' age groups (25-59, with a peak among the 45-54 year olds). The sharpest contrast according to age, however, is in the 'personal taking' category: here, the youngest are the most tolerant, the oldest are the strictest.

Perhaps the most intriguing differences are to be found between men's and women's judgements. While men more strongly condemn the relatively clear-cut wrongdoing in the 'corporate misconduct' category, it is 'opportunism' that women judge in much stricter terms. It is tempting to speculate that men, who tend to dominate senior positions in business, might be more likely to see these actions as inevitable in a competitive world, while women might be more likely to be the victims than the practitioners of opportunistic tactics in business life. Other studies have also shown that men tend to see right and wrong in terms of relatively sharp, formal distinctions and women to see subtle gradations of wrongdoing, defined in terms of situations and complex interpersonal considerations.* A tendency for women to condemn more strongly than men the 'borderline' actions in the opportunism category is consistent with that argument.** These gender differences will be increasingly interesting to study as women move in greater numbers into top decision-making roles. Will they adopt conventional outlooks on business practices; or will they, through their own distinctive outlooks, help to change the 'business culture'?

## Conclusions

A decade and more of economic transitions and changes in government policy have materially changed Britain in many ways. It is unlikely, however, that they have fundamentally altered the British public's

---

*   Gilligan (1982) especially Chapter 3. But Timms' (1992) EVSSG data show a different pattern, with women just as likely as men to voice straightforward, categorical ethical judgements. On this point see also Noddings (1984).

**  So is the fact that male respondents (particularly young ones) are more likely to go to extremes in their judgements, choosing 'nothing wrong' or 'very seriously wrong' much more often than women do.

orientation toward private enterprise and its judgement of what is and is not 'proper' conduct in the marketplace. To the extent that our data illuminate important aspects of people's views on business, we find no consistent trend towards an 'enterprise culture', nor for that matter towards any new British tolerance of greed. Nor, despite apparently growing concerns about the behaviour of some players in the business world, do we see clear evidence of an anti-business backlash. Although more people are worried about the power of business and industry nowadays than in the early 1980s, concern about the power of government is now even more widespread.

The severity of public judgements of some practices is clear cut: any firm who knowingly causes pollution will attract strong public censure. People also have strong feelings about the ways in which profits of enterprise should be used, but nine out of ten believe that their priorities are not shared by the enterprises themselves. Social standards of right and wrong in business do not clash with those laid down in the law, but they do, at times, reach beyond the law.

There are subtle subgroup differences in perceptions of right and wrong in business - some of these between generations, some reflecting ideology, gender or class. These differences are unlikely to be the stuff of grand controversy, nor do they portend any imminent revolution of attitudes to, and expectations of, private enterprise in a market economy. Nonetheless they will continue to be an important factor in determining a national consensus on the 'proper' role of the marketplace and business in society.

This limited exploration of public attitudes to a range of business transactions suggests that, even after more than a decade of aggressively pro-business, pro-enterprise rhetoric, and of major changes in both the domestic and the world economies in that direction, there is still more stability than change both in British values in respect of the limits of private enterprise, and in how people view self-interest.

If we see the past decade's upheavals in a longer perspective, this apparent stability is hardly surprising: Britain was the first nation to industrialise, and the first to encounter the difficult transitions to post-industrial life. The nation has thus had a longer time than any other to adjust to the ethical dilemmas of the marketplace, and to form, test and revise the balance between the imperatives of business and the needs of the wider society. This balance can adjust itself in important ways, as the politics of the past decade has shown; but to the extent that pragmatism remains a strong element of British life and culture (Christoph, 1965, p. 631; Heath and Topf, 1987; Norton, 1991, pp. 34-35), we should not expect to find massive shifts in values.

Comparisons between people in different age groups point to the potential for change. But our evidence suggests that such changes will be gradual, not disruptive and abrupt. And in a world where ideologies and fundamental contrasts have recently had a way of crumbling, a capacity for gradual adaptation should perhaps not be undervalued. If the world is indeed becoming more committed to vigorous private enterprise, and at the same time a bit more wary of the dangers of business excess, a workable balance needs to be found between public and private interests (Mackie, 1977). New 'rules' will have to be formulated which are grounded not only in the law but in consensual social values as well. This seems to be a genuine possibility in contemporary Britain.


## Notes

1. We do not have direct evidence as to what proportion of respondents to the 1991 *British Social Attitudes* survey would qualify as 'post-materialist', but Inglehart (1990) places Britain in a tie for fourth place among twelve major economic powers in 1986-87, in terms of the strength of post-materialism of its citizens.

2. However, the relatively tolerant response is probably conditional: follow-up interviews in 1987 with a group of respondents to the 1984 survey who had been asked a similar question about getting a relative a job "with the [local] council" showed that much depended upon whether the relative is qualified for the job (Johnston, 1991).
   It is interesting to note that judgements of that 1984 item regarding a *council* job were a good deal more strict than those for the private sector job: for nepotism in council hiring, the results were 'Nothing wrong', 11 per cent; 'A bit wrong', 19 per cent; 'Wrong', 45 per cent; and 'Seriously wrong', 23 per cent, on the four-point scale used that year.

3. This item is of particular interest from an American vantage-point. Responses to survey questions indicate that in the American north-east at least, few people would have qualms about keeping the money.

4. We have divided the sample into seven-year age groups to reflect the elapsed time between 1984, when the question was first asked, and 1991. By comparing each 1984 age-group to the next oldest age-group in 1991 (for example, people aged 32-38 in 1984 will have become 39-45 by 1991) we can make a tentative comparison of inter-generational change *versus* life-cycle changes. However, we must remember that these are not the same individuals.


## References

Christoph, J. B. (1965), 'Consensus and Cleavage in British Political Ideology', *American Political Science Review, 59.*

Dunleavy, P., Gamble, A. and Peele, G. (1990), *Developments in British Politics 3,* London: MacMillan.

Eisenstadt, A.S. (1978), 'Political Corruption in American History: Some Further Thoughts', in Eisenstadt, A. S., Hoogenboom, A. and Trefousse, H. L., *Before Watergate: Problems of Corruption in American History,* Brooklyn, N.Y.: Brooklyn College Press.

Esping-Anderson, G. (1990), *The Three Worlds of Welfare Capitalism,* Cambridge: Polity Press.

Gilligan, C. (1982), *In a Different Voice: Psychological Theory and Women's Development.* Cambridge, MA: Harvard University Press.

Heath, A. and McMahon, D. (1991), 'Consensus and dissensus', in Jowell, R., Brook, L. and Taylor, B. with Prior, G. (eds.), *British Social Attitudes: the 8th Report,* Aldershot: Dartmouth.

Heath, A. and Topf, R. (1987), 'Political Culture', in Jowell, R., Witherspoon, S. and Brook, L., *British Social Attitudes: the 1987 Report,* Aldershot: Gower.

Held, V. (1984), *Rights and Goods: Justifying Social Action,* London: Collier Macmillan.

Inglehart, R. (1977), *The Silent Revolution: Changing Values and Political Styles among Western Publics,* Princeton, N.J.: Princeton University Press.

Inglehart, R. (1990), *Culture Shift in Advanced Industrial Society,* Princeton, N.J.: Princeton University Press.

Johnston, M. (1986), 'Right and Wrong in American Politics: Popular Conceptions of Corruption', *Polity,* 18/3, pp. 367-391.

Johnston, M. (1988), 'The Price of Honesty', in Jowell, R., Witherspoon, S. and Brook L. (eds.), *British Social Attitudes: the 5th Report,* Aldershot: Gower.

Johnston, M. (1991), 'Right and Wrong in British Politics': "Fits of Morality" in Comparative Perspective', *Polity,* 24/1, pp. 1-25.

Johnston, M. and Wood, D. (1985), 'Right and Wrong in Public and Private Life', in Jowell, R. and Witherspoon, S. (eds.), *British Social Attitudes: the 1985 Report,* Aldershot: Gower.

Jowell, R. and Topf, R. (1988) 'Trust in the Establishment', in Jowell, R., Witherspoon, S. and Brook, L. (eds.), *British Social Attitudes: the 5th Report,* Aldershot: Gower

Kavanagh, D. (1987), *Thatcherism and British Politics: The End of Consensus?,* Oxford: Oxford University Press.

Kavanagh, D. and Seldon, A. (eds.) (1989), *The Thatcher Effect: A Decade of Change,* Oxford: Oxford University Press.

Mackie, J.L. (1977), *Ethics: Inventing Right and Wrong,* Harmondsworth: Penguin.

Noddings, N. (1984), *Caring: A Feminine Approach to Ethics and Moral Education,* London: University of California Press.

Norton, P. (1991), *The British Polity (2nd edition),* London: Longman.

Riddell, P. (1991), *The Thatcher Era and its Legacy,* Oxford: Blackwell.

Timms, N. (1992), *Family and Citizenship: Values in Contemporary Britain,* Aldershot: Dartmouth.

Young, H. (1990), *One of Us: A Biography of Margaret Thatcher,* London: MacMillan.

Young, K. (1991), 'Shades of Green', in Jowell, R., Brook, L. and Taylor B. with Prior, G. (eds.), *British Social Attitudes: the 8th Report,* Aldershot: Dartmouth.

## Bibliographic note

A very useful general survey of business ethics issues and concepts can be found in

Mahoney, J. (1990), *Teaching Business Ethics in the UK, Europe and the USA: A Comparative Study,* London: Athlone Press.

Other major works include:

Benson, G.C.S. (1982), *Business Ethics in America,* Lexington, Mass.: Lexington Books.

Bowie, N.E. (1982), *Business Ethics,* London: Prentice-Hall.

DeGeorge, R.T. and Pichler, J.A. (eds.) (1978), *Ethics, Free Enterprise, and Public Policy: Original Essays on Moral Issues in Business,* Oxford: Oxford University Press.

Desjardins, J.R. and McCall, J.J. (2nd ed. 1990), *Contemporary Issues in Business Ethics,* Belmont, Ca.: Wadsworth.

Donaldson, J. (1989), *Key Issues in Business Ethics,* London: Academic Press.

Donaldson, T. (1989), *The Ethics of International Business,* Oxford: Oxford University Press.

Engelbourg, S. (1980), *Power and Morality: American Business Ethics 1840-1914,* London: Greenwood Press.

Freeman, R.E. (ed.) (1991), *Business Ethics: The State of the Art,* Oxford: Oxford University Press.

McHugh, F. (1988), *Keyguide to Information Sources in Business Ethics,* London: Mansell Nichols.

Marsh, P.D.V. (1980), *Business Ethics*, London: Associated Business Press.
Sufrin, S.C. (1980), *Management of Business Ethics*, London: Kennikat Press.
Willmer, M.A.P. and Keiser, J. (1982), *The Ethics of Deviousness*, Manchester Business School.
Winfield, M. (1990), *Minding Your Own Business: Self-Regulation and Whistleblowing in British Companies*, London: Social Audit.

## Acknowledgements

The author and editors thank Colgate University for its support, under the Sloan Foundation's Program in the New Liberal Arts, toward the costs of data acquisition, and Professors Jack Mahoney and Noel Timms for their helpful comments on the questions, and on various drafts of this chapter.

## 7.1 RESULTS OF FACTOR ANALYSIS (VARIMAX ROTATION)

| Variable name* | Abuse of position | Opportunism | Personal taking | Corporate/ professional misconduct |
|---|---|---|---|---|
| DIRSICK | .81450 | .22831 | .14285 | .07913 |
| JEMPSICK | .81046 | .26355 | .18679 | .04151 |
| CHARG300 | .54017 | -.09190 | .21078 | .32194 |
| COCARUSE | .09845 | .64666 | .11199 | .14147 |
| CIGSPYNG | .07761 | .59573 | .04921 | .11585 |
| STRKTAXI | .26804 | .58759 | -.02466 | .17520 |
| JBENEPOT | -.07752 | .57414 | .28400 | .01348 |
| FORBRIBE | .16736 | .49588 | .14442 | .29253 |
| INSUR150 | .26162 | .18588 | .64511 | -.05938 |
| STORCHKP | .19963 | .11607 | .64314 | -.05633 |
| CLAIM75 | .33437 | -.13110 | .56862 | .33355 |
| MANGIF75 | -.11225 | .04856 | .55766 | .36554 |
| VATCHEAT | -.00566 | .29077 | .54421 | .09282 |
| DELAYDRG | .25408 | .18067 | -.07713 | .71402 |
| LWINDEAL | .13489 | .24396 | .20385 | .61909 |
| BREWRYPR | -.11426 | .20174 | .24579 | .53530 |
| FACPOLUT | .42451 | .15536 | -.17858 | .53019 |
| Eigenvalues | 4.43851 | 1.50331 | 1.38597 | 1.14691 |

*See Appendix III for the full question wording of these variables.

## 7.2  COMPARISONS OF FACTOR SCORES OF VARIOUS POPULATION SUBGROUPS*

| | Abuse of position | | Oppor- tunism | | Personal taking | | Corporate/ professional misconduct | |
|---|---|---|---|---|---|---|---|---|
| | Mean | N | Mean | N | Mean | N | Mean | N |
| **Party identification:** | | | | | | | | |
| Conservative | .1124 | 493 | | | | | | |
| Labour | -.0974 | 480 | | | | | | |
| *Significance (across all party groups)* | *p =.0071* | | | | | | | |
| **'Private enterprise is the best solution':** | | | | | | | | |
| Agree strongly | | | -.2326 | 49 | | | | |
| Agree | | | -.1530 | 374 | | | | |
| Neither | | | -.0314 | 433 | | | | |
| Disagree | | | .1678 | 288 | | | | |
| Disagree strongly | | | .2053 | 37 | | | | |
| *Significance* | | | *p = .0002* | | | | | |
| **Age group:** | | | | | | | | |
| 18-24 | | | | | -.5175 | 180 | -.1854 | 180 |
| 25-34 | | | | | -.3098 | 268 | .1039 | 268 |
| 35-44 | | | | | -.0293 | 233 | .1234 | 233 |
| 45-54 | | | | | .1362 | 221 | .1752 | 221 |
| 55-64 | | | | | .2315 | 198 | .0220 | 198 |
| 65+ | | | | | .3521 | 295 | .2188 | 295 |
| *Significance* | | | | | *p = .0000* | | *p = .0000* | |
| **Socio-economic group:** | | | | | | | | |
| Professional/ employer/manager | | | -.2788 | 268 | | | | |
| Intermediate non-manual | | | .0065 | 169 | | | | |
| Junior non-manual | | | .0647 | 279 | | | | |
| Skilled manual | | | -.0569 | 270 | | | | |
| Semi-skilled manual | | | .2025 | 252 | | | | |
| Unskilled manual | | | .2821 | 95 | | | | |
| *Significance* | | | *p = .0002* | | | | | |
| **Gender:** | | | | | | | | |
| Male | | | -.2101 | 650 | | | .1470 | 650 |
| Female | | | .1823 | 749 | | | -.1276 | 749 |
| *Significance* | | | *p = .0000* | | | | *p = .0000* | |

\* Mean factor scores can be interpreted as a measure of how strictly a group tended to judge a given category of actions. For the whole sample, the means for the factor scores are zero. A negative score does not indicate positive approval of a category of actions, but rather a comparatively low level of disapproval.

# 8 Community relations in Northern Ireland

*Tony Gallagher* *

In the late 1980s, government policy on community relations in Northern Ireland was established with three main aims: increasing the level of cross-community, that is Protestant/Catholic, contact; encouraging greater mutual understanding of and respect for the different cultures and traditions in the province; and trying to achieve equality of opportunity and equity of treatment for everyone (CCRU, 1991). In line with these objectives a number of specific programmes have been established.

The Central Community Relations Unit (CCRU) of the Northern Ireland Civil Service sponsors policies designed to improve community relations. The Northern Ireland Community Relations Council (NICRC) provides financial support and advice to community groups, encourages Protestant/Catholic contact schemes and, through the Cultural Traditions Group, attempts to enhance knowledge of and respect for cultural pluralism in Northern Ireland (Hayes, 1991).

The Department of Education in Northern Ireland (DENI) funds a Cross-Community Contact Scheme to encourage joint work between schools and youth clubs across the religious divide. Contact programmes have also been established by voluntary agencies such as the Northern Ireland Voluntary Trust (McCartney, 1990) and Co-operation North (Murray and O'Neill, 1991).

There have also been specific economic and social programmes targeted on areas of special need, such as the Making Belfast Work initiative. In

* Lecturer in Educational Research in the School of Education at The Queen's University, Belfast.

1991 the then Secretary of State announced that Targeting Social Need (TSN) was to be the third public expenditure priority for Northern Ireland, alongside the existing priorities of security and strengthening the economy (Brooke, 1991). The aim of the TSN initiative is to target government policies and programmes more sharply on those areas or sections of the community suffering the highest levels of disadvantage and deprivation, thereby indirectly reducing existing social and economic differentials between Protestants and Catholics in Northern Ireland. As part of this initiative, government departments are required to monitor the impact of their policies on the two communities.

In 1989, the first year in which the *British Social Attitudes* survey was extended to cover Northern Ireland, two major pieces of legislation with a community relations dimension, the Education Reform Order and the Fair Employment Act, were introduced in Northern Ireland. This chapter will draw upon data from the three annual *Northern Ireland Social Attitudes* surveys conducted so far, to offer an initial assessment of the legislation's impact. But first we will follow past reports on the Northern Ireland data (Curtice and Gallagher, 1990; Gallagher, 1991)* by examining evidence on aspects of social division in Northern Ireland and, in particular, the way in which attitudes are informed by, and organised around, religious identity.

### Social identity and social division in Northern Ireland

Any assessment of reform measures, such as those in education and fair employment, has to be made in the wider context of continuing social division in Northern Ireland. So we begin by examining evidence for the religious basis of political identity and social affiliation in Northern Ireland; the extent of trust accorded to governmental and other social institutions; attitudes to the constitutional future of Northern Ireland; and general perceptions of the state of community relations.

#### Political identity

In 1989 we reported the extent to which religion is closely associated with party politics in Northern Ireland, and commented that "cross-sectarian voting in Northern Ireland is virtually non-existent" (Curtice and

---

* It should be noted that two separate reports have been published on the Northern Ireland data, covering a much wider range of topics than can be addressed here (Stringer and Robinson, 1991, 1992). A third *Northern Ireland Social Attitudes* report will be published in 1993, and will contain a chapter by the same author covering many of the issues addressed here.

Gallagher, 1989, p. 194). The results of the later surveys confirm that the religious basis of political partisanship remains strong, with only the Alliance party attracting a significant degree of cross-community support. Thus, only a handful of Catholics in any of the survey years have ever reported identifying with one of the unionist parties, hardly any Protestants support the SDLP, and none supports Sinn Fein. There has been a decline in the proportion of Catholics who say they identify with no political party, from 28 per cent in 1989 to 16 per cent in 1991, whereas this figure has increased slightly among Protestants; perhaps our comment on the 1989 findings that the Northern Irish parties had a weak hold upon the electorate (Curtice and Gallagher, 1990, p. 192) is not as true as it was.

**Political partisanship in Northern Ireland (Northern Ireland parties only)**

| | | Religious affiliation | | | | | |
|---|---|---|---|---|---|---|---|
| | | Protestant | | | Catholic | | |
| | All* | 1989 | 1990 | 1991 | 1989 | 1990 | 1991 |
| | % | % | % | % | % | % | % |
| Official Unionist | 30 | 52 | 54 | 51 | 1 | * | - |
| Democratic Unionist | 8 | 19 | 16 | 14 | 1 | - | - |
| Alliance | 10 | 10 | 8 | 9 | 7 | 8 | 9 |
| SDLP | 18 | - | - | 1 | 44 | 43 | 49 |
| Sinn Fein | 4 | - | - | - | 7 | 7 | 10 |
| Worker's party | 1 | 1 | 1 | 1 | 5 | 3 | 2 |
| None | 17 | 10 | 13 | 13 | 28 | 23 | 16 |

* The three per cent who support some other party, and the nine per cent who did not know or did not answer are not shown in this table, so columns do not sum to 100 per cent

Further evidence to support this view is that the proportion of Northern Irish respondents who say they identify with British political parties has declined slightly over the three survey years: in 1989, 27 per cent of respondents in Northern Ireland said they identified with one of the three main British parties, with 19 per cent identifying with the Conservatives. By 1991 the level of identification with British parties was 21 per cent, with only 13 per cent saying they identified with the Conservatives. So our results do not suggest that people in Northern Ireland are turning to British political parties in preference to local parties.

### *Social affiliation*

The continuing importance of religion in Northern Ireland is illustrated also by patterns of social affiliation. In 1989 we asked respondents how close they felt to people who were born in the same area, who were of the same social class, of the same religious background, of the same race, who lived in the same area and who shared the same political beliefs. We found that a higher proportion in Northern Ireland, in comparison with Britain, said they were very or fairly close to each of these groups. The largest difference in response was found for "people of the same religious background", to whom 64 per cent in Northern Ireland, but only 36 per cent in Britain, said they felt very or fairly close. Results in 1991 were almost identical to those in 1989.

*Trust in government*

We also find continuing differences between Protestants and Catholics in Northern Ireland in the amount of trust they place in government. In 1989 and 1991 we asked respondents how much they would trust government to act in the best interests of Northern Ireland under different sorts of constitutional arrangements.
   First, we asked about the present arrangement:

> *Under direct rule from Britain, as now, how much do you generally trust British governments of any party to act in the best interests of Northern Ireland?*

We then asked two parallel questions about possible future arrangements:

> *If there was self-rule, how much do you think you would generally trust a Stormont government...*

> *And if there were a united Ireland, how much do you think you would generally trust an Irish government...*

Results for both Protestants and Catholics in Northern Ireland are shown below:

|  | Religious affiliation | | | |
|  | Protestant | | Catholic | |
| **% saying they would trust each government 'just about always' or 'most of the time'** | **1989** | **1991** | **1989** | **1991** |
|---|---|---|---|---|
| British government under direct rule | 33 | 40 | 15 | 22 |
| Stormont government under self-rule | 67 | 73 | 20 | 31 |
| Irish government in united Ireland | 9 | 14 | 36 | 45 |

Two features stand out: first, in each of the three putative arrangements there has been an increase since 1989 in the expressed level of trust among both Protestants and Catholics. That said, it remains true that while Protestants express a relatively high degree of trust in a local Stormont government, Catholics in general are not particularly trusting of government under *any* condition.

The degree of Protestant trust in the British government appears to be closely linked to the alternative options considered. Thus, when we asked respondents whether they generally find themselves on the side of the British or of the Irish government when there is an argument between Britain and the Republic of Ireland, we found that 83 per cent of Protestants, but only 13 per cent of Catholics, would generally support the British government. In contrast, only one per cent of Protestants and 36 per cent of Catholics say they would generally support the Irish government.

## Confidence in institutions

In 1991 we asked about the confidence respondents had in a range of social institutions. The figure below shows proportions expressing "complete confidence" or "a great deal of confidence" in each institution, in Northern Ireland and Britain.

**Confidence in institutions: Britain and Northern Ireland**

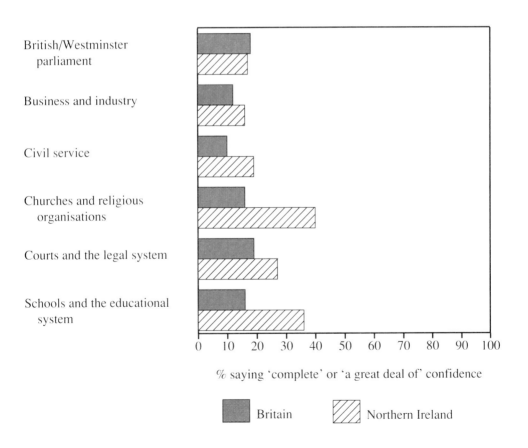

In general, the proportion of British respondents expressing this level of confidence in any of the institutions is fairly low (20 per cent or less).  In Northern Ireland a much higher degree of confidence is expressed in schools (36 per cent) and the churches (40 per cent) than in Britain, while the levels of confidence in the civil service and the courts are a little higher in Northern Ireland.

Looking just at respondents in Northern Ireland, we see in the figure below that Protestants are more likely than Catholics to express this amount of confidence in the courts (Protestants: 36 per cent;  Catholics; 14 per cent) and in parliament (Protestants: 26 per cent;  Catholics: 7 per cent).

**Confidence in institutions: Protestants and Catholics in Northern Ireland**

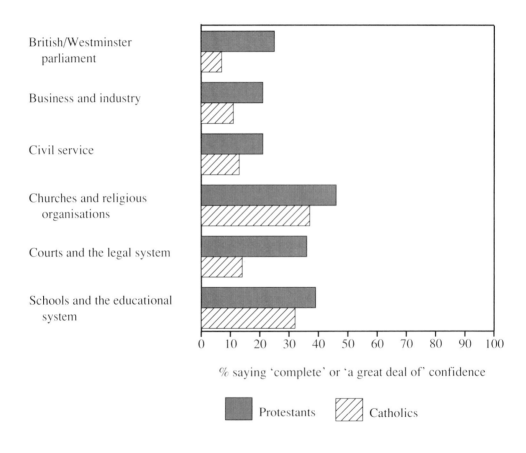

% saying 'complete' or 'a great deal of' confidence

Protestants        Catholics

The most striking feature of this figure, however, is the consistently high level of support among Protestant *and* Catholics in Northern Ireland in schools and the churches. There are, of course, parallel schools systems for Protestants and Catholics in Northern Ireland (Cormack, Gallagher and Osborne, 1991). These responses appear to reinforce the significance of the basic division in Northern Irish society centred on religious identity, in that respondents express greatest confidence in the two social institutions which, arguably, underpin this division.

## Constitutional issues

Past reports in this series have drawn attention to divisions within Northern Ireland, and between Northern Ireland and Britain, on the constitutional future of the province. Our 1991 surveys show that these divisions continue. First, we can see that there remains a basic division between respondents in Northern Ireland and in Britain on the issues of a united Ireland and a withdrawal of British troops:

|  | Britain | | | Northern Ireland | | |
|---|---|---|---|---|---|---|
|  | 1989 | 1990 | 1991 | 1989 | 1990 | 1991 |
| **% saying that:** | | | | | | |
| There should be a united Ireland | 55 | 56 | 54 | 24 | 25 | 22 |
| British troops should be withdrawn | 59 | 60 | 58 | 32 | 32 | 25 |

The most important feature of both sets of figures is the stability of responses. But the data for Northern Ireland do suggest a slight decline in support for the withdrawal of troops between 1989 and 1991. We also find a continuing chasm between Protestant and Catholic preferences:

|  | Religious affiliation | |
|---|---|---|
|  | Protestant | Catholic |
| **% in Northern Ireland saying that:** | | |
| There should be a united Ireland | 4 | 53 |
| The Union should be maintained | 92 | 35 |
| British troops should be withdrawn | 11 | 49 |
| British troops should *not* be withdrawn | 86 | 38 |

As we have commented before (Gallagher, 1991, p. 61), however, Catholic opinion is much more ambivalent than is Protestant opinion on these issues. Although a majority of Catholics favour the reunification of Ireland, still more than a third of them want to maintain the Union. This contrasts with 92 per cent of Protestants who wish to maintain the Union and only four per cent who do not. Similarly, Catholics, unlike

Protestants, are relatively evenly divided on the question of British troop withdrawal: more favour withdrawal than not, but the margin is small. Among Protestants, in contrast, the margin is very large in favour of maintaining the *status quo.*

*Perceptions of community relations*

The evidence so far provides a salutary reminder of the extent of social division in Northern Ireland. But when we turn to perceptions in Northern Ireland of the state of community relations between Protestants and Catholics compared to five years ago, we see some signs of optimism that community relations are improving:

**Perception of community relations in Northern Ireland...**

|  | Northern Ireland | | | | | | Britain | |
|---|---|---|---|---|---|---|---|---|
|  | Religious affiliation | | | | | | | |
|  | Protestant | | | Catholic | | | | |
| ... compared to five years ago | 1986* | 1989 | 1991 | 1986* | 1989 | 1991 | 1989 | 1991 |
|  | % | % | % | % | % | % | % | % |
| better | 11 | 20 | 28 | 9 | 23 | 31 | 14 | 20 |
| about the same | 41 | 50 | 53 | 45 | 44 | 50 | 51 | 52 |
| worse | 47 | 26 | 15 | 46 | 31 | 16 | 26 | 16 |
| ... in five years time |  | % | % |  | % | % | % | % |
| better |  | 22 | 29 |  | 30 | 40 | 14 | 20 |
| about the same |  | 56 | 55 |  | 51 | 50 | 55 | 59 |
| worse |  | 16 | 10 |  | 16 | 4 | 19 | 9 |

* Source: Smith (1987)

In 1986, in the aftermath of political protests against the Anglo-Irish Agreement, almost a half of Protestants and Catholics in Northern Ireland felt that community relations were getting worse. By 1991 the number holding this view had dropped to a little over one in six. Undoubtedly, part of this change has been due to the drop in political tensions over this period. All the same, it is noteworthy that the proportion saying that community relations have improved over the past five years has increased dramatically, with approaching three times as many Protestants *and* Catholics believing them to have improved than believed so in 1986. Moreover, in 1991 40 per cent of Catholics and 29 per cent of Protestants say that they expect community relations in Northern Ireland to be better in five years time, while only four per cent of Catholics and 10 per cent of Protestants say they expect community relations to be worse. The overall pattern of these results suggests that community relations are changing for the better; this may be attributed to many factors including the changing political climate in Northern Ireland, but it seems likely that the community relations initiatives described at the beginning of this chapter may have had some impact.

We now go on to look at public response to the initiatives in more detail.

## Community relations policy in Northern Ireland

We outlined earlier the various community relations initiatives in operation in Northern Ireland. Here we are particularly interested in the two legislative measures enacted in 1989; the Fair Employment Act and the Education Reform Order.

The 1989 Fair Employment Act significantly strengthened the 1976 Act which outlawed direct discrimination in employment, provided a mechanism whereby individuals could seek redress for cases of alleged discrimination, and encouraged employers to establish fair employment practices in recruitment and promotion. The 1989 Act went considerably further. Among its measures was the establishment of a Fair Employment Commission (FEC). The Act outlawed indirect discrimination in employment on the basis of religious affiliation or political belief, and widened the scope of affirmative action measures to redress imbalances within workforces. For present purposes, however, we are primarily interested in the Act's establishment of compulsory monitoring of workforces. In 1990 and 1991 all employers with more than 25 employees were required to register with the FEC, monitor the religious composition of their workforces and submit annual returns to the FEC. In 1992 this requirement was extended to employers with more than ten employees. At the time of our first survey these measures had been proposed and the opportunity was taken to assess attitudes to them; two years later, with the legislation implemented, we asked the same questions again to examine how much, if at all, attitudes had changed.

The second major piece of legislation, the Education Reform Order (1989), was the Northern Ireland version of the Education Reform Act (1988). As in England and Wales, the Northern Ireland Reform Order introduced a common curriculum and the devolution of greater financial management to schools (McClure, 1992), but whereas the Act covering England and Wales appeared to move away from the practice of multiculturalism in education (Cross, 1990), the Northern Ireland Reform Order contained a number of measures which were directly designed to help improve community relations. It obliged government, for the first time, to support initiatives to increase the number of integrated schools in Northern Ireland, that is, schools explicitly catering for both Protestants and Catholics. However, in recognition of the fact that, for the foreseeable future, most pupils in Northern Ireland will continue to be educated in non-integrated schools, the Reform Order introduced two cross-curricular themes on Education for Mutual Understanding (EMU) and Cultural Heritage to the common curriculum. Both of these themes specifically address issues of social division in Northern Ireland.

*Attitudes to fair employment*

We first look at attitudes to fair employment generally, and then go on to examine the pattern of attitudes to religious monitoring.

Although only one in ten Catholics and one in five Protestants admit to any personal prejudice against people of a different religious denomination, large majorities of both groups feel that prejudice against Catholics and against Protestants does exist. Views are more evenly divided, however, when we ask about the relative chances Protestants and Catholics have of getting a job:

> *Do Protestants and Catholics in Northern Ireland who apply for the same jobs have the **same** chance of getting a job or are their chances of getting a job different?*

|                 | 1989 | 1991 |
|-----------------|------|------|
|                 | %    | %    |
| Same chance     | 48   | 49   |
| Different chance| 42   | 40   |

Women are more likely than men to say that the chances Protestants and Catholics have of getting a job are the same, as are those who are either employed or retired in comparison with those who are unemployed. Perhaps not surprisingly, views on employment chances differ somewhat according to party identification: thus, 64 per cent of those who identify with the Official Unionist Party (OUP) say that the chances are equal, while 59 per cent of those who identify with the nationalist SDLP say that the chances are different. More fundamental than party differences are differences in perceptions between Protestants and Catholics:

> *Do Protestants and Catholics in Northern Ireland who apply for the same jobs have the **same** chance of getting a job or are their chances of getting a job different?*

|                 | Religious affiliation | | | | | |
|-----------------|-------|-------|-------|-------|-------|-------|
|                 | Protestant | | | Catholic | | |
|                 | 1986* | 1989 | 1991 | 1986* | 1989 | 1991 |
|                 | % | % | % | % | % | % |
| Same chance     | 68 | 60 | 62 | 26 | 30 | 29 |
| Different chance| 27 | 30 | 30 | 67 | 60 | 59 |

\* Source: Smith (1987)

Most Catholics continue to believe that Catholics and Protestants have a different chance of getting a job, while most Protestants believe they have the same chance. But the gap has diminished slightly since 1986.

Among those who feel employment chances are different, a clear majority feels that Protestants are more likely than Catholics to get a job: in 1991, 55 per cent of respondents felt this as opposed to only 23 per cent who felt that Catholics are more likely to get jobs than Protestants. Once again, views on this vary according to party identification: for instance 54 per cent of OUP identifiers say that Catholics are more likely than Protestants to get jobs while 84 per cent of SDLP identifiers say the reverse is more likely. And once again the views of Protestants and Catholics are far apart:

*Which group is more likely to get a job?*

| | | | | | Religious affiliation | | |
|---|---|---|---|---|---|---|---|
| | | Protestant | | | | Catholic | |
| | 1986[†] | 1989 | 1991 | | 1986[†] | 1989 | 1991 |
| | % | % | % | | % | % | % |
| Protestants | 28 | 31 | 26 | | 84 | 84 | 82 |
| Catholics | 25 | 39 | 49 | | - | * | 2 |
| Don't know/depends | 46 | 20 | 18 | | 16 | 10 | 11 |

[†] Source: Smith (1987). Percentages are based on those saying that chances are different
* = less than 0.5%

Overwhelmingly, Catholics feel that they bear the brunt of disadvantage. Protestants differ in their attitudes in two ways: first, the majority of Protestants feel that the labour market *does* provide equal opportunity; and secondly, of the minority of Protestants who believe that the labour market is unfair, roughly half think that Catholics are more likely to get a job, and one quarter that Protestants are. It seems that some Protestants believe in the existence of a segregated labour market where each side looks after its own (Osborne, 1991). Moreover, the proportion of Protestants believing that Catholics are at a relative *advantage* in the labour market has almost doubled since 1986; this may indicate a mistaken belief that the measures contained in the 1989 Fair Employment Act provide for positive discrimination in favour of Catholics (Cassidy, 1991).

So far we had asked only about the relative chances of Protestants and Catholics in the labour market. As a further check we asked respondents about perceived discrimination by employers against Protestants and Catholics separately.

**% believing that many employers are more likely to give jobs to...**

**Religious affiliation**

|                    | Protestant | | Catholic | |
|--------------------|-----------|------|---------|------|
|                    | 1989      | 1991 | 1989    | 1991 |
| ... Protestants    | %         | %    | %       | %    |
| a lot              | 6         | 11   | 26      | 31   |
| a little           | 43        | 50   | 54      | 53   |
| hardly at all      | 42        | 32   | 13      | 9    |
| ... Catholics      | %         | %    | %       | %    |
| a lot              | 13        | 13   | 5       | 9    |
| a little           | 44        | 54   | 43      | 57   |
| hardly at all      | 33        | 26   | 42      | 25   |

Overall, a majority of both Catholics and Protestants feel that many employers exhibit at least *some* religious prejudice in offering jobs. Eighty-four per cent of Catholics and 67 per cent of Protestants believe that employers are likely to discriminate against their denomination. Moreover, the proportion of both Catholics and Protestants believing this has risen since 1989. On the other hand, in 1989 around half of both Protestants and Catholics felt that many employers were more likely to give jobs to people in their own communities; and in 1991 this view too was even more prevalent, with about three in five Protestants and two in three Catholics endorsing it.

The survey results so far point to a fairly widespread perception in Northern Ireland that the labour market does not provide equal opportunities. It is clear too that this view is held to a different extent among Protestants and Catholics. There is, nonetheless, a consensus in favour of equal opportunity in employment. In 1991, when we asked respondents whether Protestants and Catholics who apply for the same job *should* have an equal chance, an overwhelming 92 per cent of Catholics and 97 per cent of Protestants said they should. This is important since there is evidence that, even in the quite recent past, some people were prepared to justify differential labour market opportunities in Northern Ireland (Nelson, 1975).

So the pattern of perceptions on the extent of fairness or unfairness in the Northern Ireland labour market is differentiated by denomination. But this phenomenon co-exists with a general belief that labour market opportunity *should* be fair. Given this background we now turn to attitudes to the Fair Employment legislation in Northern Ireland and, in particular, the measure requiring employers to monitor the religious composition of their workforces. At the time of the 1989 *Northern Ireland Social Attitudes* survey, the Bill was still under consideration by parliament, but we were able to ask respondents whether they supported or opposed a Fair Employment Law which would require employers to keep records of their employees' religion and make sure there was no discrimination.    In 1991 the same question was asked but this time referred to *the* Fair Employment Law:

**% saying they support or oppose the Fair Employment Law\* requiring employers to keep records of the religion of their employees**

|  | All | | Protestant | | Catholic | |
|---|---|---|---|---|---|---|
|  | **Religious affiliation** | | | | | |
|  | **1989** | **1991** | **1989** | **1991** | **1989** | **1991** |
|  | % | % | % | % | % | % |
| Support strongly | 31 | 45 | 20 | 31 | 47 | 67 |
| Support just a bit | 19 | 26 | 20 | 28 | 16 | 21 |
| Oppose just a bit | 12 | 10 | 14 | 14 | 10 | 4 |
| Oppose strongly | 26 | 13 | 33 | 20 | 16 | 3 |

\* In 1989, a Fair Employment Law

In 1989 around one in four Catholics opposed statutory religious monitoring of workforces, compared to nearly a half of Protestants.  By 1991 we see that opposition has dwindled within both communities. Indeed, support from Catholics has risen 25 percentage points since 1989, and perhaps more significantly, a majority of Protestants (59 per cent) support statutory monitoring in 1991, compared with 40 per cent in 1989.

   In line with these findings we see that support for religious monitoring of workforces has increased among SDLP identifiers from 71 per cent in 1989, to 89 per cent in 1991.  More significantly, perhaps, support among OUP identifiers has increased from 37 per cent in 1989 to 58 per cent in 1991.  While support for monitoring is strong across all age-groups, it is strongest among those aged 18-34.

   As already noted, at the time of the 1991 survey only firms with workforces of more than 25 employees were obliged to practice religious monitoring.  So it was possible that employees' attitudes could have been associated with participation or non-participation.  This is indeed the case, but it is among those employed in large workplaces that the level of support for statutory monitoring has increased most.

**% supporting or opposing the Fair Employment Law**

|  | Less than 10 | | 10-24 | | 25 or more | |
|---|---|---|---|---|---|---|
|  | **Number of employees at their workplace** | | | | | |
|  | **1989** | **1991** | **1989** | **1991** | **1989** | **1991** |
|  | % | % | % | % | % | % |
| Support | 53 | 64 | 53 | 75 | 48 | 74 |
| Oppose | 39 | 30 | 41 | 22 | 41 | 21 |

So far the main test of the success or failure of the 1989 Fair Employment Act has been the willingness of employers to collect information and submit returns to the Fair Employment Commission.

The FEC has published two rounds of monitoring data, for 1990 and 1991 (FEC, 1991; 1992) and, in this period, only one employer made a public, if temporary, stand in refusing to disclose monitoring figures. To that extent then, the monitoring provisions of the 1989 Act have been successfully implemented. Moreover the results of our survey point to a widening acceptance of monitoring within both communities.

## Education

As noted, the Education Reform (Northern Ireland) Order (1989) incorporated many of the reform measures already established in England and Wales, but with a number of different emphases to take account of issues peculiar to Northern Ireland. Thus the Northern Ireland reforms committed government to support the development of integrated schools for Protestants and Catholics by making it possible for an existing denominational school to adopt integrated status through a parental vote. In addition, the proposed common curriculum for Northern Ireland includes two compulsory cross-curricular themes with a community relations dimension, both of which are intended to reflect the pluralism of Northern Irish society. As part of these curricular initiatives, contact schemes between existing non-integregated schools are encouraged, though not compulsory.

In 1989 and 1991 we asked two sets of questions on educational issues. The first set covered attitudes to Protestant/Catholic contact and, in particular, attitudes to mixed or integrated schools, and the second explored attitudes to a plural curriculum.

In their analysis of attitudes to cross-community contact on the 1989 *Northern Ireland Social Attitudes* survey, Gallagher and Dunn (1991) found that, while most respondents favoured greater contact, there was in fact a relatively low level of cross-community contact in many aspects of social life. This general pattern of responses is confirmed by the results of the 1991 survey. But we find a high level of support for a pro-active approach to community relations: 90 per cent or more say that government and public bodies should do more to teach Catholic and Protestant children greater respect for each other and to create better community relations generally. We find also a high level of support for greater activity by governments and politicians on all sides to improve community relations.

When we move on to the specific area of education we find a similar picture. When asked whether they preferred more mixing or more separation in schools, a clear majority in both communities favoured more mixing. And in the Catholic community the majority for integrating more schools has grown.

| | Religious affiliation | | | |
| | Protestant | | Catholic | |
| % saying they favour more mixing in ... | 1989 | 1991 | 1989 | 1991 |
|---|---|---|---|---|
| ... primary schools | 65 | 67 | 68 | 74 |
| ... secondary and grammar schools | 68 | 69 | 73 | 81 |

Furthermore, over 60 per cent of both Catholics and Protestants feel that the government should actually *encourage* mixed schooling, and fewer than one in ten of both communities feel that the government should *discourage* mixed schooling.

However, on the question of whether respondents would prefer to send their *own* children to a mixed-religion school we find a more divided picture:

| | Religious affiliation | | | |
| | Protestant | | Catholic | |
| % saying they would prefer to send their children to a school that is ... | 1989 | 1991 | 1989 | 1991 |
|---|---|---|---|---|
| | % | % | % | % |
| ... own religion only | 41 | 45 | 37 | 42 |
| ... mixed religion | 52 | 50 | 54 | 49 |

Support for integrated schooling for one's own children drops to about a half among both Protestants and Catholics; and support has certainly not increased since 1989; if anything it has declined. So the proportion supporting the *principle* of integrated education and government encouragement of integration is somewhat higher than the proportion who would volunteer to try it out themselves.

Integrated schools in Northern Ireland are sometimes criticised for appealing only to the middle-classes. Our evidence does not lend support to this view. In 1989, 53 per cent of respondents in manual occupations and 60 per cent of those in non-manual occupations said they would prefer to send their children to a mixed-religion school. By 1991 these proportions had fallen to 48 per cent and 54 per cent respectively.

We now turn to the issue of a plural curriculum for schools in Northern Ireland. In 1989 and 1991 we asked respondents whether they believed that all pupils in secondary and grammar schools should have to study certain subjects. These included aspects of history, religious beliefs and Irish language and culture:

| | Religious affiliation | | | |
| | Protestant | | Catholic | |
| % agreeing that all secondary school pupils should have to study | 1989 | 1991 | 1989 | 1991 |
|---|---|---|---|---|
| The history of ... | | | | |
|     Northern Ireland | 74 | 80 | 69 | 82 |
|     Britain | 81 | 85 | 63 | 68 |
|     the Republic of Ireland | 51 | 57 | 71 | 73 |
| Protestant religious beliefs | 37 | 49 | 52 | 57 |
| Catholic religious beliefs | 29 | 35 | 60 | 63 |
| Religious beliefs in general* | | 71 | | 78 |
| Irish language and culture | 13 | 18 | 59 | 64 |

Most respondents believe that history teaching should reflect the overlap of interests in Northern Ireland. Thus majorities of both Catholics and Protestants agree that all post-primary pupils should be taught the history of Northern Ireland, Britain and the Republic of Ireland. There are, however, predictable differences in the degree of support reflecting community loyalties, with more Protestants than Catholics supporting the teaching of British history, and more Catholics than Protestants supporting the teaching of the history of the Irish Republic. Nonetheless the level of support for each of these two aspects of the history curriculum has risen between 1989 and 1991 for *both* religious groups.

When the focus switches to the next three items - the teaching of religious beliefs - the pattern is a little different. First, the level of support for such teaching, among both Protestants and Catholics, has risen between 1989 and 1991. Still, only around one-third of Protestants believe that all post-primary pupils should be taught Catholic religious beliefs, while more than a half (57 per cent) of Catholics favour the teaching to all of Protestant religious beliefs. That said, the proportion of Protestants who are *not* in favour of teaching Catholic religious beliefs to all post-primary school pupils has fallen from 52 per cent in 1989, to 42 per cent in 1991.

On the teaching of the Irish language and culture, Protestant opposition remains strong, with only 18 per cent believing it should be taught to all post-primary pupils.

Responses on these issues are also linked to party identification. As indicated above, supporters of all main political parties show high, and

---

* In 1989 this item was phrased "Non-denominational religious beliefs - not specifically Catholic or Protestant", which 39 per cent of Protestants and 53 per cent of Catholics agreed all secondary school pupils should have to study. In 1991 the wording was changed to "Religious beliefs in general - not specifically Catholic or Protestant". It seems likely that the change in wording has affected the distribution of responses, so that 1989 and 1991 figures for this item are not comparable; thus the 1989 figures have been omitted from the table itself.

increasing, levels of support for teaching the history of Northern Ireland and Britain. This is also true of teaching the history of the Republic of Ireland for all but DUP identifiers: among this group opinion is fairly evenly divided. In contrast, 58 per cent of OUP identifiers agree, and the level of agreement is higher still among Alliance and SDLP identifiers and among those who identify with no political party.

The pattern of responses is, however, a little more complex when we turn to the teaching of religious beliefs and Irish language and culture to all children:

**% saying they agree or disagree with the teaching to all children of ...**

| | | ...Protestant religious beliefs | | ...Catholic religious beliefs | | ...Irish language and culture | |
|---|---|---|---|---|---|---|---|
| | | 1989 | 1991 | 1989 | 1991 | 1989 | 1991 |
| **Party identification:** | | | | | | | |
| **DUP** | agree: | 52 | 60 | 29 | 25 | 13 | 15 |
| | disagree: | 32 | 21 | 54 | 57 | 69 | 73 |
| **OUP** | agree: | 40 | 50 | 35 | 37 | 13 | 13 |
| | disagree: | 41 | 30 | 46 | 40 | 70 | 71 |
| **SDLP** | agree: | 51 | 58 | 64 | 64 | 55 | 64 |
| | disagree: | 23 | 31 | 15 | 27 | 19 | 18 |
| **Alliance** | agree: | 31 | 51 | 33 | 48 | 21 | 30 |
| | disagree: | 58 | 32 | 57 | 33 | 56 | 40 |
| **None** | agree: | 39 | 44 | 39 | 42 | 44 | 43 |
| | disagree: | 44 | 36 | 44 | 35 | 41 | 35 |

Three main features are apparent from this table. First, the pattern of responses confirms the wide divergence of views on the teaching of Irish language and culture in schools; the extent of *disagreement* on this issue varies by 50 percentage points or more between those who identify with the SDLP and those who identify with either of the two main unionist parties. Secondly, these data show that DUP identifiers are particularly opposed to a plural curriculum in Northern Ireland. A clear majority of DUP identifiers *disagree* with the teaching of Irish language and culture, and with the teaching of Catholic religious beliefs, while a majority *agree* with the teaching of Protestant religious beliefs. While OUP identifiers are no less opposed to the teaching of Irish language and culture, they are more evenly divided on the teaching of Catholic religious beliefs.

The third main feature of these data concern those who identify with the Alliance party or who identify with no political party in Northern Ireland. It is among these two (small) groups of respondents that some of the most interesting changes in opinion have occurred. For example, in 1989 most Alliance supporters disagreed with the teaching of Protestant or Catholic religious beliefs (even-handedly), but in 1991 opinion had switched towards agreement (again even-handed). It may be that, in 1989, these respondents took the view that schools in Northern

Ireland should not dwell on issues that were potentially divisive.  Now
they seem to support the plural curriculum proposed by the educational
reforms.


**Conclusion**

In the three years since the *Northern Ireland Social Attitudes* survey was
launched, there have been significant developments in community
relations policy.  Our survey provides an opportunity to offer an initial
assessment of the impact of some of these measures, alongside an
examination of more general patterns of social attitudes in Northern
Ireland.

First, although aspects of the 1989 Fair Employment Act proved
controversial when initially proposed, in particular the provision requiring
employers to monitor the religious composition of their workforces, public
support for religious monitoring in Northern Ireland is now widespread.
These measures were already supported by a majority of Catholics in
1989, and that support has now consolidated and strengthened.  Perhaps
more significantly, Protestants' views on religious monitoring have
switched from opposition to support.

Second, we examined attitudes to a number of education reforms
introduced in 1989 and found a high degree of support for initiatives to
encourage greater contact and mutual respect among Protestants and
Catholics.  But a higher proportion agreed with the principle of mixed-
religion schools than would themselves actually prefer to send their
children to such schools.  Only one-half of respondents favour integrated
schooling for their own children.  Attitudes to a plural curriculum in
Northern Ireland are somewhat more diverse.  In general, Catholics are
more supportive than Protestants.  There is *general* support for pluralism
in the history curriculum, but somewhat more reluctance among
Protestants when it comes to the teaching of Catholic religious beliefs.
And, there is substantial Protestant opposition to the compulsory teaching
of Irish language and culture in secondary schools.

We uncovered too a variety of political and identity issues which
highlight the extent of social division in Northern Ireland.  Thus, religious
identity continues to underpin political partisanship and attitudes to the
constitutional future of Northern Ireland.  When results from Northern
Ireland and Britain are compared, we find just how much religion forms
a basis for social affiliation in Northern Ireland in contrast to Britain.
This carries over to the relatively high level of confidence the Northern
Irish have in socio-religious institutions such as churches and schools.
Nonetheless, the latest survey also points to an apparent optimism in
Northern Ireland that community relations are improving and are likely
to improve in the near future.  And, on the evidence we have, the
optimism may well be justified.  In several areas, according to our data,
positive change is not only possible but has begun taking place.

# References

Brooke, P. (1991), 'Opening Address', in Central Community Relations Unit (CCRU), *The Review of Employment Equity in Northern Ireland*, Belfast: CCRU.

Cassidy, F. (1991), 'Affirmative Action Options', Fair Employment Commission Paper presented to the IRS conference, Belfast.

Central Community Relations Unit (CCRU) (1991), *Community Relations in Northern Ireland*, Belfast: CCRU.

Cormack, R. J., Gallagher, A. M. and Osborne, R. D. (1991), 'Religious Affiliation and Educational Attainment in Northern Ireland: The Financing of Schools in Northern Ireland', Annex E in *Sixteenth Report of the Standing Advisory Commission of Human Rights*, House of Commons Paper 488, London: HMSO.

Cross, M. (ed.) (1990), 'Race and Educational Reform: Special Issue,' *New Community*, 16(3), pp. 331-446.

Curtice, J. and Gallagher, T. (1990), 'The Northern Irish Dimension', in Jowell, R., Witherspoon, S. and Brook, L. with Taylor, B. (eds.), *British Social Attitudes: the 7th Report*, Aldershot: Gower.

Fair Employment Commission (FEC) (1991), *A Profile of the Workforce in Northern Ireland: A Summary of the 1990 Monitoring Returns*, Belfast: FEC.

Fair Employment Commission (FEC) (1992), *A Profile of the Northern Ireland Workforce: Summary of the 1991 Monitoring Returns*, Belfast: FEC.

Gallagher, T. (1991), 'Justice and the Law in Northern Ireland', in Jowell, R., Brook, L. and Taylor, B. with Prior, G. (eds.), *British Social Attitudes: the 8th Report*, Aldershot: Dartmouth.

Gallagher, A. M. and Dunn, S. (1991), 'Community Relations in Northern Ireland: Attitudes to Contact and Integration', in Stringer, P. and Robinson, G. (eds.), *Social Attitudes in Northern Ireland 1990/91 Edition*, Belfast: Blackstaff.

Hayes, M. (1991), *Whither Cultural Diversity?*, Belfast: Community Relations Council.

MacClure, S. (1992), *Education Reformed: A Guide to the Education Reform Act*, London: Hodder and Stoughton.

McCartney, C. (1990), *Making Ripples: An Evaluation of the Inter-Community Contact Grant Scheme of the Northern Ireland Voluntary Trust*, Coleraine: University of Ulster.

Murray, D. and O'Neill, J. (1991), *Peace Building in a Political Impasse: Cross Border Links in Ireland*, Coleraine: University of Ulster.

Nelson, S. (1975), 'Protestant "Ideology" Considered: The Case of "Discrimination"', in Crewe, I. (ed.), *British Political Sociology Yearbook Volume 2: The Politics of Race*, London: Croom Helm.

Osborne, R. D. (1991), 'Discrimination and Fair Employment', in Stringer, P. and Robinson, G. (eds.), *Social Attitudes in Northern Ireland 1990/91 Edition*, Belfast: Blackstaff.

Smith, D. J. (1987), *Equality and Inequality in Northern Ireland, Part 3: Perceptions and Views*, London: Policy Studies Institute.

Stringer, P. and Robinson, G. (eds.) (1991), *Social Attitudes in Northern Ireland 1990/91 Edition*, Belfast: Blackstaff.

Stringer, P. and Robinson, G. (eds.) (1992), *Social Attitudes in Northern Ireland: The Second Report 1991-1992*, Belfast: Blackstaff.

# Acknowledgements

SCPR, our colleagues at the Policy Planning and Research Unit (PPRU), Belfast and at the Centre for Social Research (CSR) at Queen's University, Belfast, are grateful for the funding from the Central

Comunity Relations Unit and the Nuffield Foundation, which has enabled us to extend the *British Social Attitudes* survey series to Northern Ireland.

Fieldwork in Northern Ireland was again carried out by PPRU with its usual skill and efficiency, and we extend our thanks to the PPRU interviewers. In addition, we are grateful to our colleagues in SCPR, PPRU and CSR for their help in developing the Northern Ireland version of our questionnaire.

# 9 Class, race and opportunity

*Ken Young* [*]

One of the most hotly-contested questions in post-war Britain has been the extent to which the social policies of the welfare state, together with progressive taxation and a changing social climate, have brought about equality of opportunity. Sought by successive Labour and Conservative governments, it might almost be said that equality of opportunity has been the *leitmotif* of modern domestic politics, whether the issue is the relief of extreme poverty, or the constriction of ordinary life by limited horizons and racial prejudice. Britain has long been widely perceived as a class-based society, both by foreign critics and by domestic reformers (Tawney, 1931; Westergaard and Resler, 1975; Weiner, 1982). All three major political parties concede the point by employing, in their different ways, the rhetoric of equality of opportunity.

John Major's aspiration to create a classless society is just the latest and most explicit of such commitments. Whether or not such ambitions lie within the grasp of *any* government (or indeed are logically consistent with other aspirations) are important questions but not to be dealt with here. What we can do is assess the magnitude of the task. Much recent commentary conveys an impression that the Prime Minister has made a canny choice: by riding the tide of social change, which is surely tending towards the erosion of class, his strategy (it is claimed) is heading towards ineluctable success. However, as this chapter shows, social class divisions are by no means as fluid as is sometimes thought. Rather, class appears

[*] Professor of Politics and Vice-Principal, Queen Mary and Westfield College, University of London.

to be a pervasive, persistent and immutable feature of British social life (Reid, 1989).

If the divisions of social class were the sole concern of egalitarians, the problem of eradicating them would still be formidable enough. Yet the old problems of poverty, exclusion and discrimination took on a new form with the arrival, principally in the 1950s and early 1960s, of economic migrants from the Caribbean and the Indian sub-continent and later of dispossessed refugees from East Africa. The clichéd Disraelian reference to the 'two nations' gained a new significance as successive surveys uncovered the extent of prejudice towards and discrimination against minority groups in what was increasingly accurately described as 'black and white Britain'.

We do not deal in the *British Social Attitudes* series with the measurable realities of exclusion and discrimination; other surveys, most notably by the Policy Studies Institute, have helped to establish the facts of discrimination and disadvantage (Daniel, 1968; Smith, 1976; Brown, 1984). But we have asked, in most survey rounds since 1983, a series of questions about class identification and racial prejudice; about the extent to which social class and race are perceived to affect opportunities; and about the extent to which their effects are seen to be increasing or diminishing.

When we ask respondents how 'close' they feel to other people of the same social class, ethnic group, area, age, religious background or political beliefs, most people choose class or race in preference to the other characteristics. And it was the pre-eminence of class and race in social divisions that prompted us to present and discuss our findings on class, race and opportunity more fully this year than previously and to take stock of the trends in British society which they reveal. Practical policy and political rhetoric alike will need in future to accommodate themselves to the picture which emerges.

## A sense of class

That it is feasible to ask questions about the effects of a person's social class on their opportunities, and to elicit answers from the great majority - around 98 per cent - of respondents, testifies to the ubiquity of a sense of class. Nor is this ready ability to locate oneself in the class structure a mere convenience. The majority (58 per cent) of respondents to our 'solidarity' question profess to feeling 'very' or 'fairly close' to other people of the same social class background as themselves, with manual workers slightly more inclined than people in non-manual jobs to feel a 'very close' affinity.

Equally striking is the *persistence* of this sense of class. Despite great changes in the patterns of work and the continuing contraction of blue-collar or manual employment,[1] the expectation that class divisions would thereby be eroded has yet to be fulfilled. Certainly there is little indication in the last eight years that subjective (or self-assigned) social class has responded to changes in these and other patterns. Rather, the picture is one of remarkable stability.

> *Most people see themselves as belonging to a particular social class. Please look at this card and tell me which social class you would say you belong to.*

|  | 1983 | 1984 | 1985 | 1986 | 1987 | 1989 | 1991 |
|---|---|---|---|---|---|---|---|
|  | % | % | % | % | % | % | % |
| Upper middle | 1 | 2 | 2 | 1 | 2 | 1 | 2 |
| Middle | 24 | 25 | 26 | 24 | 26 | 28 | 27 |
| Upper working | 23 | 19 | 19 | 21 | 21 | 21 | 18 |
| Working | 46 | 48 | 47 | 48 | 46 | 44 | 46 |
| Poor | 3 | 3 | 4 | 3 | 3 | 3 | 4 |
| Don't know | 3 | 2 | 2 | 2 | 1 | 2 | 2 |

Thus around two-thirds of our respondents have classified themselves as 'upper working class' or 'working class' every year since 1983. And almost all the rest (around a quarter) classify themselves as middle class.

The apparent fixity of the overall distribution of social class identity is not in itself evidence of social immobility, for it is possible that a high level of upward and downward mobility - in the sense of change in personal fortunes - might be self-cancelling and thus concealed within this pattern. We have therefore regularly followed up with the question: "Which social class would you say your parents belonged to when you started at primary school?" If we compare the social class to which respondents assign themselves with that to which they judge their parents to have belonged, we see a modicum of movement both over the last eight years and from schooldays to the present.

|  | 1983 | | 1991 | |
|---|---|---|---|---|
|  | Parents' social class | Own social class | Parents' social class | Own social class |
|  | % | % | % | % |
| Upper middle | 2 }18 | 1 }26 | 3 }21 | 2 }29 |
| Middle | 16 | 24 | 19 | 27 |
| Upper working | 12 }70 | 23 }69 | 11 }70 | 18 }64 |
| Working | 58 | 46 | 59 | 46 |
| Poor | 9 | 3 | 7 | 4 |
| Don't know | 2 | 3 | 1 | 2 |

In 1983, virtually the same proportion of respondents said they were working or upper working class as said their parents were; by 1991 there was a gap of six percentage points.

It is perhaps surprising, given the changes in lifestyle and increase in living standards that most respondents will have witnessed over their lifetimes, that the sense of social mobility is not more widespread. As many as 82 per cent of respondents do not consider themselves to have crossed the boundary between the working and middle classes; around one in ten claim to have achieved a degree of upward social mobility, and four per cent claim to have moved downward. Although there are advances on the 1983 survey, this is hardly a society in flux, in which ebb and flow across class boundaries simply creates an *impression* of stability. Rather, the reality is mundane: people generally consider themselves to have remained pretty much in the class into which they were born. A sense of class in Britain thus resembles an inherited characteristic, like race or gender, from which it is self-evidently very difficult to escape.

### Social class and opportunities today

In *The 1986 Report* we showed the extent to which respondents to the first three surveys saw Britain as a class-bound society (Airey and Brook, 1986). The overall picture at that stage was one of little change over the years, but of increasing pessimism as to the extent to which social class determines opportunities. That brief interim report referred to the revealed pattern of class *discrimination*. Although this term is technically justifiable, it is probably better reserved for situations in which opportunities are actually limited by exclusionary judgements or behaviour, based on perceived class features such as accent or appearance.[2]

Perhaps we should not be surprised to find large numbers of people believing that social class affects an individual's opportunities in life, for there is a degree of circularity in the claim: an individual's social class is perceived as a bundle of life chances, which may be greater and more lavish, or less and more constricted, than those of another. The important issue is whether or not individuals can overcome the initial disadvantages of class background to secure their own advancement in life, which is a matter of movement at the margin. It is of great interest, then, whether or not that margin of freedom is seen as broadening or remaining static over the course of time.

We asked: "To what extent do you think a person's social class affects his or her opportunities in Britain today?" As the next table shows, only between a quarter and a third of respondents in each survey round regard social class as unimportant, and while the responses have fluctuated, they have done so within so small a range that no trend can confidently be discerned. Even the 1991 figures which appear to indicate a notable increase in the perception of class disadvantage to the highest levels since the survey series began, might well be just another fluctuation.

**Effect of social class on opportunities, 1983-81**

|              | 1983 | 1984 | 1985 | 1986 | 1987 | 1989 | 1991 |
|--------------|------|------|------|------|------|------|------|
|              | %    | %    | %    | %    | %    | %    | %    |
| A great deal | 25   | 25   | 29   | 24   | 28   | 27   | 27   |
| Quite a lot  | 45   | 38   | 37   | 40   | 39   | 42   | 47   |
| Not very much| 25   | 28   | 27   | 28   | 27   | 25   | 21   |
| Not at all   | 3    | 6    | 4    | 5    | 5    | 4    | 3    |

These aggregate figures conceal differences between sub-groups within the sample. The over-64s, for instance, are rather less inclined to concede importance to social class than are younger respondents; Labour and - to a rather greater extent - Liberal Democrat identifiers see class as a more important shaper of opportunities than do Conservative identifiers; manual workers have a sharper sense of class disadvantage than do non-manual workers.

In each of our survey years we also asked supplementary questions about whether social class has a greater effect on opportunities today than it did ten years previously, and whether it will be more important or less important in ten years' time. Paradoxically, despite the sharper sense of class disadvantage registered in 1991, the perception of the *past* importance of social class has changed in the other direction. That is, although people are more inclined now than in previous years to see class as important, four out of five think it was *even more important* ten years ago than it is now. Moreover, the 1991 results show the highest expectation since the 1983 survey that class will be less important in ten years' time than it is today; one in three respondents make this forecast.

Asking about the importance of class today, in the past and in the future, enables us to ascertain respondents' views of the overall trend. Not surprisingly, most see the importance of class as relatively constant, or subject to a linear trend: few consider that the direction of change will alter. The table below summarises these shifting perceptions of change. Our surveys in the mid-1980s revealed the greatest pessimism about the persistence of class divisions. Now, it seems, there is at least a sense that Britain is moving, albeit gradually, away from a situation in which opportunities are rigidly circumscribed by birth.

| The effect of social class on opportunities is now: | 1983 % | 1987 % | 1991 % |
|---|---|---|---|
| worse than past - will get still worse | 10 | 16 | 10 |
| worse than past - will stay same | 8 }21 | 7 }25 | 7 }20 |
| worse than past - will get better | 4 | 2 | 2 |
| same as past - will get worse | 5 | 6 | 3 |
| same as past - will stay same | 33 }45 | 31 }42 | 30 }38 |
| same as past - will get better | 8 | 5 | 7 |
| better than past - will get worse | 1 | 1 | 1 |
| better than past - will stay same | 9 }30 | 9 }28 | 12 }40 |
| better than past - will get still better | 20 | 17 | 25 |

Again, it is important to consider where these changes in the direction of a greater optimism are to be found. As the table below shows, people in every social class have become more sanguine, but it is principally white-collar workers who are most likely to proclaim that class is losing its importance.

**Importance of social class compared with recent past, 1985-1991**

| Percentage point change since 1985 in % saying: | All | I/II | Social Class III non-manual | III manual | IV/V |
|---|---|---|---|---|---|
| More important | -5 | -6 | -6 | -9 | - |
| Less important | +11 | +15 | +14 | +8 | +4 |
| No change | -5 | -8 | -8 | +1 | -2 |

We can expect, on this evidence, further shifts in the same direction for (as already noted) the class structure is itself changing slowly away from manual towards non-manual occupations. Thus the perception of 'classlessness' - itself a relative, rather than an absolute term - is likely to continue to increase.

So, John Major's commitment to a classless society has on its side not only trends in British society but also their knock-on effects on the pattern of social expectations. Nevertheless, such movement as there is is not being driven by changing perceptions, nor - according to our surveys -by dramatic increases in what might be termed *achieved mobility*, but by slow changes in the occupational structure leading to an expectation of improvement. Yet these changes are too gradual, and the expectations too fragile, to guarantee any eventual political payoffs. They must also be read against the bedrock belief that Britain is still a class-bound society in which a person's social origins are one of the primary determinants of his or her opportunities.

## Racial prejudice and discrimination

If class mobility seems beyond the reach of the great majority of white people, those from black and Asian minorities have the additional factors of racial prejudice and discrimination to contend with. In 1984, in the first *British Social Attitudes* report, we reported high levels of awareness of racial discrimination and a surprisingly high proportion of respondents who were prepared to admit to personal prejudice against blacks and Asians (Airey, 1984).

We asked all respondents: "First, thinking of Asians - that is, people whose families were originally from India and Pakistan - who now live in Britain. Do you think there is a lot of prejudice against them in Britain nowadays, a little, or hardly any?" We then followed with a parallel question about "black people - that is people whose families were originally from the West Indies or Africa". The responses can be compared with those to the question about social class and opportunities, for the run of answers from 1983 to 1991 show a similar remarkable stability in the perceptions of racial prejudice. Around half the respondents think there is a lot of prejudice against black people, and slightly more think this to be the case for Asians. A further third think there is a little prejudice against both. Even more remarkably, only a very small proportion of the British - fewer than one in ten both eight years ago and now - see their society as prejudice-free.

| | **Perceived prejudice against:** | | | | | |
| | **Asians** | | | **Blacks** | | |
| | 1983 | 1987 | 1991 | 1983 | 1987 | 1991 |
| | % | % | % | % | % | % |
| A lot | 54 | 62 | 58 | 50 | 57 | 50 |
| A little | 37 | 30 | 35 | 40 | 33 | 41 |
| Hardly any | 6 | 6 | 4 | 7 | 7 | 7 |
| Don't know/ other answer | 3 | 2 | 3 | 3 | 2 | 3 |

We also asked a pair of more specific questions about the extent to which people of Asian and West Indian origin 'are not given jobs these days because of their race'. Prior to 1991, each of the readings showed that around 60 per cent of the sample believed that such discrimination existed. The latest figures suggest something of an increase in perceptions of discrimination (64 per cent in respect of Asians and 69 per cent in respect of West Indians). This may or may not signal a trend.

Another indication of the extent of perceived disadvantage is given by our 1990 question, reported in *The 8th Report* (Brook and Cape, 1991, pp. 189-90) on the treatment that an innocent 'black person' or an innocent 'white person' might expect from the courts. Forty-two per cent of respondents (58 per cent of the small number of black and Asian respondents) thought a black person was more likely to be found guilty of a crime they did not commit than was a white person. Interestingly, expectations about *class* disadvantage by the criminal justice system are even more widespread; 56 per cent think a poor person more likely to be found guilty than a rich person of a crime they did not commit.

As with social class, the consistent year-on-year figures for the perceived *extent* of prejudice mask a quite different picture of the perceived *trend* in levels of prejudice, at its highest in the mid 1980s. Since then there has been a sharp decline in the proportion of respondents thinking that prejudice is more widespread now than five years earlier. As many as a quarter of respondents to the most recent survey (the largest proportion in the time series) believe that there is less prejudice today than five years ago.

**Prejudice in Britain today, compared with five years ago**

|                | 1983 | 1984 | 1985 | 1986 | 1987 | 1989 | 1990 | 1991 |
|----------------|------|------|------|------|------|------|------|------|
|                | %    | %    | %    | %    | %    | %    | %    | %    |
| More now       | 45   | 40   | 38   | 49   | 50   | 31   | 32   | 24   |
| Less now       | 16   | 20   | 20   | 12   | 13   | 21   | 20   | 24   |
| About the same | 36   | 37   | 39   | 36   | 35   | 44   | 45   | 50   |

These changes in perceptions of immediate past trends are complemented by a shift towards greater optimism for the future. Asked if there will be more, less, or about the same amount of racial prejudice in Britain in five years time, responses for 1991 show that for the first time in the survey series, optimists outnumber pessimists; but as in the case of past trends, those who perceive stasis comfortably outnumber those who perceive change in either direction.

**Prejudice in Britain in five years' time, compared with today**

|                     | 1983 | 1984 | 1985 | 1986 | 1987 | 1989 | 1990 | 1991 |
|---------------------|------|------|------|------|------|------|------|------|
|                     | %    | %    | %    | %    | %    | %    | %    | %    |
| More in 5 years' time | 42   | 40   | 42   | 46   | 46   | 32   | 37   | 21   |
| Less                | 17   | 18   | 18   | 13   | 12   | 19   | 20   | 25   |
| About the same      | 36   | 38   | 35   | 36   | 37   | 45   | 39   | 50   |

We do not have data for 1980-81, the years in which serious disturbances - generally seen as racial in nature - broke out in British cities. However, there were further riots in 1985, leading perhaps to a short-lived increase in pessimism as to the future of race relations in Britain. The following table provides a possible indication of such an upheaval in expectations.

| Racial prejudice in Britain is now: | 1983 % | 1987 % | 1991 % |
|---|---|---|---|
| worse than past - will get still worse | 30 ⎫ | 36 ⎫ | 13 ⎫ |
| worse than past - will stay same | 10 ⎬43 | 10 ⎬48 | 8 ⎬23 |
| worse than past - will get better | 3 ⎭ | 2 ⎭ | 2 ⎭ |
| same as past - will get worse | 10 ⎫ | 9 ⎫ | 7 ⎫ |
| same as past - will stay same | 21 ⎬36 | 22 ⎬34 | 33 ⎬49 |
| same as past - will get better | 4 ⎭ | 3 ⎭ | 8 ⎭ |
| better than past - will get worse | 1 ⎫ | 1 ⎫ | 1 ⎫ |
| better than past - will stay same | 5 ⎬16 | 4 ⎬12 | 8 ⎬24 |
| better than past - will get still better | 10 ⎭ | 7 ⎭ | 15 ⎭ |

The latest figures should be interpreted with caution until future results establish whether or not they represent a trend or just another fluctuation. But on the face of it, there does appear to have been a very sharp drop in pessimism about the future of race relations in Britain.

We also asked respondents to rate their own levels of racial prejudice, enabling us to make comparisons both over time and between different social groups. Some movement since 1983 is discernible, and the 1991 figures show a decrease in reported prejudice. Still, almost a third of the sample admit to being either 'very prejudiced' or 'a little prejudiced' against people of other races.

*How would you describe yourself ... as very prejudiced against people of other races, a little prejudiced or not prejudiced at all?*

|  | 1983 % | 1987 % | 1991 % |
|---|---|---|---|
| Very prejudiced | 4 | 4 | 2 |
| A little prejudiced | 31 | 34 | 29 |
| Not prejudiced at all | 64 | 60 | 68 |

Small changes in overall response mask larger shifts among population subgroups. Only a quarter of Labour identifiers admit to any degree of prejudice, compared with a third of Liberal Democrats and as many as 40 per cent of Conservatives. This represents a widening of party differences since 1983. Fewer women than men admit to racial prejudice; 72 per cent claim to be 'not prejudiced at all', compared with 63 per cent of men. Women are also slightly more gloomy about both past and future trends in the prevalence of discrimination (although this, interestingly, is a recent development).

We examined the data for evidence of whether racial prejudice was more common among the older generations, but the age relationship was in fact slight. However, this bald finding may be misleading, and may owe more to the fact that, having grown up in a different social climate, less explicit on matters of race, older people may understand 'prejudice' in different ways. Indeed, our other indirect indicators of prejudice - attitudes to matters of policy or social contact - show older people to be *substantially* more prejudiced than younger people. We may come closer to eliciting 'actual' prejudice when we ask rather sharper questions about how people would react to the admission of people from ethnic minority groups into positions of authority at work or into the intimacy of the family.

We asked half of the respondents who described themselves as 'white' whether they thought 'most white people' would mind if a suitably qualified person of Asian origin were appointed as their boss; and then whether they thought most white people would mind if one of their close relatives were to marry a person of Asian origin; we then also asked if they would *personally* mind in each case. The remaining half of the 'white' respondents were asked parallel questions to gauge feelings about West Indian bosses and marriage partners.

Our findings show that respondents make a sharp distinction between inter-racial contact in the workplace and in the family, both in their assumptions about other people's reactions and in their own reactions. Many more respondents thought that 'most white people' would object to a West Indian or Asian person marrying into their family than thought they would object to a West Indian or Asian boss.

| | 1983 | 1984 | 1986 | 1989 | 1991 |
|---|---|---|---|---|---|
| **% saying 'most white people' would mind 'a little' or 'a lot':** | | | | | |
| **Person of West Indian origin...** | | | | | |
| ... as boss | 54 | 58 | 54 | 53 | 51 |
| ... in the family | 79 | 81 | 76 | 78 | 75 |
| **Person of Asian origin...** | | | | | |
| ... as boss | 54 | 54 | 56 | 57 | 52 |
| ... in the family | 77 | 76 | 79 | 80 | 74 |

Asked whether they themselves would mind, respondents display both a greater claimed level of *personal* egalitarianism than they attribute to other people, and a movement in favour of greater egalitarianism more particularly in respect of West Indians. Intense personal hostility (that is, mind 'a lot') to a black or Asian marrying into the family has dropped around 10 points between 1983 and 1991. Such movement is, however, small relative to the high levels of reported prejudice; for instance, as many as two in five people would still mind, and half of those 'a lot', if a close relative were to choose a black or Asian marriage partner.

| % of respondents minding 'a little' or 'a lot': | 1983 | 1984 | 1986 | 1989 | 1991 |
|---|---|---|---|---|---|
| **Person of West Indian origin:** | | | | | |
| ... as boss | 20 | 20 | 18 | 20 | 12 |
| ... in the family | 57 | 51 | 46 | 52 | 44 |
| **Person of Asian origin:** | | | | | |
| ... as boss | 19 | 22 | 17 | 20 | 14 |
| ... in the family | 51 | 53 | 50 | 49 | 43 |

The large differences between the relatively widespread acceptability of a West Indian or Asian boss and the widespread opposition to a West Indian or Asian marriage partner suggests that there is less prejudice at the workplace compared with that which lurks at home. Interestingly, the respondent's employment sector appears to make little difference to the acceptability of a boss from an ethnic minority; so there is little sign here of any effects of the generally higher profile accorded to equal opportunities in public sector organisations.

A clue as to just how good a measure of prejudice the self-rated question is can be found in the following table. It turns out to be a very sound predictor of whether or not people display racist preferences, insofar as it clearly distinguishes between the highly prejudiced and the slightly prejudiced. Whereas there is almost no propensity among those who describe themselves as *non*-prejudiced to object to a black or Asian boss, around a third even of this group *would* mind a black or Asian marrying into their family; on the other hand, this compares with some three-quarters of those who describe themselves as prejudiced, around one in three of whom would also object to a black or Asian boss.

| % of respondents minding 'a little' or 'a lot': | All | Self rated prejudice | |
|---|---|---|---|
| | | Prejudiced* | Non-prejudiced |
| **Person of West Indian origin:** | | | |
| ... as boss | 12 | 29 | 3 |
| ... in the family | 44 | 72 | 31 |
| **Person of Asian origin:** | | | |
| ... as boss | 14 | 33 | 5 |
| ... in the family | 43 | 74 | 29 |

* Prejudiced 'a lot' or 'a little'

As in 1984, those who describe themselves as 'prejudiced' are also more likely to ascribe prejudice to 'most people', although (as before) the pattern is not nearly so distinct.

The overall pattern of the results reported above would lead us to expect inter-generational differences in willingness to accept a West Indian or Asian person marrying into the family, and this is indeed very much the case. Respondents aged 55 and over, whether male or female, are more than twice as likely as those aged under 35 to say that they would mind 'a lot'.

| Whether respondents would mind: | All | Men | | | Women | | |
|---|---|---|---|---|---|---|---|
| | | 18-34 | 35-54 | 55+ | 18-34 | 35-54 | 55+ |
| **a West Indian person in the family** | % | % | % | % | % | % | % |
| Mind a lot | 20 | 7 | 17 | 25 | 11 | 18 | 36 |
| Mind a little | 24 | 23 | 28 | 26 | 12 | 28 | 24 |
| Not mind | 53 | 69 | 49 | 42 | 76 | 53 | 36 |
| **an Asian person in the family** | % | % | % | % | % | % | % |
| Mind a lot | 21 | 13 | 22 | 29 | 13 | 15 | 29 |
| Mind a little | 22 | 13 | 24 | 26 | 17 | 29 | 23 |
| Not mind | 53 | 70 | 53 | 41 | 69 | 51 | 41 |

## Race relations policies

Race relations policy, backed up by law, seeks to reduce discrimination and, in the longer term, to reduce prejudice. Since the mid-1960s British policies on race have been characterised by two purportedly complementary strands (Brown, 1983; Young, 1983). The first of these is the tightening of immigration controls to stabilise the number of 'immigrants' in Britain. The second is the introduction of measures to help secure equality of opportunity through anti-discrimination laws, and through funding programmes targeted on areas in which ethnic minorities are concentrated.

How well has support for these policies stood up over the years? A number of questions in the survey series provide evidence. We can assess support for anti-discrimination laws from a question we ask regularly as to whether or not respondents support a law against 'racial discrimination, that is giving unfair preference to a particular race...'. We also ask regularly whether Britain gives 'too much', 'too little' or 'about the right amount' of 'help to Asians and West Indians who have settled in this country'. And we have a regular question too on support for restricting or allowing more immigration of Asian and West Indian people (and other nationalities, not mentioned here). The time-series of answers to each of the four questions is shown below.

| % supporting: | 1983 | 1984 | 1986 | 1989 | 1990 | 1991 |
|---|---|---|---|---|---|---|
| Anti-discrimination law | 69 | 70 | 65 | 68 | 68 | 76 |
| More or same aid to Asians and West Indians | 62 | n/a | 60 | 56 | 61 | 62 |
| Less Asian immigration | 71 | 74 | 68 | 67 | 62 | n/a |
| Less West Indian immigration | 67 | 69 | 64 | 62 | 58 | n/a |

n/a = not asked

Apart from the 1991 upturn in support for the law against racial discrimination, support for the three strands of race policy has remained firm throughout the series. There is virtually no support for increased settlement, and large majorities support continued restriction of immigration. That these majorities have reduced somewhat is not surprising when considered against the substantial fall in the rate of immigration from the Indian subcontinent and the Caribbean.[3] But large majorities also support the anti-discrimination law and the policy of helping those people who have settled in Britain from India, Pakistan and the West Indies. The public appears therefore broadly to support the 'restrict and aid' strategies of successive governments.

On this issue there are much stronger associations with the age of the respondent than on any other race-related measure, stronger by far than those with party identification which are often thought to be the key influence on views about immigration. The table below shows stronger backing among younger respondents (under 35) for the generally ill-supported proposition that *more* aid should be provided to help people who have settled in Britain, as well as markedly more liberal attitudes than those held by respondents aged over 55 on all four measures.

| | Age | | | | | |
|---|---|---|---|---|---|---|
| | 18-24 | 25-34 | 35-44 | 45-54 | 55-64 | 65+ |
| % supporting (1991): | | | | | | |
| Anti-discrimination law | 85 | 82 | 82 | 73 | 69 | 67 |
| More aid to people who have settled | 27 | 20 | 9 | 8 | 8 | 7 |
| % supporting (1990):* | | | | | | |
| Less WI immigration | 41 | 51 | 56 | 60 | 72 | 64 |
| Less Asian immigration | 50 | 59 | 59 | 62 | 73 | 67 |

*These questions were not asked in 1991

As usual, we cannot tell whether this marks the start of a new mood of liberalism in Britain or whether the young will revert as they get older.

**Class and political protest**

We now return to the subject of class, viewed from another angle. In the first of this series, *The 1984 Report*, we introduced the concept of political efficacy, an individual's sense that he or she has the resources and the confidence to shape, either alone or with others, the course of events (Young, 1984). In their pioneering study of *The Civic Culture*, Gabriel Almond and Sidney Verba had explored this sense of efficacy - or personal political competence, as they termed it - noting that many people feel themselves to have no avenues of influence open to them, or consider governmental affairs to lie beyond their reach (Almond and Verba, 1963). We reproduced Almond and Verba's key question on political efficacy - the extent to which the respondent would take action to oppose some "harmful or unjust" law that was under consideration - in our 1983 survey, repeated it in 1986 and again in 1991. The responses in that first year indicated that such social resources as occupation, education and income, as well as employment status and unionisation, bore heavily upon the individual's sense of political power or powerlessness, and upon the strategies he or she might choose to influence events.

Faced with the prospect of a proposed law they considered to be unjust or harmful, respondents were invited to choose up to eight courses of action in response. These fell into two groups. First were those whose effectiveness was not contingent upon any other like-minded people acting similarly but was entirely personal: contacting their MP, speaking to an influential person, contacting a government department, or contacting the press, radio or television. The second group of strategies depended for their effectiveness upon collective action: signing a petition, raising the issue in an organisation, taking part in a protest or demonstration, or forming a group of like-minded people.

Comparing the results for the three survey rounds, we find some notable increases in the extent to which people generally are prepared to exert themselves against a proposed unjust or harmful action by government by engaging in some course of action - whether lobbying someone, signing a petition or demonstrating - and a continuing fall in the proportion who say they would do nothing (from 32 per cent in the unprompted 1959 study to a mere handful in 1991)[4].

| % taking each action | 1983 | 1986 | 1991 |
|---|---|---|---|
| **Personal action:** | | | |
| Contact MP | 46 | 52 | 48 |
| Speak to influential person | 10 | 15 | 17 |
| Contact government department | 7 | 12 | 11 |
| Contact radio, TV or newspaper | 14 | 15 | 14 |
| **Collective action:** | | | |
| Sign petition | 54 | 65 | 78 |
| Raise issue in an organisation I belong to | 9 | 10 | 9 |
| Go on a protest or demonstration | 8 | 11 | 14 |
| Form a group of like-minded people | 6 | 8 | 7 |
| **None of these** | 12 | 10 | 6 |

These figures confirm the expectation raised by the 1983 figures, that Britain is becoming a more active and assertive society certainly by comparison with the 1960s. Almond and Verba's original conclusions about political acquiesence in Britain have been overturned by cultural change (see Topf, 1989; Almond and Verba, 1980).

*The 1984 Report* explored some of the more striking differences in the responses of different social groups, although many others - including sharp contrasts between the age groups among both men and women - were not reported due to the constraints of space. That report also developed a simple formula for the separate summary of personal and collective political efficacy scores, calculated as follows:

$$\frac{P - i}{n} \quad \text{or} \quad \frac{C - i}{n}$$

where P is the number of 'personal' actions mentioned, C the number of 'collective' actions, $i$ is the number of persons choosing none of the proffered courses of action and $n$ is the total number of respondents in that sub-group. The Personal Action Index (PAI) and Collective Action Index (CAI) scores below thus permit a sharp differentiation between groups, being sensitive both to the total number of actions chosen from among the portfolio and to the number of abstainers. The scores for the whole sample in each year illustrate the changes.

| | 1983 | 1986 | 1992 |
|---|---|---|---|
| Personal Action Index (PAI) score | 0.64 | 0.83 | 0.84 |
| Collective Action Index (CAI) score | 0.65 | 0.83 | 1.01 |

Turning to the sub-groups, and taking our principal interest in class comparisons first, we see the persistence of marked disparities in the PAI and CAI scores according to social class. For the PAI scores in particular, the gradients are predictable and quite steep.

|  | PAI | | | CAI | | |
|---|---|---|---|---|---|---|
|  | 1983 | 1986 | 1991 | 1983 | 1986 | 1991 |
| Social Class: | | | | | | |
| I | 0.83 | 0.96 | 1.15 | 0.86 | 1.02 | 1.06 |
| II | 0.83 | 1.07 | 1.07 | 0.76 | 0.97 | 1.21 |
| III Non-manual | 0.75 | 0.87 | 0.95 | 0.55 | 0.77 | 1.00 |
| III Manual | 0.59 | 0.69 | 0.75 | 0.61 | 0.75 | 0.98 |
| IV | 0.52 | 0.67 | 0.71 | 0.37 | 0.54 | 0.76 |
| V | 0.35 | 0.63 | 0.52 | 0.91 | 0.89 | 1.01 |
| All | 0.64 | 0.83 | 0.84 | 0.65 | 0.83 | 1.01 |

Our earlier findings of social class differences in perceived opportunities and in the expectation of fair treatment by social institutions are therefore reinforced by the discrepancies in personal political efficacy between the social classes.

Class is by no means the only source of difference in personal political efficacy. Gender inequalities and gender differences have often been discovered in the course of this series, and women's sense that they lack political clout is reflected in men's and women's 1991 PAI scores of 0.91 and 0.78 respectively. Men and women do not, however, differ in their CAI scores (1.00 for men and 1.01 for women in 1991).

This is also a realm in which age matters. People in the youngest and oldest age groups lack the political resources of those in the middle-age groups, the young because they have yet to acquire a stable place in society and to experience the influence it bestows, the old because they have to some extent lost it (through absence from the labour market or, for many of the oldest, through dependency) and also because their formative experiences were those of a more quiescent, accepting generation. The combination of age and gender is apparent from the following table, which shows men of all age groups except the very oldest to have high personal and collective political efficacy scores, while women have a more expected pattern with efficacy at its peak in the 25-44 age groups, and particularly low efficacy scores in the oldest age group.

**PAI and CAI scores by age within sex, 1991**

|  | PAI | | CAI | |
|  | Men | Women | Men | Women |
|---|---|---|---|---|
| Age group: | | | | |
| 18-24 | 0.94 | 0.62 | 1.21 | 1.11 |
| 25-34 | 0.97 | 0.90 | 1.03 | 1.23 |
| 35-44 | 0.83 | 0.96 | 1.10 | 1.22 |
| 45-54 | 1.00 | 0.87 | 1.07 | 1.11 |
| 55-64 | 1.00 | 0.82 | 1.01 | 0.89 |
| over 65 | 0.75 | 0.48 | 0.69 | 0.51 |

The number of ethnic minority respondents in any one survey round is too small to enable us to make a corresponding calculation, but this is an issue which would amply repay separate study. What is clear so far is that political efficacy is affected more by social class status and its correlates (income, education) than by even the sharply contrasting age and gender groups. Class, then, is paramount in shaping political competence and the willingness to resist unwelcome legislative changes. We would expect race to matter too, particularly for the older generations many of whom may still think of themselves as 'immigrants' - with the inevitable deficit in active citizenship that such a label implies.

## Conclusions

Class politics have traditionally been associated with the Labour movement, although they make only a faltering appearance nowadays at the fringes of debate within the Labour Party. The most striking recent political change has been the assumption by the Conservative Party, or rather by John Major in particular, of the class mantle in the form of a determination to transform Britain into a "classless society". Mr. Major's programme runs counter to the conventional Conservative view as articulated by such traditionalists as Lord St. John of Fawsley:

> I think that class is largely an irrelevancy in contemporary British society. Some people may use it as an excuse for their own failures, but I think we have very largely a mobile society, a society open to talent. The talented child or young person is able to reach the top of any profession or any activity to which that child sets his or her mind, provided that the ability is there.... We talk a lot about class in British society, but I think its significance socially is very small (quoted in Reid, 1989, p. 294).

This view does not tally with the British public's view of itself. Perceived inequalities based on class persist, as do differences in subjective class identities and inequalities of expectation. They easily eclipse any marginal changes in social mobility.

True, the alignments of class and race arise from a variety of sources. Some are comparatively benign, including the sense of identity and solidarity with other people perceived to be in some way like ourselves; but at worst, they cramp aspirations and limit the horizons of opportunity. Yet others have a more sinister aspect, with class or racial prejudice and discrimination giving rise to social and economic exclusions which are overwhelmingly recognised by the public as realities of life in modern Britain. Perceptions of Britain as an unequal society are deeply embedded and no portrait of social division in Britain would be complete that did not take them into account.

Moreover, because these inequalities extend to the political realm, the prospects for change are remote - unless, that is, the determination to create a classless society extends beyond the eradication of overt discrimination and self-limitation to the expansion of political resources to the "dispossessed".

Conservative ministers have certainly used the term 'empowerment' in the more limited context of representation and community self-management in, for example, the recent City Challenge schemes. As we suggested in *The 1984 Report* (Young, 1984), the issue of empowerment consists both of changing aspirations and of redressing inequalities in political influence. The sharp class variations in the sense of personal efficacy or competence must, to some extent, reflect personal and community *experiences* of dealing with government and public bodies, experiences which are notably less rewarding for people with little social status. The commitment to a Citizen's Charter would on this analysis certainly help but it will require a far wider and more rigorous application if it is to address the class inequalities in political influence. Birth, wealth and connection will surely continue to have a main heading on political power as long as they are expected - and thus permitted - to do so.

## Notes

1.   For instance, the proportion of *British Social Attitudes* respondents in non-manual occupations has risen from 44 per cent in 1984 to 50 per cent in 1991.

2.   It is more appropriate to adopt the usage of *discrimination* and *disadvantage*, already well-established in the field of race relations. *Disadvantage* refers to a less competitive position in the economy, arising from the transmitted failure to acquire the means of ensuring material well-being. *Discrimination* refers to deliberate exclusionary judgements which deprive people of benefits to which they are entitled. It may or may not arise from *prejudice* or hostility. The term *indirect discrimination* is used in both policy and law to refer to the maintenance of practices or requirements which have the effect of excluding people drawn from groups which have a less-than-proportionate likelihood of meeting them; indirect discrimination is thus an unintended consequence of institutional selectivity in situations where disadvantage exists, and may or may not be held justifiable. The misunderstandings of indirect discrimination are well-recorded, and the utility of the concept of disadvantage is well-proven. For these reasons, the term discrimination is best reserved to the narrower meaning of direct and deliberate acts of exclusion.

3.   The annual average flow of immigrants from the New Commonwealth and Pakistan fell by 10,000, or about 30 per cent, between 1975-9 and 1985-9, largely as a result of increasing restrictions on entry (CSO, 1992).

4.   Topf (1989) provides a searching discussion of the meaning of these data, but overlooks the fact that the 1959 study was based on an unprompted question. Thus only limited comparison between the Almond and Verba study and our own series is possible.

## References

Airey, C. (1984), 'Social and Moral Values' in Jowell R. and Airey, C. (eds.), *British Social Attitudes: the 1984 Report*, Aldershot: Gower.

Airey, C. and Brook, L. (1986), 'Interim Report: Social and Moral Issues' in Jowell, R., Witherspoon, S. and Brook, L. (eds.), *British Social Attitudes: the 1986 Report*, Aldershot: Gower.

Almond, G. A. and Verba, S. (1963), *The Civic Culture*, Princeton, N.J.: Princeton University Press.

Almond, G. A. and Verba, S. (1980), *The Civic Culture Revisited: an Analytic Study*, Boston: Little, Brown.

Brook, L. and Cape, E. (1991), 'Interim Report: Civil Liberties', in Jowell, R., Brook, L. and Taylor, B. with Prior, G. (eds.), *British Social Attitudes: the 8th report*, Aldershot: Dartmouth.

Brown, C. (1983), 'Ethnic Pluralism in Britain: the Demographic and Legal Background' in Glazer, N. and Young, K. (eds.), *Ethnic Pluralism and Public Policy*, London: Heinemann.

Brown, C. (1984), *Black and White Britain: the Third PSI Survey*, London: Heinemann.

Central Statistical Office (CSO) (1992), *Social Trends 22*, London: HMSO.

Daniel, W. W. (1968), *Racial Discrimination in England*, Harmondsworth: Penguin.

Reid, I. (1989), *Social Class Differences in Britain, 3rd edition*, London: Fontana.

Smith, D. J. (1976), *The Facts of Racial Disadvantage*, Political and Economic Planning (PEP), Volume XLII, Broadsheet No. 560, London: PEP.

Tawney, R. J. (1931), *Equality*, London: Unwin.

Topf, R. (1989), 'Change and Political Culture in Britain' in Gibbins, J. R. (ed.), *Contemporary Political Culture: Politics in a Postmodern Age*, London: Sage.

Weiner, M. J. (1982), *English Culture and the Decline of the Industrial Spirit, 1850-1980*, Cambridge: CUP.

Westergaard, J. and Resler, J. (1975), *Class in a Capitalist Society*, London: Heinemann.

Young, K. (1983), 'Ethnic Pluralism and the Policy Agenda in Britain' in Glazer, N. and Young, K. (eds.), *Ethnic Pluralism and Public Policy*, London: Heinemann.

Young, K. (1984), 'Political Attitudes' in Jowell, R. and Airey, C. (eds.) *British Social Attitudes: the 1984 report*, Aldershot: Gower.

## Acknowledgement

In 1990, the Home Office agreed to provide financial support for the BSA survey series. This has ensured that the series can continue to include questions (such as ones on racial prejudice and discrimination, first asked in 1983) of interest to the Home Office. SCPR is grateful for its support.

# 10 Interim report: Charitable giving

*Steven Barnett and Susan Saxon-Harrold* [*]

> Our policies of wider ownership are yielding richer fruit year by year. I want to see charities get a good share of the wealth that is now beginning to cascade down and across the generations.

These words from John Major to the 1991 Charities Conference demonstrate the government's continuing commitment to the credo that people should be entitled to benefit from lower taxation, but should in return be prepared to give some of their extra income to charity. It is in effect a sort of implicit bargain with tax-payers: government welfare provision has to be rationed, so any additional needs should be met by the generosity of private individuals. This is part of the policy of 'active citizenship', designed to replace the 'dependency culture'.

The post-war welfare state consensus, sustained by both Labour and Conservative administrations, has been that certain basic provisions - such as a proper education, access to decent health care, a place to live and a basic income - are the responsibility of government. This has been an agreed agenda, even if the means of meeting it have often been hotly debated, and the fulfilment of each objective has until recently been thought to be just round the corner. The Thatcher governments of the 1980s fractured that consensus somewhat, for instance in ceding to charities a growing responsibility for areas previously in the exclusive domain of government. Hospitals and schools began to compete with more traditional animal welfare and foreign aid organisations in the

---

[*]   Steven Barnett is an independent researcher and visiting lecturer at Goldsmith's College, University of London; Susan Saxon-Harrold is Head of Research at the Charities Aid Foundation.

urgency and the originality of their charitable appeals; the £65 million raised by Great Ormond Street Hospital's Wishing Well appeal was a startling example of the potential income which could be generated. According to one published report (Directory of Social Change, 1992) "many hospital appeals now stress that if not enough money is raised, lives will be lost. Charity has assumed a life-saving role".

This shift in government philosophy has thus created a different and more competitive environment for charities. In part this may be because behind the new policy is a crucial assumption: that a rolling back of state responsibility will be matched by a growing generosity among 'active citizens' anxious to fill the gap. If this fails to happen, we might expect both 'traditional' charities and the new welfare appeals to suffer, so harming their beneficiaries.

In practice, there could be many factors which make people disinclined to heed government exhortations to part with at least some of the fruits of tax cuts. Indeed, for many of the less well-off the tax burden is little or no lighter than a decade ago. Many, of course, *have* benefited; but the very concept of charity might be anathema to some, seeming to discourage self-sufficiency which they have been glad to see the government rediscover. Some may feel that there is little point in tax cuts if they are not entitled to reap the benefits themselves. Others, influenced perhaps by adverse publicity surrounding the collapse of War on Want in April 1990, may be dubious about the way in which charities are run, and feel that their donations would be squandered on administration, excessive advertising and inefficient practices. On a purely practical level, some may simply feel overwhelmed by the proliferation of organisations and worthy causes asking for their financial support. As the White Paper (Home Office, 1989) which preceded the 1992 Charities Act put it:

> Since [1960] the charity world has changed dramatically. There has been an enormous increase in the number and variety of charities and a substantial increase in the funds flowing through them... Charities are being registered by the Charity Commission at the rate of one every 30 minutes of the working day.

But there could be a more fundamental reason why people resist some kinds of charity appeals. Successive *British Social Attitudes* surveys have demonstrated the public's persistent attachment to the principles of collective provision underwritten by taxation. Yet governments of the 1980s and beyond have just as persistently been attached to the notion that individuals should assume at least some of the task of welfare provision. This apparent conflict could lead to seriously underfunded pockets of welfare provision, notably less popular causes which the public would be unlikely to choose as targets of their generosity.

It is these potential problems that make it important to understand how British people feel towards charitable giving, and then to monitor how those feelings shift over time.

## Who gives and how?

Less than three per cent of respondents said they had *not* given money to charity in any way in the previous year. It is in the nature of such questions that people's recollections are never entirely reliable, either through genuine inability to pin down their activities to within a given period or through a reluctance (despite careful question wording) to appear mean. So we may have underestimated the proportion who made no charitable donations in the last year, but we have no comparable data against which to check this.[1]

Perhaps more interesting than the total numbers who have given money are the ways in which they chose to give. In its reports on its own surveys, the Charities Aid Foundation (CAF) makes a useful distinction between 'philanthropic' donations - involving contributions with no prospect of material return - and giving through purchases, which involve transactions of some kind (Halfpenny, 1991). The table below follows that distinction.

**Ways given money to charity in the past year**

|  | % |
|---|---|
| **Purchases** | |
| Buying raffle tickets | 82 |
| Buying goods in sale/fête | 37 |
| Buying goods in charity shop | 34 |
| Attending an event in aid of charity | 31 |
| Buying goods from charity catalogue | 22 |
| **Philanthropy** | |
| Sponsoring someone in fund-raising | 68 |
| Giving in door-to-door collection | 63 |
| Giving in street collection | 60 |
| Giving in church collection | 35 |
| Giving to TV or radio appeal | 18 |
| **None of these ways** | 3 |

Thus buying raffle tickets with its element of excitement and chance of reward is, over the course of a year, the most popular form of giving.

Beyond that, the prevalent forms of contribution tend to be philanthropic, with around two-thirds saying they had sponsored someone and close to that proportion saying they had given in door-to-door or street collections. A third had given in church collections in the past year. Despite the proliferation of broadcast appeals through 'telethons', live concerts and so on, personal solicitation still appears to be more successful in prompting individuals to give. But the table above shows only the most common channels of contribution, not the most successful in terms of amounts raised. (We did not ask for amounts given.) According to CAF's statistics, covenants raise the most in sheer monetary terms, while church collections provide the largest slice of philanthropic donations (Halfpenny, 1991).[2]

Just as the numbers of people making any donation might be subject to exaggeration, so the number of ways in which they give may also be inflated, and the data should therefore be treated with some caution. As the next table shows, nearly half the population claim to have given to charity in five ways or more in the year preceding the interview, and a further third to have given in three or four ways.

**Number of ways given money to charity in the last year**

|                    | %  |
|--------------------|----|
| 0, 1 or 2 ways     | 19 |
| 3 or 4 ways        | 33 |
| 5 or 6 ways        | 28 |
| 7 to 10 ways       | 20 |

The number of ways people give varies according to sub-group and probably differs as much as a result of varying opportunities or resources as from different dispositions. Thus, not surprisingly, the youngest and oldest age-groups tend to find fewer ways in which to make donations, probably because they lack the kind of social networks that provide opportunities to give. Both these age-groups are probably less likely to be cajoled into giving. Analysis by social class also shows predictable differences, with manual workers giving in fewer ways than non-manual workers. Although these differences may partly reflect differences in disposable income, we should note that data from the most recent CAF household survey suggest that the number of methods of giving are unlikely to correlate strongly with total amount given.[3]

There is a close correlation between educational attainment and the number of different ways of contributing, with 72 per cent of degree-holders saying they gave in five ways or more, compared with 33 per cent of those with no qualifications. And income disparities do not explain this variation, since the same pattern emerges when we control for income. Research in the United States (Hodgkinson and Weitzmann, 1990) has also established a close association between level of educational attainment and disposition to give (as well as actual amounts given). As we shall see when examining attitudes to charities in general, education emerges as one of the most powerful determinants of values and priorities.

## Government and charities

Government might be keen to devolve some of the responsibility for areas of public expenditure to voluntary donations, but to what extent does the British public approve or disapprove? And how do people's perceptions of what can legitimately be devolved change according to the nature of the cause?

The surveys carried out by CAF between 1988 and 1992 have found that the public is overwhelmingly of the opinion that government should not rely on charities to raise needed money: attitudes on this issue hardened between 1987 and 1988/89, but since then appear to have remained fairly constant.[4]  In the *British Social Attitudes* survey we tested the same proposition, asking respondents how much they agreed or disagreed with the statement that "the government should do less for the needy and encourage charities to do more instead".   This required active disagreement by those who wanted to affirm the government's role.  In the event, over three-quarters (77 per cent) disagreed and 15 per cent gave a neutral answer.  Only six per cent were prepared to agree to a smaller role for government in the alleviation of need.

To address the same issue more specifically we presented respondents with six areas of expenditure and invited them to say whether the money needed should be raised from government (entirely or mainly), from charities (entirely or mainly) or equally from both.  The six 'causes' ranged from health service expenditure, traditionally associated with government, to animal welfare, traditionally associated with charities.

|  | | Funding should be | | |
| --- | --- | --- | --- | --- |
|  | | entirely/mainly from government | shared equally | entirely/mainly from charity |
| Kidney machines | % | 93 | 5 | 1 |
| Housing for homeless | % | 86 | 9 | 2 |
| Lifeboats | % | 65 | 21 | 12 |
| Protecting rare animals | % | 29 | 36 | 27 |
| Holidays for disabled people | % | 31 | 34 | 30 |
| Food aid to poor countries | % | 29 | 34 | 30 |

Contrary to our expectations, responses did not shift gradually across the spectrum from a belief in almost complete dependence on government to one in almost complete dependence on charity.  Rather, they fell into two distinct groups with one item towards the middle.  In respect of two causes - kidney machines and housing for the homeless (representing traditional 'core' welfare areas) - the vast majority felt that the government should be integrally involved, and the distinctions were only a matter of whether they should be exclusively or just predominantly in the government's domain.  On funding for lifeboats, opinion was more divided.   Even though this is a cause traditionally associated with charities, most people (two-thirds) still feel it should be entirely or mainly the government's responsibility, and only one in eight thought it should be entirely or mainly the responsibility of charity.  As for the other three causes, responses are split more evenly, around a third of respondents favouring each option.

This division of opinion suggests that those areas in which support for *government* funding is greatest concern the alleviation of human suffering or, indeed, saving lives in Britain. Food aid, concerned as it is with these goals in poorer countries, is less popular as a government responsibility, but perhaps some respondents did not immediately appreciate the underlying reasons for food aid. Starker, more explicit question wording (for example, "money to feed starving people in poor countries") might have changed the pattern of responses.

Even so, it is likely that for many people the borders of the UK represent an appropriate boundary for government expenditure, and that human suffering which takes place outside those boundaries should not be accorded the same priority. The geographical limits to our sense of human suffering - or at least to our attitudes to the alleviation of that suffering - require more exploration. The concept of 'remoteness' could well be an important factor affecting people's priorities for government spending, applicable as much *within* the UK as outside it. Causes closer to home - within people's own neighbourhood or region and with which they more easily identify - may perhaps evoke a greater enthusiasm than causes elsewhere in Britain, let alone in other countries.

Although overall priorities for government *versus* charitable spending can be divided broadly into these three categories, this neat classification works less well for some sections of the population than for others. We looked first at the two causes which were considered, overwhelmingly, to be government's responsibility. Two groups of respondents emerged as being distinctive and interesting. First, as the next table illustrates, Labour and Liberal Democrat identifiers have similar views on this issue, while Conservative identifiers are predictably less likely to support heavy dependence on government funding for either cause.

| | | Party identification | | |
| | All | Conservative | Liberal Democrat | Labour |
|---|---|---|---|---|
| **Funding for kidney machines should come:** | % | % | % | % |
| Entirely from government | 59 | 50 | 65 | 66 |
| Mainly from government | 35 | 41 | 31 | 29 |
| Equally from both | 5 | 7 | 4 | 4 |
| **Funding for housing for homeless people should come:** | % | % | % | % |
| Entirely from government | 43 | 31 | 48 | 53 |
| Mainly from government | 43 | 49 | 41 | 39 |
| Equally from both | 9 | 12 | 9 | 6 |

Thus, fewer than a third of Conservatives support total dependence on government funding for housing the homeless, compared to around half of Labour and Liberal Democrat identifiers. Funding for lifeboats reveals a similar division along party political lines.

Another group which differs notably from the rest are junior non-manual workers, often said to represent one of the heartlands of the 'Thatcherite revolution'. They are noticeably less likely than average to favour complete reliance on government spending in all three areas. But the difference is again particularly marked in respect of housing homeless people. (Thirty four per cent of the junior non-manual workers favour total reliance on government compared with an overall average of 43 per cent.)

Secondly, the differences according to religious affiliation are particularly intriguing because of the confused relationship between church and state, especially in relation to the churches' perceived role as champion of the disadvantaged. Several times during the 1980s the church and the government have come near to full-blown rows. Once was upon the publication of controversial conclusions by a Commission established in 1983 by the (then) Archbishop of Canterbury. The following extract, for instance, was seen by many as an undisguised attack on the prevailing ethos of the 1980s and, by association, on government policy.

> The Church cannot supplant the market or the state. It can ... mobilise its own resources in a way that accords high priority to the poor. It must by its example and its exertions proclaim the ethic of altruism against egotism, of community against self-seeking, and of charity against greed *(Faith in the City, 1985).*

Our aim was to find out first whether religious affiliation in itself steers people towards charity *versus* government, and secondly whether there are any striking differences between people belonging to the different religious denominations.

The next table shows that religious affiliation does seem to matter - but not that much. Those with no religious affiliation are a little more likely to favour funding entirely from government, and Roman Catholics (in particular) are more inclined than those in the C of E towards government funding. Although the differences are not large, they do lend some credibility to the cliché about the Church of England being the Conservative Party at prayer. We also examined the data to see whether or not religious attendance, or belief in God, might be more powerful discriminators than religion *per se* or denomination. The answer appears to be 'no'.

|                                                     | All | Church of England | Roman Catholic | Other Christian | None |
|-----------------------------------------------------|-----|-------------------|----------------|-----------------|------|
|                                                     | %   | %                 | %              | %               | %    |
| **Funding for kidney machines should come:**        |     |                   |                |                 |      |
| Entirely from government                            | 59  | 54                | 61             | 61              | 64   |
| Mainly from government                              | 35  | 39                | 32             | 31              | 32   |
| Equally from both                                   | 5   | 6                 | 6              | 6               | 2    |
|                                                     | %   | %                 | %              | %               | %    |
| **Funding for housing for homeless people should come:** |     |                   |                |                 |      |
| Entirely from government                            | 43  | 38                | 51             | 41              | 47   |
| Mainly from government                              | 43  | 47                | 39             | 42              | 41   |
| Equally from both                                   | 9   | 9                 | 5              | 12              | 9    |

Associations with level of educational attainment are less straightforward, but graduates in particular are also more inclined towards government funding. Age, too, has a bearing upon attitudes, but only insofar as 18-24 year olds are particularly inclined to favour government responsibility for housing homeless people (52 per cent compared to 43 per cent overall).

In general, the three causes on which attitudes are more evenly distributed between the relative obligations of government and charity are also the three on which sub-group differences tend to be smaller.

### Attitudes to self-sufficiency and the role of charities

For some people, charity seems to represent the unacceptable face of dependency rather than generosity. The role of charitable giving, particularly in relation to its effect on the recipients of charity, has been debated since at least Victorian times, fuelled over the last decade by the resurgence in liberal economic thinking. Even so, most people in Britain tend to reject the notion that self-sufficiency is, in itself, desirable come what may: 43 per cent disagree that "people should look after themselves and not rely on charities": still, 28 per cent agree, and as many as a quarter have no opinion either way.

Perversely, but predictably perhaps, the oldest and poorest members of the sample (overlapping groups), who might be perceived as closest to requiring material support themselves, are the most ardent believers in self-sufficiency. Three times as many of those aged over 65 agree with this statement as do 18-24 year-olds, (47 per cent compared with 15 per cent); and nearly twice as many in the lowest income group as in the highest (40 per cent compared with 22 per cent). Despite the statement's resonance with some of the political rhetoric of the 1980s, however, the correlations with party affiliation are not as strong as might have been expected.

*People should look after themselves and not rely on charities*

|  | | Agree ('strongly' or 'just') | Neither | Disagree ('strongly' or 'just') |
|---|---|---|---|---|
| **All** | % | 28 | 25 | 43 |
| | | | | |
| **Party identification:** | | | | |
| Conservative | % | 33 | 25 | 39 |
| Liberal Democrat | % | 22 | 26 | 50 |
| Labour | % | 25 | 23 | 47 |

The greatest division of opinion is between two groups with diametrically opposite value orientations towards the welfare state. Based on their responses to a number of 'scale' questions included in the questionnaire, we are able to score people according to how 'welfarist' they are, or how 'individualist' in their general beliefs and values.[5] That the scale works is demonstrated by the fact that 57 per cent of individualists agree that "people should look after themselves", while only 14 per cent of welfarists feel that way. This association is, of course, predictable but it uncovers something of a contradiction since these same 'individualists' are also less likely to favour government expenditure on the NHS or on housing for the homeless, and more likely to want charities to undertake a greater share of those burdens. Among this group are also the strongest advocates of the dependency theory, and presumably regard dependence on charity (from voluntary donations) as the lesser evil.

Despite government entreaties to think of others when disposing of their newly-gained wealth, six people in ten are prepared to endorse another proposition included in the survey, that it is *not* everyone's responsibility to give what they can to charity (rising to over two-thirds of Conservative supporters).[6] Younger people once again are more inclined to take a more altruistic stance than older people (on the grounds, some might say, that the young have less to be altruistic with), while the essentially Christian doctrine of giving what one can to charity finds no more agreement among those with a religious affiliation than those without.

There is, therefore, no evidence of a widespread sense of society's moral responsibility to give generously to charities. In 1990, evidence from CAF seemed to suggest that charitable giving in Britain might actually be in decline, leading to widespread talk of 'compassion fatigue' - a concept that was never clearly defined, but conveyed a sense of universal weariness with acts of generosity. Longer-term evidence would be needed to prove that people's inclination to give had been systematically eroded, and perhaps a more likely explanation is 'compassion confusion', the numbing effect of the profusion of charitable appeals.

For instance, three-quarters of the sample agreed that "there are so many charities that it is difficult to decide which to give to", and only one in ten disagreed. We cannot, of course, tell whether this sense of being somewhat overwhelmed has any impact on people's attitude to charitable causes in general - or to acts of generosity towards individual charities. It may be that there has *always* been an acute sense of competition for charitable donations, and that the very high profile of certain charity appeals in the mass media in recent years has just made this competition more visible.

Another potentially damaging perception of charities is that some of them at least have been characterised as wasteful and inefficient. Following adverse publicity in the mid-1980s, the government established the 'Efficiency Scrutiny of the Supervision of Charities' which reported in 1987 under Sir Philip Woodfield. The results of his deliberations included a recommendation that the Charity Commission should come down more heavily on organisations where there was evidence of dealing with incompetence and abuse.

It is therefore hardly surprising, though perhaps a little sobering, that over a third of the public should agree that "most charities are wasteful in their use of funds". A further third remains neutral and less than a quarter actively disagree. As the next table shows, there is a very strong relationship between this negative view of charities and both age and educational attainment. More than twice as many over 65s as 18-24 year-olds believe that charities are wasteful, and the same is true of those with low or no educational qualifications, compared with those who have degrees. Moreover, age matters after controlling for education, and vice-versa.

*Most charities are wasteful in their use of funds*

|  | | Agree ('strongly' or 'just') | Neither | Disagree ('strongly' or 'just') |
|---|---|---|---|---|
| **All** | % | 36 | 33 | 24 |
| **Age:** | | | | |
| 18-24 | % | 22 | 33 | 40 |
| 25-44 | % | 31 | 38 | 27 |
| 45-64 | % | 42 | 28 | 23 |
| 65+ | % | 48 | 31 | 11 |
| **Highest qualifications:** | | | | |
| Degree | % | 21 | 30 | 47 |
| Professional | % | 34 | 37 | 26 |
| 'A' level/'O' level | % | 32 | 33 | 32 |
| CSE or equivalent | % | 43 | 37 | 13 |
| None | % | 44 | 30 | 15 |

This could be related to individual experience - for instance, that younger and better-qualified people have had more direct experience of working with charities. Or it could be a result of adverse publicity in newspapers that are read by older and less qualified people alike. CAF's figures (CAF, 1991) demonstrate that only eight per cent of expenditure by the top 400 charities goes on administration or general costs, and a further eight per cent on fundraising, leaving 84 per cent of expenditure for direct charitable purposes. Public perception is rather different, according to CAF's most recent survey: on average, their respondents believed that only 47 per cent of donations reach the needy for home-based charities and only 39 per cent for third world charities.[7] It seems therefore that charities need to do more (perhaps to spend more) to convince the public that they are working effectively.

That the charitable horizons of the British tend towards the parochial is strongly endorsed by public reaction to the proposition that "we should support more charities which benefit people in Britain, rather than people overseas". Over half agreed and fewer than a quarter disagreed. As before, these general attitudes conceal major variations between the social classes. Fewer than half of those in professional/managerial and intermediate non-manual grades agree with the statement compared with two-thirds of the semi-skilled and unskilled.

*We should support more charities which benefit people in Britain, rather than people overseas*

|  |  | Agree ('strongly' or just) | Neither agree nor disagree | Disagree ('strongly' or just) |
|---|---|---|---|---|
| **All** | % | 56 | 17 | 24 |
| **Socio-economic group:** |  |  |  |  |
| Professional/managerial | % | 48 | 20 | 31 |
| Intermediate non-manual | % | 42 | 17 | 38 |
| Junior non-manual | % | 51 | 21 | 25 |
| Skilled manual | % | 65 | 15 | 17 |
| Semi-skilled manual | % | 67 | 14 | 14 |
| Unskilled manual | % | 66 | 5 | 18 |

The difference becomes even more marked according to education: only a quarter of those with degrees compared to over two-thirds of those with few or no qualifications agree with the statement.

Given the extensive television news reports these days of sometimes harrowing scenes from around the world, watched by people from all sections of society, the magnitude of these differences is perhaps surprising. They suggest a very localised sense of priority in attitudes to charities which, with the proliferation of appeals from local institutions such as hospitals, colleges and schools as well as traditional fund-raising organisations (for example, Shelter and Age Concern) may place international charities like Oxfam at an increasing disadvantage.

## Conclusions

When President Reagan cut federal grant aid, he said that he expected philanthropy to make up the balance.  Americans had a moral responsibility, he said, having enjoyed tax cuts throughout his administration, to bestow some proportion of their increased wealth on areas of spending from which government was withdrawing.  His appeal went largely unheeded, and a number of welfare projects and formerly state-supported institutions suffered funding crises as a result.

There is a danger that British philanthropy may prove equally resistant to being boosted, and the evidence presented here suggests some of the reasons why.[8]  Perhaps the most fundamental problem is an enduring conviction that certain areas of expenditure are simply not appropriate for reliance on charities, and that - in particular - government should not evade responsibility for its citizens who are in need.  The problem is compounded by the irony that those who are most enthusiastic about switching the expenditure burden from government to charity are also the most likely to entertain fears about the dangers of charity.  They are, it seems, people who worry about the effects of the 'dependency culture' in general, whether the agent of that dependence is government or charity.

Additional problems are likely to be created by the sheer profusion of charities.  The registration rate of two charities an hour mentioned in the White Paper (Home Office, 1989) is likely to escalate with the arrival of opted-out schools and trust hospitals.  There is also likely to be a proliferation in university appeals.  It is clear from the evidence presented here that the sheer volume creates confusion amongst potential donors, and that it might act as a disincentive to giving.

The new demands being made by schools and hospitals - and the increasing sophistication and creativity with which their fund-raising appeals are being handled - also have implications for charities working in other areas.  Their practical and symbolic value for local communities is likely to give them an advantage over charities which are perhaps more remote or less visible in their work.  Our evidence lends weight to the conventional wisdom about the parochialism of the British, and suggests that international charities are already at a severe disadvantage.[9]  It could be that the notion of active citizenship simply becomes a means of compensating for reductions or shortfalls in government spending at home.  Even so, as in the USA, the ultimate effect may well be to leave traditional causes (such as medical research, housing for the homeless and so on) significantly worse off than they were.  Moreover there is evidence from our data that, among some groups within the population, this is a matter of no great concern:  certainly those without a higher education are less convinced about the benefits of giving, and more prone to believe that charitable funds are wasted.  It is the educated *élite* on the whole, rather than the masses, who have a relatively benign attitude towards charities and charitable giving.

The moral responsibility arguments of active citizenship that were pursued by Mrs Thatcher in the UK and Mr Reagan in the USA were presumably predicated on a view that the beneficiaries of new-found wealth would voluntarily divert some of it into charitable causes. This does not appear either to have happened to any marked degree, nor to be that plausible a proposition to a sceptical public - especially, we suspect, during a recession when many people will have difficulty in convincing themselves that they *are* better off. On our evidence, formidable additional obstacles will need to be cleared, even in boom times, before most people would be willing to devote increases in their real incomes to causes that they feel should 'properly' be funded from taxation.

## Notes

1.  The regular surveys of charitable giving run by the Charities Aid Foundation (CAF) ask about donations given by households over the previous month. Around 20 per cent say they have not given, a discrepancy between these surveys and ours which is not surprising given the different time-scales. Differences can also arise in respondent definitions of charity, and according to whether a prompted list of methods of giving is shown (as on BSA). For a full discussion of the methodological problems involved in asking about charitable giving, see Halfpenny (1989).
2.  The more recent *International Survey of Giving* (CAF, 1992) reports that the amount raised by covenants in Britain fell back in 1991/92.
3.  Correlation is unlikely to be strong since there is considerable variation between giving methods in the median donation. In response to a television appeal, for example, it is £5 compared to 25p for a shop counter collection and 50p for a street collection. Full details can be found in CAF (1992), p. 19.
4.  In their four surveys of individual giving and volunteering (CAF, 1988-1992), CAF asked respondents to agree or disagree with the following statement: "The government ought to help more, not rely on charities to raise needed money." The proportions agreeing over the four surveys were 1987: 80 per cent; 1988/89: 89 per cent; 1989/90: 88 per cent; 1990/91: 86 per cent.
5.  The welfarist scale, derived from factor analysis carried out by Heath *et al* (1986), was constructed from Qs. 2.38a-h of Version A of the 1991 self-completion questionnaire. Responses were scored from 1 to 5 and summed. Not answered and 'don't know' responses were excluded from the base.
6.  There is a big disparity between this finding and results of a similar statement in CAF surveys, couched in positive rather than negative terms ("It is the responsibility of people to give what they can to charity"). Over half *agree* with this statement. Maybe these statements are not simple antitheses but rather two philosophical positions which might not be wholly incompatible. The lesson is that question-wording, particularly perhaps in relation to statements containing moral obligation, is enormously important.
7.  Respondents to the most recent CAF survey (CAF, 1992, p. 48), were asked - separately for home and third world charities - how much they think gets to the cause for every £1 they give. Twenty six per cent said they did not know for the former and 32 per cent for the latter. The medians given of 47 per cent and 39 per cent represent typical amounts among those who offered a figure.
8.  After some sharp increases in voluntary income during the early to mid-1980s, the top 200 charities have reported almost no real increase towards the end of the decade (CAF, 1991). In grossing up the evidence of their four household surveys, CAF has

concluded that "the most that can be said is that our charity surveys provide little evidence of any real increase in individual charitable giving over the four-year period 1987 to 1991" (CAF, 1992).

9.  Further hard evidence comes from analysis of voluntary income to the top 400 charities. The proportion of all voluntary donations going to international aid agencies declined slightly from 20 per cent in 1988/89 to 19 per cent in 1989/90. Over the same period, voluntary contributions to education increased by 58 per cent and to medicine and health by 17 per cent (CAF, 1991).

## References

CAF (1992), *International Survey of Giving*, London: CAF.

CAF (1991), *Charity Trends 1991, 14th Edition*, London: CAF.

CAF (1990), *Charity Household Survey 1988/89: Findings from a National Survey*, London: CAF.

CAF (1988), *Charity Household Survey, 2nd Edition: Findings from a National Survey*, London: CAF.

Faith in the City, A Call for Action by Church and Nation, *Report of a Commission on Urban Priority Areas* (1985), London: Church House Publishing.

*Charity and NHS Reforms (1992)*, London: Directory of Social Change.

*Efficiency Scrutiny of the Supervision of Charities* (1987), [Report Commissioned from Sir Philip Woodfield by the Home Secretary and Economic Secretary to the Treasury], London: HMSO.

Halfpenny, P. (1989), 'The Charities Aid Foundation Household Survey: an Evaluation of Methods and Findings' in Lee, N. (ed.), *Sources of Charity Finance*, London: Charities Aid Foundation.

Halfpenny, P. (1991), 'Individual Giving in Britain, 1987-1990', in *Charity Trends*, 14, London: Charities Aid Foundation.

Heath, A., Jowell, R., Curtice, J. and Witherspoon, S. (1986), *End of Award Report to the ESRC: Methodological Aspects of Attitude Research*, London: SCPR.

Hodgkinson, V. A. and Weitzmann, M. S. (1990), *Giving and Volunteering in the United States: Findings from a National Survey*, Washington: Independent Sector.

Home Office (1989), *Charities: A Framework For The Future*, London: HMSO.

## Acknowledgement

We are grateful to the Charities Aid Foundation for its funding to enable us to include these questions on charities. Susan Saxon-Harrold contributed to this chapter in a personal capacity: the views represented here are not necessarily those of the Charities Aid Foundation.

# 11 Interim report: The national health

*Nick Bosanquet* *

Among the leading political issues over the last decade has been the performance of the NHS and its future as a public service. Public concern has been reflected in parliamentary time: from 1986 to 1992 the NHS was the subject of more early day motions and occupied more parliamentary time than any other subject. This sort of sustained concentration is new. In earlier periods, such conflict as there was over the NHS was usually to do with issues such as nurses' pay rather than with intrinsic issues such as health planning or funding. Successive plans for reorganising health services, under discussion from 1968 onwards, received little public attention. True, some issues intrinsic to the NHS very briefly received political prominence, such as the introduction of prescription charges in 1951 and the debate over the future of private practice in 1975, but these controversies are around a generation apart.

The period since 1983, when the *British Social Attitudes* series began, thus provides a unique opportunity to assess how public attitudes to the NHS have fared during such sustained political conflict about its future direction. The nature of the conflict has changed during the period: from 1983 to 1989 it was mainly about funding, waiting lists and patient care - that is about the performance and standards of existing services. But from 1989 the focus shifted to the government's proposed reforms: fundamental changes were being debated and then introduced, such as 'fund-holding' by general practices and 'opting out' by hospitals. These

* Professor of Health Policy, Royal Holloway and Bedford New College, University of London.

rekindled suspicions and accusations that the government was implicitly attempting to create a two-tier health service no longer free to all and with differential access to services according (in effect) to income rather than need.

So changing attitudes have to be seen against a background of these two intense but overlapping periods of controversy and debate. As we have noted in previous Reports (see especially Bosanquet, 1984, 1988; Taylor-Gooby, 1990), public attitudes to the NHS changed substantially between 1983 and 1989. First, there was an increase in commitment to the 'principle' of the NHS. Secondly, the public gave a higher and higher place to health services in its priorities for extra government spending. Younger people especially took this view. Thirdly, there was a steadily rising sense of dissatisfaction with specific aspects of the NHS, particularly with hospital services.

As we shall see, the NHS has become a little less prominent in the public mind since 1989, as the debate has moved from the relatively accessible issues of performance standards to the more remote and technical issues of wholesale reorganisation and the introduction of 'internal markets'. This may be partly a question of crowding out: economic problems have come to the forefront, as has education. On the other hand, public opinion may also have reacted positively to the fact that a new approach to the NHS is being adopted on which judgement ought to be suspended.

## Access to the NHS

We turn now to assess changes in more detail, beginning with the general principle of free, open access to the NHS. The high level of public support we found in 1983 for the principle of free treatment for everyone at the point of delivery has increased further. At that time two-thirds of respondents opposed the idea of a two-tier service, with access to free services being limited to lower income groups. By 1989 almost three-quarters were against it and there was no further rise in 1990. (We did not ask that question in the 1991 survey.)

*It has been suggested that the National Health Service should be available only to those with lower incomes. This would mean that contributions and taxes could be lower and most people would then take out medical insurance and pay for health care. Do you support or oppose this idea?*

|         | 1983 | 1986 | 1989 | 1990 |
|---------|------|------|------|------|
|         | %    | %    | %    | %    |
| Support | 29   | 27   | 22   | 22   |
| Oppose  | 64   | 67   | 74   | 74   |

In 1983 opposition to a two-tier health service was strongest among those with high incomes (who on the surface had most to lose), and it is even more true now than it was.  But opposition has also increased among people with lower incomes, so that by 1990 views of those in the top income quartile were virtually identical to those in the bottom quartile. Taylor-Gooby (1990) reported similar findings in some detail, so we will not rehearse them here.  The only point worth adding here is that the continuing growth during the 1980s in public support for the principle of free and open access to the NHS by 1990 had apparently begun to peak - but not to reverse itself.

## Public spending priorities

Between 1983 and 1989 health services also gained strongly as a priority for additional public expenditure.  The proportion naming health as the first priority rose 24 percentage points over these six years.  Since 1989, however, the *relative* priority given to health spending has dropped sharply, as the next table shows.

### First priority for extra spending, 1983-91*

|                          | 1983 | 1986 | 1989 | 1990 | 1991 |
|                          | %    | %    | %    | %    | %    |
|--------------------------|------|------|------|------|------|
| Health                   | 37   | 47   | 61   | 56   | 48   |
| Education                | 24   | 27   | 19   | 24   | 28   |
| Housing                  | 7    | 7    | 7    | 6    | 7    |
| Social security benefits | 6    | 7    | 9    | 5    | 4    |

* A further six spending areas are specified in the question but not shown here; none was nominated as top priority by more than a handful of respondents

We should be cautious about overinterpreting these figures.  Health remains comfortably the public's chief priority for extra spending.  But its prominence seemed to peak in 1989 (at around 60 per cent) and, at around 50 per cent now, its relative position is less dominant than it was. Could it be that the debate on the future structure of the NHS has gone some way towards alleviating public concern?  Of course, many of the reforms were hardly in place at the time of our 1991 fieldwork round, but attention was heavily focused on their introduction.  Another factor is that education has grown sharply as a priority since 1989.  This is shown clearly in the next table, which combines first *and* second priorities for extra public spending.

**% naming each as first or second priority for extra spending, 1983-91**

|                          | 1983 | 1986 | 1989 | 1990 | 1991 |
|--------------------------|------|------|------|------|------|
| Health                   | 63   | 75   | 83   | 81   | 74   |
| Education                | 50   | 57   | 55   | 60   | 62   |
| Housing                  | 20   | 21   | 21   | 20   | 21   |
| Social security benefits | 12   | 11   | 14   | 13   | 11   |

Health is still comfortably the main priority, but education is once again a strong competitor (as it had been in 1983 but not since).  There are few signs of increasing concern about other issues - even ones such as housing and social security benefits which have also been hotly debated in recent years.

The shift away since 1989 from such overwhelming concern with health is particularly noteworthy because it took place during a period in which public attitudes in general continued to move decisively in favour of more tax to finance extra social spending.

*Suppose the government had to choose between the three options on this card, which do you think it should choose?*

|                                                                      | 1983 | 1986 | 1989 | 1990 | 1991 |
|----------------------------------------------------------------------|------|------|------|------|------|
|                                                                      | %    | %    | %    | %    | %    |
| Reduce taxes and spend less on health, education and social benefits | 9    | 5    | 3    | 3    | 3    |
| Keep taxes and spending on these services at the same level as now   | 54   | 44   | 37   | 37   | 29   |
| Increase taxes and spend more                                        | 32   | 46   | 56   | 54   | 65   |

So while from 1990 to 1991 the high priority given to the health service fell somewhat, support for higher taxation for social spending still rose. It seems that from 1983 to 1989 public concern about welfare services had focused itself mainly on the health service and that, since then, concern has widened - primarily to encompass education too (see Halsey, 1991.)

Between 1983 and 1989 much of the impetus behind the rise in priority for health spending came from younger respondents.  Older respondents had always given strong support to more health spending.  But enthusiasm for more spending on education has now also risen most among younger respondents, creating more than one serious contender for first priority. This was true too for people with higher incomes and for the educationally well-qualified.  Indeed, by 1991 it was education, not health, that was named as the highest priority for extra spending among graduates.

## Satisfaction with aspects of the NHS

*The public's verdict*

Reflecting our earlier findings, the period between 1983 and 1989 saw a steady rise in dissatisfaction with the NHS as a whole, with the largest upsurge coming between 1983 and 1986, *before* the main increase in public calls for extra spending.  By 1989 dissatisfaction seemed to have peaked and since then  it has abated somewhat.

**Satisfaction with the NHS, 1983-91**

|                              | 1983 | 1986 | 1989 | 1990 | 1991 |
|------------------------------|------|------|------|------|------|
|                              | %    | %    | %    | %    | %    |
| Very satisfied               | 11   | 6    | 6    | 7    | 7    |
| Quite satisfied              | 44 }55 | 34 }40 | 30 }36 | 30 }37 | 33 }40 |
| Neither satisfied nor dissatisfied | 20 | 19 | 18 | 15 | 19 |
| Quite dissatisfied           | 18   | 23   | 25   | 27   | 23   |
| Very dissatisfied            | 7 }25 | 16 }39 | 21 }46 | 20 }47 | 18 }41 |

Nonetheless it remains uncomfortably high, particularly among certain sub-groups.  In 1991 dissatisfaction was greatest among graduates (51 per cent of whom were 'very' or 'quite' dissatisfied); it was particularly marked among those with high household incomes, and among those covered by private health insurance (all overlapping groups).  There was also greater dissatisfaction in London and the south-east (where there is a high concentration of the well-off) than in northern England and Scotland.  Among the population as a whole then, but particularly among certain sub-groups, (notably the well-educated middle classes) the health service is seen to be getting worse; could it be that the new 'consumer consciousness' has simply resulted in higher expectations of performance which have so far not materialised?

Respondents were also asked about particular services such as out-patient treatment and in-patient care.  Again, there was a sharp rise in dissatisfaction with each between 1983 and 1986 but since then attitudes have shown little change.  The latest figures are shown below, still indicating that outpatient services are of particular concern.

**Satisfaction with NHS in-patient and out-patient services, 1991**

| | In-patient | Out-patient |
|---|---|---|
| | % | % |
| Very satisfied | 25 }64 | 15 }52 |
| Quite satisfied | 39 | 37 |
| Neither | 16 | 15 |
| Quite dissatisfied | 9 }13 | 18 }26 |
| Very dissatisfied | 4 | 8 |

While the controversies and exposure surrounding the NHS may have served to heighten discontent with the NHS as a whole, they seem to have had less effect on perceptions of specific services. In respect of primary care for instance, there has even been some decline in levels of dissatisfaction (which were already low to start with): in 1983, 13 per cent were dissatisfied with family doctors and by 1991 this proportion had fallen to nine per cent. Satisfaction with dentists, health visitors and district nurses also remained very high.

*The insider's view*

We conducted a special analysis of change in attitudes among the small sub-sample of respondents who were NHS employees (admittedly only 168 cases) and found that their attitudes were distinctive. In particular, between 1987 and 1991 health staff (covering all those at all levels employed in the NHS) became more concerned about standards in hospital services and more likely to stress the need for improvement in the 'general condition of hospital buildings' and in hospital accident and emergency departments. They also showed increased worry about the quality of nursing care in hospitals (some of them were, of course, nurses): the proportion calling for improvement rose from 29 to 38 per cent over the four-year period during which concern in the population generally rose from 21 to 25 per cent. Moreover, as the next table shows, NHS staff were more likely than the public at large to be dissatisfied with both NHS in-patient and out-patient services.

**Satisfaction with NHS in-patient and out-patient services, 1991**

| | In-patient | | Out-patient | |
|---|---|---|---|---|
| | All | NHS staff | All | NHS staff |
| | % | % | % | % |
| Very/quite satisfied | 64 | 63 | 52 | 47 |
| Neither | 16 | 12 | 15 | 17 |
| Very/quite dissatisfied | 13 | 21 | 26 | 32 |

As far as both in-patient and out-patient services are concerned, the ratio of satisfied to dissatisfied is noticeably higher among the public than it is among NHS staff. As far as primary care is concerned, however, NHS staff attitudes were not so distinctive. The high proportion of NHS staff satisfied with local doctors, for instance, was virtually the same as that of the population as a whole.

So NHS staff seem, on our evidence, to have reacted in a distinctive way to the debate on NHS reforms. On the one hand, the proportion of staff dissatisfied with the NHS fell from 67 to 50 per cent between 1990 and 1991 (a greater decrease than that in the population generally - from 47 to 41 per cent) and the proportion satisfied rose from 21 to 34 per cent; but at the same time many NHS staff have become more inclined to register concern about specific aspects of the service. Perhaps the controversies and reforms have propelled them towards greater support for the NHS as an institution, and to feel increasing frustration at those aspects of the service which seem to let it down.

## Issues for the mid-1990s

The 1990s are surely unlikely to see a repetition of the generalised political conflict over the NHS that we witnessed during the 1980s. The major political parties are no longer offering sharply contrasting positions on its structure and management, and the issues of the 1990s are thus likely to be more local, and more concerned with specific aspects of the service.

### Primary health care

One effect of the reforms is likely to be an increased role for primary care. This will start from a base of generally favourable attitudes to family doctors, but with some long-running criticism of particular aspects such as appointment systems:

**Aspects of primary care seen as in need of improvement, 1987-91**

|                                                   | 1987 | 1989 | 1990 | 1991 |
|---------------------------------------------------|------|------|------|------|
| % saying that each is in need of improvement ('a lot' or 'some')* |      |      |      |      |
| GPs' appointment systems                          | 47   | 45   | 41   | 44   |
| Amount of time GP gives to each patient           | 33   | 34   | 31   | 29   |
| Waiting areas at GPs' surgeries                   | n/a  | n/a  | 28   | 27   |
| Being able to choose which GP to see              | 29   | 30   | 27   | 26   |
| Quality of medical treatment by GPs               | 26   | 27   | 24   | 26   |

* The order of the items is according to the amount of criticism they attracted in 1991. The question about waiting areas was not asked in 1987 or 1989.

New policies are now in place with the aim of improving the quality of service and care in general practice. For example, most practices are now taking part in medical audits and it has become easier for patients to change GPs. We await further rounds of this series to discover what impact the large investment now being made in improvements will actually have on consumer attitudes.

Secondary care is also likely to change both in location and in how it is organised. There will be a reduction in numbers of large hospitals in city centres and an increase in day treatment. Day services, which already amount to a fifth of all admissions, are now likely to be concentrated in a few large cities. In the long term, services could become more effective and accessible, but public attitudes may be influenced by the traumatic adjustment at the outset.

*Competition with the private sector*

From 1983 to 1990 there was an increase from 11 per cent to 17 per cent in the proportion of respondents covered by private health insurance. For just over half of those privately insured (53 per cent), cover was a perk that came with the job. By 1991 this upward trend had halted, with 15 per cent covered overall, perhaps in part because the recession has reduced employers' willingness to pay. Predictably, of course, it is those who are best off who are covered: 29 per cent of those with degrees and 41 per cent of those with incomes above £26,000 a year, compared with seven per cent of the least well qualified and four per cent of those in the lowest income group.

The 1991 survey provides new material on detailed perceptions of the role of the private sector. New questions covered medical, nursing and hotel aspects of care. The questions were intended to act as a benchmark to allow us to monitor into the 1990s public perceptions of the strengths and weaknesses of NHS hospitals and private hospitals. We asked:

*From what you know or have heard, how would you compare NHS treatment in an NHS hospital with private treatment in a private hospital?*

| | | NHS hospitals are: | | Private hospitals are: | | | | |
|---|---|---|---|---|---|---|---|---|
| | | Much better | A little better | No differ-ence | A little better | Much better | DK/ NA | MEAN* SCORE |
| Being able to deal with unexpected medical complications | % | 14 | 8 | 26 | 6 | 9 | 38 | 2.00 |
| Quality of nursing care | % | 6 | 5 | 29 | 13 | 17 | 30 | 1.81 |
| Having the latest medical equipment | % | 9 | 7 | 14 | 14 | 22 | 33 | 1.68 |
| Amount of information given by doctor about the patient's condition | % | 5 | 4 | 22 | 14 | 18 | 37 | 1.51 |
| Quality of medical treatment | % | 7 | 5 | 28 | 14 | 16 | 30 | 1.34 |
| Quality and choice of food | % | 6 | 4 | 7 | 11 | 43 | 29 | 1.31 |
| Waiting time before an operation can take place | % | 7 | 3 | 5 | 7 | 50 | 28 | 1.27 |

* The mean score was derived from scoring 'NHS hospitals much better' = +5 to 'Private hospitals much better' = +1 ('don't know' and 'not answered' are omitted). In this table the items have been ordered according to the mean score of each.

Reassuringly perhaps, around a third of respondents admitted that they knew too little about the differences between the two sectors to be able to say which was the better.

Predictably, there was a vote of confidence for the hotel services provided by the private sector. For instance, 54 per cent of all respondents (and three in four of those expressing a view) thought that the food in private hospitals was better. As expected too, nearly four in five respondents who expressed a view also perceived private hospitals as having shorter waiting times. Less predictably, perhaps, private hospitals were perceived as being better than NHS hospitals on all aspects of care except coping with unexpected medical complications. Within the internal market there will certainly be more competition between private and NHS hospitals and, on our evidence to date, patients will be all too eager to sample the attractions of private hospitals - given the fact that their perceived disadvantages are not all that apparent. This of course, leaves aside entirely questions of cost.

**Conclusions**

The changes in attitudes we have noted since 1989 give some clues to how perceptions of the health service may alter during the 1990s. First, the NHS is unlikely to have the same prominence as in the 1980s. With responsibility for assessing needs and buying services shifting out of the 'ownership' of Westminster and Whitehall, there may well be a decline in general public interest. (There is even the possibility -remote though it seems at present - of a new political consensus.) One of the effects of the internal market is likely to be that NHS funding and access will come to be seen as a series of local problems rather than as a single national one. The 'health crisis' may go the way of the public housing crisis, which shifted to local and more autonomous public enterprise, which in turn led to a change in public perceptions. Centralisation and politicisation are inextricably linked; thus changes in structure are likely to lead to changes in attitude. However, one important *caveat* remains. The NHS will inevitably face squeezes as a result of the enduring problems of the British economy, and no amount of structural change will disguise a shortfall in resources. This will doubtless help to ensure that the NHS does stay prominently on the national political agenda, although perhaps not as prominently as in the recent past.

The new incentives built into the NHS reforms may lead to changes which will be cumulative in their impact on attitudes. As already noted, primary care is likely to have a much more conspicuous role. Already the GPs' response to fund holding has been much more positive than once predicted in some quarters, turning it from an experimental programme into one that is likely to cover 50 per cent of the population by 1995. The new purchasing authorities may by then be in a position to manage an integrated budget covering primary as well as secondary care, and they are likely to invest further in primary care. The family doctor service, among the most popular of those provided by the NHS, is likely to continue to attract loyalty from its patients with whom it has regular contact.

The new NHS is likely to place greater emphasis on local ability to manage a way out of trouble and to meet performance standards. There will thus be less incentive and less opportunity to shift problems upwards towards national government. In addition, the new emphasis on health promotion, and on *personal* responsibility for lifestyle changes, will work to depoliticise health care still further. The government has already been surprisingly successful in shifting responsibility for decisions about priorities in the delivery of services from national to local institutions. So the 1990s seem likely to show a much greater preoccupation with the doings of local managers and with the needs of patients in diverse localities and client groups.

A more pluralistic system of health care in Britain may well lead to some intense *local* conflicts, but the age of national confrontation over broad collective issues seems to be passing. The successive health service crises of the 1980s were 'owned' by government. From now on, ownership is likely to pass to local doctors, managers and patients.

For the private sector this change presents continuing problems of adjustment to a new environment. There is every likelihood, for instance, that it will find its medium technology hospital treatment increasingly uncompetitive in the new marketplace. The private sector's best prospect seems to lie in new kinds of partnership with the public sector in the acute services. It is also more likely to expand further in long-term care of elderly people. Here, as elsewhere, its reputation will depend on whether it is able to maintain quality in care. The new marketplace in the health services may well, in effect, be a series of local marketplaces, each of which will depend on local initiatives. We might well find in future rounds, therefore, that the sense of national consensus about the NHS begins to give way to a much more diverse set of attitudes and responses which depend more on where you live than on what you believe in principle.

## References

Bosanquet, N. (1984), 'Social Policy and the Welfare State', in Jowell, R. and Airey, C. (eds.), *British Social Attitudes: the 1984 Report*, Aldershot: Gower.

Bosanquet, N. (1988), 'An Ailing State of National Health', in Jowell, R., Witherspoon, S. and Brook, L. (eds.), *British Social Attitudes: the 5th Report*, Aldershot: Gower.

Bosanquet, N. (1989), 'Public Opinion and the Welfare State', in Millard, F. (ed.), *Social Welfare and the Market*, London: STICERD/LSE.

Halsey, A. H. (1991), 'Failing Education?', in Jowell, R., Brook, L. and Taylor, B. with Prior, G. (eds.), *British Social Attitudes: the 8th Report*, Aldershot: Dartmouth.

Taylor-Gooby, P. (1990), 'Social Welfare: The Unkindest Cuts', in Jowell, R., Witherspoon, S. and Brook, L. with Taylor, B. (eds.), *British Social Attitudes: the 7th Report*, Aldershot: Gower.

## Acknowledgement

SCPR is grateful to the Department of Health for its financial support which helps to ensure that we can continue to include questions on health care.

# Appendix I
# Technical details of the surveys

## British Social Attitudes

Since 1986 the generosity of the Sainsbury Family Charitable Trusts has enabled us to interview around 3,000 respondents a year, a substantial increase from the 1,700 to 1,800 interviewed in the first three years of the survey series. Core questions were asked of all respondents, and the remaining questions were asked of a random half sample of around 1,500 respondents each - version A of one half, version B of the other. The structure of the questionnaire is shown in Appendix III.

### Sampling experiment

In 1991 we decided to investigate the effect of using a different sampling frame. All previous BSA samples had been drawn from the electoral register (ER). This time, half of the BSA sample was drawn from ER, and half from the Postcode Address File (PAF).

In recent years, concern has been growing among survey researchers about deficiencies in the coverage of ER, not only of individuals in the adult population but also of addresses. ER is known to have certain biases in coverage: registration rates are particularly low among young people and ethnic minorities, and in inner cities. There is also evidence that coverage of the register has worsened in recent years. PAF is a list of addresses - postal delivery points - compiled by the Post Office. It has greater coverage of addresses than ER, with no detectable bias in coverage.

Because of these differences, a change from ER to PAF as a sampling frame may have an effect on response rates, on the demographic and socio-economic structure of the respondent 'population', and hence on the distribution of responses to particular questions. Effects such as these would be particularly serious for a time-series such as *British Social Attitudes*, where it is important to maintain year-on-year consistency. It would thus be unwise to move directly from ER to PAF without attempting to assess what effects, if any, the change to a new sampling frame might have on the distribution of responses. For this reason, it was decided to conduct a 'splicing' experiment, drawing half of the BSA sample from each sampling frame. The Market Research Development Fund contributed towards the marginal costs of this experiment, and we are grateful to them for their support. Extensive analysis of the results of using the different sampling frames is underway, and will shortly be published.

**Sample design**

The *British Social Attitudes* survey is designed to yield a representative sample of adults aged 18 or over. For practical reasons, the sample is confined to those living in private households. People living in institutions (though not in private households at such institutions) are excluded, as are households whose addresses were not on the electoral register (ER half) or the Postcode Address File (PAF half).

The sampling method involved a multi-stage design, with four separate stages of selection.

*Selection of parliamentary constituencies*

At the first stage, 176 parliamentary constituencies were selected from all those in England, Scotland and Wales. In Scotland, the four constituencies north of the Caledonian Canal were excluded: their geographically scattered inhabitants are prohibitively costly to interview.

Before selection, constituencies were stratified according to information held in SCPR's constituency datafile, compiled from information in OPCS *Monitors*, and including a variety of social indicators. The stratification factors used in the 1991 survey were:

- Registrar General's Standard Region
- Population density (persons per hectare) with variable banding used according to region, in order to make the strata roughly equal in size[1]
- Ranking by percentage of homes that were owner-occupied, from the 1981 Census figures

Constituencies were then selected systematically with probability of selection proportionate to size of electorate. The 176 selected constituencies were then allocated alternately to the ER and PAF halves of the sample, 88 constituencies to each.

## Electoral register sample

### Selection of polling districts

Fieldwork was timed to start in mid-March, so the sample was drawn from the 1990 registers, which were just reaching the end of their period of currency.

Within most of the 88 constituencies selected for the ER sample a single polling district was chosen. Any polling district with fewer than 500 electors was combined with one or more other polling districts before the selection stage, so that in some constituencies a combination of polling districts was selected. Polling districts were chosen with probability proportionate to size of electorate.

### Selection of addresses

Twenty-six addresses were selected in each of the 88 polling districts. The ER sample issued to interviewers was therefore 88 x 26 = 2288 addresses.

The addresses in each polling district were selected by starting from a random point on the list of electors and, treating the list as circular, choosing each address at a fixed interval. The fixed interval was calculated for each polling district separately to generate the correct number of addresses.

By this means, addresses were chosen with probability proportionate to their number of listed electors. At each sampled address the names of all electors given on the register were listed, and the name of the individual on which the sampling interval had landed was marked with an asterisk. This person is known as the 'starred elector'. Each starred elector was allocated a serial number.

### Selection of individuals

The electoral register is an unsatisfactory sampling frame of *individuals,* although it is regarded as reasonably complete as a frame of *addresses.* So a further selection stage was required to convert the listing of addresses into a sample of individuals.

Interviewers were instructed to call at the address of each starred elector and to list all those eligible for inclusion in the sample - that is, all persons currently aged 18 or over and resident at the selected household.

In households where the list of people eligible to take part in the survey was the same as the electoral register listing, the interviewer was instructed to interview the starred elector. Where there was a difference between the household members named in the register and those eligible to take part in the survey (because there had been movement into or out of the address after the compilation of the electoral register, or because some people were not registered) the interviewer selected one respondent by a random selection procedure (using a computer-generated Kish grid). Where there were two or more households at the selected address, interviewers were required to identify the household of the starred elector, or the household occupying the part of the address where he or she used to live, and to select a household using a Kish grid; then they followed the same procedure to select a person for interview.

## Postcode Address File sample

### Selection of ward segments

In order to select a PAF segment equivalent in size to a polling district, a two-stage procedure was adopted. First, within each of the selected constituencies, a single ward was selected. Any ward containing fewer than 1500 addresses was combined with a contiguous ward (from within the same constituency) before the selection stage, so that in some constituencies a ward group was selected. Wards (or ward groups) were then selected with probability proportionate to the number of addresses listed in the PAF.

Then, within each selected ward (or ward group) the PAF addresses were listed in alphanumeric order of postcode, and the list was split into three equal-sized segments. One of the segments was then selected at random.

### Selection of addresses

Twenty-eight addresses were selected in each of the 88 ward segments. The PAF sample was therefore 88 x 28 = 2464 addresses. More addresses were selected on the PAF half of the sample than on the ER half, because a greater proportion of 'deadwood' addresses (such as unoccupied addresses or those that are business premises only) are listed on PAF than on ER.

The addresses in each ward segment were selected by starting from a random point on the list of addresses, and choosing each address at a fixed interval. The fixed interval was calculated for each ward segment separately in order to generate the correct number of addresses.

*Selection of individuals*

Interviewers called at each address selected from the PAF, and listed all those eligible for inclusion in the sample - that is, all persons currently aged 18 or over and resident at the selected address.

The interviewer then selected one respondent by a random selection procedure (using a Kish grid). Where there were two or more households or 'dwelling units' at the selected address, interviewers first had to select one household or dwelling unit using a Kish grid; they then followed the same procedure to select a person for interview.

## Questionnaire versions

Alternate serial numbers were allocated to the A or B half of the sample. Odd serial numbers were allocated to the A sample, and even serial numbers to the B sample, so that each questionnaire version was assigned to 2,376 addresses. This meant that each interviewer (and each sampling point) had both A and B addresses.

## Weighting

Before analysis, the data were weighted. Weighting procedures differed for the ER and PAF halves of the sample.

*Electoral register sample*

The weighting took account of any differences between the number of people listed on the register (which determined the initial selection probability) and the number found at the address. Such differences were found in 28 per cent of addresses, in each of which data were weighted by the number of persons aged 18 or over currently living at the address divided by the number of electors listed on the register for that address. The vast majority of such weights was between 0.25 and 2.0. Weights below 0.25 were applied in only four cases, and weights above 2.0 in only eight cases. At 72 per cent of addresses the number of persons listed on the register and the number found at the address matched, so that the effective weight was one. The unweighted base (the number of persons interviewed) for the electoral register sample was 1,477 and the weighted base was 1,418.

*Postcode Address File sample*

The Postcode Address File does not list the number of persons at each address, and so the selection probabilities could not take size of household into account. So the data were weighted to take account of the fact that individuals living in large households had a lower chance than individuals in small households of being included in the sample. In addition, the PAF does not contain any information about how many households or 'dwelling units' are present at each address; in some cases several dwelling units have the same postal address. To compensate for this, the weighting has to take account of the number of dwelling units at an address, as well as the number of adults in the selected unit.

This means that the weights applied to the PAF sample are, in general, larger than those applied to the ER sample. All the weights fell within a range between one and 20, and the average weight applied was 2.0. In order to retain the original sample structure, the weighted PAF sample was scaled down to make the number of weighted productive cases exactly equal to the number of weighted cases in the ER sample.

The unweighted base (the number of persons interviewed) for the PAF half of the sample was 1,441 and the weighted base was 1,418. The distribution of weights used is shown below:

| Weight | No. | % | Scaled weight |
|--------|-----|------|---------------|
| 1 | 415 | 28.8 | 0.490 |
| 2 | 789 | 54.8 | 0.980 |
| 3 | 153 | 10.6 | 1.470 |
| 4 | 59 | 4.1 | 1.961 |
| 5 | 6 | 0.4 | 2.451 |
| 6 | 7 | 0.5 | 2.941 |
| 7 | 1 | 0.1 | 3.431 |
| 8 | 5 | 0.3 | 3.921 |
| 10 | 1 | 0.1 | 4.901 |
| 12 | 1 | 0.1 | 5.882 |
| 14 | 2 | 0.1 | 6.862 |
| 16 | 1 | 0.1 | 7.842 |
| 20 | 1 | 0.1 | 9.803 |

## Fieldwork

Interviewing was carried out mainly during March, April and May 1991, with 16 per cent of interviews taking place later.

Fieldwork was conducted by interviewers drawn from SCPR's regular panel. All interviewers attended a one-day briefing conference to familiarise them with the selection procedures and questionnaires.

The average interview length was, for version A of the questionnaire, 60 minutes, and for version B, 59 minutes.

The final response achieved is shown below:

|  | No. | % |
|---|---|---|
| Addresses issued | 4752 | |
| Vacant, derelict, other out of scope | 374 | |
| In scope | 4378 | 100.0 |
| Interview achieved | 2918 | 66.7 |
| Interview not achieved | 1460 | 33.3 |
| Refused | 1120[2] | 25.6 |
| Not contacted | 182[3] | 4.2 |
| Other non-response | 158 | 3.6 |

The response rate achieved with the A version of the questionnaire was the same as with the B version, at 67 per cent. The response rate on the ER half of the sample was 67 per cent, and that on the PAF half, 66 per cent. Overall response rates ranged between 75 per cent in the South-West, and 62 per cent in Greater London and 61 per cent in the South-East.

As in earlier rounds of the series, respondents were asked to fill in a self-completion questionnaire which was, whenever possible, collected by the interviewer. Otherwise, the respondent was asked to post it to SCPR. If necessary, up to three postal reminders were sent to obtain the self-completion supplement.

Four hundred and thirty-seven respondents (15 per cent of those interviewed) did not return their self-completion questionnaire. Versions A and B of the self-completion questionnaire were both returned by the same proportion of respondents - 85 per cent. Since the overall proportion returning a self-completion questionnaire was high we decided against additional weighting to correct for non-response.

## Advance letter experiment

As an experiment to test the effect on response rates, a letter was sent to a random two-thirds of the selected households in the *British Social Attitudes* sample. (Every third address, beginning with the third, did not receive the advance letter.) The letter briefly described the purpose of the survey and the coverage of the questionnaire, and asked for co-operation when the interviewer called. The effect of the advance letter on overall response was apparently negligible. The response rate among respondents who had been sent the advance letter was 67 per cent; among those who had not been sent the advance letter, it was 66 per cent. For further details, see Brook, Taylor and Prior (1992).

**Analysis variables**

A number of standard analyses have been used in the tables that appear both in the text and at the end of the chapters of this report. The analysis groups requiring further definition are set out below.

*Region*

The Registrar General's 10 Standard Regions have been used, except that we have distinguished between Greater London and the remainder of the South-East. Sometimes these have been grouped into what we have termed 'compressed region': 'Northern' includes the North, North-West and Yorkshire and Humberside. East Anglia is included in the 'South', as is the South-West.

*Change to Standard Occupational Classification (SOC)*

Respondents are classified according to their own occupation, not that of a 'head of household'. Their spouses or partners are similarly classified. The main social class variables used in the analyses in this report are Registrar General's Social Class and Socio-economic Group (SEG).

In previous years, *British Social Attitudes* occupation coding has been carried out according to the OPCS *Classification of Occupations 1980* (CO80). In 1991, OPCS introduced a new occupation coding schema, the *Standard Occupational Classification* (SOC), and the new schema was used for the occupation coding on the 1991 BSA survey. SOC has a hierarchical structure, consisting of 371 Unit Groups which can be aggregated into 77 Minor Groups,, 22 Sub-major Groups and 9 Major Groups. The reasons why a new schema was developed are explained in OPCS (1991a, 1991b).

Social Class and SEG were rebased on SOC by OPCS according to the principle of maximum continuity; that is, the number of jobs (and hence persons) allocated to the same Social Class or SEG category as when they were based on CO80 was maximised.

In practice, OPCS have established that overall, 2.3 per cent of jobs were assigned to a different Social Class due to the rebasing on SOC, and 2.0 per cent of jobs to a different Socio-economic Group (see OPCS, 1991b). While the net redistribution of cases due to rebasing on SOC is small, most of the change is concentrated in particular categories, so the impact of change on those categories can be substantial (see OPCS, 1991b, p. 15). In practice, however, analysts can be confident that the change to SOC does not affect year-on-year comparability of social class variables in the *British Social Attitudes* survey.

*Registrar General's Social Class*

Each respondent's Social Class is based on his or her current or last occupation. So all respondents in paid work at the time of the interview, or waiting to take up a paid job already offered, or retired, or seeking work, or looking after the home, have their occupation (present, future or last as appropriate) classified into Occupational Unit Groups, according to the OPCS Standard Occupational Classification 1991. The combination of occupational classification with employment status generates the six Social Classes:

| | | |
|---|---|---|
| I | Professional, etc. occupations | |
| II | Managerial and technical occupations | } 'Non-manual' |
| III (Non-manual) | Skilled occupations | |
| III (Manual) | Skilled occupations | |
| IV | Partly skilled occupations | } 'Manual' |
| V | Unskilled occupations | |

In this report we have usually collapsed them into four groups: I & II, III Non-manual, III Manual, IV & V.

The remaining respondents are grouped as 'never worked/not classifiable', but are not shown in the tables. For some analyses, it may be more appropriate to classify respondents according to their *current* social class, which takes into account only their present economic position. In this case, in addition to the six social classes listed above, the remaining respondents not currently in paid work fall into one of the following categories: 'not classified', 'retired', 'looking after the home', 'unemployed' or 'others not in paid occupations'.


*Socio-economic Group*

As with Social Class, each respondent's SEG is based on his or her current or last occupation. SEG aims to bring together people with jobs of similar social and economic status, and is derived from a combination of employment status and occupation. The full SEG classification identifies 18 categories, but in this Report we have usually condensed these into groups:

- Professionals, employers and managers
- Intermediate non-manual workers
- Junior non-manual workers
- Skilled manual workers
- Semi-skilled manual workers
- Unskilled manual workers

As with Social Class, the remaining respondents are grouped as 'never worked/not classifiable', but are not shown in the tables.

*Goldthorpe schema*

The Goldthorpe schema classifies occupations by their 'general comparability', considering such factors as sources and levels of income, economic security, promotion prospects, and level of job autonomy and authority.    We have developed a programme which derives the Goldthorpe classification from the SOC unit groups combined with employment status.  Two versions of the Goldthorpe schema are coded. The full schema has 11 categories, and the 'compressed schema' combines these into five classes:

- Salariat (professional and managerial)
- Routine non-manual workers (office and sales)
- Petty bourgeoisie (the self-employed, including farmers, with and without employees)
- Manual foremen and supervisors
- Working class (skilled, semi-skilled and unskilled manual workers, personal service and agricultural workers)

There is a residual category of those who have never had a job or who have given insufficient information.

The Goldthorpe schema has also been rebased on SOC (see Goldthorpe and Heath, 1992).  The new schema was not available in time to be incorporated into analyses in this report, but it has now been added to the dataset, and so can be used by secondary analysts with access to the data.

*Industry*

All respondents whose occupation could be coded were allocated a Standard Industrial Classification (SIC, 1980). Two-digit class codes were applied.  Respondents were also classified as working in public sector services, public sector manufacturing and transport, private sector manufacturing or private sector non-manufacturing, by cross-analysing SIC categories with responses to a question about the type of employer for whom they worked.  As with Social Class, SIC may be generated on the basis of the respondent's current occupation only, or on his or her most recently-classifiable occupation.

*Party identification*

Respondents can be classified as identifying with a particular political party, or party grouping, on one of three counts: if they consider themselves supporters of the party (Q.2a,d), or as closer to it than to others (Q.2b,d), or as more likely to support it in the event of a general election (Q.2c).  The three groups are generally described respectively as *partisans, sympathisers,* and *residual identifiers.* The three groups combined are referred to in both text and tables as 'identifiers'.

Liberal Democrat identifiers (in spring 1991) also include those nominating the 'Social and Liberal Democrat Party' or the 'Liberal Party'. Mentions of 'Alliance' or 'Independent Liberal' or 'Independent SDP' were coded in the 'Other party' category.

*Other analysis variables*

These are taken directly from the questionnaire, and to that extent are self-explanatory. The principal ones used in the in-text tables are:

| | |
|---|---|
| Sex (Q.901a) | Highest educational qualification |
| Age (Q.901b) | obtained (Q.907,908) |
| Household income (Q.917a) | Marital status (Q.900) |
| Economic position (Q.12) | Religion (Q.103 (A version)/Q.116 (B version)) |

**Sampling errors**

No sample precisely reflects the characteristics of the population it represents because of both sampling and non-sampling errors. If a sample were designed as a random sample (if every adult had an equal and independent chance of inclusion in the sample) then we could calculate the sampling error of any percentage, $p$, using the formula:

$$s.e\ (p) = \sqrt{\frac{p(100\text{-}p)}{n}}$$

where $n$ is the number of respondents on which the percentage is based. Once the sampling error had been calculated, it would be a straightforward exercise to calculate a confidence interval for the true population percentage. For example, a 95 per cent confidence interval would be given by the formula:

$$p \pm 1.96 \times s.e.(p)$$

Clearly, for a simple random sample (srs), the sampling error depends only on the values of $p$ and $n$. However, simple random sampling is almost never used in practice because of its inefficiency in terms of time and cost.

As noted above, the *British Social Attitudes* sample, like that drawn for most large-scale surveys, was clustered according to a stratified multi-stage design into 176 polling districts (or combinations or equivalents of polling districts). With a complex design like this, the sampling error of a percentage giving a particular response is not simply a function of the number of respondents in the sample and the size of the percentage; it also depends on how that percentage response is spread within and between polling districts. The complex design may be assessed relative to simple random sampling by calculating a range of design factors (DEFTs) associated with it, where

$$\text{DEFT} = \sqrt{\frac{\text{Variance of estimator with complex design, sample size n}}{\text{Variance of estimator with srs design, sample size n}}}$$

and represents the multiplying factor to be applied to the simple random sampling error to produce its complex equivalent. A design factor of one means that the complex sample has achieved the same precision as a simple random sample of the same size. A design factor greater than one means the complex sample is less precise than its simple random sample equivalent.

If the DEFT for a particular characteristic is known, a 95 per cent confidence interval for a percentage may be calculated using the formula:

$$p \pm 1.96 \times \textit{complex sampling error (p)}$$

$$= p \pm 1.96 \times \text{DEFT} \times \sqrt{\frac{p(100\text{-}p)}{n}}$$

Calculations of sampling errors and design effects were made using the World Fertility Survey 'Clusters' programme.

The table below gives examples of the DEFTs and confidence intervals calculated. For most attitudinal questions asked of the whole sample, we can see that the confidence interval is usually around plus or minus two per cent of the survey proportion; so we can be 95 per cent certain that the true population proportion is within two per cent (in either direction) of the proportion we report. However, for certain variables (those most associated with the area a person lives in) we find the confidence interval is plus or minus three per cent or more. This is particularly so for party identification and housing tenure. For instance, Labour identifiers and local authority tenants tend to be concentrated within certain areas; consequently there is proportionately more variation in a clustered sample than there would be in a simple random sample. But for most variables, especially attitudinal ones, the use of standard statistical tests of significance (based on the assumption of simple random sampling) is unlikely to be misleading. The table below also shows that, when questions were asked of only half the sample, confidence intervals are correspondingly greater.

| Classification variables | | % (*p*) | Complex standard error of *p* (%) | 95 per cent confidence interval | DEFT |
|---|---|---|---|---|---|
| Q.2 | **Party identification** | | | | |
| | Conservative | 34.8 | 1.56 | 31.7 - 37.9 | 1.77 |
| | Liberal Democrat | 12.2 | 0.81 | 10.6 - 13.8 | 1.34 |
| | Labour | 35.3 | 1.51 | 32.3 - 38.3 | 1.71 |
| A100 /B104 | **Housing tenure** | | | | |
| | Owns | 66.2 | 1.87 | 62.5 - 69.9 | 2.14 |
| | Rents from local authority | 21.1 | 1.67 | 17.8 - 24.4 | 2.20 |
| | Rents privately | 11.1 | 1.28 | 8.6 - 13.6 | 2.10 |
| A101 /B114 | **Religion** | | | | |
| | No religion | 35.1 | 1.19 | 32.8 - 37.4 | 1.34 |
| | Church of England | 35.6 | 1.34 | 33.0 - 38.2 | 1.50 |
| | Catholic | 10.1 | 0.71 | 8.7 - 11.5 | 1.25 |
| Q.906 | **Age of completing continuous full-time education** | | | | |
| | 16 or under | 67.8 | 1.46 | 64.9 - 70.7 | 1.69 |
| | 17 or 18 | 16.1 | 0.87 | 14.4 - 17.8 | 1.27 |
| | 19 or over | 13.0 | 0.94 | 11.2 - 14.8 | 1.51 |
| **Attitudinal variables** | | | | | |
| Q.5 | **Benefits for the unemployed are...** | | | | |
| | ... too low | 52.6 | 1.37 | 49.9 - 55.3 | 1.43 |
| | ... too high | 26.7 | 1.18 | 24.4 - 29.0 | 1.33 |
| Q.59a | **Health care should be the same for everyone** | 54.3 | 1.66 | 51.0 - 57.6 | 1.27 |
| B62 | **Expect unemployment to go up** | 71.4 | 1.38 | 68.7 - 74.1 | 1.16 |
| B71f | **Concern about the 'greenhouse effect'** | | | | |
| | Very concerned | 40.9 | 1.61 | 37.7 - 44.1 | 1.21 |
| | A bit concerned | 37.2 | 1.54 | 34.2 - 40.2 | 1.17 |
| | Not very concerned | 13.6 | 1.13 | 11.4 - 15.8 | 1.20 |
| | Not at all concerned | 4.5 | 0.76 | 3.0 - 6.0 | 1.34 |
| A2.04 | **Pre-marital sex always or mostly wrong** | 17.6 | 1.21 | 15.2 - 20.0 | 1.06 |
| A2.05 | **Extra-marital sex always or mostly wrong** | 82.7 | 1.56 | 79.6 - 85.8 | 1.56 |

These calculations are based on the total sample from the 1991 survey (2,836 weighted, 2,918 unweighted), or on A respondents (1,414 weighted, 1,473 unweighted) or B respondents (1,422 weighted, 1,445 unweighted). As the examples above show, sampling errors for proportions based only on the A or B sample, or on subgroups within the sample, are somewhat larger than they would have been, had the questions been asked of everyone.

## Notes

1.  The population density bands used were as follows:

| Region | Density banding (persons per hectare) |
|---|---|
| North<br>North-West } | Under 6; 6-13; over 13 |
| Yorks and Humberside | Under 8; 8-21; over 21 |
| West Midlands | Under 5; 5-34; over 34 |
| East Midlands<br>East Anglia }<br>South-West | Under 2; 2-10; over 10 |
| South-East | Under 4; 4-8; over 8 |
| Greater London | Under 40; 40-65; over 65 |
| Wales }<br>Scotland | Under 2; 2-10; over 10 |

2.  'Refusals' comprise refusals before selection of an individual at the address, refusals to the office, refusal by the selected person, 'proxy' refusals (on behalf of the selected respondent) and broken appointments after which the selected person could not be recontacted.
3.  'Non-contacts' comprise households where no-one was contacted, and those where the selected person could not be contacted (never found at home, known to be away on business, on holiday, in hospital, and so on).

## Northern Ireland Social Attitudes

In 1991 for the third year the *British Social Attitudes* survey was extended to include Northern Ireland, with funding from the Nuffield Foundation and the Central Community Relations Unit in Belfast. In 1991, as in previous years, core questions were asked in both surveys, but in addition there was a special module in the Northern Ireland questionnaire; in 1991 this module was mainly concerned with community relations (Qs. 76-97 on the interview questionnaire and Qs.2.38-2.42 on the self-completion questionnaire). To maintain the time-series, many items from the 1989 and 1990 surveys were repeated. Some of these questions were asked in Britain too (Version A, Qs.71-78), so allowing us to compare the attitudes of those living in Northern Ireland with the attitudes of people in Britain. The structure of the Northern Ireland questionnaire, and its relationship to the British questionnaire, is shown in Appendix III.

Representatives from SCPR, the Policy Planning and Research Unit (PPRU) in Belfast (which also carried out the sampling and the fieldwork), the Centre for Social Research at Queen's University in Belfast (which reports separately on the Northern Ireland results), and the Central Community Relations Unit met in the months before fieldwork to plan the survey and design the questionnaire module. As with all questionnaire modules, however, final responsibility for its coverage and wording remains with SCPR.*

## Sample design

The survey was designed to yield a representative sample of all adults aged 18 or over living in private households in Northern Ireland.

The sample was drawn from the rating list, the most up-to-date listing of private households, made available to PPRU for research purposes. People living in institutions (though not in private households in such institutions) are excluded.

Before addresses were selected, the rating list file was stratified into three geographical areas: Belfast, East Northern Ireland and West Northern Ireland. Within each of these strata a simple random sample of addresses was selected, with probability proportionate to the number of addresses in that stratum. A combination of the small geographical size of Northern Ireland, the generally low population density (outside the Greater Belfast area) and the extent of coverage of PPRU's panel of interviewers mean that it is not necessary to cluster addresses within areas. Addresses were selected from a computer-based copy of the list using a random-number-generation routine. The issued sample was 1,400 addresses.

## *Selection of individuals*

The rating list provides a good sampling frame of *addresses*, but contains no information about the number of *people* living at an address. So a further selection stage was required to convert the listing of addresses to a listing of individuals.

Interviewers were instructed to call at each address issued in their assignments. They then had to list all people resident at the address who were eligible for inclusion in the sample: that is, all persons currently aged 18 or over living at the address. From this listing of eligible adults, the interviewer selected one respondent by a random selection procedure (using a computer-generated Kish grid).

In Northern Ireland, addresses could not be selected with probability proportionate to the size of the household (as with the electoral register

---

* For further information about the technical details of the *Northern Ireland Social Attitudes* survey, see Sweeney (1993).

sampling used in *British Social Attitudes*). So before analysis, the data were weighted to adjust for the fact that individuals living in large households had a lower chance than individuals in small households of being included in the sample. This means that the weights applied to the Northern Ireland sample are, in general, larger than those applied to the British one. All the weights fell within a range between one and nine, and the average weight applied was 2.08. In order to retain the actual number of interviews, the weighted sample was scaled back to the size of the unweighted sample, yielding a total of 906 interviews and an average scaled weight of 1. The distribution of weights used is shown below:

| No. of adults aged 18 and over | Weight | No. | % | Scaled weight |
|---|---|---|---|---|
| 1 | 1 | 236 | 26.0 | 0.482 |
| 2 | 2 | 480 | 53.0 | 0.963 |
| 3 | 3 | 110 | 12.1 | 1.445 |
| 4 | 4 | 58 | 6.4 | 1.927 |
| 5 | 5 | 14 | 1.5 | 2.408 |
| 6 | 6 | 5 | 0.6 | 2.890 |
| 7 | 7 | 2 | 0.2 | 3.372 |
| 9 | 9 | 1 | 0.1 | 4.335 |

Thus, 26 per cent of households had only one adult present, 53 per cent were two-adult households, and so on.

## Fieldwork

Fieldwork in Northern Ireland began in late February 1991. Ninety-two per cent of interviews were carried out in February and March, 1991, with the remaining 64 interviews carried out later.

Fieldwork was conducted by interviewers drawn from PPRU's panel. All interviewers attended a one-day briefing conference to familiarise them with the selection procedures and the questionnaires. The interview took on average 67 minutes to administer.

### Overall response

|  | No. | % |
|---|---|---|
| Addresses issued | 1400 | |
| Vacant, derelict, other out of scope | 107 | |
| In scope | 1293 | 100.0 |
| Interview achieved | 906 | 70.1 |
| Interview not achieved | 387 | 29.9 |
| Refused | 282 | 21.8 |
| Not contacted | 54 | 4.2 |
| Other non-response | 51 | 3.9 |

As in the *British Social Attitudes* survey, respondents were asked to fill in a self-completion questionnaire which was, whenever possible, collected by the interviewer. Otherwise, the respondent was asked to post it direct to a Northern Ireland Post Office Box from which it was forwarded, through PPRU to SCPR. If necessary, up to two postal reminders were sent to obtain the self-completion questionnaire from those who had not returned it. In all, 848 respondents returned the self-completion questionnaire, 94 per cent of those interviewed.

*Advance letter*

A letter was sent to all the selected households in the *Northern Ireland Social Attitudes* sample shortly before fieldwork began. This briefly described the purpose of the survey and the coverage of the questionnaire, and asked for co-operation when the interviewer called.

## Analysis variables

Analysis variables were mostly the same as those used in the British survey. There were two exceptions. Questions about party identification included Northern Irish political parties; and the *Northern Ireland Social Attitudes* questionnaire carried some questions about mixed or integrated schooling (Qs.902-903).

## Sampling errors

Because the *Northern Ireland Social Attitudes* survey is a simple random sample, there are no complex sampling errors to calculate. The sampling error of any percentage, *p*, can be calculated using the formula:

$$s.e \ (p) \ = \ \sqrt{\frac{p(100-p)}{n}}$$

## References

Brook, L., Prior, G. and Taylor, B. (1992), *British Social Attitudes, 1991 Survey: Technical Report*, London: SCPR.
Goldthorpe, J. and Heath, A. (1992), 'Revised Class Schema 1992', *Working Paper No.13*, London: JUSST.
OPCS (1991a), *Standard Occupational Classification, Volume 1*, London: HMSO.
OPCS (1991b), *Standard Occupational Classification, Volume 3*, London: HMSO.
Sweeney, K. (1993), 'Technical Details of the Survey', in Stringer, P. and Robinson, G., (eds.), *Social Attitudes in Northern Ireland: the 3rd Report*, (forthcoming).

# Appendix II
# Notes on the tabulations

1. Figures in the tables are from the 1991 survey unless otherwise indicated.
2. Tables at the end of chapters and within the text are percentaged as indicated.
3. In tables, '\*' indicates less than 0.5 per cent but greater than zero, and '-' indicates zero.
4. When findings based on the responses of fewer than 50 respondents are reported in the text, reference is made to the small base size. Any percentages based on fewer than 50 respondents (unweighted) are bracketed in the tables.
5. Percentages equal to or greater than 0.5 have been rounded up in all tables (eg. 0.5 per cent = one per cent, 36.5 per cent = 37 per cent).
6. In many tables the proportions of respondents answering 'don't know' or not giving an answer are omitted. This, together with the effects of rounding and weighting, means that percentages will not always add to 100 per cent.
7. 'Liberal Democrat' identifiers in the tables include those nominating (in spring 1991) the Social and Liberal Democrat Party or the Liberal Party.
8. The self-completion questionnaire was not completed by 15 per cent of respondents in Britain and by six per cent of respondents in Northern Ireland (see Appendices I and III). Percentage responses to the self-completion questionnaire are based on all those who completed it.

# Appendix III
# The questionnaires

As explained in Appendix I, two different versions of the questionnaire were administered in Britain (each with its own self-completion supplement), and a separate questionnaire was administered in Northern Ireland (also with its supplement). The diagrams that follow show the structure of the questionnaires and the topics covered (not all of which are reported in this volume).

All six questionnaires (interview and self-completion) are reproduced on the following pages. We have removed the keying codes and inserted instead the percentage distribution of answers to each question. We have also included the SPSS variable name, bracketed and in italics, beside each question. Percentages for the core questions are based on the total sample (2,836 weighted in Britain and 906 weighted and unweighted in Northern Ireland), while those for questions in versions A and B are based on the appropriate subsamples (1,414 and 1,422 weighted). We reproduce first version A of the interview questionnaire in full; then those parts of version B that differ; the two versions of the self-completion questionnaire follow. In the last part of Appendix III we reproduce the interview questionnaire administered in Northern Ireland and its self-completion supplement. Figures do not necessarily add up to 100 because of weighting and rounding, or for one or more of the following reasons:

(i) Some sub-questions are filtered - that is, they are asked of only a proportion of respondents. In these cases the percentages add up (approximately) to the proportions who were asked them. Where, however, a *series* of questions is filtered, we have indicated the weighted base at the beginning of that series (for example, all employees), and throughout derived percentages from that base.

(ii)   If the (unweighted) base for a question is less than 50, frequencies (the *number* of people giving each response) are shown, rather than percentages.

(iii)  At a few questions, respondents were invited to give more than one answer and so percentages may add to well over 100 per cent. These are clearly marked by interviewer instructions on the questionnaires. In addition, percentage signs follow each figure.

As reported in Appendix I, the *British Social Attitudes* self-completion questionnaire was not completed by 15 per cent of respondents who were successfully interviewed. To allow for comparisons over time, the answers in the supplement have been repercentaged on the base of those respondents who returned it (for version A: 1,221 weighted; for version B: 1,207 weighted). This means that the figures are comparable with those given in all earlier reports in this series except in *The 1984 Report*, where the percentages need to be recalculated if comparisons are to be made.

The *Northern Ireland Social Attitudes* self-completion questionnaire was not completed by six per cent of respondents to the main questionnaire. Again the answers in the supplement have been repercentaged on the base of those who returned it (848 weighted and unweighted).

A module on religious beliefs and attitudes, developed as part of SCPR's involvement in the *International Social Survey Programme*, was fielded in the self-completion supplement, on version A of the British supplement, and also on the *Northern Ireland Social Attitudes* supplement (Qs. 2.01-35).

## Structure of the questionnaires
## Britain
### Interview questionnaire
### Both versions

Section 1.   Newspaper readership
             Party political identification
             Welfare State
             National Health Service

Section 2.   Economic activity
             Labour market participation
             Gender issues at the workplace
             Employee training

| **Version A** | **Version B** |
|---|---|
| Section 3.   Social security, pensions and maintenance | Section 3.   European Community Economic issues and policies Perceptions of own household income |
| Section 4.   Right and wrong in business transactions | |
| Section 5.   Northern Ireland | Section 4.   Environment |
| Section 6.   Class and race | Section 5.   Health and lifestyle |
| Section 7.   Gender | Section 6.   Politics and participation |
| Section 8.   Charitable giving | |
| Section 9.   Crime | Section 7.   Housing (long) |
| Section 10.  Housing (short) | |

### Both versions

Version A, Section 11 }   Religious denomination
Version B, Section 8  }   and attendance

Version A, Section 12 }   Demographics and other
Version B, Section 9  }   classificatory variables

### Self-completion questionnaire

| **Version A** | **Version B** |
|---|---|
| Qs. 2.01-35 *ISSP* module: religion | B. 2.01-03  National Health Service* |
| Qs. 2.36-37 National Health Service* | B. 2.04     Welfarism* |
| Q. 2.38     Welfarism* | B. 2.05-15  Training and the workplace* |
| Qs. 2.39-49 Training and the workplace* | B. 2.16-26  Environment |
| Qs. 2.50-51 Business and profits | B. 2.27     Health and lifestyle |
| Qs. 2.52-53 Northern Ireland | B. 2.28-34  Politics, participation and institutions |
| Qs. 2.54-58 Gender issues | |
| Qs. 2.59-62 Attitude scales | B. 2.35-36  Attitude scales |
| | B. 2.37-39  Housing |

*These questions were asked on both versions on the self-completion questionnaire

## Northern Ireland

### Interview questionnaire

Section 1.    Newspaper readership
Welfare state
National Health Service

Section 2.    Economic activity
Labour market participation
Gender issues at the workplace

Section 3.    European Community
Economic issues and policies
Perceptions of own household income

Section 4.    Health and lifestyle

Section 5.    Northern Ireland module:

Religious prejudice and discrimination
Religious segregation*
Evenhandedness of security forces*
Integrated schooling*
Community relations*
Security operations*
Party political identification (*NISA* version)*
Constitutional issues

Section 6.    Gender

Section 7.    Charitable giving

Section 8.    Housing (short)

Section 9.    Religious denomination and attendance

Section 10.   Demographics and other classificatory variables

### Self-completion questionnaire

Qs. 2.01-36   Religion
Q. 2.37      Health and lifestyle
Qs. 2.38-42   Northern Ireland module*
Qs. 2.43-47   Gender issues
Q. 2.48      Charitable giving
Q. 2.49      Left-right and liberal-authoritarian scales

* These questions were asked in Northern Ireland only;
all others were also asked in Britain.

A

SCPR
SOCIAL & COMMUNITY PLANNING RESEARCH

Head Office: 35 NORTHAMPTON SQUARE,
LONDON EC1V 0AX Telephone 071 250 1866

Field and DP Office: BRENTWOOD, ESSEX
Northern Field Office: DARLINGTON, CO. DURHAM

Spring 1991

P1135/Britain

**BRITISH SOCIAL ATTITUDES:**

**1991 SURVEY**

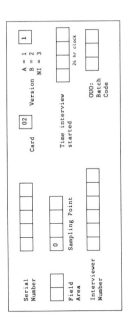

Serial Number

Field Area    0

Sampling Point

Interviewer Number

Card    02    Version    A = 1
B = 2
NI = 3        1

Time interview started        24 hr clock

OUO:
Batch
Code

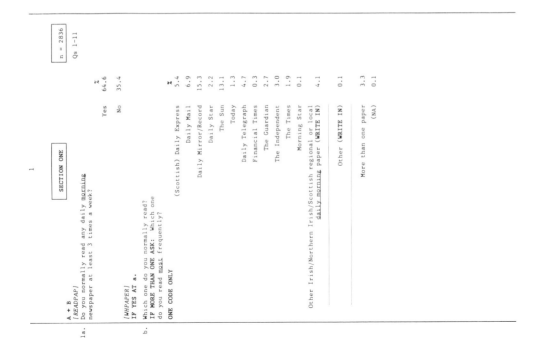

1

n = 2836
Qs 1-11

**SECTION ONE**

**A + B**
*[READPAP]*
1a. Do you normally read any daily <u>morning</u> newspaper at least 3 times a week?

| | % |
|---|---|
| Yes | 64.6 |
| No | 35.4 |

*[WHPAPER]*
**IF YES AT a.**
b. Which one do you normally read?
IF MORE THAN ONE ASK: Which one do you read <u>most</u> frequently?
ONE CODE ONLY

| | % |
|---|---|
| (Scottish) Daily Express | 5.4 |
| Daily Mail | 6.9 |
| Daily Mirror/Record | 15.3 |
| Daily Star | 2.2 |
| The Sun | 13.1 |
| Today | 1.3 |
| Daily Telegraph | 4.7 |
| Financial Times | 0.3 |
| The Guardian | 2.7 |
| The Independent | 3.0 |
| The Times | 1.9 |
| Morning Star | 0.1 |
| Other Irish/Northern Irish/Scottish regional or local <u>daily morning</u> paper (**WRITE IN**) | 4.1 |
| Other (**WRITE IN**) | 0.1 |
| More than one paper | 3.3 |
| (NA) | 0.1 |

---

2

n = 2836

**A + B**
*[SUPPARTY]*
**ASK ALL**
2a. Generally speaking, do you think of yourself as a supporter of any one political party?

| | % |
|---|---|
| Yes | 47.4 |
| No | 52.6 |

*[CLOSEPTY]*
**IF NO AT a.**
b. Do you think of yourself as a little closer to one political party than to the others?

| | % |
|---|---|
| Yes | 26.3 |
| No | 25.9 |
| (NA) | 0.4 |

**IF NO AT b.**
c. If there were a general election tomorrow, which political party do you think you would be most likely to support? CODE ONE ONLY UNDER c. & d.

IF ALLIANCE, OR INDEPENDENT LIBERAL OR INDEPENDENT SDP, CODE 'OTHER PARTY' AND WRITE IN

**IF YES AT a. OR b.**
d. Which one? CODE ONE ONLY UNDER c. & d.
IF ALLIANCE OR INDEPENDENT LIBERAL OR INDEPENDENT SDP, CODE OTHER PARTY AND WRITE IN

*[PARTYID1]*

| | c. & d. % |
|---|---|
| Conservative | 34.8 |
| Labour | 35.3 |
| Liberal Democrat/Liberal/SLD | 12.2 |
| Scottish Nationalist | 2.0 |
| Plaid Cymru | 0.2 |
| Green Party | 1.9 |
| Other party (**WRITE IN**) | 0.2 |
| Other answer (**WRITE IN**) | 0.8 |
| None | 7.4 |
| Refused/unwilling to say | 3.4 |
| DK/Undecided | 1.7 |
| (NA) | 0.2 |

*[IDSTRNG]*
**IF ANY PARTY CODED AT c. & d.**
e. Would you call yourself very strong ... (QUOTE PARTY NAMED) ... fairly strong, or not very strong?

| | % |
|---|---|
| Very strong | 8.4 |
| Fairly strong | 34.7 |
| Not very strong | 42.8 |
| (Don't know) | 0.3 |
| (NA) | 3.0 |

n = 2836

## Page 4

A + B

[DOLE]

5. Opinions differ about the level of benefits for the unemployed. Which of these two statements comes closest to your own view ... READ OUT ...

|  | % |
|---|---|
| ... benefits for the unemployed are too low and cause hardship | 52.6 |
| OR - benefits for the unemployed are too high and discourage people from finding jobs? | 26.7 |
| (Neither) | 7.4 |
| (Both - some hardship, but because wages are low, no incentive) | 0.7 |
| (Both - some people benefit, others suffer) | 3.1 |
| (About right - in between the two) | 1.1 |
| Other (WRITE IN) | 0.3 |
| (Don't know) | 7.5 |
| (NA) | 0.7 |

[TAXSPEND]

CARD C

6. Suppose the government had to choose between the three options on this card. Which do you think it should choose?

|  | % |
|---|---|
| Reduce taxes and spend less on health, education and social benefits | 3.4 |
| Keep taxes and spending on these services at the same level as now | 28.5 |
| Increase taxes and spend more on health, education and social benefits | 64.9 |
| (None) | 1.5 |
| (Don't know) | 1.6 |
| (NA) | 0.1 |

[NHSSAT]

CARD D

7. All in all, how satisfied or dissatisfied would you say you are with the way in which the National Health Service runs nowadays? Choose a phrase from this card.

|  | % |
|---|---|
| Very satisfied | 6.7 |
| Quite satisfied | 33.0 |
| Neither satisfied nor dissatisfied | 19.3 |
| Quite dissatisfied | 23.0 |
| Very dissatisfied | 17.7 |
| (Don't know) | 0.2 |
| (NA) | 0.1 |

## Page 3

A + B

ASK ALL

CARD A

3. Here are some items of government spending. Which of them, if any, would be your highest priority for extra spending? And which next? Please read through the whole list before deciding.

ONE CODE ONLY IN EACH COLUMN

|  | [SPEND1] Highest priority % | [SPEND2] Next highest % |
|---|---|---|
| Education | 28.5 | 33.3 |
| Defence | 1.5 | 2.1 |
| Health | 47.8 | 25.8 |
| Housing | 7.5 | 13.4 |
| Public transport | 1.3 | 3.9 |
| Roads | 1.4 | 3.3 |
| Police and prisons | 2.0 | 4.1 |
| Social security benefits | 4.5 | 6.4 |
| Help for industry | 3.9 | 6.0 |
| Overseas aid | 0.6 | 0.6 |
| (None of these) | 0.3 | 0.3 |
| (Don't know) | 0.5 | 0.7 |
| (NA) | 0.2 | 0.1 |

CARD B

4. Thinking now only of the government's spending on social benefits like those on the card. Which, if any, of these would be your highest priority for extra spending? And which next?

ONE CODE ONLY IN EACH COLUMN

|  | [SOCBEN1] Highest priority % | [SOCBEN2] Next highest % |
|---|---|---|
| Retirement pensions | 41.0 | 21.7 |
| Child benefits | 16.9 | 17.9 |
| Benefits for the unemployed | 9.8 | 12.6 |
| Benefits for disabled people | 24.4 | 33.8 |
| Benefits for single parents | 6.9 | 11.7 |
| (None of these) | 0.4 | 0.9 |
| (Don't know) | 0.6 | 1.1 |
| (NA) | 0.1 | 0.3 |

n = 2836

6

A + B
[INPAT1] - INPAT6]
ASK ALL

CARD E

11. Now suppose you had to go into your local NHS hospital for observation, and maybe an operation.

From what you know or have heard, please say whether you think ...

READ OUT a.-f. AND CODE ONE FOR EACH

n = 2836

| | Definitely would | Probably would | Probably would not | Definitely would not | (Don't know) | (NA) |
|---|---|---|---|---|---|---|
| a. ... the hospital doctors would tell you all you may feel you need to know? | % 19.1 | 48.6 | 22.5 | 7.0 | 2.7 | 0.2 |
| b. ... the hospital doctors would take seriously any views you may have on the sorts of treatment available? | % 12.9 | 44.1 | 29.1 | 6.8 | 6.9 | 0.2 |
| c. ... the operation would take place on the day it was booked for? | % 10.6 | 47.3 | 27.7 | 7.2 | 6.8 | 0.3 |
| d. ... you would be allowed home only when you were really well enough to leave? | % 17.9 | 46.1 | 23.8 | 8.0 | 3.9 | 0.3 |
| e. ... the nurses would take seriously any complaints you may have? | % 23.6 | 54.6 | 12.8 | 3.8 | 5.0 | 0.2 |
| f. ... the hospital doctors would take seriously any complaints you may have? | % 21.4 | 53.9 | 16.1 | 3.4 | 5.0 | 0.2 |

5

A + B
CARD D AGAIN

8. From your own experience, or from what you have heard, please say how satisfied or dissatisfied you are with the way in which each of these parts of the National Health Service runs nowadays.

READ OUT a.-f. AND CODE ONE FOR EACH

n = 2836

| | Very satis-fied | Quite satis-fied | Neither satisfied nor dissatis-fied | Quite dissatis-fied | Very dissatis-fied | (DK) | (NA) |
|---|---|---|---|---|---|---|---|
| a. [GPSAT] First, local doctors/GPs? | % 33.7 | 48.9 | 7.7 | 6.7 | 2.6 | 0.3 | 0.1 |
| b. [DENTSAT] National Health Service dentists? | % 20.2 | 47.3 | 16.1 | 8.6 | 3.6 | 3.9 | 0.4 |
| c. [HVSAT] Health visitors? | % 11.9 | 27.0 | 29.4 | 5.8 | 1.7 | 22.9 | 1.3 |
| d. [DNSAT] District nurses? | % 18.1 | 28.5 | 27.7 | 2.9 | 0.7 | 20.8 | 1.3 |
| e. [INPATSAT] Being in hospital as an in-patient? | % 24.9 | 38.9 | 16.3 | 9.4 | 3.9 | 5.8 | 0.7 |
| f. [OUTPASAT] Attending hospital as an out-patient? | % 15.2 | 37.1 | 15.5 | 18.1 | 8.4 | 5.2 | 0.6 |

9. [PRIVMED] Are you covered by a private health insurance scheme, that is an insurance scheme that allows you to get private medical treatment? For example: BUPA or PPP.

%
Yes    15.4
No     84.6

10. [PRIVPAID] IF YES AT Q.9 Does your employer (or your husband's/wife's employer) pay the majority of the cost of membership of this scheme?

%
Yes            8.1
No             7.1
(Don't know)   0.2

7

**SECTION TWO**

n = 2836

A + B

*[RECONACT]*
CARD F

12. Which of these descriptions applies to what you were doing last week, that is, in the seven days ending last Sunday? PROBE: Any others?
CODE ALL THAT APPLY IN COLUMN I

IF ONLY ONE CODE AT I, TRANSFER IT TO COLUMN II
IF MORE THAN ONE AT I, TRANSFER HIGHEST ON LIST TO II

Q.12

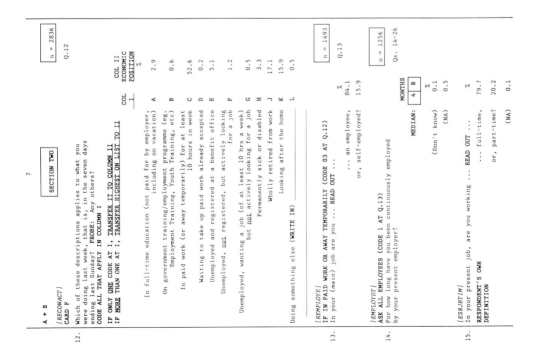

| | COL I | COL II ECONOMIC POSITION % |
|---|---|---|
| In full-time education (not paid for by employer, including on vacation) | A | 2.9 |
| On government training/employment programme (eg. Employment Training, Youth Training, etc) | B | 0.6 |
| In paid work (or away temporarily) for at least 10 hours in week | C | 52.6 |
| Waiting to take up paid work already accepted | D | 0.2 |
| Unemployed and registered at a benefit office | E | 5.1 |
| Unemployed, not registered, but actively looking for a job | F | 1.2 |
| Unemployed, wanting a job (of at least 10 hrs a week) but not actively looking for a job | G | 0.5 |
| Permanently sick or disabled | H | 3.3 |
| Wholly retired from work | J | 17.1 |
| Looking after the home | K | 15.9 |
| Doing something else (WRITE IN) | L | 0.5 |

*[REMPLOYE]*
IF IN PAID WORK OR AWAY TEMPORARILY (CODE 03 AT Q.12)

13. In your (main) job are you ... READ OUT ...

n = 1493

Q.13

%
... an employee, 84.1
or, self-employed? 15.9

*[EMPLOYDT]*
ASK ALL EMPLOYEES (CODE 1 AT Q.13)

14. For how long have you been continuously employed by your present employer?

n = 1256

Qs. 14-26

MONTHS
MEDIAN: 4 8

%
(Don't know) 0.1
(NA) 0.5

*[ESRJBTIM]*
15. In your present job, are you working ... READ OUT ...
RESPONDENT'S OWN DEFINITION

%
... full-time, 79.7
or, part-time? 20.2
(NA) 0.1

---

8

n = 1256

A + B

*[EJBHOURS]*
16. How many hours a week do you normally work in your (main) job?
(IF RESPONDENT CANNOT ANSWER ASK ABOUT LAST WEEK)

HOURS
MEDIAN: 3 8

(NA) 4.0%

*[EJBHRCAT]*
%
10-15 hours a week 5.8
16-23 hours a week 10.2
24-29 hours a week 3.6
30 or more hours a week 80.2
(NA) 0.3

*[WAGENOW]*
17a. How would you describe the wages or salary you are paid for the job you do - on the low side, reasonable, or on the high side? IF LOW: Very low or a bit low?

%
Very low 8.7
A bit low 19.7
Reasonable 62.6
On the high side 8.7
Other answer (WRITE IN) -
(NA) 0.3

*[PAYGAP]*
CARD G
b. Thinking of the highest and the lowest paid people at your place of work, how would you describe the gap between their pay, as far as you know? Please choose a phrase from this card.

%
Much too big a gap 15.7
Too big 27.9
About right 43.4
Too small 4.1
Much too small a gap 0.4
(Other answer) 0.2
(Don't know) 7.6
(NA) 0.7

*[WAGEXPCT]*
18. If you stay in this job, would you expect your wages or salary over the coming year to ... READ OUT ...

%
... rise by more than the cost of living, 19.3
rise by the same as the cost of living, 46.9
rise by less than the cost of living, 23.9
or, not to rise at all? 7.2
(Will not stay in job) 0.7
(Don't know) 1.8
(NA) 0.1

9

n = 1256

**19.** A + B *[NUMEMP]*
Over the coming year do you expect your workplace to be ... **READ OUT** ...

|  | % |
|---|---|
| ... increasing its number of employees, | 18.1 |
| reducing its number of employees, | 25.7 |
| or, will the number of employees stay about the same? | 53.9 |
| Other answer (**WRITE IN**) _____ | 0.2 |
| (Don't know) | 1.7 |
| (NA) | 0.4 |

**20a.** *[LEAVEJOB]*
Thinking now about your own job. How likely or unlikely is it that you will leave this employer over the next year for any reason? Is it ... **READ OUT** ...

|  | % |
|---|---|
| ... very likely, | 13.1 |
| quite likely, | 12.0 |
| not very likely, | 30.1 |
| or, not at all likely? | 44.3 |
| (Don't know) | 0.3 |
| (NA) | 0.2 |

**b.** IF VERY OR QUITE LIKELY AT a.
CARD H
Why do you think you will leave? Please choose a phrase from this card or tell me what other reason there is.
CODE ALL THAT APPLY

|  | % |
|---|---|
| *[WHYGO1]* Firm will close down | 1.2 |
| *[WHYGO2]* I will be declared redundant | 4.6 |
| *[WHYGO3]* I will reach normal retirement age | 1.3 |
| *[WHYGO4]* My contract of employment will expire | 1.5 |
| *[WHYGO5]* I will take early retirement | 1.2 |
| *[WHYGO6]* I will decide to leave and work for another employer | 10.7 |
| *[WHYGO7]* I will decide to leave and work for myself, as self-employed | 0.9 |
| *[WHYGO10]* I will leave to look after home/children/relative | 2.0 |
| *[WHYGO8]* Other answer (**WRITE IN**) _____ | 2.9 |
| (Don't know) | 0.3 |
| (NA) | 0.2 |

**21a.** ASK ALL EMPLOYEES
*[EUNEMP]*
During the last <u>five years</u> - that is since March 1986 - have you been unemployed and seeking work for any period?

|  | % |
|---|---|
| Yes | 19.4 |
| No | 80.5 |
| (NA) | 0.1 |

---

10

n = 1256

MONTHS
[0] [5]

**21b.** A + B
*[EUNEMPT]*
IF YES AT a.
For how many months in total during the last five years?

MEDIAN: months [0] [5]

| (NA) | 0.4% |
|---|---|

**22a.** *[WPUNIONS]*
ASK ALL EMPLOYEES
At your place of work are there unions, staff associations, or groups of unions recognised by the management for negotiating pay and conditions of employment?

|  | % |
|---|---|
| Yes | 57.9 |
| No | 41.3 |
| (Don't know) | 0.4 |
| (NA) | 0.5 |

**b.** *[WPUNIONW]*
IF YES AT a.
On the whole, do you think these unions or staff associations do their job well or not?

|  | % |
|---|---|
| Yes | 35.1 |
| No | 18.8 |
| (Don't know) | 3.7 |
| (NA) | 1.1 |

**23a.** *[INDREL]*
ASK ALL EMPLOYEES
In general how would you describe relations between management and other employees at your workplace
... **READ OUT** ...

|  | % |
|---|---|
| ... very good, | 33.6 |
| quite good, | 44.7 |
| not very good, | 16.3 |
| or, not at all good? | 4.7 |
| (Don't know) | 0.2 |
| (NA) | 0.5 |

**b.** *[WORKRUN]*
And in general, would you say your workplace was ... **READ OUT** ...

|  | % |
|---|---|
| ... very well managed, | 24.9 |
| quite well managed, | 54.7 |
| or, not well managed? | 19.6 |
| (Don't know) | 0.3 |
| (NA) | 0.5 |

**24.** Now for some more general questions about your work.
*[EMPEARN]*
For some people their job is simply something they do in order to earn a living. For others it means much more than that. On balance, is your present job
... **READ OUT** ...

|  | % |
|---|---|
| ... just a means of earning a living, | 31.9 |
| or, does it mean much more to you than that? | 67.6 |
| (Don't know) | 0.2 |
| (NA) | 0.3 |

11

A + B
[EWORK1 - EWORK1O]
CARD I

25a. Now I'd like you to look at the statements on the card and tell me which ones best describe your own reasons for working at present. Any others? CODE ALL THAT APPLY IN COL a.
IF MORE THAN ONE REASON ASK b. OTHERS GO TO Q.26

b. And which one of these would you say is your main reason for working? CODE ONE IN COL b.

[EWRKMAIN]

| | a. Reasons for working % | b. Main Reason % |
|---|---|---|
| Working is the normal thing to do | 25.0% | 4.1 |
| Need money for basic essentials such as food, rent or mortgage | 69.4% | 53.8 |
| To earn money to buy extras | 39.6% | 9.3 |
| To earn money of my own | 28.8% | 7.1 |
| For the company of other people | 29.7% | 2.8 |
| I enjoy working | 55.9% | 13.5 |
| To follow my career | 34.8% | 8.0 |
| For a change from my children or housework | 9.3% | 0.8 |
| Other (WRITE IN) | 1.0% | 0.2 |
| (Don't know) | - | 0.1 |
| (NA) | 0.2% | 0.4 |

[SAYJOB]
ASK ALL EMPLOYEES
26a. Suppose there was going to be some decision made at your place of work that changed the way you do your job. Do you think that you personally would have any say in the decision about the change, or not?

| | % |
|---|---|
| Yes | 53.9 |
| No | 42.5 |
| (It depends/don't know) | 3.4 |
| (NA) | 0.2 |

[MUCHSAY]
IF YES AT a.
b. How much say or chance to influence, the decision do you think you would have ... READ OUT ...

| | % |
|---|---|
| ... a great deal, | 12.6 |
| quite a lot, | 22.7 |
| or, just a little? | 17.7 |
| (It depends/don't know) | 0.8 |
| (NA) | 0.3 |

[MORESAY]
ASK ALL EMPLOYEES
c. Do you think you should have more say in decisions affecting your work, or are you satisfied with the way things are?

| | % |
|---|---|
| Should have more say | 44.5 |
| Satisfied with way things are | 53.9 |
| (Don't know) | 1.2 |
| (NA) | 0.4 |

n = 1256

---

12

n = 641

Qs. 27 and 28

A + B
IF RESPONDENT IS MAN, ASK Q.27
IF RESPONDENT IS WOMAN, GO TO Q.29
ASK MALE EMPLOYEES [EMSMEWRK]
27. Where you work, are there any women doing the same sort of work as you?

| | % |
|---|---|
| Yes | 41.5 |
| No | 58.2 |
| (Works alone) | 0.1 |
| (No-one else doing the same job) | 0.3 |

[EMSEXWRK]
28a. Do you think of your work as ... READ OUT ...

| | % |
|---|---|
| ... mainly men's work, | 35.4 |
| mainly women's work, | 0.3 |
| or, work that either men or women do? | 64.3 |
| Other (WRITE IN) | - |
| (Don't know) | - |

[EMWOMCLD]
IF MAINLY MEN'S WORK (CODE 1 AT a.)
b. Do you think that women could do the same sort of work as you?

| | % |
|---|---|
| Yes | 20.7 |
| No | 14.4 |
| (Don't know) | 0.2 |
| (NA) | 0.2 |

[EMWOMWILD]
IF YES OR DON'T KNOW AT b.
c. Do you think that women would be willing to do the same sort of work as you?

| | % |
|---|---|
| Yes | 10.8 |
| No | 8.1 |
| (Don't know) | 1.7 |

## 13

**A + B**
*[EWSEXWRK]*
**ASK FEMALE EMPLOYEES**

29. Where you work, are there any men doing the same sort of work as you?

|  | % |
|---|---|
| Yes | 42.2 |
| No | 53.6 |
| (Works alone) | 0.3 |
| (No-one else doing the same job) | 1.5 |
| (NA) | 2.3 |

*[EWSEXHRK]*
30a. Do you think of your work as ... READ OUT ...

|  | % |
|---|---|
| ... mainly women's work, | 26.0 |
| mainly men's work, | 1.1 |
| or, work that either men or women do? | 71.9 |
| Other (**WRITE IN**) | 0.1 |
| (Don't know) | 0.1 |
| (NA) | 0.6 |

*[EWMENCLD]*
IF MAINLY WOMEN'S WORK (CODE 1 AT a.)
b. Do you think that men could do the same sort of work as you?

|  | % |
|---|---|
| Yes | 24.2 |
| No | 1.5 |
| (Don't know) | 0.2 |
| (NA) | 0.2 |

*[EWMENWLD]*
IF YES OR DON'T KNOW AT b.
c. Do you think that men would be willing to do the same sort of work as you?

|  | % |
|---|---|
| Yes | 11.2 |
| No | 12.4 |
| (Don't know) | 0.7 |
| (NA) | 0.2 |

*[ECOURSE]*
**ASK ALL EMPLOYEES**

31a. In the last two years, have you been on any courses or had other formal training, which was part of your work or helpful to your work?

INTERVIEWER: ANY TRAINING WHICH IS RELATED TO RESPONDENT'S PAST, PRESENT, OR FUTURE WORK MAY BE COUNTED, BUT DO NOT INCLUDE LEISURE COURSES OR HOBBIES WHICH ARE NOT JOB-RELATED

|  | % |
|---|---|
| Yes, had training related to work | 50.4 |
| No, had none | 49.4 |
| (NA) | 0.1 |

## 14

**A + B**
*[ECOURSET]*
IF YES AT a.

31b. In all, about how many full days have you spent in this kind of training over the last two years?

PROBE FOR TOTAL TIME SPENT IN JOB-RELATED TRAINING IN PAST OR PRESENT JOB; WRITE IN AS APPROPRIATE.

IF LESS THAN ½ DAY, WRITE IN "000"

MEDIAN:  DAYS  | 1 | 0 |

|  | % |
|---|---|
| (Don't know) | 0.2 |
| (NA) | 0.2 |

*[EXPCOURS]*
**ASK ALL EMPLOYEES**

32a. Over the next two years, do you expect to have any (more) courses or training for your work?

|  | % |
|---|---|
| Yes, expect to | 45.1 |
| No, don't expect to | 48.8 |
| (Don't know/depends) | 5.6 |
| (NA) | 0.4 |

*[ELKCOURS]*
b. And apart from what you expect, would you like to have any (more) courses or formal training for your work in the next two years, or are you not that bothered?

|  | % |
|---|---|
| Yes, would like to | 51.9 |
| No, not that bothered | 46.4 |
| (Don't know/depends) | 1.4 |
| (NA) | 0.4 |

IF YES AT b.
CARD J
c. Here are some possible benefits of training. Which, if any, is the main reason why you would like to do more training? And which next?

ONE CODE ONLY IN EACH COLUMN

|  | *[EYTRAIN1]* Main reason % | *[EYTRAIN2]* Next reason % |
|---|---|---|
| To make work more interesting | 8.7 | 14.4 |
| To earn more money | 3.2 | 8.4 |
| To improve chances of promotion | 9.7 | 9.0 |
| To improve chances of getting a better job | 6.1 | 8.0 |
| To learn new sorts of skills | 23.9 | 11.2 |
| Other (main) reason (**WRITE IN**) | 0.2 | - |
| Other (next) reason (**WRITE IN**) | - | 0.2 |
| (None of these) | - | 0.5 |
| (NA) | 0.1 | 0.4 |

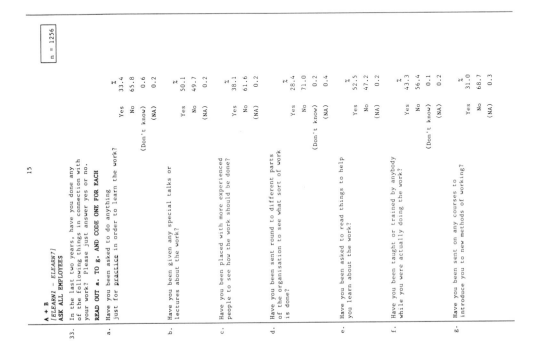

## 15

n = 1256

A + B
[ELEARN1 - ELEARN7]
ASK ALL EMPLOYEES

33. In the last two years, have you done any of the following things in connection with your work? Please just answer yes or no.
READ OUT a. TO g. AND CODE ONE FOR EACH

a. Have you been asked to do anything just for practice in order to learn the work?

|   | % |
|---|---|
| Yes | 33.4 |
| No | 65.8 |
| (Don't know) | 0.6 |
| (NA) | 0.2 |

b. Have you been given any special talks or lectures about the work?

|   | % |
|---|---|
| Yes | 50.1 |
| No | 49.7 |
| (NA) | 0.2 |

c. Have you been placed with more experienced people to see how the work should be done?

|   | % |
|---|---|
| Yes | 38.1 |
| No | 61.6 |
| (NA) | 0.2 |

d. Have you been sent round to different parts of the organisation to see what sort of work is done?

|   | % |
|---|---|
| Yes | 28.4 |
| No | 71.0 |
| (Don't know) | 0.2 |
| (NA) | 0.4 |

e. Have you been asked to read things to help you learn about the work?

|   | % |
|---|---|
| Yes | 52.5 |
| No | 47.2 |
| (NA) | 0.2 |

f. Have you been taught or trained by anybody while you were actually doing the work?

|   | % |
|---|---|
| Yes | 43.3 |
| No | 56.4 |
| (Don't know) | 0.1 |
| (NA) | 0.2 |

g. Have you been sent on any courses to introduce you to new methods of working?

|   | % |
|---|---|
| Yes | 31.0 |
| No | 68.7 |
| (NA) | 0.3 |

## 16

n = 1256

A + B
[EPENSOFR]

34a. As far as you know, does your present employer offer any pension scheme for employees?

|   | % |
|---|---|
| Yes | 74.7 |
| No | 23.0 |
| (Don't know) | 2.2 |
| (NA) | 0.1 |

b. [EPENSPAY]
IF YES AT a.
Do members of this scheme have to contribute part of their wages or salaries towards it, or not?

|   | % |
|---|---|
| Yes | 59.3 |
| No | 12.1 |
| (Don't know) | 3.2 |
| (NA) | 0.2 |

c. [EPENSMEM]
Are you a member of this scheme?

|   | % |
|---|---|
| Yes | 53.7 |
| No | 20.7 |
| (Don't know) | 0.2 |
| (NA) | 0.1 |

d. [EPENSADD]
IF YES AT c.
On top of any contributions you have to make, do you make any additional voluntary contributions to this scheme?

|   | % |
|---|---|
| Yes | 6.8 |
| No | 46.5 |
| (Don't know) | 0.4 |
| (NA) | 0.2 |

ASK ALL SELF-EMPLOYED (CODE 02 AT Q.12)

n = 237
Qs.35-44

35. [SSRJBTIM]
In your present job, are you working... READ OUT ...
RESPONDENT'S OWN DEFINITION

|   | % |
|---|---|
| ... full-time, | 82.8 |
| or, part-time? | 16.4 |
| (NA) | 0.8 |

36. [SJBHOURS]
How many hours a week do you normally work in your (main) job?
(IF RESPONDENT CANNOT ANSWER, ASK ABOUT LAST WEEK)

MEDIAN: HOURS 4 5

|   | % |
|---|---|
| (Varies) | 1.0 |
| (Don't know) | 0.8 |
| (NA) | 5.1 |

[SJBHRCAT]

|   | % |
|---|---|
| 10-15 hours a week | 7.0 |
| 16-23 hours a week | 5.8 |
| 24-29 hours a week | 4.3 |
| 30 or more hours a week | 82.6 |
| (NA) | 0.3 |

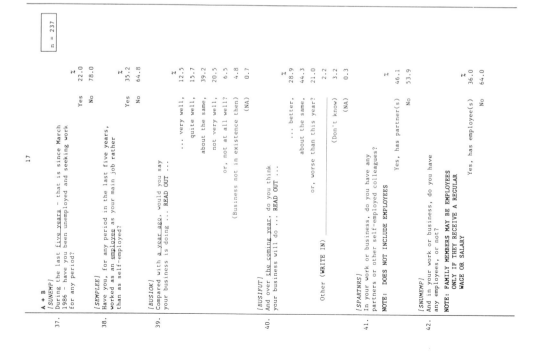

**17**

n = 237

**A + B**
[SUNEMP]
37. During the last five years - that is since March 1986 - have you been unemployed and seeking work for any period?

|  | % |
|---|---|
| Yes | 22.0 |
| No | 78.0 |

[SEMPLEE]
38. Have you, for any period in the last five years, worked as an employee as your main job rather than as self-employed?

|  | % |
|---|---|
| Yes | 35.2 |
| No | 64.8 |

[BUSIOK]
39. Compared with a year ago, would you say your business is doing ... READ OUT ...

|  | % |
|---|---|
| ... very well, | 12.5 |
| quite well, | 15.7 |
| about the same, | 39.2 |
| not very well, | 20.5 |
| or, not at all well? | 6.5 |
| (Business not in existence then) | 4.8 |
| (NA) | 0.7 |

[BUSIFUT]
40. And over the coming year, do you think your business will do ... READ OUT ...

|  | % |
|---|---|
| ... better, | 28.9 |
| about the same, | 44.3 |
| or, worse than this year? | 21.0 |
| Other (WRITE IN) _____ | 2.2 |
| (Don't know) | 3.2 |
| (NA) | 0.3 |

[SPARTNRS]
41. In your work or business, do you have any partners or other self-employed colleagues?
**NOTE: DOES NOT INCLUDE EMPLOYEES**

|  | % |
|---|---|
| Yes, has partner(s) | 46.1 |
| No | 53.9 |

[SNUMEMP]
42. And in your work or business, do you have any employees, or not?
**NOTE: FAMILY MEMBERS MAY BE EMPLOYEES ONLY IF THEY RECEIVE A REGULAR WAGE OR SALARY**

|  | % |
|---|---|
| Yes, has employee(s) | 36.0 |
| No | 64.0 |

**18**

n = 237

**A + B**
[SEMPEARN]
43. For some people their job is simply something they do in order to earn a living. For others it means much more than that. On balance, is your present job ... READ OUT ...

|  | % |
|---|---|
| ... just a means of earning a living, | 22.4 |
| or, does it mean much more to you than that? | 77.2 |
| (NA) | 0.4 |

**CARD K**
[SWORKI - SWORKIO]
44a. Now I'd like you to look at the statements on the card and tell me which ones best describe your own reasons for working at present. Any others? CODE ALL THAT APPLY IN COL a.

**IF MORE THAN ONE REASON ASK b.  OTHERS GO TO Q.57.**
[SWRKMAIN]
b. And which one of these would you say is your main reason for working? CODE ONE IN COL b.

| | a. Reasons for working % | b. Main Reason % |
|---|---|---|
| Working is the normal thing to do | 32.8 | 4.6 |
| Need money for basic essentials such as food, rent or mortgage | 73.2 | 57.1 |
| To earn money to buy extras | 39.3 | 5.3 |
| To earn money of my own | 21.9 | 5.3 |
| For the company of other people | 17.8 | 0.7 |
| I enjoy working | 70.5 | 19.1 |
| To follow my career | 24.7 | 5.4 |
| For a change from my children or housework | 6.0 | 0.7 |
| Other reasons (WRITE IN) _____ | 2.0 | 1.3 |
| (DK/NA) | 0.6 | 0.4 |

**SELF-EMPLOYED NOW GO TO Q.57**

n = 1343

Q.45 only

**ASK ALL NOT IN PAID WORK (CODES 01-02 OR 04-11 AT Q.12)**
[NPWORKIO]
45. In the seven days ending last Sunday, did you have any paid work of less than 10 hours a week?

|  | % |
|---|---|
| Yes | 6.2 |
| No | 66.1 |
| (NA) | 27.6 |

**INTERVIEWER CHECK:**
**RESPONDENT IS:**

|  | % |
|---|---|
| IN FULL-TIME EDUCATION, CODE 01 AT Q.12 | 2.9 |
| PERMANENTLY SICK OR DISABLED, CODE 08 AT Q.12 | 3.3 |
| DOING SOMETHING ELSE, CODE 11 AT Q.12 | 0.5 |
| ON GOVERNMENT PROGRAMME, CODE 02 AT Q.12 | 0.6 |
| WAITING TO TAKE UP PAID WORK, CODE 04 AT Q.12 | 0.2 |
| UNEMPLOYED, CODES 05,06,07 AT Q.12 | 6.8 |
| WHOLLY RETIRED FROM WORK, CODE 09 AT Q.12 | 17.1 |
| LOOKING AFTER THE HOME, CODE 10 AT Q.12 | 15.9 |

19

**A + B**

*[WGUNEMP]*
**ASK ALL ON GOVERNMENT PROGRAMME OR WAITING TO TAKE UP PAID WORK**
**(CODES 02,04 AT Q.12)**

n = 23
Q.46 only

46. During the last five years - that is since March 1986 - have you been unemployed and seeking work for any period?

|  | % |
|---|---|
| Yes | 71.8 |
| No | 24.0 |
| (NA) | 4.2 |

*[UUNEMP]*
**ASK ALL UNEMPLOYED (CODES 05,06,07 AT Q.12)**

n = 193
Qs. 47-50

47a. In total how many months in the last five years - that is, since March 1986 - have you been unemployed and seeking work?

MEDIAN: | 1 | 8 | MONTHS

|  | % |
|---|---|
| (NA) | 4.0% |

b. How long has this present period of unemployment and seeking work lasted so far?

MEDIAN: | 1 | 2 | MONTHS

|  | % |
|---|---|
| (NA) | 4.5% |

48. How confident are you that you will find a job to match your qualifications ... **READ OUT** ...

|  | % |
|---|---|
| ... very confident, | 18.2 |
| quite confident, | 24.7 |
| not very confident, | 24.9 |
| or, not at all confident? | 29.2 |
| (NA) | 2.9 |

49a. Although it may be difficult to judge, how long from now do you think it will be before you find an acceptable job?

MEDIAN: | 0 | 7 | MONTHS

|  | % |
|---|---|
| Never | 14.1 |
| (Don't know) | 31.3 |
| (NA) | 3.6 |

---

20

**A + B**

*[UJOBCHNC]*
49b. Do you think that there is a real chance nowadays that you will get a job in this area, or is there no real chance nowadays?

n = 193

|  | % |
|---|---|
| Real chance | 43.5 |
| No real chance | 52.6 |
| (Don't know) | 0.8 |
| (NA) | 3.2 |

*[UNEMEARN]*
50. For some people work is simply something they do in order to earn a living. For others it means much more than that. In general, do you think of work as ... **READ OUT** ...

|  | % |
|---|---|
| ... just a means of earning a living, | 38.9 |
| or, does it mean much more to you than that? | 58.0 |
| (Don't know) | 0.8 |
| (NA) | 2.4 |

**ASK ALL WHOLLY RETIRED FROM WORK (CODE 09 AT Q.12)**

n = 486
Qs. 51-54

*[EMPLPEN]*
51a. Do you receive a pension from any past employer?

|  | % |
|---|---|
| Yes | 52.1 |
| No | 44.8 |
| (NA) | 3.0 |

b. **IF NO AT a.**
May I just check, are you ...
**READ OUT** ...

|  | % |
|---|---|
| ... married, | 25.3 |
| or, not married? | 22.6 |

*[SEMPLPEN]*
c. **IF MARRIED**
Does your *husband/wife* receive a pension from any past employer?

|  | % |
|---|---|
| Yes | 8.8 |
| No | 15.8 |
| (NA) | 0.4 |

*[PRPENGET]*
d. **ASK ALL WHOLLY RETIRED FROM WORK**
And do you receive a pension from any private arrangements you have made in the past, that is apart from the state pension or one arranged through an employer?

|  | % |
|---|---|
| Yes | 6.1 |
| No | 91.0 |
| (Don't know) | 0.1 |
| (NA) | 2.8 |

*[SPRPNGET]*
e. **IF MARRIED. OTHERS GO TO Q.52**
And does your *husband/wife* receive a pension from any private arrangements *he/she* has made in the past, that is apart from the state pension or one arranged through an employer?

|  | % |
|---|---|
| Yes | 3.7 |
| No | 20.4 |
| (NA) | 1.3 |

22

n = 452

**A + B**
*[FTJOBSER]*
IF NO AT Q.55

56a. How seriously in the past five years have you considered getting a <u>full-time</u> job ... **READ OUT** ...

**PROMPT, IF NECESSARY: FULL-TIME IS 30+ HOURS A WEEK**

|  | % |
|---|---|
| ... very seriously, | 1.2 |
| quite seriously, | 3.3 |
| not very seriously, | 4.8 |
| or, not at all seriously? | 51.9 |
| (NA) | 6.4 |

*[PTJOBSER]*
b. IF 'NOT VERY' OR 'NOT AT ALL' SERIOUSLY AT a. How seriously, in the past five years, have you considered getting a <u>part-time</u> job? ... **READ OUT** ...

|  | % |
|---|---|
| ... very seriously, | 2.6 |
| quite seriously, | 3.0 |
| not very seriously, | 5.2 |
| or, not at all seriously? | 45.2 |
| (NA) | 7.1 |

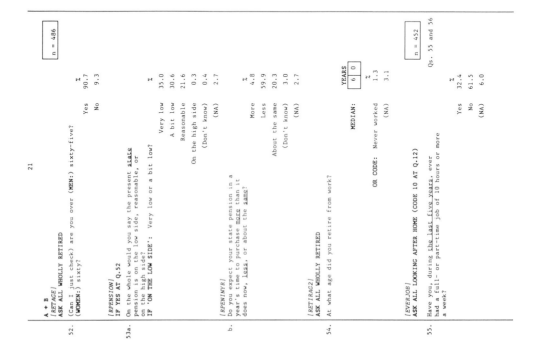

---

21

n = 486

**A + B**
*[RETAGE]*
ASK ALL WHOLLY RETIRED

52. (Can I just check) are you over (**MEN:**) sixty-five? (**WOMEN:**) sixty?

|  | % |
|---|---|
| Yes | 90.7 |
| No | 9.3 |

*[RPENSION]*
IF YES AT Q.52

53a. On the whole would you say the present <u>state</u> pension is on the low side, reasonable, or on the high side?
IF 'ON THE LOW SIDE': Very low or a bit low?

|  | % |
|---|---|
| Very low | 35.0 |
| A bit low | 30.6 |
| Reasonable | 21.6 |
| On the high side | 0.3 |
| (Don't know) | 0.4 |
| (NA) | 2.7 |

*[RPENINYR]*
b. Do you expect your state pension in a year's time to purchase <u>more</u> than it does now, <u>less</u>, or about the <u>same</u>?

|  | % |
|---|---|
| More | 4.8 |
| Less | 59.9 |
| About the same | 20.3 |
| (Don't know) | 3.0 |
| (NA) | 2.7 |

*[RETIRAG2]*
ASK ALL WHOLLY RETIRED

54. At what age did you retire from work?

MEDIAN: YEARS 6 0

|  | % |
|---|---|
| OR CODE: Never worked | 1.3 |
| (NA) | 3.1 |

n = 452

*[EVERJOB]*
ASK ALL LOOKING AFTER HOME (CODE 10 AT Q.12)

55. Have you, during <u>the last five years</u>, ever had a full- or part-time job of 10 hours or more a week?

|  | % |
|---|---|
| Yes | 32.4 |
| No | 61.5 |
| (NA) | 6.0 |

Qs. 55 and 56

23

**SECTION THREE**

n = 1414
Qs. A57-A65

**ASK ALL**

[UBPOOR]
A57a. Think of a married couple without children living only on unemployment benefit. Would you say that they are ... READ OUT ...

|  | % |
|---|---|
| ... really poor, | 17.0 |
| hard up, | 49.6 |
| have enough to live on, | 19.5 |
| or, have more than enough? | 1.1 |
| (Don't know) | 12.7 |

b. [PENSPOOR]
Now thinking of a married couple living only on the state pension. Would you say they are ... READ OUT ...

|  | % |
|---|---|
| ... really poor, | 23.6 |
| hard up, | 54.3 |
| have enough to live on, | 16.9 |
| or, have more than enough? | 0.4 |
| (Don't know) | 4.8 |

A58a. [POORUB40]
Now thinking of a married couple without children living on £60 per week. Would you say they are ... READ OUT ...

|  | % |
|---|---|
| ... really poor, | 41.2 |
| hard up, | 47.7 |
| have enough to live on, | 8.3 |
| or, have more than enough? | 0.1 |
| (Don't know) | 2.5 |
| (NA) | 0.2 |

b. [POORSPNO]
And what about a pensioner couple living on £75 per week. Would you say they are ... READ OUT ...

|  | % |
|---|---|
| ... really poor, | 22.3 |
| hard up, | 52.7 |
| have enough to live on, | 22.4 |
| or, have more than enough? | 0.6 |
| (Don't know) | 2.0 |

A59a. [SAMEHLTH]
Do you think that health care should be the same for everyone, or should people who can afford it be able to pay for better health care?

|  | % |
|---|---|
| Same for everyone | 54.3 |
| Able to pay for better | 43.7 |
| (Don't know) | 1.7 |
| (NA) | 0.3 |

---

24

A59b. [SAMEHLTH]
Should the quality of education be the same for all children, or should parents who can afford it be able to pay for better education?

|  | % |
|---|---|
| Same for everyone | 55.2 |
| Able to pay for better | 42.9 |
| (Don't know) | 1.7 |
| (NA) | 0.3 |

c. [SAMEPENS]
And do you think that pensions should be the same for everyone, or should people who can afford it be able to pay for better pensions?

|  | % |
|---|---|
| Same for everyone | 31.0 |
| Able to pay for better | 64.7 |
| (Don't know) | 4.2 |
| (NA) | 0.1 |

A60a. INTERVIEWER CHECK Q.12, PAGE 7. IS RESPONDENT WHOLLY RETIRED FROM WORK (CODE 09 AT Q.12)?

|  | % |
|---|---|
| Yes | 19.5 |
| No | 80.5 |

b. [PENSPAST]
ASK ALL EXCEPT THOSE WHOLLY RETIRED FROM WORK
As far as you know, do you have any pension entitlements built up for you through any past employer? I mean, of course, apart from the basic state pension.

INTERVIEWER: EXCLUDE PENSION THROUGH PRESENT EMPLOYER

|  | % |
|---|---|
| Yes | 17.2 |
| No | 57.9 |
| (Don't know) | 0.8 |
| (NA) | 4.5 |

A61a. [PPPCONTR]
ASK ALL EXCEPT THOSE WHOLLY RETIRED FROM WORK
Do you contribute to any (other) private or personal pension scheme - apart from the state pension or any pension arranged through an employer?

|  | % |
|---|---|
| Yes | 16.7 |
| No | 59.7 |
| (Don't know) | 0.0 |
| (NA) | 4.0 |

n = 1414

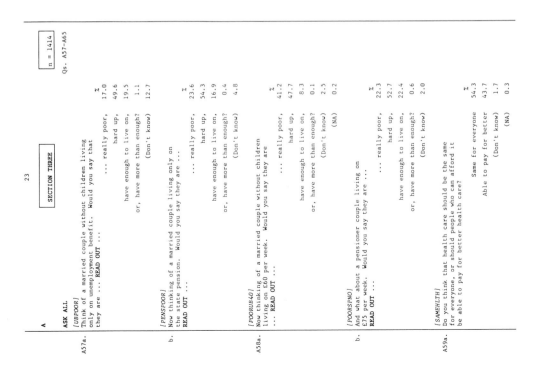

26

A

**CARD M**

A64. I will now read out a list of statements. For each one, please tell me, from this card, how much you agree or disagree.

n = 1414

| | Agree strongly | Agree | Neither agree nor disagree | Disagree | Disagree strongly | (Don't know) | (NA) |
|---|---|---|---|---|---|---|---|
| *[SAVFRRET]*<br>a. The government should encourage people to provide something for their own retirement instead of relying only on the state pension | % 19.2 | 54.9 | 9.2 | 13.1 | 2.2 | 1.1 | 0.3 |
| *[PNGVABAN]*<br>b. The government is gradually abandoning its responsibility to provide adequate old age pension | % 13.5 | 36.0 | 11.7 | 29.2 | 5.2 | 4.0 | 0.4 |
| *[PNYNGBTR]*<br>c. Younger people nowadays are able to make better pension arrangements because they have more choice | % 13.2 | 72.4 | 6.3 | 5.4 | 0.5 | 1.9 | 0.3 |
| *[STPENWOR]*<br>d. State pensions used to provide a better standard of living than they do nowadays | % 5.8 | 33.7 | 17.3 | 25.8 | 3.3 | 13.8 | 0.3 |

A65. Now a few questions about couples who divorce.

Imagine a married couple who divorce. They have a child at primary school who remains with the mother.

*[MTCDADSH]*
a. Do you think that the father should be made to make maintenance payments to support the child?

|  | % |
|---|---|
| Yes | 92.5 |
| No | 3.0 |
| (Don't know) | 4.3 |
| (NA) | 0.2 |

*[MTDPDINC]*
b. If he does make maintenance payments for the child, should the amount depend on the father's income, or not?

|  | % |
|---|---|
| Yes | 90.8 |
| No | 7.7 |
| (Don't know) | 1.4 |
| (NA) | 0.1 |

*[MTDPMINC]*
c. Do you think the amount of maintenance should depend on the mother's income, or not?

|  | % |
|---|---|
| Yes | 67.5 |
| No | 28.9 |
| (Don't know) | 3.3 |
| (NA) | 0.2 |

---

25

A

*[PPPPAST]*
IF 'NO' AT a.

A61b. Have you ever contributed to any (other) **private** or personal pension scheme in the past – **again, apart** from the state pension or any pension arranged through an employer?

n = 1414

|  | % |
|---|---|
| Yes | 6.9 |
| No | 52.7 |
| (Don't know) | 0.0 |
| (NA) | 4.1 |

ASK ALL
CARD L
*[PENWHOSH]*

A62a. Please say, from this card, who you think should be **mainly** responsible for ensuring that people have an adequate retirement pension.

|  | % |
|---|---|
| Mainly the government | 53.7 |
| Mainly employers | 8.2 |
| Shared equally | 31.8 |
| Some other arrangement | 5.5 |
| (Don't know) | 0.8 |
| (NA) | 0.1 |

*[PENOTHSH]*
IF 'OTHER ARRANGEMENT' AT a.

b. What other kind of arrangement is that?
(WRITE IN)

|  | % |
|---|---|
| (Make own arrangements) | 4.4 |
| (Other answer) | 1.1 |

*[STPENIS]*
A63a. Would you say that the state pension for a retired couple nowadays **is**, on its own ...
**READ OUT** ...

|  | % |
|---|---|
| ... more than enough for their basic needs, | 0.8 |
| just enough for their basic needs, | 41.7 |
| or, less than enough for their basic needs? | 51.7 |
| (Don't know) | 5.4 |
| (NA) | 0.3 |

*[STPENSHD]*
b. And would you say that the state pension for a retired couple nowadays **should**, on its own, be ...
**READ OUT** ...

|  | % |
|---|---|
| ... more than enough for their basic needs, | 61.5 |
| just enough for their basic needs, | 33.1 |
| or, less than enough for their basic needs? | 3.2 |
| (Don't know) | 1.9 |
| (NA) | 0.3 |

## 27

n = 1414

**A** [MTDPMREH]

A65d. Suppose the mother re-marries. Should the father go on paying maintenance for the child, should he stop, or should it depend on the new husband's income?

%

| | |
|---|---|
| Continue | 42.5 |
| Stop | 16.3 |
| Depends | 38.4 |
| (Don't know) | 2.6 |
| (NA) | 0.2 |

e. [MTIFCOHB]

Now suppose that the same couple had been living together, but had not actually been married. Do you think you would have answered differently about whether the father should make maintenance payments for the child, or would your answers have been much the same?

%

| | |
|---|---|
| Different | 6.7 |
| Much the same | 91.2 |
| (Don't know) | 2.0 |
| (NA) | 0.1 |

## 28

SECTION FOUR

n = 1414

Qs. A66-A70

**A**

CARD N

A66. Suppose a big British firm made a large profit in a particular year.

a. [PROFTDO1]

Which one of these things do you think it would be most likely to do?

RECORD IN COL a.

b. [FSTPRIOR]

Now which one do you think should be its first priority?

RECORD IN COL b.

CODE ONE ONLY IN EACH COLUMN

| | a. Most likely to do % | b. First priority % |
|---|---|---|
| Increase dividends to the shareholders | 34.4 | 3.2 |
| Give the employees a pay rise | 6.3 | 26.6 |
| Cut the prices of its products | 3.8 | 13.8 |
| Invest in new machinery or new technology | 20.1 | 25.7 |
| Improve the employees' working conditions | 2.4 | 11.5 |
| Research into new products | 6.4 | 5.0 |
| Invest in training for the employees | 2.3 | 11.1 |
| Give a bonus to top management | 20.0 | 0.4 |
| (None of these) | 0.2 | 0.2 |
| (Don't know) | 2.9 | 2.0 |
| (NA) | 1.2 | 0.5 |

CARD O

A67. I am now going to read out some situations that might come up. Which of the phrases on this card comes closest to what you think of each situation?

READ OUT a. TO n. AND CODE ONE FOR EACH

| | | Nothing wrong | Bit wrong | Wrong | Seriously wrong | Very seriously wrong | (Don't know) | (NA) |
|---|---|---|---|---|---|---|---|---|
| a. | [CLAIM75] A company employee exaggerates his claims for travel expenses over a period and makes £75 | % 3.4 | 14.8 | 49.9 | 20.6 | 10.2 | 0.8 | 0.4 |
| b. | [MANGIF75] A company manager accepts a Christmas present worth £75 from a firm from which he buys products | % 33.0 | 20.0 | 31.4 | 10.0 | 4.0 | 1.2 | 0.4 |
| c. | [CHARG300] A milkman slightly overcharges customers over a period and makes £300 | % 0.2 | 2.0 | 25.9 | 43.0 | 28.3 | 0.2 | 0.4 |

## A

n = 1414

| | Nothing wrong | Bit wrong | Wrong | Seriously wrong | Very seriously wrong | (Don't know) | (NA) |
|---|---|---|---|---|---|---|---|
| A67d. [BREWRYPR] Two large breweries get together and agree to raise their prices at the same time | % 16.8 | 10.4 | 35.8 | 20.4 | 13.5 | 2.8 | 0.4 |
| e. [JBENEPOT] An employee uses his influence to get a relative a job at his workplace | % 43.6 | 22.2 | 23.7 | 5.4 | 3.4 | 1.1 | 0.6 |
| f. [STRKTAXI] A private taxi firm puts up its fares during a public transport strike | % 7.4 | 13.0 | 42.1 | 24.7 | 11.7 | 0.6 | 0.5 |
| g. [JEMPSICK] A junior employee makes a habit of taking time off as sick leave when he is not ill | % 0.6 | 5.4 | 44.8 | 33.3 | 15.1 | 0.3 | 0.5 |
| h. [DIRSICK] A company director makes a habit of taking time off as sick leave when he is not ill | % 1.2 | 3.8 | 33.9 | 36.6 | 23.7 | 0.4 | 0.4 |
| i. [FORBRIBE] A British firm competing for a contract in a foreign country offers large gifts of money to officials | % 6.5 | 10.0 | 33.3 | 28.5 | 19.5 | 1.7 | 0.5 |
| j. [LWINDEAL] A lawyer is told by a client that the client's firm is about to annouce big profits. The lawyer buys shares in that firm before the announcement is made | % 5.1 | 6.1 | 28.9 | 29.3 | 28.7 | 1.5 | 0.4 |
| k. [DELAYDRG] A drug company delays supplies of an important new drug in order to keep its price high | % 0.8 | 1.9 | 25.1 | 32.9 | 38.0 | 0.9 | 0.4 |
| l. [COCARUSE] A company provides its directors with expensive company cars even though they are hardly ever used for work | % 13.0 | 11.1 | 40.3 | 20.5 | 13.3 | 1.4 | 0.4 |
| m. [FACPOLUT] A factory discovers that it is polluting a nearby river and does nothing about it | % 0.0 | 0.4 | 9.2 | 29.6 | 60.0 | 0.4 | 0.4 |
| n. [CIGSPYNG] A tobacco manufacturer sponsors a national event popular with young people to get publicity | % 15.6 | 11.4 | 32.9 | 19.4 | 19.4 | 1.0 | 0.4 |

## A

n = 1414

CARD O AGAIN

Still using this card, please say which comes closest to what you think about these situations.

| | Nothing wrong | Bit wrong | Wrong | Seriously wrong | Very seriously wrong | (Don't know) | (NA) |
|---|---|---|---|---|---|---|---|
| A68a. [VATCHEAT] A householder is having a repair job done by a local plumber. He is told that if he pays cash he will not be charged VAT. So he pays cash. [VATDO] | % 26.5 | 27.6 | 35.7 | 5.2 | 2.9 | 1.6 | 0.4 |

b. Might you do this if the situation came up?

| | % |
|---|---|
| Yes | 71.3 |
| No | 22.6 |
| (Don't know) | 5.2 |
| (NA) | 0.9 |

| | Nothing wrong | Bit wrong | Wrong | Seriously wrong | Very seriously wrong | (Don't know) | (NA) |
|---|---|---|---|---|---|---|---|
| A69a. [STORCHKP] A man gives a £5 note for goods he is buying in a big store. By mistake, he is given change for a £10 note. He notices but keeps the change. [STORCHDO] | % 7.7 | 15.3 | 59.0 | 11.0 | 6.3 | 0.3 | 0.4 |

b. Might you do this if the situation came up?

| | % |
|---|---|
| Yes | 24.6 |
| No | 71.9 |
| (Don't know) | 3.0 |
| (NA) | 0.5 |

| | Nothing wrong | Bit wrong | Wrong | Seriously wrong | Very seriously wrong | (Don't know) | (NA) |
|---|---|---|---|---|---|---|---|
| A70a. [INSUR150] In making an insurance claim, a man whose home has been burgled exaggerates the value of what was stolen by £150. [INSDO150] | % 6.4 | 19.9 | 54.5 | 13.1 | 5.1 | 0.6 | 0.4 |

b. Might you do this if the situation came up?

| | % |
|---|---|
| Yes | 24.4 |
| No | 71.1 |
| (Don't know) | 4.0 |
| (NA) | 0.5 |

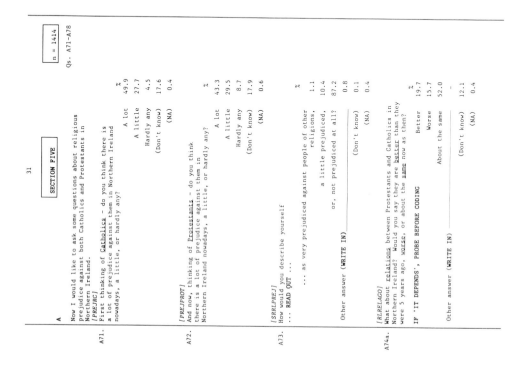

31

n = 1414

Qs. A71-A78

SECTION FIVE

A

Now I would like to ask some questions about religious prejudice against both Catholics and Protestants in Northern Ireland.

A71. [PREJRC]
First thinking of Catholics - do you think there is a lot of prejudice against them in Northern Ireland nowadays, a little, or hardly any?

| | % |
|---|---|
| A lot | 49.9 |
| A little | 27.7 |
| Hardly any | 4.5 |
| (Don't know) | 17.6 |
| (NA) | 0.4 |

A72. [PREJPROT]
And now, thinking of Protestants - do you think there is a lot of prejudice against them in Northern Ireland nowadays, a little, or hardly any?

| | % |
|---|---|
| A lot | 43.3 |
| A little | 29.5 |
| Hardly any | 8.7 |
| (Don't know) | 17.9 |
| (NA) | 0.6 |

A73. [SRRLPREJ]
How would you describe yourself ... READ OUT ...

| | % |
|---|---|
| ... as very prejudiced against people of other religions, | 1.1 |
| a little prejudiced, | 10.4 |
| or, not prejudiced at all? | 87.2 |
| (Don't know) | 0.1 |
| (NA) | 0.4 |

Other answer (WRITE IN)

A74a. [RLRELAGO]
What about relations between Protestants and Catholics in Northern Ireland? Would you say they are better than they were 5 years ago, worse, or about the same now as then?

IF 'IT DEPENDS', PROBE BEFORE CODING

| | % |
|---|---|
| Better | 19.7 |
| Worse | 15.7 |
| About the same | 52.0 |
| | - |
| (Don't know) | 12.1 |
| (NA) | 0.4 |

Other answer (WRITE IN)

32

n = 1414

A

A74b. [RLRELFUT]
And what about in 5 years time? Do you think relations between Protestants and Catholics will be better than now, worse than now, or about the same as now?

IF 'IT DEPENDS', PROBE BEFORE CODING

| | % |
|---|---|
| Better than now | 19.8 |
| Worse than now | 9.4 |
| About the same | 58.8 |
| | 0.2 |
| (Don't know) | 11.0 |
| (NA) | 0.8 |

Other answer (WRITE IN)

c. [RELGALWY]
Do you think that religion will always make a difference to the way people feel about each other in Northern Ireland?

| | % |
|---|---|
| Yes | 86.0 |
| No | 6.4 |
| | 0.8 |
| (Don't know) | 5.5 |
| (NA) | 1.3 |

Other answer (WRITE IN)

A75. [OWNMXSCH]
If you were deciding where to send your children to school, would you prefer a school with children of only your own religion, or a mixed-religion school?

PROBE IF NECESSARY: Say if you did have school-age children.

| | % |
|---|---|
| Own religion only | 13.6 |
| Mixed-religion school | 80.1 |
| (Don't know) | 5.0 |
| (NA) | 1.3 |

A76. [BRTIRSDE]
When there is an argument between Britain and the Republic of Ireland, do you generally find yourself on the side of the British or of the Irish government?

IF 'IT DEPENDS', PROBE BEFORE CODING

| | % |
|---|---|
| Generally British government | 54.6 |
| Generally Irish government | 6.7 |
| It depends (AFTER PROBE) | 10.4 |
| (Neither) | 18.6 |
| (Don't know/can't say) | 9.0 |
| (NA) | 0.7 |

## 34

n = 1414 | Qs. A79-A85a

**SECTION SIX**

**A**

**Now moving on to the subject of social class in Britain.**

*[SCCOPPORT]*

**A79a.** To what extent do you think a person's social class affects his or her opportunities in Britain today ... READ OUT ...

|  | % |
|---|---|
| ... a great deal, | 26.9 |
| quite a lot, | 47.0 |
| not very much, | 21.4 |
| or, not at all? | 2.9 |
| Other answer (WRITE IN) | 0.4 |
| (Don't know) | 1.1 |
| (NA) | 0.3 |

*[SCIMPAGO]*

**b.** Do you think social class is <u>more</u> or <u>less</u> important now in affecting a person's opportunities than it was 10 years ago, or has there been no real change?

|  | % |
|---|---|
| <u>More</u> important now | 20.0 |
| <u>Less</u> important now | 38.5 |
| No change | 40.2 |
| (Don't know) | 1.1 |
| (NA) | 0.2 |

*[SCIMPFUT]*

**c.** Do you think that in 10 years' time social class will be <u>more</u> or <u>less</u> important than it is now in affecting a person's opportunities, or will there be no real change?

|  | % |
|---|---|
| <u>More</u> important in 10 years' time | 13.5 |
| <u>Less</u> important in 10 years' time | 34.4 |
| No change | 49.9 |
| (Don't know) | 1.9 |
| (NA) | 0.3 |

**CARD Q**

*[SRSOCCL]*

**A80a.** Most people see themselves as belonging to a particular social class. Please look at this card and tell me which social class you would say <u>you</u> belong to? RECORD ANSWER IN COL a.

*[PRSOCCL]*

**b.** And which social class would you say your <u>parents</u> belonged to when you started at primary school? RECORD ANSWER IN COL b.

|  | a. Self % | b. Parents % |
|---|---|---|
| Upper middle | 1.9 | 2.8 |
| Middle | 27.1 | 18.6 |
| Upper working | 18.0 | 11.1 |
| Working | 46.2 | 58.7 |
| Poor | 4.0 | 7.2 |
| (Don't know) | 2.0 | 1.0 |
| (NA/Refused) | 0.8 | 0.6 |

---

## 33

n = 1414

**A**

*[UNTDIREL]*

**A77.** At any time in the next 20 years, do you think it is likely or unlikely that there will be a united Ireland? PROBE: Very *likely/unlikely* or quite *likely/unlikely*?

|  | % |
|---|---|
| Very likely | 3.8 |
| Quite likely | 19.8 |
| Quite unlikely | 27.8 |
| Very unlikely | 35.5 |
| (Even chance) | 9.1 |
| (Don't know) | 3.4 |
| (NA) | 0.5 |

**CARD P**

*[GOVINTNI]*

**A78a.** Under direct rule from Britain, as now, how much do you generally trust <u>British governments</u> of <u>any</u> party to act in the best interests of Northern Ireland? CODE ONE ONLY IN COL a.

*[STRINTNI]*

**b.** If there was self-rule, how much do you think you would generally trust a <u>Stormont government</u> to act in the best interests of Northern Ireland? CODE ONE ONLY IN COL b.

*[IREINTNI]*

**c.** And if there was a united Ireland, how much do you think you would generally trust an <u>Irish government</u> to act in the best interests of Northern Ireland? CODE ONE ONLY IN COL c.

|  | a. British govt. % | b. Stormont govt. % | c. Irish govt. % |
|---|---|---|---|
| Just about always | 5.2 | 5.0 | 6.2 |
| Most of the time | 32.6 | 31.0 | 35.4 |
| Only some of the time | 37.7 | 31.0 | 29.8 |
| Rarely | 12.0 | 10.6 | 9.6 |
| Never | 3.8 | 3.4 | 3.4 |
| (Don't know/can't say) | 8.3 | 18.4 | 14.9 |
| (NA) | 0.6 | 0.7 | 0.7 |

n = 1414

35

**A**
**CARD R**
*[RACEORIG]*
AB1. To which of these groups do you consider you belong?
CODE ONE ONLY

|  |  | % |
|---|---|---|
| **Black:** | of **African** or **Caribbean** or **other** origin | 1.4 |
| **Asian:** | of **Indian** origin | 1.4 |
|  | of **Pakistani** origin | 0.5 |
|  | of **Bangladeshi** origin | 0.1 |
|  | of **Chinese** origin | 0.1 |
|  | of **other** origin | 0.2 |
|  | (WRITE IN) |  |
| **White:** | of **British** origin | 89.7 |
|  | of **Irish** origin | 2.6 |
|  | of **other** origin | 3.4 |
|  | (WRITE IN) |  |
|  | Refused | 0.1 |
|  | (NA) | 0.3 |

Now I would like to ask you some questions about racial prejudice in Britain.
*[PREJAS]*
A82a. First, thinking of **Asians** – that is, people whose families were originally from India and Pakistan – who now live in Britain. Do you think there is a lot of prejudice against them in Britain nowadays, a little, or hardly any?

|  | % |
|---|---|
| A lot | 58.1 |
| A little | 34.8 |
| Hardly any | 4.3 |
| (Don't know) | 2.4 |
| (NA) | 0.3 |

*[PREJBLK]*
b. And **black** people – that is people whose families were originally from the West Indies or Africa – who now live in Britain. Do you think there is a lot of prejudice against them in Britain nowadays, a little, or hardly any?

|  | % |
|---|---|
| A lot | 49.6 |
| A little | 40.7 |
| Hardly any | 7.0 |
| (Don't know) | 2.4 |
| (NA) | 0.3 |

*[PREJNOW]*
c. Do you think there is generally **more** racial prejudice in Britain now than there was 5 years ago, **less**, or about the **same** amount?

|  | % |
|---|---|
| More now | 24.0 |
| Less now | 24.1 |
| About the same | 49.7 |
| Other answer (WRITE IN) |  |
| (Don't know) | 1.3 |
| (NA) | 0.3 |

36

*[PREJFUT]*
d. Do you think there will be **more**, **less** or about the **same** amount of racial prejudice in Britain in 5 years time compared with now?

|  | % |
|---|---|
| More in 5 years | 21.2 |
| Less | 25.4 |
| About the same | 49.5 |
| Other answer (WRITE IN) |  |
| (Don't know) | 2.7 |
| (NA) | 0.4 |

*[SRPREJ]*
e. How would you describe yourself ... READ OUT ...

|  | % |
|---|---|
| ... as very prejudiced against people of other races, | 2.3 |
| a little prejudiced, | 28.7 |
| or, not prejudiced at all? | 67.6 |
| Other answer (WRITE IN) | 0.5 |
| (Don't know) | 0.4 |
| (NA) | 0.4 |

*[ASJOB]*
A83a. On the whole, do you think people of Asian origin in Britain are **not** given job these days **because** of their race ... READ OUT ...

|  | % |
|---|---|
| ... a lot, | 18.8 |
| little, | 45.0 |
| or – hardly at all? | 29.1 |
| (Don't know) | 6.3 |
| (NA) | 0.7 |

*[WIJOB]*
b. And on the whole, do you think people of West Indian origin in Britain are **not** given jobs these days **because** of their race ... READ OUT ...

|  | % |
|---|---|
| ... a lot, | 23.1 |
| a little, | 46.4 |
| or, hardly at all? | 23.7 |
| (Don't know) | 6.4 |
| (NA) | 0.4 |

*[RACELAW]*
A84a. There is a law in Britain **against** racial discrimination, that is against giving unfair preference to a particular race in housing, jobs and so on. Do you generally **support** or **oppose** the idea of a law for this purpose?

|  | % |
|---|---|
| Support | 75.9 |
| Oppose | 20.7 |
| (Don't know) | 2.5 |
| (NA) | 0.9 |

*[IMMHELP]*
b. Do you think, on the whole, that Britain gives **too little** or **too much** help to Asians and West Indians who have settled in this country, or are present arrangements about right?

|  | % |
|---|---|
| Too little | 12.8 |
| Present arrangements right | 49.3 |
| Too much | 30.0 |
| Other answer (WRITE IN) | 0.7 |
| (Don't know) | 6.7 |
| (NA) | 0.6 |

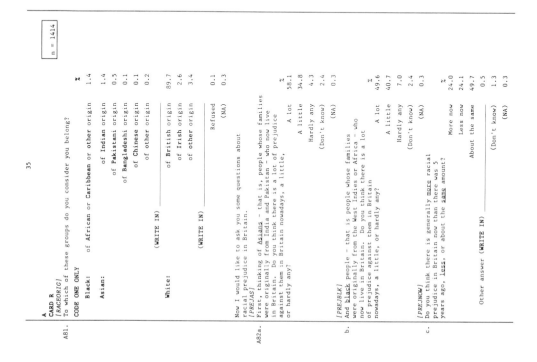

37

**A85a. INTERVIEWER CHECK:**

| | % |
|---|---|
| Respondent is white (CODE 07, 08 or 09 AT Q.81) | 95.8 |
| Other (CODES 01-06 or 97 AT Q.81) | 3.7 |
| (Refused/NA) | 0.4 |

n = 1414

*[RACERSO]*
IF RESPONDENT IS WHITE    n = 1354

b. INTERVIEWER: REFER TO LAST DIGIT OF SAMPLING POINT (SP ON LABEL)    Q.A85b only

    IF ODD: Ask Version X (Q.86a-d.)   1   ASK Q.86a.-d.   [n = 747]
                          AND RING CODE

    IF EVEN OR ZERO: Ask Version Y (Q.86e.-h.)   2   GO TO Q.86e.-h.   [n = 607]
                                 AND RING CODE

---

**VERSION X**    n = 747    Qs. A86 a-d

*[OBOSSAS]*
A86a. Do you think **most** white people in Britain would mind or not mind if a suitably qualified person of Asian origin were appointed as their boss? IF 'WOULD MIND': A lot or a little? RECORD IN COL. a.

*[SBOSSAS]*
b. And you personally? Would you mind or not mind? IF 'WOULD MIND': A lot or a little? RECORD IN COL. b.

*[OMARAS]*
c. Do you think that **most** white people in Britain would mind or not mind if one of their close relatives were to marry a person of Asian origin? IF 'WOULD MIND': A lot or a little? RECORD IN COL. c.

*[SMARAS]*
d. And you personally? Would you mind or not mind? RECORD IN COL. d. THEN GO TO Q.87 IF 'WOULD MIND': A lot or a little?

| | BOSS | | MARRIAGE | |
|---|---|---|---|---|
| | a. Most people % | b. Self % | c. Most people % | d. Self % |
| Mind a lot | 21.5 | 5.6 | 36.7 | 20.6 |
| Mind a little | 30.5 | 8.0 | 37.3 | 22.4 |
| Not mind | 43.6 | 84.3 | 21.4 | 53.2 |
| Other answer | 1.7 | 0.9 | 1.9 | 2.5 |
| (Don't know) | 2.4 | 1.0 | 2.4 | 1.1 |
| (NA) | 0.3 | 0.1 | 0.3 | 0.1 |

WRITE IN: a.

b.

c.

d.

---

38

**VERSION Y**    n = 607    Qs. A86e-h

*[OBOSSWI]*
A86e. Do you think **most** white people in Britain would mind or not mind if a suitably qualified person of **black or West Indian** origin were appointed as their boss? IF 'WOULD MIND': A lot or a little? RECORD IN COL. e.

*[SBOSSWI]*
f. And you personally? Would you mind or not mind? IF 'WOULD MIND': A lot or a little? RECORD IN COL. f.

*[OMARWI]*
g. Do you think that **most** white people in Britain would mind or not mind if one of their close relatives were to marry a person of **black or West Indian** origin? IF 'WOULD MIND': A lot or a little? RECORD IN COL. g.

*[SMARWI]*
h. And you personally? Would you mind or not mind? IF 'WOULD MIND': A lot or a little? RECORD IN COL. h.

| | BOSS | | MARRIAGE | |
|---|---|---|---|---|
| | e. Most people % | f. Self % | g. Most people % | h. Self % |
| Mind a lot | 16.1 | 3.9 | 38.0 | 20.0 |
| Mind a little | 34.8 | 7.8 | 36.7 | 23.9 |
| Not mind | 45.3 | 86.3 | 19.6 | 53.1 |
| Other answer | 1.0 | 0.4 | 1.1 | 1.3 |
| (Don't know) | 1.5 | 0.6 | 3.2 | 0.6 |
| (NA) | 1.3 | 1.1 | 1.5 | 1.1 |

WRITE IN: e.

f.

g.

h.

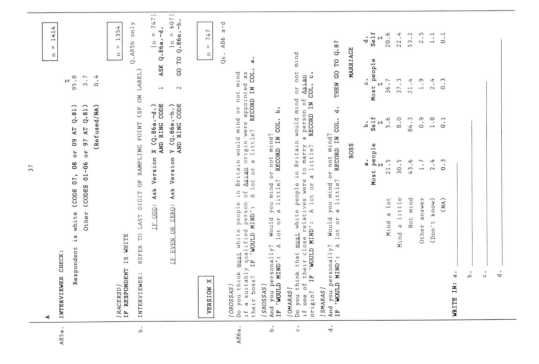

## 39

## SECTION SEVEN

n = 1414

Qs. A87-A93

**A87.** IF INTERVIEWING IN ENGLAND OR WALES, ASK ABOUT "BRITAIN". IF INTERVIEWING IN SCOTLAND, ASK ABOUT "SCOTLAND".
[DIVORCE]
Do you think that divorce in *Britain/Scotland* should be ... READ OUT ...

|  | % |
|---|---|
| ... easier to obtain than it is now, | 10.3 |
| more difficult, | 34.8 |
| or, should things remain as they are? | 48.4 |
| (Don't know) | 6.2 |
| (NA) | 0.3 |

**A88.** [SEXLAW]
There is a law in Britain against sex discrimination, that is against giving unfair preference to men - or to women - in employment, pay and so on. Do you generally support or oppose the idea of a law for this purpose?

|  | % |
|---|---|
| Support | 84.7 |
| Oppose | 13.3 |
| (Don't know) | 1.7 |
| (NA) | 0.4 |

**A89a.** [MARSTAT - See Q900a]
Can I just check your own marital status? At present are you ... READ OUT ...
CODE FIRST TO APPLY

|  | % |
|---|---|
| ... married, | 60.7 |
| living as married, | 5.6 |
| separated or divorced, | 6.3 |
| widowed, | 8.2 |
| or, not married? | 19.1 |
| (NA) | 0.1 |

**b.** And are there any children under 16 years old in this household?

|  | % |
|---|---|
| Yes | 57.4 |
| No | 42.6 |

n = 1414

**A90.** IF MARRIED OR LIVING AS MARRIED (CODES 1 OR 2 AT Q.89a) ASK Q.90. OTHERS GO TO Q.91

I would like to ask about how you and your *husband/wife/partner* generally share some family jobs. Who *does* the household shopping: mainly the man, mainly the woman or is the task shared equally?
RECORD ANSWER IN GRID BELOW AND CONTINUE WITH b. - g.

CODE ONE FOR EACH ITEM

[DOCHORE1 - DOCHORE7]

|  | | Mainly man | Mainly woman | Shared equally | Someone else | (NA) |
|---|---|---|---|---|---|---|
| a. | Household shopping? % | 5.1 | 30.0 | 31.3 | 0.4 | 0.2 |
| b. | ... who makes the evening meal? % | 5.9 | 47.0 | 13.6 | - | 0.5 |
| c. | ... who does the evening dishes? % | 18.6 | 22.1 | 25.0 | 0.3 | 0.9 |
| d. | ... who does the household cleaning? % | 2.5 | 45.4 | 18.2 | 0.6 | 0.3 |
| e. | ... who does the washing and ironing? % | 1.7 | 56.4 | 8.0 | 0.4 | 0.5 |
| f. | ... who repairs the household equipment? % | 54.9 | 4.2 | 6.5 | 0.7 | 0.8 |
| g. | ... who organises the household money and payment of bills? % | 21.1 | 26.9 | 18.5 | - | 0.5 |

[DOCHILD1, DOCHILD2]
IF CHILD(REN) AT Q.89b., ASK h. - i. OTHERS GO TO Q.91

|  | | Mainly man | Mainly woman | Shared equally | Someone else | (NA) |
|---|---|---|---|---|---|---|
| h. | ... who looks after the child(ren) when they are sick? % | 0.3 | 14.6 | 9.5 | - | 0.1 |
| i. | ... who teaches the child(ren) discipline? % | 2.3 | 4.2 | 17.9 | - | 0.1 |

**A91.** ASK ALL

(Now) I would like to ask about how you think family jobs *should* generally be shared between men and women. Who do you think *should* do the household shopping: mainly the man, mainly the woman, or should the task be shared equally?
RECORD ANSWER IN GRID BELOW AND CONTINUE WITH b. - i.

CODE ONE FOR EACH ITEM

[SHCHORE1 - SHCHORE7]

|  | | Mainly man | Mainly woman | Shared equally | (Don't know) | (NA) |
|---|---|---|---|---|---|---|
| a. | Household shopping? % | 0.8 | 22.0 | 75.9 | 0.2 | 1.1 |
| b. | ... who should make the evening meal? % | 1.0 | 39.1 | 57.5 | 0.8 | 1.6 |
| c. | ... who should do the evening dishes? % | 11.5 | 11.0 | 75.5 | 0.2 | 1.9 |
| d. | ... who should do the household cleaning? % | 0.7 | 35.6 | 62.2 | 0.2 | 1.3 |
| e. | ... who should do the washing and ironing? % | 0.3 | 57.9 | 40.0 | 0.3 | 1.5 |
| f. | ... who should repair the household equipment? % | 66.3 | 0.8 | 31.0 | 0.4 | 1.4 |
| g. | ... organise the household money and payment of bills? % | 17.0 | 14.4 | 66.2 | 0.5 | 1.9 |

[SHCHILD1, SHCHILD2]

|  | | Mainly man | Mainly woman | Shared equally | (Don't know) | (NA) |
|---|---|---|---|---|---|---|
| h. | ... look after the child(ren) when they are sick? % | 0.4 | 36.8 | 59.8 | 0.3 | 2.7 |
| i. | ... who should teach the child(ren) discipline? % | 8.2 | 3.9 | 85.0 | 0.2 | 2.7 |

42

n = 1414
Qs. A94 - A9

SECTION EIGHT

**ASK ALL**
**CARD T**

A94a. On this card are ways in which people are asked to give to charity. Some people are not able to give. How about you: in which, if any, of these ways have you given money to charity in the last year? Any others? PROBE UNTIL 'No'.
CODE ALL THAT APPLY

| | Given in last year |
|---|---|
| [CHARRAFF] Buying raffle tickets | 81.9% |
| [CHARFETE] Buying goods in a sale or fete | 37.3% |
| [CHARSHOP] Buying goods in a charity shop | 33.9% |
| [CHARCAT] Buying goods from a charity catalogue | 22.2% |
| [CHARDOOR] Giving in a door-to-door collection | 62.5% |
| [CHARST] Giving in a street collection | 60.3% |
| [CHARCH] Giving in a church collection | 35.1% |
| [CHARTVRD] Giving to a TV or radio appeal | 17.9% |
| [CHARSPON] Sponsoring someone in a fundraising event | 67.9% |
| [CHAREVNT] Attending an event in aid of charity | 30.8% |
| [CHARNONE] (None of these) | 2.5% |
| (NA) | 0.3% |

[CHAROTHR]
b. And are there any other ways you have given money to charity in the last year, such as special appeals, collection tins in shops or pubs, covenants, or some other way?

| | % |
|---|---|
| No, none | 56.2 |
| (Yes, given in a pub collection) | 5.1 |
| (Yes, given in a shop collection) | 5.9 |
| (Yes, given in other collection/ type of collection not stated) | 5.4 |
| (Yes, given by covenant) | 4.9 |
| (Yes, given by regular subscription/payment) | 2.6 |
| (Yes, given to special/direct appeals) | 7.5 |
| (Yes, other donations than those listed above) | 2.4 |
| (Yes, in more than one of these ways) | 5.7 |
| (DK/NA) | 4.3 |

41

n = 1414

A92. [PROMOTE]
Some people think that women are generally less likely than men to be promoted at work, even when their qualifications and experience are the same. Do you think this happens ... READ OUT ...

| | % |
|---|---|
| ... a lot, | 43.2 |
| a little, | 40.6 |
| or, hardly at all? | 10.9 |
| (Don't know) | 4.9 |
| (NA) | 0.4 |

CARD S

A93a. [MWORK1 - MWORK10]
I'd like you to look at the statements on this card. In general, which ones do you think best describe the reasons why many married women work? Any others? CODE ALL THAT APPLY. RECORD IN COL. a.

IF MORE THAN ONE REASON MENTIONED AT a., ASK b. OTHERS GO TO Q.94

[MWKMAIN]
b. And which one of these would you say is generally the main reason why married women work? RECORD IN COL. b.

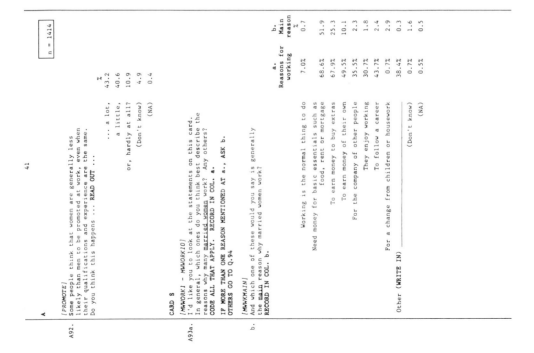

| | a. Reasons for working % | b. Main reason % |
|---|---|---|
| Working is the normal thing to do | 7.0% | 0.7 |
| Need money for basic essentials such as food, rent or mortgage | 68.6% | 51.9 |
| To earn money to buy extras | 67.9% | 25.3 |
| To earn money of their own | 49.5% | 10.1 |
| For the company of other people | 35.5% | 2.3 |
| They enjoy working | 30.7% | 1.8 |
| To follow a career | 43.7% | 2.4 |
| For a change from children or housework | 38.4% | 2.9 |
| Other (WRITE IN) _____ | 0.7% | 0.3 |
| (Don't know) | 0.7% | 1.6 |
| (NA) | 0.5% | 0.5 |

43

A

CARD U

n = 1414

A95. Here are some things on which money is spent. For each one, please tell me where you think the money should come from.

READ OUT a. TO f. AND CODE ONE FOR EACH

| | Entirely from government | Mainly from government | Shared equally | Mainly from charities | Entirely from charities | From somewhere else | (Don't know) | (NA) |
|---|---|---|---|---|---|---|---|---|
| a. [KIDNEYSH] Kidney machines for NHS hospitals | % 58.5 | 34.6 | 5.0 | 0.8 | 0.1 | 0.1 | 0.4 | 0.4 |
| b. [HOMELSSH] Housing for homeless people | % 43.0 | 43.0 | 8.8 | 1.4 | 0.2 | 1.6 | 1.3 | 0.6 |
| c. [FODAIDSH] Food aid to poor countries | % 10.5 | 18.8 | 34.3 | 25.0 | 4.9 | 4.3 | 1.3 | 0.8 |
| d. [DISHOLSH] Holidays for disabled people | % 10.3 | 20.9 | 34.1 | 26.3 | 4.1 | 2.2 | 1.4 | 0.6 |
| e. [LIFEBTSH] Lifeboats | % 32.5 | 32.4 | 21.1 | 9.5 | 2.3 | 1.2 | 0.6 | 0.4 |
| f. [RANIMLSH] Protecting rare animals | % 11.2 | 19.1 | 36.2 | 21.5 | 5.8 | 4.0 | 1.8 | 0.4 |

44

SECTION NINE

n = 1414

Qs. A96-A97

Now a few questions about crime.

CARD V

A96. Here are some possible ways of helping to prevent crime in Britain. How effective do you think each one is?

READ OUT a.-k. AND CODE ONE FOR EACH

| | Very effective | Quite effective | Not very effective | Not at all effective | (Don't know) | (NA) |
|---|---|---|---|---|---|---|
| a. [STIFRSNT] Stiffer sentences generally | % 27.5 | 39.3 | 27.3 | 3.9 | 1.5 | 0.5 |
| b. [LSVIOLTV] Less violence and crime on television | % 22.0 | 37.2 | 31.7 | 7.3 | 1.1 | 0.6 |
| c. [CAREPROP] People taking more care of their property | % 35.4 | 50.8 | 10.6 | 1.9 | 0.8 | 0.6 |
| d. [MORRELIG] People taking religion more seriously | % 8.6 | 22.5 | 36.0 | 29.0 | 3.3 | 0.6 |
| e. [NGHWATCH] More schemes like Neighbourhood Watch | % 24.1 | 58.9 | 12.8 | 1.4 | 2.3 | 0.5 |
| f. [PRISNMOR] Sending more people to prison | % 11.8 | 23.7 | 49.2 | 11.7 | 2.9 | 0.7 |
| g. [PRISNLSS] Sending fewer people to prison | % 1.5 | 24.4 | 45.8 | 19.5 | 8.2 | 0.6 |
| h. [FAMDISCP] Firmer discipline in families | % 56.6 | 36.4 | 4.5 | 1.3 | 0.7 | 0.5 |
| i. [SCHDISCP] Firmer discipline in schools | % 55.6 | 35.5 | 6.6 | 1.2 | 0.6 | 0.5 |
| j. [MORPOLIC] More police on the beat | % 55.0 | 38.6 | 4.6 | 0.5 | 0.7 | 0.5 |
| k. [REDUCPOV] Reducing poverty | % 39.1 | 41.1 | 13.9 | 2.9 | 2.4 | 0.6 |

A97. [FINELEVL] Suppose two people were found guilty of a similar offence. One earns a lot, the other doesn't.

Should the offender on the low income be given a smaller fine than the one on the high income, or should the fine be the same for both?

%

38.3

57.9

Other (WRITE IN) _____ 0.7

(It depends) 0.9

(Don't know) 1.5

(NA) 0.6

45

A + B
ASK ALL
[HOMETYPE]

| SECTION TEN |
|---|

n = 2836

Qs. A98-A100

98a. Now a few questions on housing
INTERVIEWER CODE FROM OBSERVATION AND CHECK WITH RESPONDENT
Would I be right in describing this accommodation as a ...
READ OUT ONE THAT YOU THINK APPLIES

%
... detached house or bungalow 20.1
... semi-detached house or bungalow 37.3
... terraced house 25.8
self-contained, purpose built flat/maisonette (inc. in tenement block) 10.5
... self-contained converted flat/maisonette 4.8
... room(s) - not self-contained 0.3
Other (WRITE IN) _____ 0.5
(NA) 0.6

b. [HOMEEST]
May I just check, is your home part of a housing estate? (SCOTLAND: or scheme?)
NOTE: MAY BE PUBLIC OR PRIVATE; RESPONDENT'S OWN DEFINITION

%
Yes, part of estate 43.7
No 55.3
(Don't know) 0.1
(NA) 1.0

99a. [HOMEIYR]
How long have you lived in your present home ... READ OUT ...

%
... less than a year, 8.3
or, one year or more? 91.2
(Don't know) 0.1
(NA) 0.4

b. [HOMENYR]
IF 'ONE YEAR OR MORE' AT a.
How many years?
PROBE FOR BEST ESTIMATE

MEDIAN: | 0 | 8 | YEARS
(DK/NA) 0.5%

100. ASK ALL
[TENURE1]
Does your household own or rent this accommodation?
PROBE AS NECESSARY

IF OWNS: Outright or on a mortgage?
IF RENTS: From whom?

%
Owns: Own (leasehold/freehold) outright 24.6
Buying (leasehold/freehold) on mortgage 41.7
Rents: Local Authority 20.9
New Town Development Corporation 0.2
Housing Association 2.1
Property company 0.7
Employer 1.0
Other organisation 1.5
Relative 0.6
Other individual 5.3
Rent free: Rent free, squatting, etc. 0.8
(Don't know) 0.1
(NA) 0.5

Note: Qs. 98, 99 and 100 were also asked on the B Version
of the questionnaire as Qs. 98, 99 and 104.

---

46

A + B

| SECTION ELEVEN |
|---|

n = 2836

Qs. A101-A103

ASK ALL

101. [RELIGION]
Do you regard yourself as belonging to any
particular religion? IF YES: Which?
CODE ONE ONLY - DO NOT PROMPT

%
No religion 35.1
Christian - no denomination 3.7
Roman Catholic 10.1
Church of England/Anglican 35.6
Baptist 1.0
Methodist 2.9
Presbyterian/Church of Scotland 4.5
Free Presbyterian 0.1
Brethren 0.1
United Reform Church (URC)/Congregational 0.8
Other Protestant (WRITE IN) _____ 1.7
Other Christian (WRITE IN) _____ 0.5
Hindu 0.9
Jewish 0.3
Islam/Muslim 1.3
Sikh 0.3
Buddhist 0.1
Other non-Christian (WRITE IN:) 0.2
Refused/unwilling to say 0.4
(NA) 0.4

47

n = 2836

A + B

102. IF 'REFUSED' AT Q.101 (CODE 97) GO TO Q.900
ASK ALL OTHERS
[FAMRELIG]
In what religion, if any, were you brought
up? PROBE IF NECESSARY: What was your
family's religion?
CODE ONE ONLY - DO NOT PROMPT

%
No religion 5.9
Christian - no denomination 3.2
Roman Catholic 13.9
Church of England/Anglican 53.8
Baptist 1.8
Methodist 5.6
Presbyterian/Church of Scotland 7.3
Free Presbyterian 0.2
Brethren 0.3
United Reform Church (URC)/Congregational 1.3
Other Protestant (WRITE IN) _____ 1.5
Other Christian (WRITE IN) _____ 0.5
Hindu 1.0
Jewish 0.5
Islam/Muslim 1.3
Sikh 0.3
Buddhist 0.1
Other non-Christian (WRITE IN) _____ 0.1
Refused/unwilling to say -
(NA) 1.2

103. IF ANY RELIGION AT Q.101 OR Q.102, ASK Q.103; OTHERS GO TO Q.900
[CHATTEND]
Apart from such special occasions as weddings, funerals
and baptisms, how often nowadays do you attend services
or meetings connected with your religion?
PROBE AS NECESSARY

%
Once a week or more 11.3
Less often but at least once in two weeks 2.4
Less often but at least once a month 6.4
Less often but at least twice a year 12.5
Less often but at least once a year 6.6
Less often 3.7
Never or practically never 48.5
Varies too much to say 0.5
Refused/unwilling to answer 0.1
Don't know -
(NA) 2.8

Note: Qs. 101-103 were also asked on the B version of the
questionnaire as Qs. 114-116

48

n = 2836
Qs.900 - 912a

A + B
SECTION TWELVE

900a. [MARSTAT]
Can I just check whether at present you are
... READ OUT ...
CODE FIRST TO APPLY
%
... married, 60.7
living as married, 5.6
separated or divorced, 6.3
widowed, 8.2
or, not married? 19.1
(NA) 0.1

b. [HOUSEHLD]
Finally, a few questions about you and
your household. Including yourself, how
many people live here regularly as
members of this household?
CHECK INTERVIEWER MANUAL FOR DEFINITION OF
HOUSEHOLD IF NECESSARY.
MEAN: 0 3

901. Now I'd like to ask for a few details about
each person in your household. Starting with
yourself, what was your age last birthday?
WORK DOWN COLUMNS OF GRID FOR EACH HOUSEHOLD MEMBER

| | Resp. | 2 | 3 | 4 | 5 | 6 | 7 | 8 | 9 | 10 |
|---|---|---|---|---|---|---|---|---|---|---|

a. [RSEX]
[P2SEX - P1OSEX]
Sex:
%
Male 45.7
Female 54.3

b. [RACE]
[P2AGE - P10AGE]
Age last birthday:

c. [P2REL - P10REL]
Relationship to
respondent:
Spouse/partner
Son/daughter
Parent/parent-in-law
Other relative
Not related

d. [RRESP]
[P2RESP - P10RESP]
HOUSEHOLD MEMBER
WITH LEGAL RESPON-
SIBILITY FOR          %
ACCOMMODATION    Yes   80.3
(INC. JOINT AND   No   17.4
SHARED)          (NA)   2.3

CHECK THAT NUMBER OF PEOPLE IN GRID EQUALS NUMBER GIVEN
AT Q.900b

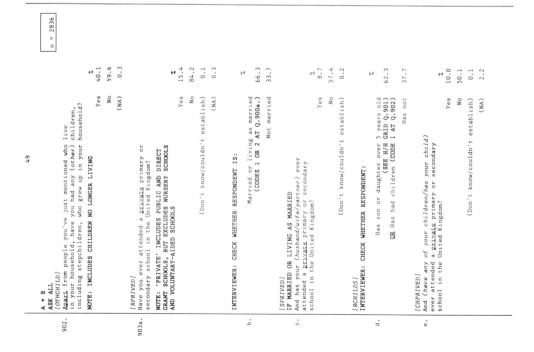

n = 2836

**49**

A + B
ASK ALL
*[OTHCHILD]*
902. Apart from people you've just mentioned who live in your household, have you had any (other) children, including stepchildren, who grew up in your household?
NOTE: INCLUDES CHILDREN NO LONGER LIVING

|  | % |
|---|---|
| Yes | 40.1 |
| No | 59.6 |
| (NA) | 0.3 |

*[RPRIVED]*
903a. Have you ever attended a private primary or secondary school in the United Kingdom?
NOTE: 'PRIVATE' INCLUDES PUBLIC AND DIRECT GRANT SCHOOLS, BUT EXCLUDES NURSERY SCHOOLS AND VOLUNTARY-AIDED SCHOOLS

|  | % |
|---|---|
| Yes | 15.4 |
| No | 84.2 |
| (Don't know/couldn't establish) | 0.1 |
| (NA) | 0.3 |

b. INTERVIEWER: CHECK WHETHER RESPONDENT IS:

|  | % |
|---|---|
| Married or living as married (CODES 1 OR 2 AT Q.900a.) | 66.3 |
| Not married | 33.7 |

*[SPRIVED]*
IF MARRIED OR LIVING AS MARRIED
c. And has your (husband/wife/partner) ever attended a private primary or secondary school in the United Kingdom?

|  | % |
|---|---|
| Yes | 8.7 |
| No | 57.4 |
| (Don't know/couldn't establish) | 0.2 |

*[RCHILD5]*
d. INTERVIEWER: CHECK WHETHER RESPONDENT:

|  | % |
|---|---|
| Has son or daughter over 5 years old (SEE H/H GRID Q.901) OR Has had children (CODE 1 AT Q.902) | 62.3 |
| Has not | 37.7 |

*[CHPRIVED]*
e. And (have any of your children/has your child) ever attended a private primary or secondary school in the United Kingdom?

|  | % |
|---|---|
| Yes | 10.0 |
| No | 50.1 |
| (Don't know/couldn't establish) | 0.1 |
| (NA) | 2.2 |

n = 2836

**50**

A + B
ASK ALL
904a. INTERVIEWER: IS THIS A SINGLE PERSON HOUSEHOLD - RESPONDENT ONLY PERSON AT Q.901 (p.48)

|  | % |
|---|---|
| Yes | 13.5 |
| No | 86.5 |

*[DUTYRESP]*
IF NO AT a.
b. Who is the person mainly responsible for general domestic duties in this household?

|  | % |
|---|---|
| Respondent mainly | 35.6 |
| Someone else mainly (WRITE IN RELATIONSHIP TO RESP.) | 32.4 |
| Duties shared equally (WRITE IN BY WHOM) | 17.0 |
| (NA) | 1.5 |

(See derived variable *[EISEDUTY]* for gender and relationship of persons other than the respondent)

*[CHLDINHH]*
905a. INTERVIEWER: IS THERE A CHILD UNDER 16 YEARS IN HOUSEHOLD? SEE H/H GRID, Q.901

|  | % |
|---|---|
| Yes | 30.7 |
| No | 69.3 |

*[CHLDRESP] + [EISECHLD]*
IF YES AT a.
b. Who is the person mainly responsible for the general care of the child(ren) here?

|  | % |
|---|---|
| Respondent mainly | 13.7 |
| Someone else mainly (WRITE IN RELATIONSHIP TO RESP.) | 10.1 |
| Care shared equally (WRITE IN BY WHOM) | 6.2 |
| (NA) | 0.7 |

(See derived variable *[EISECHLD]* for gender and relationship of persons other than the respondent)

*[TEA]*
ASK ALL
906. How old were you when you completed your continuous full-time education?
PROBE AS NECESSARY

|  | % |
|---|---|
| 15 or under | 42.5 |
| 16 | 25.4 |
| 17 | 8.6 |
| 18 | 7.5 |
| 19 or over | 13.0 |
| Still at school | 0.3 |
| Still at college, polytechnic, or university | 2.4 |
| Other answer (WRITE IN:) | - |
| (NA) | 0.4 |

51

A + B
CARD XI
[SCHQUAL]

907a. Have you passed any of the examinations on this card?

n = 2836

|  | % |
|---|---|
| Yes | 51.3 |
| No | 48.5 |
| (NA) | 0.2 |

IF YES AT a.
b. Which ones? Any others?
CODE ALL THAT APPLY

|  | % |
|---|---|
| [EQUAL1] CSE Grades 2-5 } GCSE Grades D-G | 15.8 |
| [EQUAL2] CSE Grade 1 / GCE O' level / GCSE Grades A-C / School certificate / Scottish (SCE) Ordinary / SUPE Ordinary / Scottish School-leaving Certificate lower grade / Northern Ireland Junior Certificate | 41.9 |
| [EQUAL3] GCE A' level/S' level / Higher school certificate / Matriculation / Scottish SCE/SLC/SUPE at higher grade / Northern Ireland Senior Certificate | 19.3 |
| [EQUAL4] Overseas School Leaving Exam/Certificate | 1.6 |

ASK ALL
CARD X2 [PSCHQUAL]

908a. And have you passed any of the exams or got any of the qualifications on this card?

|  | % |
|---|---|
| Yes | 43.6 |
| No | 56.2 |
| (NA) | 0.1 |

IF YES AT a.
b. Which ones? Any others?
CODE ALL THAT APPLY [EQUAL5 - EQUAL17]

|  | % |
|---|---|
| Recognised trade apprenticeship completed | 7.8 |
| RSA/other clerical, commerical qualification | 10.1 |
| City & Guilds Certificate - Craft/Intermediate/Ordinary/ Part I | 7.7 |
| City & Guilds Certificate - Advanced/Final/Part II or Part III | 4.0 |
| City & Guilds Certificate - Full technological | 1.3 |
| BEC/TEC General/Ordinary National Certificate (ONC) or Diploma (OND) | 3.8 |
| BEC/TEC Higher/Higher National Certificate (HNC) or Diploma (HND) | 3.4 |
| Teacher training qualification | 3.8 |
| Nursing qualification | 3.5 |
| Other technical or business qualification/certificate | 6.3 |
| University or CNAA degree or diploma | 8.7 |
| Other recognised academic or vocational qualification | 1.6 |
| (Other qualification/DK/NA) | 1.3 |

52

A + B

909. INTERVIEWER: REFER TO ECONOMIC POSITION OF RESPONDENT (Q.12, p.7)

n = 2836

|  | % |  |
|---|---|---|
| RESPONDENT IS IN PAID WORK (CODE 03) | 52.6 | ASK ABOUT PRESENT JOB |
| RESPONDENT IS WAITING TO TAKE UP PAID WORK (CODE 04) | 0.2 | ASK ABOUT FUTURE JOB |
| ALL OTHERS (CODES 01-02; 05-11) | 47.2 | ASK ABOUT PAST JOB |

910. Now I want to ask you about your (present/future/last) job. CHANGE TENSES FOR (BRACKETED) WORDS AS APPROPRIATE.

a. What (is) your job?
PROBE AS NECESSARY: What (is) the name or title of the job?
IF 'NEVER HAD JOB', WRITE IN AND GO TO Q.911

b. What kind of work (do) you do most of the time?
IF RELEVANT: What materials/machinery (do) you use?

c. What training or qualifications (are) needed for that job?

d. [RSUPER]
(Do) you directly supervise or (are) you directly responsible for the work of any other people?

|  | % |
|---|---|
| (Yes) | 32.5 |
| No | 66.4 |
| (Don't know) | 0.3 |
| (NA) | 0.8 |

IF YES: How many? MEDIAN: [0 0 0 5]

e. [REMPLOYEE]
Can I just check: (are) you ... READ OUT ...

|  | % |
|---|---|
| ... an employee, | 85.1 |
| or, self-employed? | 11.3 |
| (NA) | 0.5 |

n = 2836

## 53

**A + B**
*[RSECTOR]*
**IF EMPLOYEE (CODE 1 AT e.)**
**CARD X1**

910f. Which of the types of organisation on this card (do) you work for?

**CODE FIRST TO APPLY**

|  | % |
|---|---|
| Private firm or company | 54.0 |
| Nationalised industry/public corp. | 4.9 |
| Local Authority/Local Education Authority | 12.7 |
| Health Authority/NHS hospital | 5.6 |
| Central Government/Civil Service | 4.1 |
| Charity or Trust | 1.3 |
| Other (WRITE IN:) | 2.3 |
| (Don't know) | 0.1 |
| (NA) | 0.2 |

g. *[PREMISES]* is where you (work) your employer's only premises, or (are) there other premises elsewhere?

|  | % |
|---|---|
| Employer's only premises | 20.5 |
| Employer has other premises elsewhere | 61.4 |
| (Don't know) | 1.2 |
| (NA) | 2.0 |

**ASK ALL WHO HAVE EVER WORKED**
h. What (does) your employer (IF SELF-EMPLOYED: you) make or do at the place where you usually (work) (from)?
**IF FARM, GIVE NO. OF ACRES**

i. *[REMPWORK]* Including yourself, how many people (are) employed at the place where you usually (work) (from)?
**IF SELF-EMPLOYED:** (Do) you have any employees?
**IF YES:** How many?

|  | % |
|---|---|
| (No employees) | 6.3 |
| Under 10 | 19.3 |
| 10-24 | 14.4 |
| 25-99 | 20.4 |
| 100-499 | 19.6 |
| 500 or more | 14.8 |
| (Don't know) | 1.1 |
| (NA) | 1.1 |

j. *[RPARTFUL]* (Is) the job ... READ OUT ...

|  | % |
|---|---|
| ... full-time (30+ HOURS) | 75.3 |
| or, part-time (10-29 HOURS)? | 20.5 |
| (NA) | 1.1 |

## 54

**A + B**

**O.U.O.**
**RESPONDENT'S OCCUPATIONAL DETAILS**

911a. *[UNIONSA]*
**ASK ALL**
Are you <u>now</u> a member of a trade union or staff association?

**CODE FIRST TO APPLY**

|  | % |
|---|---|
| Yes: trade union | 20.6 |
| Yes: staff association | 4.0 |
| No | 74.9 |
| (NA) | 0.6 |

b. *[UNIONEVR]*
**IF NO AT a.**
Have you <u>ever</u> been a member of a trade union or staff association?

**CODE FIRST TO APPLY**

|  | % |
|---|---|
| Yes: trade union | 28.0 |
| Yes: staff association | 3.1 |
| No | 43.4 |
| (NA) | 0.9 |

912a. **INTERVIEWER:**
**RESPONDENT IS:**

|  | % |
|---|---|
| Married or living as married (CODES 1 OR 2 AT Q.900a.) | 66.3 |
| All others | 33.7 |

n = 2836

OFFICE USE ONLY

OC
ES
SEG
SC/NM.M
SIC
HG
SOC

## 55

A + B

n = 1881

Qs 912b - 914

**912b.** [SECONACT]
CARD X4
Which of these descriptions applied to what your (husband/wife/partner) was doing last week, that is the seven days ending last Sunday? PROBE: Any others? CODE ALL THAT APPLY IN COL. I
IF ONLY ONE CODE AT I, TRANSFER IT TO COL. II
IF MORE THAN ONE AT I, TRANSFER HIGHEST ON LIST TO II

| | COL I | COL II ECONOMIC POSITION % |
|---|---|---|
| In full-time education (not paid for by employer, including on vacation) | A | 0.3 |
| On government training/employment programme e.g. Employment Training, Youth Training programme etc.) | B | 0.3 |
| In paid work (or away temporarily) for at least 10 hours in week | C | 59.1 |
| Waiting to take up paid work already accepted | D | 0.3 |
| Unemployed and registered at a benefit office | E | 3.4 |
| Unemployed, not registered, but actively looking for a job | F | 0.3 |
| Unemployed, wanting a job (of at least 10 hrs a week), but not actively looking for a job | G | 0.5 |
| Permanently sick or disabled | H | 3.1 |
| Wholly retired from work | J | 15.7 |
| Looking after the home | K | 16.3 |
| Doing something else (WRITE IN) | L | 0.4 |
| (NA) | | 0.2 |

**c.** [SLASTJOB]
IF CODES 01-02, OR 05-11 AT b.
How long ago did your (husband/wife/partner) last have a paid job (other than the government programme you mentioned) of at least 10 hours a week?

| | % |
|---|---|
| Within past 12 months | 5.1 |
| Over 1, up to 5 years ago | 9.7 |
| Over 5, up to 10 years ago | 9.1 |
| Over 10, up to 20 years ago | 8.0 |
| Over 20 years ago | 5.1 |
| Never had a paid job of 10+ hours a week | 2.7 |
| (NA) | 0.7 |

## 56

A + B

n = 1881

**913.** INTERVIEWER:
REFER TO ECONOMIC POSITION OF SPOUSE/PARTNER (Q.912b.)

| | % | |
|---|---|---|
| SPOUSE/PARTNER IS IN PAID WORK (CODE 03) | 59.1 | ASK ABOUT PRESENT JOB |
| SPOUSE/PARTNER IS WAITING TO TAKE UP PAID WORK (CODE 04) | 0.3 | ASK ABOUT FUTURE JOB |
| ALL OTHERS (CODES 01-02; 05-11) | 40.6 | ASK ABOUT LAST JOB |

**914a.** Now I want to ask you about your (husband's/wife's/partner's) (present, future, last) job. CHANGE (BRACKETED) WORDS AS APPROPRIATE
What (is) (his/her) job?
PROBE AS NECESSARY: What (is) the name or title of that job?
IF 'NEVER HAD A JOB', WRITE IN AND GO TO Q.915

**b.** What kind of work (does) (he/she) do most of the time?
IF RELEVANT: What materials/machinery (does) (he/she) use?

**c.** What training or qualifications (are) needed for that job?

**d.** [SSUPER]
(Does) (he/she) directly supervise or (is) (he/she) directly responsible for the work of any other people?

| | % |
|---|---|
| (Yes) | 35.5 |
| No | 60.6 |
| (NA) | 1.3 |
| (Don't know) | 2.6 |

IF YES: How many? MEDIAN | 0 | 6 |

**e.** [SEMPLOYE]
(Is) (he/she) ... READ OUT ...

| | % |
|---|---|
| ... an employee, | 84.6 |
| or, self-employed? | 11.8 |
| (Don't know) | 0.1 |
| (NA) | 0.7 |

57

**A + B**

[SSECTOR]
IF SPOUSE/PARTNER IS EMPLOYEE (CODE 1 AT e.)

CARD X5

914f. Which of the types of organisation on this card (does) (he/she) work for?

| | % |
|---|---|
| Private firm or company | 54.2 |
| Nationalised industry/public corporation | 6.1 |
| Local Authority/Local Education Authority | 12.1 |
| Health Authority/NHS hospital | 5.2 |
| Central Government/Civil Service | 4.2 |
| Charity or Trust | 0.6 |
| Other (WRITE IN) | 1.8 |
| (Don't know) | 0.1 |
| (NA) | 0.9 |

ASK ALL WHOSE SPOUSE/PARTNER HAS EVER WORKED
g. What (does) the employer (IF SELF-EMPLOYED: (he/she)) make or do at the place where (he/she) usually (works) (from)?
IF FARM, GIVE NO. OF ACRES

[SEMPWORK]
h. Including (him-/herself), roughly how many people (are) employed at the place where (he/she) usually (works) (from)?

IF YES: How many?

| | % |
|---|---|
| (No employees) | 5.9 |
| Under 10 | 18.1 |
| 10-24 | 12.7 |
| 25-99 | 19.5 |
| 100-499 | 19.7 |
| 500 or more | 15.8 |
| (Don't know) | 3.5 |
| (NA) | 2.0 |

IF SELF-EMPLOYED: (Does) (he/she) have any employees?

[SPARTFUL]
i. (Is) the job ... READ OUT ...

| | % |
|---|---|
| ... full-time (30+ HOURS) | 74.1 |
| or, part-time (10-29 HOURS)? | 19.6 |
| (Don't know) | 0.1 |
| (NA) | 3.3 |

n = 1881

---

58

**A + B**

O.U.O.
SPOUSE'S OCCUPATIONAL DETAILS

[CAROWN]
ASK ALL
915. Do you, or does anyone else in your household own or have the regular use of a car or a van?

| | % |
|---|---|
| Yes | 73.4 |
| No | 26.5 |
| (NA) | 0.1 |

[ANYBENFT]
CARD X6
916a. Have you or anyone in this household received any of the state benefits on this card during the last five years?

| | % |
|---|---|
| Yes | 82.3 |
| No | 17.5 |
| (NA) | 0.2 |

b. IF YES AT a. Any others?
Which ones?
CODE ALL THAT APPLY

| | % |
|---|---|
| [BENEFT1] Child benefit | 39.5 |
| [BENEFT2] Maternity benefit or allowance | 8.5 |
| [BENEFT3] One-parent benefit | 4.5 |
| [BENEFT4] Family credit | 3.6 |
| [BENEFT5] State retirement or widow's pension | 25.9 |
| [BENEFT6] State supplementary pension | 1.7 |
| [BENEFT15] Community Charge rebate/Poll Tax rebate or benefit | 17.9 |
| [BENEFT7] Invalidity or disabled pension or benefit | 8.0 |
| [BENEFT8] Attendance/Invalid care/Mobility allowance | 4.6 |
| [BENEFT9] State Sickness or injury benefit | 10.3 |
| [BENEFT10] Unemployment benefit | 16.4 |
| [BENEFT11] Income support | 16.0 |
| [BENEFT12] Housing benefit (rate or rent rebate) | 16.0 |
| [BENEFT13] Other state benefit(s) volunteered (WRITE IN) | 0.4 |
| (NA) | 0.2 |

59

n = 2836

**A + B**

ASK ALL

**917a.** CARD X7 [HHINCOME]
Which of the letters on this card represents the total income of your household from all sources before tax? Please just tell me the letter.
NOTE: INCLUDES INCOME FROM BENEFITS, SAVINGS, ETC.
CODE ONE IN COLUMN a.

**b.** INTERVIEWER: CHECK Q.12, PAGE 7:

| | % |
|---|---|
| RESPONDENT IS IN PAID WORK (CODE 03) | 52.6 |
| ALL OTHERS | 47.4 |

**c.** [REARN]
Which of the letters on this card represents your own gross or total earnings, before deduction of income tax and national insurance?
ONE CODE IN COLUMN c.

| | | | a. Household income % | c. Own earnings % |
|---|---|---|---|---|
| Less than £3,999 pa | Q | = | 8.3 | 6.2 |
| £4,000 - £5,999 pa | T | = | 10.9 | 5.8 |
| £6,000 - £7,999 pa | O | = | 7.0 | 5.7 |
| £8,000 - £9,999 pa | K | = | 5.7 | 5.6 |
| £10,000 - £11,999 pa | L | = | 6.2 | 5.4 |
| £12,000 - £14,999 pa | B | = | 6.9 | 6.7 |
| £15,000 - £17,999 pa | Z | = | 7.7 | 4.7 |
| £18,000 - £19,999 pa | M | = | 4.8 | 2.2 |
| £20,000 - £22,999 pa | F | = | 5.3 | 1.8 |
| £23,000 - £25,999 pa | J | = | 4.2 | 1.4 |
| £26,000 - £28,999 pa | D | = | 3.9 | 1.0 |
| £29,000 - £31,999 pa | H | = | 2.9 | 0.9 |
| £32,000 - £34,999 pa | C | = | 3.1 | 0.3 |
| £35,000 pa or more | G | = | 6.0 | 1.0 |
| (Refused/Don't know) | | | 10.6 | 2.3 |
| (NA) | | | 6.5 | 1.4 |

**918.** [OWNSHARE]
ASK ALL
Do you (or your husband/wife/partner) own any shares quoted on the Stock Exchange, including unit trusts?

| | % |
|---|---|
| Yes | 28.4 |
| No | 70.6 |
| (Don't know) | 0.1 |
| (NA) | 0.8 |

**919a.** [PHONE]
Is there a telephone in (your part of) this accommodation?

| | % |
|---|---|
| Yes | 88.4 |
| No | 11.3 |
| (NA) | 0.3 |

60

n = 2836

**A + B**
[TELNUM]
IF YES AT a.

**919b.** A few interviews on any survey are checked by a supervisor to make sure that people are satisfied with the way the interview was carried out. In case my supervisor needs to contact you, it would be helpful if we could have your telephone number.
IF NUMBER GIVEN
WRITE ON THE ARF - NOT HERE!

| | % |
|---|---|
| Number given | 80.1 |
| Number refused | 6.5 |
| (NA) | 1.8 |

**920a.** ASK ALL
[SAMPLTYP]
INTERVIEWER CHECK:
Sample type of this address is:
(SAMPLE TYPE IS 'ST' ON ADDRESS LABEL)

| | % |
|---|---|
| 1 or 3 | 69.1 |
| 2 or 4 | 30.9 |

IF CODE 1 AT a.
SHOW ADVANCE LETTER
[LETTERRM]

**b.** In March we sent your household a letter, giving advance notice that an interviewer would be calling to ask for an interview. The letter looked like this (SHOW).
Do you remember receiving this letter?

| | % |
|---|---|
| Yes, remembers letter | 44.3 |
| No, does not | 23.2 |
| Other (WRITE IN) _____ | 1.4 |
| (NA) | 0.3 |

**c.** ASK ALL
[LETTERPR]
If you were given a choice, would you have preferred ... READ OUT ...

| | % |
|---|---|
| ... to have a letter in advance saying an interviewer would call, | 56.5 |
| or, to have an interviewer simply call round, | 3.1 |
| or, wouldn't it really matter? | 38.6 |
| (Don't know) | 0.4 |
| (NA) | 1.3 |

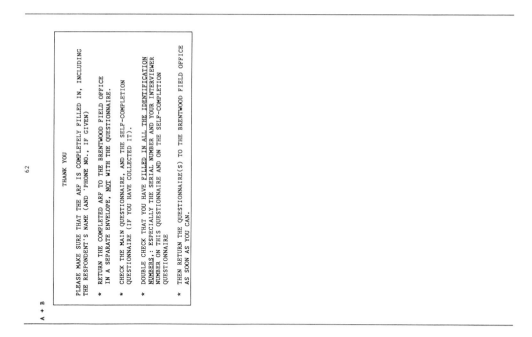

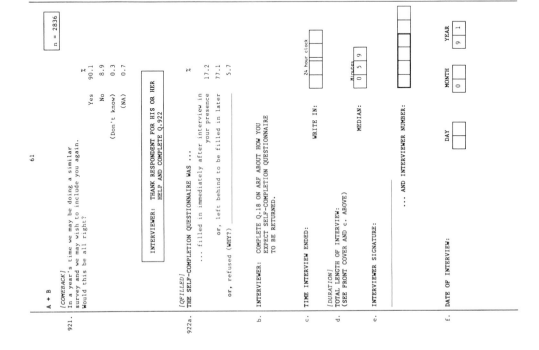

B

SCPR
SOCIAL & COMMUNITY PLANNING RESEARCH

Head Office: 35 NORTHAMPTON SQUARE,
LONDON EC1V 0AX  Telephone 071-250 1866

Field and DP Office: BRENTWOOD, ESSEX
Northern Field Office: DARLINGTON, CO. DURHAM

Spring 1991

P1135/Britain

**BRITISH SOCIAL ATTITUDES:**

**1991 SURVEY**

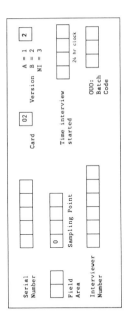

Serial
Number

Field
Area          0

Interviewer
Number

Card    02     Version   A = 1
                         B = 2
                         NI = 3

Sampling Point

Time interview
started            24 hr clock

OUO:
Batch
Code

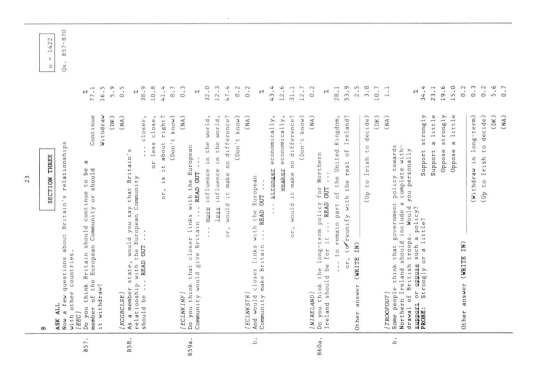

**n = 1422**

**n = 1422   Qs. B57-B70**

## SECTION THREE

**B**
ASK ALL.
Now a few questions about Britain's relationships with other countries.

*[EEC]*
B57. Do you think Britain should continue to be a member of the European Community or should it withdraw?

%
Continue 77.1
Withdraw 16.5
(DK) 5.9
(NA) 0.5

*[ECGBCLSE]*
B58. As a member state, would you say that Britain's relationship with the European Community should be ... **READ OUT** ...

%
... closer, 38.9
or less close, 41.4
or, is it about right? 10.8
(Don't know) 8.7
(NA) 0.3

*[ECLNKINF]*
B59a. Do you think that closer links with the European Community would give Britain ... **READ OUT** ...

%
... more influence in the world, 32.0
less influence in the world, 12.3
or, would it make no difference? 47.4
(Don't know) 8.2
(NA) 0.2

*[ECLNKSTR]*
b. And would closer links with the European Community make Britain ... **READ OUT** ...

%
... stronger economically, 43.4
weaker economically, 12.6
or, would it make no difference? 31.1
(Don't know) 12.7
(NA) 0.2

*[NIRELAND]*
B60a. Do you think the long-term policy for Northern Ireland should be for it ... **READ OUT** ...

%
... to remain part of the United Kingdom, 28.1
or, to reunify with the rest of Ireland? 53.9
Other answer (WRITE IN) 2.5
(Up to Irish to decide) 3.8
(DK) 10.7
(NA) 1.1

*[TROOPOUT]*
b. Some people think that government policy towards Northern Ireland should include a complete withdrawal of British troops. Would you personally **support** or **oppose** such a policy?
**PROBE:** Strongly or a little?

%
Support strongly 34.4
Support a little 23.1
Oppose strongly 19.6
Oppose a little 15.0
Other answer (WRITE IN) 0.2
(Withdraw in long-term) 0.3
(Up to Irish to decide) 0.2
(DK) 5.6
(NA) 0.7

---

**B**
B61. Now I would like to ask you about two economic problems - inflation and unemployment.
*[PRICES]*
First, inflation: in a year from now, do you expect prices generally to have gone up, to have stayed the same, or to have gone down?

%
IF GONE UP OR GONE DOWN: To have gone up by a lot 42.7
By a lot or a little? To have gone up by a little 40.7
To have stayed the same 7.6
To have gone down by a little 6.7
To have gone down by a lot 0.9
(Don't know) 1.1
(NA) 0.3

*[UNEMP]*
B62. Second, unemployment: in a year from now, do you expect unemployment to have gone up, to have stayed the same, or to have gone down?

%
IF GONE UP OR GONE DOWN: To have gone up by a lot 42.0
By a lot or a little? To have gone up by a little 29.5
To have stayed the same 16.7
To have gone down by a little 7.7
To have gone down by a lot 2.3
(Don't know) 1.6
(NA) 0.3

*[UNEMPINF]*
B63a. If the government **had** to choose between keeping down inflation or keeping down unemployment, to which do you think it should give highest priority?

%
Keeping down inflation 41.4
Keeping down unemployment 54.5
Other answer (WRITE IN) 0.3
Both equal 2.1
(DK) 1.3
(NA) 0.4

*[CONCERN]*
b. Which do you think is of the most concern to **you and your family** ... **READ OUT** ...

%
... inflation, 62.2
or, unemployment? 34.4
Other (WRITE IN) 0.2
(Don't know) 1.2
Neither 0.1
Both equal 1.4
(NA) 0.5

*[INDUSTRY]*
B64. Looking ahead over the next year, do you think Britain's general industrial performance will improve, stay much the same, or decline?

%
IF IMPROVE OR DECLINE: Improve a lot 3.7
By a lot or a little? Improve a little 17.0
Stay much the same 38.6
Decline a little 23.0
Decline a lot 11.6
(Don't know) 5.9
(NA) 0.2

26

n = 1422

**B**
[SRINC]

B68a. Among which group would you place yourself
... READ OUT ...

|  | % |
|---|---|
| ... high income, | 3.4 |
| middle income, | 47.9 |
| or, low income? | 47.4 |
| (DK) | 0.5 |
| (NA) | 0.8 |

**CARD M**
[HINCDIFF]

b. Which of the phrases on this card would you
say comes closest to your feelings about your
household's income these days?

|  | % |
|---|---|
| Living comfortably on present income | 26.2 |
| Coping on present income | 46.7 |
| Finding it difficult on present income | 17.6 |
| Finding it very difficult on present income | 8.8 |
| Other (WRITE IN) | 0.1 |
| (DK) | 0.1 |
| (NA) | 0.5 |

[HINCPAST]

B69. Looking back over the last year or so, would you
say your household's income has ... READ OUT ...

|  | % |
|---|---|
| ... fallen behind prices, | 54.6 |
| kept up with prices, | 35.8 |
| or, gone up by more than prices? | 7.8 |
| (Don't know) | 1.2 |
| (NA) | 0.5 |

[HINCXPCT]

B70. And looking forward to the year ahead, do you
expect your household's income will ...
READ OUT ...

|  | % |
|---|---|
| ... fall behind prices, | 47.3 |
| keep up with prices, | 38.6 |
| or, go up by more than prices? | 9.9 |
| (Don't know) | 3.8 |
| (NA) | 0.5 |

---

25

**B**

B65. Here are a number of policies which might help
Britain's economic problems. As I read them
out, will you tell me whether you would support
such a policy or oppose it?

READ OUT ITEMS a.-j. AND CODE ONE FOR EACH

n = 1422

|  |  | Support | Oppose | (DK) | (NA) |
|---|---|---|---|---|---|
| a. | [ECOHELP1] Control of wages by law | % 33.1 | 63.6 | 2.6 | 0.7 |
| b. | [ECOHELP2] Control of prices by law | % 60.4 | 37.2 | 1.7 | 0.7 |
| c. | [ECOHELP3] Reducing the level of government spending on health and education | % 7.3 | 91.2 | 0.6 | 0.9 |
| d. | [ECOHELPC] Government controls to cut down goods from abroad | % 66.6 | 28.2 | 3.7 | 1.5 |
| e. | [ECOHELP5] Increasing government subsidies for private industry | % 58.1 | 34.8 | 5.7 | 1.3 |
| f. | [ECOHELP7] Reducing government spending on defence | % 55.2 | 41.6 | 2.1 | 1.1 |
| g. | [ECOHELP8] Government schemes to encourage job sharing | % 69.9 | 25.5 | 3.7 | 0.9 |
| h. | [ECOHELP9] Government to set up construction projects to create more jobs | % 83.9 | 12.7 | 2.5 | 0.9 |
| i. | [ECOHELPA] Government action to cut interest rates | % 90.1 | 7.2 | 2.1 | 0.7 |
| j. | [ECOHELPB] Government controls on hire purchase and credit | % 81.2 | 15.9 | 2.2 | 0.7 |

B66. [INCOMGAP]
Thinking of income levels generally in Britain today,
would you say that the gap between those with high
incomes and those with low incomes is ... READ OUT ...

|  | % |
|---|---|
| ... too large, | 79.5 |
| about right, | 16.3 |
| or, too small? | 2.3 |
| (DK) | 1.3 |
| (NA) | 0.7 |

**CARD L**

B67. Generally, how would you describe levels of taxation?

a. Firstly for those with high incomes? Please choose a phrase from
this card. RECORD ANSWER IN COL a. [TAXH1]

b. Next for those with middle incomes? Please choose a phrase from
this card. RECORD ANSWER IN COL b. [TAXMID]

c. And lastly for those with low incomes? Please choose a phrase from
this card. RECORD ANSWER IN COL c. [TAXLOW]

| Taxes are: | a. High incomes % | b. Middle incomes % | c. Low incomes % |
|---|---|---|---|
| Much too high | 2.4 | 2.7 | 21.7 |
| Too high | 10.3 | 22.6 | 52.4 |
| About right | 35.4 | 65.5 | 20.3 |
| Too low | 39.5 | 5.4 | 2.2 |
| Much too low | 9.0 | 0.4 | 0.5 |
| (DK) | 2.9 | 3.1 | 2.2 |
| (NA) | 0.5 | 0.4 | 0.6 |

## SECTION FOUR

27

n = 1422

Qs. B71-B74

**B71.** How concerned are you about each of these environmental issues? Please choose a phrase from the card.

CARD N

READ OUT a.-j. AND CODE ONE FOR EACH

| | | Very concerned | A bit concerned | Not very concerned | Not at all concerned | (Don't know/ can't say) | (NA) |
|---|---|---|---|---|---|---|---|
| a. | [INSECTCD] ...insecticides, fertilisers and chemical sprays? | % 48.7 | 35.6 | 11.2 | 3.1 | 0.9 | 0.5 |
| b. | [SEWAGE] ...disposal of sewage? | % 63.8 | 26.5 | 5.4 | 2.5 | 1.3 | 0.4 |
| c. | [OZLAYER] ...thinning of the ozone layer? | % 51.8 | 31.7 | 9.7 | 2.7 | 3.5 | 0.7 |
| d. | [NUCPRISK] ...risks from nuclear power stations? | % 49.2 | 29.9 | 14.0 | 5.2 | 1.1 | 0.6 |
| e. | [POPGROW] ...the growth in the world's population? | % 38.1 | 35.2 | 20.1 | 4.2 | 1.8 | 0.6 |
| f. | [GRNHSEEF] ...the 'greenhouse effect' - a rise in the world's temperature? | % 40.9 | 37.2 | 13.6 | 4.5 | 3.2 | 0.7 |
| g. | [FOSLFUEL] ...using up the earth's remaining coal, oil and gas? | % 38.4 | 39.5 | 15.2 | 4.1 | 1.9 | 0.8 |
| h. | [WATRQUAL] ...the quality of drinking water? | % 49.3 | 31.5 | 13.9 | 4.2 | 0.4 | 0.7 |
| i. | [SPECLOSS] ...the loss of plant and animal species? | % 54.2 | 32.4 | 9.0 | 2.4 | 1.4 | 0.6 |
| j. | [MOVECHEM] ...the transport and disposal of dangerous chemicals? | % 65.9 | 24.5 | 6.7 | 1.4 | 1.0 | 0.5 |

28

n = 1422

**B**

CARD O

**B72a.** Do you do any of the following regularly, sometimes or not at all nowadays?

READ OUT i -xi AND CODE ONE FOR EACH AT a.

VEGETARIANS SHOULD BE CODED 1 AT v

| | | a. Does: | | | | | b. Intends to: | | | |
|---|---|---|---|---|---|---|---|---|---|---|
| | | Regu-larly | Some-times | Not at all | (No car) | (DK/NA) | Yes | No | (Don't know) | (NA) |
| i | [RECYCLDO][RECYCLFT] ...return bottles, tins, newspapers and so on for recycling? | % 32.4 | 30.8 | 36.3 | | 0.5 | 12.0 | 18.5 | 5.0 | 1.2 |
| ii | [ORGANCDO][ORGANCFT] ...buy organically-grown fruit and vegetables? | % 7.8 | 38.3 | 52.8 | | 1.1 | 7.7 | 36.8 | 5.9 | 2.9 |
| iii | [NOTESTDO][NOTESTFT] ...buy toiletries or cosmetics not tested on animals? | % 33.1 | 34.0 | 29.7 | | 3.2 | 5.0 | 18.4 | 4.6 | 2.6 |
| iv | [GRWASHDO][GRWASHFT] ...buy environment-friendly washing powders or detergents? | % 31.0 | 30.7 | 35.2 | | 3.0 | 5.9 | 22.6 | 5.5 | 1.9 |
| v | [LSMEATDO][LSMEATFT] ...choose to eat less meat? | % 25.5 | 26.7 | 47.0 | | 0.8 | 3.3 | 40.8 | 1.4 | 2.2 |
| vi | [RECPRDDO][RECPRDFT] ...choose products made out of recycled materials? | % 23.2 | 47.7 | 27.7 | | 1.4 | 4.6 | 18.1 | 3.7 | 2.0 |
| vii | [SVELECDO][SVELECFT] ...make a conscious effort to save electricity? | % 47.8 | 31.8 | 19.9 | | 0.5 | 5.9 | 11.4 | 1.6 | 1.6 |
| viii | [DRIVLSDO][DRIVLSFT] ...cut back on driving your car? | % 12.1 | 18.2 | 35.4 | 32.9 | 1.4 | 3.9 | 28.8 | 1.5 | 2.6 |
| ix | [AEROSLDO][AEROSLFT] ...buy environment-friendly aerosols? | % 55.4 | 25.8 | 17.2 | | 1.6 | 2.0 | 12.1 | 2.0 | 2.3 |
| x | [PACREFDO][PACREFFT] ...refuse unnecessary packaging or wrapping? | % 17.4 | 32.4 | 49.3 | | 0.9 | 8.3 | 32.6 | 5.4 | 3.7 |
| xi | [FRANGEDO][FRANGEFT] ...Buy free-range chicken or eggs? | % 38.7 | 33.3 | 26.7 | | 1.2 | 3.9 | 18.8 | 2.8 | 1.9 |

FOR EACH ITEM CODED 3 (NOT AT ALL) AT a.

b. Do you intend to ... READ ITEM ... in the next year or so, or not? CODE AT b. ABOVE

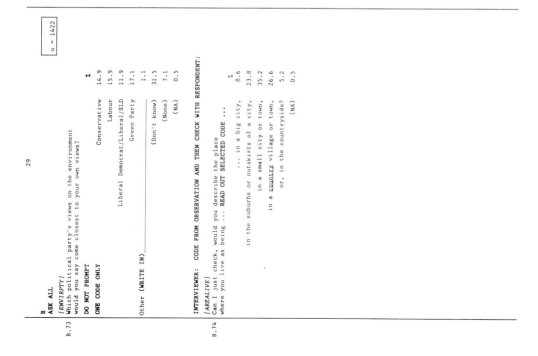

29

B
ASK ALL

*[ENVIRPTY]*
Which political party's views on the environment would you say come closest to your own views?

DO NOT PROMPT
ONE CODE ONLY

%

|  |  |
|---|---|
| Conservative | 14.9 |
| Labour | 15.9 |
| Liberal Democrat/Liberal/SLD | 11.9 |
| Green Party | 17.1 |
| Other (WRITE IN) _____ | 1.1 |
| (Don't know) | 31.5 |
| (None) | 7.1 |
| (NA) | 0.5 |

INTERVIEWER: CODE FROM OBSERVATION AND THEN CHECK WITH RESPONDENT:

B.74 *[AREALIVE]*
Can I just check, would you describe the place where you live as being ... READ OUT SELECTED CODE ...

%

|  |  |
|---|---|
| ... in a big city, | 8.6 |
| in the suburbs or outskirts of a city, | 23.8 |
| in a small city or town, | 35.2 |
| in a country village or town, | 26.6 |
| or, in the countryside? | 5.2 |
| (NA) | 0.5 |

B.73

---

30

| SECTION FIVE |
|---|

n = 1422

Qs. B75-B80b

B

B75.  *[RHEALTHY]*
ASK ALL
For your age, would you say that you lead ... READ OUT ...

%

|  |  |
|---|---|
| ... a very healthy life, | 23.4 |
| a fairly healthy life, | 63.1 |
| a not very healthy life, | 11.0 |
| or, an unhealthy life? | 2.2 |
| (Don't know) | 0.1 |
| (NA) | 0.3 |

B76.  *[FOODHLTH]*
Do you think the sort of food a person eats generally affects their health ... READ OUT ...

%

|  |  |
|---|---|
| ... a great deal, | 37.0 |
| quite a lot, | 44.9 |
| not very much, | 11.9 |
| or, hardly at all? | 4.9 |
| (Don't know) | 1.0 |
| (NA) | 0.3 |

B77a.  *[RFOODHTH]*
Thinking about the sorts of food you eat. In general, do you think your diet is ... READ OUT ...

%

|  |  |
|---|---|
| ... very healthy, | 21.7 |
| fairly healthy, | 65.8 |
| not very healthy, | 11.0 |
| or, unhealthy? | 1.0 |
| (Don't know) | 0.2 |
| (NA) | 0.3 |

b.  *[RFOODFUT]*
Do you think that you will change to a **more** healthy diet within the next two years or so? Is it ... READ OUT ...

%

|  |  |
|---|---|
| ... very likely, | 12.5 |
| fairly likely, | 25.9 |
| not very likely, | 37.6 |
| or, not at all likely? | 21.5 |
| (DK) | 1.9 |
| (NA) | 0.6 |

## 31

**B**

**B78. CARD P**
From this card, about how often these days do you eat ...

READ OUT a.-f. AND CODE ONE FOR EACH

n = 1422

| | Every day/ nearly every day | At least once a week | At least once a month | Less often | Never | (DK) | (NA) |
|---|---|---|---|---|---|---|---|
| a. [FREQMEAT] Red meat like beef, lamb or pork % | 24.5 | 57.0 | 8.1 | 3.6 | 6.4 | – | 0.4 |
| b. [FREQPOUL] Poultry like chicken or turkey % | 9.6 | 65.5 | 14.7 | 4.8 | 5.1 | – | 0.3 |
| c. [FREQFISH] Fish of any kind % | 6.6 | 60.3 | 17.3 | 7.4 | 8.0 | 0.1 | 0.3 |
| d. [FREQEGGS] Eggs % | 25.1 | 54.9 | 9.4 | 5.9 | 4.3 | – | 0.4 |
| e. [FREQCAKE] Biscuits, pastries or cakes % | 42.8 | 33.1 | 10.6 | 7.6 | 5.4 | – | 0.4 |
| f. [FREQFRUT] Fresh fruit % | 64.7 | 21.5 | 6.2 | 5.0 | 2.3 | – | 0.4 |

**B79.** Compared with two or three years ago, would you say you are now ...

READ OUT a.-i. AND CODE ONE FOR EACH

| | Yes | No | (Don't know) | (NA) |
|---|---|---|---|---|
| a. [SPREADS] ... using more low fat spreads or margarine instead of butter, or not? % | 65.9 | 33.0 | 0.5 | 0.4 |
| b. [GRILFOOD] ... eating more grilled food instead of fried food, or not? % | 68.1 | 30.3 | 0.7 | 0.8 |
| c. [FISHPOUL] ... eating more fish and poultry instead of red meat, or not? % | 52.1 | 46.3 | 0.9 | 0.7 |
| d. [SKIMMILK] ... drinking or using more semi-skimmed milk instead of full cream milk, or not? % | 49.6 | 48.7 | 1.1 | 0.7 |
| e. [BREAD] ... eating more wholemeal bread instead of white bread, or not? % | 52.7 | 46.6 | 0.2 | 0.4 |
| f. [BAKEDPOT] ... eating more boiled or baked potatoes instead of chips or roast potatoes, or not? % | 63.6 | 34.6 | 1.2 | 0.6 |

And compared with two or three years ago, would you say you are now ...

| | Yes | No | (Don't know) | (NA) |
|---|---|---|---|---|
| g. [HIFIBRE] ... eating more high fibre foods like fresh fruit and vegetables and high fibre cereals, or not? % | 62.4 | 36.7 | 0.4 | 0.4 |
| h. [SALTFOOD] ... cutting down on salty food, not? % | 46.5 | 52.7 | 0.3 | 0.5 |
| i. [XERCISE] ... taking more exercise, or not? % | 39.0 | 59.8 | 0.7 | 0.6 |

## 32

**B**
**CARD P**
[FAGSNOW]

**B80a.** Do you smoke cigarettes at all nowadays?

n = 1422
Qs. B80a.-b.

| | % |
|---|---|
| Yes | 33.8 |
| No | 66.0 |
| (NA) | 0.2 |

**b.** [PIPCGNOW] IF 'NO' AT a.
Do you smoke a pipe or cigars at all nowadays?

| | % |
|---|---|
| Yes | 3.0 |
| No | 62.7 |
| (NA) | 0.5 |

**c.** [SMOKDAY] IF 'YES' AT a.
About how many cigarettes a day do you usually smoke?

n = 481
Qs. B80c.-B82

MEDIAN  1 5

| | % |
|---|---|
| Less than one | 2.7 |
| Can't say | 0.6 |
| (NA) | 1.2 |

**d.** [SMOKMUCH] ALL SMOKERS ('YES' AT a. OR b.)
Would you describe yourself as ... READ OUT ...

| | % |
|---|---|
| ... a light smoker, | 29.9 |
| a moderate smoker, | 46.4 |
| a fairly heavy smoker, | 17.9 |
| or, a heavy smoker? | 4.8 |
| (Don't know) | – |
| (NA) | 0.8 |

**B81.** [SMOKMORE]
Compared with two or three years ago, would you say you are now smoking ... READ OUT ...

| | % |
|---|---|
| ... more, | 24.5 |
| less, | 34.5 |
| or, about the same? | 40.1 |
| (Don't know) | – |
| (NA) | 0.8 |

**B82.** [TRYSTPSM]
How likely is it that you will give up smoking within the next two years or so?
Is it ... READ OUT ...

| | % |
|---|---|
| ... very likely, | 21.4 |
| fairly likely, | 29.3 |
| not very likely, | 26.8 |
| or, not at all likely? | 19.1 |
| (Don't know) | 2.3 |
| (NA) | 0.8 |

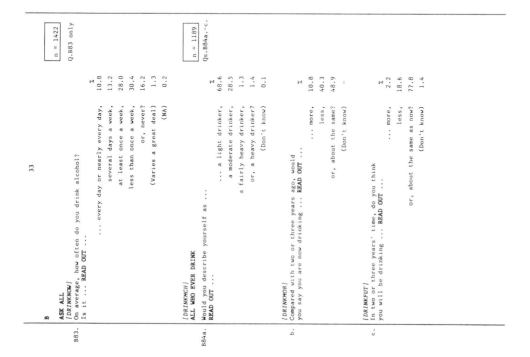

33

**B**

n = 1422

**ASK ALL**
*[DRINKNOW]*
B83. On average, how often do you drink alcohol?
Is it ... **READ OUT** ...

Q.B83 only

|  | % |
|---|---|
| ... every day or nearly every day, | 10.8 |
| several days a week, | 13.2 |
| at least once a week, | 28.0 |
| less than once a week, | 30.4 |
| or, never? | 16.2 |
| (Varies a great deal) | 1.3 |
| (NA) | 0.2 |

*[DRINKMCH]*
**ALL WHO EVER DRINK**
B84a. Would you describe yourself as ...
**READ OUT** ...

n = 1189
Qs.B84a.-c.

|  | % |
|---|---|
| ... a light drinker, | 68.6 |
| a moderate drinker, | 28.5 |
| a fairly heavy drinker, | 1.3 |
| or, a heavy drinker? | 1.4 |
| (Don't know) | 0.1 |

*[DRINKMOR]*
b. Compared with two or three years ago, would
you say you are now drinking ... **READ OUT** ...

|  | % |
|---|---|
| ... more, | 10.8 |
| less, | 40.3 |
| or, about the same? | 48.9 |
| (Don't know) | – |

*[DRINKFUT]*
c. In two or three years' time, do you think
you will be drinking ... **READ OUT** ...

|  | % |
|---|---|
| ... more, | 2.2 |
| less, | 18.6 |
| or, about the same as now? | 77.8 |
| (Don't know) | 1.4 |

34

**B**

n = 1422

**ASK ALL**
*[EXERHLTH]*
B85. Do you think the amount of exercise a person
takes generally affects their health ... **READ
OUT** ...

Qs.B85-B86

|  | % |
|---|---|
| ... a great deal, | 41.2 |
| quite a bit, | 46.5 |
| not very much, | 6.9 |
| or, hardly at all? | 3.8 |
| (Don't know) | 1.1 |
| (NA) | 0.5 |

*[RACTIVE]*
CARD Q
B86. Using this card, how physically active would you
say you are, compared with people of your age?

|  | % |
|---|---|
| Much more active than most | 18.4 |
| A bit more active | 24.2 |
| About average | 43.6 |
| A bit less active | 8.9 |
| Much less active than most | 3.5 |
| (Housebound) | 0.5 |
| (Don't know) | 0.4 |
| (NA) | 0.5 |

## SECTION SIX

n = 1422
Qs.B87-B97

**B**

**ASK ALL**
**[POLITICS]**

B87. Now I would like to ask some questions about politics.
How much interest do you generally have in what
is going on in politics ... READ OUT ...

|  | % |
|---|---|
| ... a great deal, | 10.3 |
| quite a lot, | 22.2 |
| some, | 30.7 |
| not very much, | 26.7 |
| or, none at all? | 9.6 |
| (Don't know) | 0.1 |
| (NA) | 0.4 |

**CARD R**

B88a. Suppose a law was being considered by Parliament which
you thought was really unjust and harmful. Which, if
any, of the things on this card do you think you would
do? Any others? [DOMP, DOSPK, DOGOV, DOTV, DOSIGN,
DORAIS, DOPROT, DOGRP, DONONE]
RECORD IN COL a., THEN ASK b.
CODE ALL THAT APPLY

b. And have you ever done any of the things on this card
about a government action which you thought was unjust
and harmful? Which ones? Any others? [DONEMP, DONESPK,
DONEGOV, DONETV, DONESIGN, DONERAIS, DONEPROT, DONEGRP,
DONENONE]
RECORD ALL IN COL. b.
CODE ALL THAT APPLY

|  | a. Would do % | b. Ever done % |
|---|---|---|
| Contact my MP | 48.4 | 16.7 |
| Speak to influential person | 17.0 | 5.3 |
| Contact a government department | 11.3 | 4.3 |
| Contact radio, TV or newspaper | 13.5 | 3.8 |
| Sign a petition | 77.8 | 52.5 |
| Raise the issue in an organisation I already belong to | 9.3 | 4.8 |
| Go on a protest or demonstration | 13.6 | 9.1 |
| Form a group of like-minded people | 6.6 | 1.7 |
| (No, none of these) | 6.4 | 36.5 |
| (NA) | 0.7 | 2.1 |

---

n = 1422

**B**

**[OBEYLAW]**

B89a. In general would you say that people should obey
the law without exception, or are there exceptional
occasions on which people should follow their
consciences even if it means breaking the law?

|  | % |
|---|---|
| Obey law without exception | 51.7 |
| Follow conscience on occasions | 46.6 |
| (DK) | 1.2 |
| (NA) | 0.5 |

b. **[BREAKLAW]**
Are there any circumstances in which you might
break a law to which you were very strongly
opposed?

|  | % |
|---|---|
| Yes | 33.9 |
| No | 57.2 |
| (Don't know) | 8.2 |
| (NA) | 0.7 |

B90. **[VOTEPROB]**
How likely do you think you are to vote in
the next General Election ... READ OUT ...

|  | % |
|---|---|
| ... very likely, | 68.0 |
| quite likely, | 18.2 |
| not very likely, | 7.2 |
| or, not at all likely? | 5.9 |
| (DK) | 0.1 |
| (NA) | 0.6 |

B91. **[COALITIN]**
Which do you think is generally better for
Britain ... READ OUT ...

|  | % |
|---|---|
| ... to have a government formed by one political party, | 56.3 |
| or, for two or more parties to get together to form a government? | 39.6 |
| (DK) | 3.4 |
| (NA) | 0.7 |

B92. **[VOTESYST]**
Some people say that we should change the voting
system to allow smaller political parties to get
a fairer share of MPs. Others say that we should
keep the voting system as it is, to produce more
effective government. Which view comes closest
to your own ... READ OUT ...

IF ASKED, REFERS TO
'PROPORTIONAL
REPRESENTATION'

|  | % |
|---|---|
| ... that we should change the voting system, | 36.6 |
| or, keep it as it is? | 57.6 |
| (Don't know) | 5.0 |
| (NA) | 0.5 |

37

**B**

**CARD S**

B93. Please choose a phrase from this card to say how you feel about ... READ OUT ...

n = 1422

Qs. B93a.-c.

| | Very strongly in favour | Strongly in favour | In favour | Neither in favour nor against | Against | Strongly against | Very strongly against | (Don't know/ can't say) | (NA) |
|---|---|---|---|---|---|---|---|---|---|
| a. [CONFEEL] ...the Conservative Party? | % 3.7 | 5.8 | 25.7 | 24.5 | 17.5 | 8.1 | 11.9 | 2.2 | 0.7 |
| b. [LABFEEL] ...the Labour Party? | % 5.6 | 6.2 | 23.1 | 27.5 | 24.0 | 7.2 | 4.1 | 1.7 | 0.6 |
| c. [LDFEEL] ...the Liberal Democrat Party? | % 1.1 | 3.6 | 18.4 | 50.3 | 17.2 | 2.5 | 1.7 | 4.5 | 0.6 |
| d. SCOTLAND [SNPFEEL] ...the Scottish Nationalist Party? n = 141 Q. B93d only | % 3.5 | 8.5 | 25.5 | 29.8 | 21.3 | 6.4 | 3.5 | 1.4 | - |
| e. WALES [PCFEEL] ...Plaid Cymru? n = 74 Q. B93e only | % 1.4 | 1.4 | 10.8 | 45.9 | 27.0 | 2.7 | 6.8 | 4.0 | - |

38

**B**

**CARD T**

B94. Please choose a phrase from this card to say how much you agree or disagree with the following statements.

READ OUT a.- f. BELOW AND CODE ONE FOR EACH

n = 1422

| | Agree strongly | Agree | Neither agree nor disagree | Disagree | Disagree strongly | (Don't know) | (NA) |
|---|---|---|---|---|---|---|---|
| a. [GOVNOSAY] People like me have no say in what the government does | % 15.6 | 45.0 | 11.5 | 23.9 | 2.6 | 1.0 | 0.6 |
| b. [LOSETCH] Generally speaking, those we elect as MPs lose touch with people pretty quickly | % 15.9 | 52.4 | 11.2 | 17.2 | 0.5 | 2.3 | 0.6 |
| c. [VOTEINTR] Parties are only interested in people's votes, not in their opinions | % 16.3 | 49.0 | 12.2 | 20.0 | 0.4 | 1.5 | 0.6 |
| d. [VOTEONLY] Voting is the only way people like me can have any say about how the government runs things | % 12.4 | 55.0 | 10.5 | 18.4 | 1.1 | 2.0 | 0.6 |
| e. [GOVCOMP] Sometimes politics and government seem so complicated that a person like me cannot really understand what is going on | % 16.3 | 49.1 | 7.8 | 22.9 | 2.1 | 1.2 | 0.6 |
| f. [PTYNTMAT] It doesn't really matter which party is in power, in the end things go on much the same | % 11.4 | 42.7 | 6.2 | 32.7 | 5.2 | 1.2 | 0.6 |

40

**B**

B96. Here is a quick quiz. For each thing I say, tell me if it is true or false. If you don't know, just say so and we will skip to the next one. Remember - true, false or don't know.

| | | | True | False | (Don't know) | (NA) |
|---|---|---|---|---|---|---|
| | | | | | n = 1422 | |
| a. | [KINNOCK]<br>The leader of the Labour Party is Neil Kinnock | % | 96.4 | 0.9 | 1.7 | 0.9 |
| b. | [MP100]<br>The number of members of parliament is about 100 | % | 13.9 | 58.8 | 26.4 | 0.9 |
| c. | [GELEC4YR]<br>The longest time allowed between elections is four years | % | 60.0 | 30.0 | 9.0 | 1.1 |
| d. | [HMSECLAW]<br>The Home Secretary is responsible to Parliament for law and order | % | 73.7 | 6.9 | 18.3 | 1.1 |
| e. | [PMQUSPCH]<br>It is the Prime Minister's job to prepare the Queen's Speech | % | 47.8 | 31.7 | 19.4 | 1.1 |
| f. | [BRITPR]<br>Britain's electoral system is based on proportional representation | % | 26.2 | 51.4 | 21.4 | 1.0 |
| g. | [WARSWPCT]<br>The Warsaw Pact is a trade agreement between Poland and Britain | % | 19.5 | 50.6 | 28.8 | 1.1 |
| h. | [CABINET]<br>Cabinet ministers are elected by the members of parliament in their party | % | 48.6 | 36.8 | 13.4 | 1.2 |
| i. | [WHOPCOMM]<br>MPs from different parties are on parliamentary committees | % | 62.4 | 8.2 | 28.2 | 1.2 |
| j. | [ELECROLL]<br>No-one is allowed to be on the electoral register in two different places | % | 81.5 | 9.2 | 8.0 | 1.3 |
| k. | [ECGBELEC]<br>Britain has separate elections for the European parliament and the British parliament | % | 74.7 | 5.8 | 18.4 | 1.0 |
| l. | [HOLNGWOM]<br>Women are not allowed to sit in the House of Lords | % | 17.2 | 69.2 | 12.4 | 1.1 |
| m. | [PMQUEEN]<br>British prime ministers are appointed by the Queen | % | 25.0 | 66.4 | 7.1 | 1.4 |
| n. | [DEPOSIT]<br>No-one may stand for parliament unless they pay a deposit | % | 67.8 | 18.2 | 12.8 | 1.2 |

---

39

**B**

CARD U

B95a. How much do you trust British governments of any party to place the needs of the nation above the interests of their own political party? [GOVTRUST]
RECORD IN COLUMN a.

b. And how much do you trust local councillors of any party to place the needs of their area above the interests of their own political party? [CLRTRUST]
RECORD IN COLUMN b.

c. How much do you trust British journalists on national newspapers to pursue the truth above getting a good story? RECORD IN COLUMN c. [PAPTRUST]

d. And how much do you trust British police not to bend the rules in trying to get a conviction? RECORD IN COLUMN d. [POLTRUST]

n = 1422

| | a.<br>Governments<br>% | b.<br>Councillors<br>% | c.<br>Journalists<br>% | d.<br>Police<br>% |
|---|---|---|---|---|
| Just about always | 3.8 | 1.3 | 1.2 | 8.5 |
| Most of the time | 29.4 | 24.1 | 12.5 | 40.9 |
| Only some of the time | 49.9 | 51.6 | 43.2 | 35.7 |
| Almost never | 13.7 | 19.6 | 39.1 | 11.3 |
| (Don't know/can't say) | 2.6 | 2.6 | 3.2 | 2.9 |
| (NA) | 0.7 | 0.7 | 0.7 | 0.7 |

41

**B**
**CARD V**

**B97.** Please use this card to say how much you agree or disagree with each of the following.

READ OUT a. - j. AND CODE ONE FOR EACH

n = 1422

| | Agree strongly | Agree | Neither agree nor disagree | Disagree | Disagree strongly | (Don't know) | (NA) |
|---|---|---|---|---|---|---|---|
| a. [REDISTRB] Government should redistribute income from the better off to those who are less well off | % 14.5 | 40.1 | 15.6 | 23.9 | 3.2 | 1.7 | 1.1 |
| b. [PRENTBST] Private enterprise is the best way to solve economic problems | % 4.9 | 37.3 | 25.0 | 24.1 | 1.5 | 6.3 | 1.0 |
| c. [BIGBUSNN] Big business benefits owners at the expense of workers | % 7.4 | 47.5 | 16.8 | 22.5 | 0.9 | 3.8 | 1.1 |
| d. [LSGOVINT] The less government intervenes, the better it is for the economy | % 3.0 | 32.1 | 25.2 | 28.9 | 1.0 | 8.7 | 1.1 |
| e. [WEALTH] Ordinary working people do not get their fair share of the nation's wealth | % 10.9 | 56.5 | 12.0 | 16.3 | 0.3 | 2.9 | 1.1 |
| f. [PRSRVBST] Even the most important public services and industries are best run by private enterprise | % 2.6 | 35.3 | 17.2 | 34.1 | 3.0 | 6.7 | 1.1 |
| g. [RICHLAW] There is one law for the rich and one for the poor | % 17.7 | 47.0 | 10.9 | 20.9 | 1.2 | 1.4 | 1.1 |
| h. [GOVNOTJB] It is not the government's responsibility to make sure there are enough jobs for everyone | % 2.3 | 29.8 | 9.3 | 48.3 | 6.6 | 2.5 | 1.1 |
| i. [INDUST4] Management will always try to get the better of employees if it gets the chance | % 11.2 | 50.7 | 11.5 | 21.9 | 0.7 | 2.8 | 1.1 |
| j. [UNEMGOOD] A bit of unemployment is good because it weakens the unions | % 1.4 | 13.6 | 12.3 | 55.5 | 10.5 | 5.7 | 1.1 |

---

42

**SECTION SEVEN**

n = 2836

Qs. 98-99

**A & B**
**ASK ALL**
[HOMETYPE]
Now a few questions on housing.
INTERVIEWER CODE FROM OBSERVATION AND CHECK WITH RESPONDENT

**98a.** Would I be right in describing this accommodation as a ... READ OUT ONE THAT YOU THINK APPLIES ...?

| | % |
|---|---|
| ... detached house or bungalow | 20.1 |
| ... semi-detached house or bungalow | 37.3 |
| ... terraced house | 25.8 |
| ... self-contained, purpose built flat/maisonette (inc. in tenement block) | 10.5 |
| ... self-contained converted flat/maisonette | 4.8 |
| ... room(s) - not self-contained | 0.3 |
| Other (WRITE IN) | 0.5 |
| (NA) | 0.6 |

**b.** [HOMEEST] May I just check, is your home part of a housing estate? (Scotland: or scheme)
NOTE: MAY BE PUBLIC OR PRIVATE; RESPONDENT'S OWN DEFINITION

| | % |
|---|---|
| Yes, part of estate | 43.7 |
| No | 55.3 |
| (DK) | 0.1 |
| (NA) | 1.0 |

**99a.** [HOMEIYR] How long have you lived in your present home ... READ OUT ...

| | % |
|---|---|
| ... less than a year, | 8.3 |
| or, one year or more? | 91.2 |
| (DK) | 0.1 |
| (NA) | 0.4 |

**b.** [HOMENYR] IF 'ONE YEAR OR MORE' AT a.
How many years?
PROBE FOR BEST ESTIMATE

MEDIAN: | 0 | 8 |  YEARS

(DK, NA)  0.5%

[HOMELGTH]

| | % |
|---|---|
| Less than a year | 8.3 |
| 1-2 years | 11.0 |
| 3-5 years | 18.6 |
| 6-10 years | 17.6 |
| 11-20 years | 21.9 |
| More than 20 years | 22.1 |

Note: Qs.98 and 99 were also asked on the A Version of the questionnaire as Qs. 98 and 99.

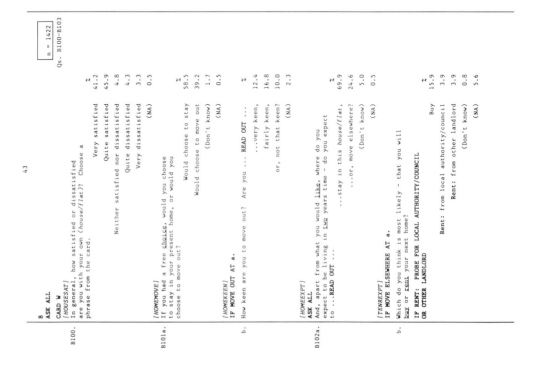

43

n = 1422
Qs. B100-B103

**B**
**ASK ALL**
**CARD W**
*[HOUSESAT]*
B100. In general, how satisfied or dissatisfied are you with your own (*house/flat*)? Choose a phrase from the card.

|  | % |
|---|---|
| Very satisfied | 41.2 |
| Quite satisfied | 45.9 |
| Neither satisfied nor dissatisfied | 4.8 |
| Quite dissatisfied | 4.3 |
| Very dissatisfied | 3.3 |
| (NA) | 0.5 |

*[HOMEMOVE]*
B101a. If you had a free **choice**, would you choose to stay in your present home, or would you choose to move out?

|  | % |
|---|---|
| Would choose to stay | 58.5 |
| Would choose to move out | 39.2 |
| (Don't know) | 1.7 |
| (NA) | 0.5 |

*[HOMEKEEN]*
**IF MOVE OUT AT a.**
b. How keen are you to move out? Are you ... READ OUT ...

|  | % |
|---|---|
| ...very keen, | 12.4 |
| fairly keen, | 16.8 |
| or, not that keen? | 10.0 |
| (NA) | 2.3 |

*[HOMEEXPT]*
**ASK ALL**
B102a. And, apart from what you would **like**, where do you expect to be living in **two** years time - do you expect to ...READ OUT ...

|  | % |
|---|---|
| ...stay in this *house/flat,* | 69.9 |
| ...or, move elsewhere? | 24.6 |
| (Don't know) | 5.0 |
| (NA) | 0.5 |

*[TENREXPT]*
**IF MOVE ELSEWHERE AT a.**
b. Which do you think is most likely - that you will **buy** or **rent** your next home?
IF RENT: PROBE FOR LOCAL AUTHORITY/COUNCIL OR OTHER LANDLORD

|  | % |
|---|---|
| Buy | 15.9 |
| Rent: from local authority/council | 3.9 |
| Rent: from other landlord | 3.9 |
| (Don't know) | 0.8 |
| (NA) | 5.6 |

44

n = 1422

**B**
*[HSEPEXPT]*
B103a. In a year from now, do you expect **house prices** in **your area** to have gone up, to have stayed the same, or to have gone down?
IF 'GONE UP' OR 'GONE DOWN'
By a lot or a little?

|  | % |
|---|---|
| To have gone up by a lot | 14.4 |
| To have gone up by a little | 50.0 |
| To have stayed the same | 24.2 |
| To have gone down by a little | 6.1 |
| To have gone down by a lot | 1.0 |
| (Don't know) | 3.5 |
| (NA) | 0.8 |

*[MINTEXPT]*
b. And in a year from now, do you expect **mortgage interest rates** (*the cost of borrowing to buy a home*) to have gone up, to have stayed the same, or to have gone down?
IF 'GONE UP' OR 'GONE DOWN'
By a lot or a little?

|  | % |
|---|---|
| To have gone up by a lot | 5.3 |
| To have gone up by a little | 19.5 |
| To have stayed the same | 13.8 |
| To have gone down by a little | 48.4 |
| To have gone down by a lot | 5.9 |
| (Don't know) | 6.3 |
| (NA) | 0.8 |

n = 2836
Q.104 only

*[TENUREI]*
104. Does your household own or rent this accommodation?
PROBE AS NECESSARY
IF OWNS: Outright or on a mortgage?
IF RENTS: From whom?

|  | % |
|---|---|
| Owns: Outright (leasehold/freehold) outright | 24.6 |
| Buying (leasehold/freehold) on mortgage | 41.7 |
| Rents: Local Authority | 20.9 |
| New Town Development Corporation | 0.2 |
| Housing Association | 2.1 |
| Property company | 0.7 |
| Employer | 1.0 |
| Other organisation | 1.5 |
| Relative | 0.6 |
| Other individual | 5.3 |
| Rent free: Rent free, squatting, etc. | 0.8 |
| (Don't know) | 0.1 |
| (NA) | 0.5 |

Note: Q. 104 was also asked on the A Version of the questionnaire as Q. 100

45

**B**
**[BUYFRMLA]**

B105a. IF CURRENTLY OWNS ACCOMMODATION (CODES 01 OR 02 AT Q.104)    n = 955    Qs. B105-B106

Did you, or the person responsible for the mortgage, buy your present home from the local authority as a tenant?

'LOCAL AUTHORITY' INCLUDES GLC, LONDON RESIDUARY BODY AND NEW TOWN DEVELOPMENT CORPORATION.

|  | % |
|---|---|
| Yes | 13.4 |
| No | 85.3 |
| (Don't know) | 0.3 |
| (NA) | 1.0 |

**[EVRBYLA1]**
IF NO AT a.

b. Have you yourself, or the person responsible for the mortgage here, ever bought any past home from the local authority as a tenant?

'LOCAL AUTHORITY' INCLUDES GLC, LONDON RESIDUARY BODY AND NEW TOWN DEVELOPMENT CORPORATION.

|  | % |
|---|---|
| Yes | 1.7 |
| No | 83.4 |
| (Don't know) | 0.1 |
| (NA) | 1.6 |

B106. ASK ALL OWNERS
INTERVIEWER CHECK:

|  | % |
|---|---|
| Respondent/household owns outright (CODE 01 AT Q.104) | 36.1 |
| Respondent/household buying on mortgage (CODE 02 AT Q.104) | 63.9 |

**[COPEMORG]**
IF BUYING ON MORTGAGE (CODE 2 AT a.)    n = 610    Q. B107a,b only

B107a. How are you and your household coping with the cost of your mortgage these days? Does it make things ... READ OUT ...

|  | % |
|---|---|
| ... very difficult, | 13.4 |
| a bit difficult, | 35.4 |
| or, not really difficult? | 47.7 |
| (Don't know) | 1.5 |
| (NA) | 2.1 |

46

**B**
**CARD X**

B107b. Suppose your monthly mortgage payments were much lower, how do you think you would use the extra money? Would you ...    n = 610    Q.B107b only

READ OUT a.-h. AND CODE ONE FOR EACH

|  |  | Very likely | Fairly likely | Not very likely | Not at all likely | (Don't know) | (NA) |
|---|---|---|---|---|---|---|---|
| a. | [BUYFRHME] Buy new things for your home? | % 29.8 | 39.0 | 18.5 | 8.4 | 2.1 | 2.1 |
| b. | [IMPRHOME] Make improvements to your present home? | % 37.2 | 34.9 | 15.2 | 8.7 | 2.0 | 2.3 |
| c. | [MOVEHSE] Move and get a bigger mortgage? | % 5.7 | 10.1 | 40.2 | 40.0 | 2.0 | 2.1 |
| d. | [SAVEMONY] Save the money in a bank or building society? | % 18.7 | 42.8 | 24.7 | 9.5 | 2.1 | 2.1 |
| e. | [INVSTMNY] Invest the money in a pension or some sort of savings plan? | % 10.5 | 26.9 | 37.7 | 20.0 | 2.8 | 2.1 |
| f. | [BUYSHARE] Buy shares or unit trusts? | % 2.1 | 16.2 | 41.1 | 35.7 | 2.6 | 2.1 |
| g. | [SPNDFAM] Spend more on yourself and your family? | % 21.5 | 51.6 | 15.9 | 6.9 | 2.0 | 2.3 |
| h. | [SPNDNEED] Spend more on day-to-day needs? | % 19.3 | 41.0 | 26.6 | 8.9 | 2.0 | 2.1 |

B108a. ALL BUYING ON MORTGAGE, RENTERS AND RENT FREE
INTERVIEWER CHECK:    n = 1077    Q.B108a only

|  | % |
|---|---|
| Respondent/household buying on mortgage (CODE 02 AT Q.104) | 56.6 |
| Respondent/household rents from LA/NTDC (CODES 03 or 04 AT Q.104) | 27.7 |
| Respondent/household rents privately, lives rent free (CODES 05-11 AT Q.104) | 15.7 |

**[CNCLBUY]**
IF LOCAL AUTHORITY OR NEW TOWN DEVELOPMENT CORPORATION TENANT (CODE 2 AT Q.108)    n = 298    Q.B108b only

b. Is it likely or unlikely that you - or the person responsible for paying the rent - will buy this (house/flat) at some time in the future?

IF LIKELY OR UNLIKELY: Very or quite?

|  | % |
|---|---|
| Very likely | 5.4 |
| Quite likely | 11.4 |
| Quite unlikely | 6.7 |
| Very unlikely | 66.1 |
| (Not allowed to buy) | 4.4 |
| (Don't know) | 2.7 |
| (NA) | 3.4 |

47

n = 467

**B**

**[RENTLEVL]**
**ASK ALL TENANTS (CODE 2 or 3 AT Q.108a.)**

Qs.B109-B113

B109. How would you describe the rent for
this accommodation? Would you say it
was ... **READ OUT** ...

|  | % |
|---|---|
| ... on the high side, | 31.2 |
| reasonable, | 57.8 |
| or, on the low side? | 6.2 |
| (Living rent free) | 2.4 |
| (Don't know) | 1.3 |
| (NA) | 0.9 |

**CARD Y**
**[PRENTREP]**

B110. In general, how satisfied are you with the standard
of repairs and maintenance your landlord provides?
Please choose a phrase from this card.

|  | % |
|---|---|
| Very satisfied | 16.3 |
| Quite satisfied | 34.3 |
| Neither satisfied nor dissatisfied | 11.1 |
| Quite dissatisfied | 22.3 |
| Very dissatisfied | 15.2 |
| (NA) | 0.9 |

**[RENTPREF]**

B111a. If you had a free choice would you choose
to rent accommodation, or would you choose
to buy?

|  | % |
|---|---|
| Would choose to rent | 30.4 |
| Would choose to buy | 64.7 |
| (Don't know) | 2.8 |
| (NA) | 2.2 |

**[RENTEXPT]**

b. And apart from what you would like, do you
expect to buy a house or a flat in the next
two years, or not?

**INCLUDES BUYING PRESENT HOUSE/FLAT**

|  | % |
|---|---|
| Yes, expect to buy | 18.1 |
| No, do not expect to buy | 74.3 |
| (Don't know) | 6.0 |
| (NA) | 1.7 |

**[EVEROWND]**

B112a. Have you ever owned your own accommodation –
that is, lived in a house or flat, which was
in your sole or joint name?

|  | % |
|---|---|
| Yes | 12.8 |
| No | 82.9 |
| (Still owns house) | 2.3 |
| (NA) | 2.0 |

**[OWNEDYRS]**
**IF YES AT a.**

b. How long ago was it that you last owned
your own house or flat?
**PROBE FOR BEST ESTIMATE**

YEARS

**MEDIAN:** | 0 | 9 |

| (NA) | 0.9% |

---

48

n = 467

**B**

**ASK ALL TENANTS** *[EVRBYLA2]*

B113. Have you yourself, or the person responsible
for paying the rent here, ever bought any
past home from the local authority as a tenant?

'LOCAL AUTHORITY' INCLUDES GLC,
LONDON RESIDUARY BODY AND NEW
TOWN DEVELOPMENT CORPORATION.

|  | % |
|---|---|
| Yes | 2.6 |
| No | 96.8 |
| (NA) | 0.6 |

**Note:** Section Eight (Qs. 114-116 on pp. 49 and 50) was also asked on
the A version of the questionnaire as Qs. 101-103 on pp. 46 and 47

A

SCPR

SOCIAL & COMMUNITY PLANNING RESEARCH

Head Office: 35 NORTHAMPTON SQUARE
LONDON EC1V 0AX Telephone 071-250 1866

Field and SP Office: BRENTWOOD, ESSEX
Northern Field Office: DARLINGTON, CO. DURHAM

P.1135/GB

## BRITISH SOCIAL ATTITUDES 1991

## SELF-COMPLETION QUESTIONNAIRE

Spring 1991

| OFFICE USE ONLY: | Sampling point |
|---|---|
| Interviewer | 0 |
| to enter: | Serial No. |
| | |
| Rec. | Interviewer No. |

### To the selected respondent:

Thank you very much for agreeing to take part in this important study - the eighth in this annual series. The study consists of this self-completion questionnaire, and the interview you have already completed. The results of the survey are published in a book each autumn; some of the questions are also being asked in twelve other countries, as part of an international survey.

*Completing the questionnaire:*

The questions inside cover a wide range of subjects, but each one can be answered simply by placing a tick (✓) in one or more of the boxes. No special knowledge is required: we are confident that everyone will be able to take part, not just those with strong views or particular viewpoints. The questionnaire should not take very long to complete, and we hope you will find it interesting and enjoyable. It should be filled in only by the person actually interviewed at your address. The answers you give will be treated as confidential and anonymous.

*Returning the questionnaire:*

Your interviewer will arrange with you the most convenient way of returning the questionnaire. If the interviewer has arranged to call back for it, please fill it in and keep it safely until then. If not, please complete it and post it back in the pre-paid, addressed envelope, AS SOON AS YOU POSSIBLY CAN.

### THANK YOU AGAIN FOR YOUR HELP.

*Social and Community Planning Research is an independent social research institute registered as a charitable trust. Its projects are funded by government departments, local authorities, universities and foundations to provide information on social issues in Britain. The British Social Attitudes Survey series has been funded mainly by the Sainsbury Family Charitable Trusts, with contributions also from government departments, the Nuffield Foundation, universities and industry. Please contact us if you would like further information.*

A

n = 1221

**A2.01** [*RUHAPPY*]
If you were to consider your life in general these days, how happy or unhappy would you say you are, on the whole?

*PLEASE TICK **ONE** BOX ONLY*

Qs. A2.01–A2.23

|  | % |
|---|---|
| Very happy | 32.5 |
| Fairly happy | 57.0 |
| Not very happy | 7.5 |
| Not at all happy | 1.4 |
| Can't choose | 0.8 |
| (NA) | 0.8 |

**A 2.02** [*GOVRESPI, GOVRESP7*]
On the whole, do you think it should or should not be the government's responsibility to ...

*PLEASE TICK **ONE** BOX ON EACH LINE*

|  | Definitely should be | Probably should be | Probably should not be | Definitely should not be | Can't choose | (NA) |
|---|---|---|---|---|---|---|
| a. Provide a job for everyone who wants one? | % 28.7 | 31.4 | 17.0 | 14.2 | 6.1 | 2.6 |
| b. Reduce income differences between the rich and poor? | % 36.5 | 30.8 | 11.0 | 12.7 | 5.4 | 3.6 |

**A 2.03** [*STIFSNT3, MURDRPEN*]
Here are some measures to deal with crime. Some people are in favour of them while others are against them. Do you agree or disagree that ...

*PLEASE TICK **ONE** BOX ON EACH LINE*

|  | Strongly agree | Agree | Neither agree nor disagree | Disagree | Strongly disagree | Can't choose | (NA) |
|---|---|---|---|---|---|---|---|
| a. People who break the law should be given stiffer sentences? | % 33.7 | 37.0 | 17.0 | 7.3 | 1.5 | 2.4 | 1.0 |
| b. People convicted of murder should be subject to the death penalty? | % 31.6 | 21.7 | 11.3 | 16.1 | 13.5 | 4.7 | 1.1 |

*Please continue ...*

A

2

n = 1221

**A 2.04** [*SEXBFMAR*]
Do you think it is wrong or not wrong if a man and a woman have sexual relations before marriage?

*PLEASE TICK **ONE** BOX ONLY*

|  | % |
|---|---|
| Always wrong | 11.1 |
| Almost always wrong | 6.5 |
| Wrong only sometimes | 14.4 |
| Not wrong at all | 61.6 |
| Can't choose | 5.7 |
| (NA) | 0.7 |

**A 2.05** [*ADULTERY*]
What about a married person having sexual relations with someone other than his or her husband or wife, is it ...

*PLEASE TICK **ONE** BOX ONLY*

|  | % |
|---|---|
| Always wrong | 58.1 |
| Almost always wrong | 24.6 |
| Wrong only sometimes | 10.7 |
| Not wrong at all | 2.6 |
| Can't choose | 3.5 |
| (NA) | 0.5 |

**A 2.06** [*SEXHOMO*]
And what about sexual relations between two adults of the same sex, is it ...

*PLEASE TICK **ONE** BOX ONLY*

|  | % |
|---|---|
| Always wrong | 52.0 |
| Almost always wrong | 7.1 |
| Wrong only sometimes | 10.1 |
| Not wrong at all | 18.8 |
| Can't choose | 11.3 |
| (NA) | 0.6 |

n = 1221

## A 2.07 [ABORLAWA, ABORLAWB]

Do you think the law should or should not allow a woman to obtain a legal abortion ...

PLEASE TICK ONE BOX ON EACH LINE

| | Definitely should allow it | Probably should allow it | Probably should not allow it | Definitely should not allow it | Can't choose | (NA) |
|---|---|---|---|---|---|---|
| a. If there is a strong chance of a serious defect in the baby? % | 73.7 | 15.8 | 2.6 | 4.3 | 3.2 | 0.5 |
| b. If the family has a very low income and can not afford any more children? % | 38.8 | 27.9 | 13.2 | 12.4 | 5.7 | 1.9 |

## A 2.08 [ABORWRGA, ABORWRGB]

Do you personally think it is wrong or not wrong for a woman to have an abortion ...

PLEASE TICK ONE BOX ON EACH LINE

| | Always wrong | Almost always wrong | Wrong only sometimes | Not wrong at all | Can't choose | (NA) |
|---|---|---|---|---|---|---|
| a. If there is a strong chance of a serious defect in the baby? % | 8.7 | 4.8 | 12.6 | 68.0 | 5.1 | 0.9 |
| b. If the family has a very low income and cannot afford any more children? % | 16.9 | 12.7 | 17.9 | 41.9 | 7.5 | 3.0 |

## A 2.09 [SEXROLE, WWFAMSUF]

How much do you agree or disagree ...

PLEASE TICK ONE BOX ON EACH LINE

| | Strongly agree | Agree | Neither agree nor disagree | Disagree | Strongly disagree | Can't choose | (NA) |
|---|---|---|---|---|---|---|---|
| a. A husband's job is to earn the money, a wife's job is to look after the home and family % | 11.9 | 20.8 | 21.2 | 25.5 | 19.0 | 1.1 | 0.4 |
| b. All in all, family life suffers when the woman has a full-time job % | 11.0 | 24.6 | 17.9 | 31.7 | 11.8 | 1.9 | 1.0 |

Please continue ...

n = 1221

## A 2.10 [TAXCHEAT, BENCHEAT]

Consider the situations listed below. Do you feel it is wrong or not wrong if ...

PLEASE TICK ONE BOX ON EACH LINE

| | Not wrong | A bit wrong | Wrong | Seriously wrong | Can't choose | (NA) |
|---|---|---|---|---|---|---|
| a. A taxpayer does not report all of his income in order to pay less income tax? % | 3.8 | 21.7 | 53.0 | 19.1 | 1.2 | 1.0 |
| b. A person gives the government incorrect information about himself to get government benefits that he is not entitled to? % | 0.5 | 7.0 | 49.4 | 41.1 | 0.9 | 1.1 |

## A 2.11 How much confidence do you have in ...

PLEASE TICK ONE BOX ON EACH LINE

| | Complete confidence | A great deal of confidence | Some confidence | Very little confidence | No confidence at all | Can't choose | (NA) |
|---|---|---|---|---|---|---|---|
| a. [PARLCONF] The British parliament? % | 4.7 | 13.6 | 43.8 | 26.8 | 7.5 | 2.6 | 0.9 |
| b. [BUSCONF] Business and industry? % | 1.0 | 11.3 | 56.6 | 20.5 | 3.5 | 5.0 | 2.0 |
| c. [CIVSCONF] The Civil Service? % | 2.6 | 7.9 | 48.4 | 26.1 | 6.4 | 6.5 | 2.2 |
| d. [CHCHCONF] Churches and religious organisations? % | 3.9 | 12.3 | 37.1 | 25.7 | 13.3 | 6.2 | 1.5 |
| e. [CORTCONF] Courts and the legal system? % | 3.2 | 15.4 | 48.3 | 22.5 | 6.8 | 2.7 | 1.2 |
| f. [SCHLCONF] Schools and the educational system? % | 3.1 | 13.1 | 48.8 | 24.7 | 6.3 | 2.7 | 1.2 |

5

n = 1221

A 2.12 How much do you agree or disagree with each of the following?

PLEASE TICK **ONE** BOX ON EACH LINE

| | Strongly agree | Agree | Neither agree nor disagree | Disagree | Strongly disagree | Can't choose | (NA) |
|---|---|---|---|---|---|---|---|
| a. [POLINGOD] Politicians who do not believe in God are unfit for public office | % 3.2 | 4.8 | 20.8 | 36.0 | 29.4 | 4.6 | 1.2 |
| b. [RIGINFVT] Religious leaders should not try to influence how people vote in elections | % 32.4 | 38.5 | 7.8 | 10.6 | 6.8 | 2.7 | 1.1 |
| c. [BETRBELF] It would be better for Britain if more people with strong religious beliefs held public office | % 4.0 | 11.7 | 25.3 | 32.7 | 20.4 | 4.6 | 1.3 |
| d. [RIGINFGV] Religious leaders should not try to influence government decisions | % 21.7 | 34.9 | 15.7 | 16.2 | 6.9 | 3.3 | 1.3 |

A 2.13 [CHCHPOWR] Do you think that churches and religious organisations in this country have too much power or too little power?

PLEASE TICK **ONE** BOX ONLY

%
Far too much power 9.0
Too much power 14.8
About the right amount of power 50.4
Too little power 8.8
Far too little power 0.9
Can't choose 14.7
(NA) 1.4

*Please continue ...*

6

n = 1221

A 2.14 [GODBELF1] Please tick one box below to show which statement comes closest to expressing what you believe about God.

PLEASE TICK **ONE** BOX ONLY

%
I don't believe in God 10.2
I don't know whether there is a God and I don't believe there is any way to find out 13.8
I don't believe in a personal God, but I do believe in a Higher Power of some kind 12.7
I find myself believing in God some of the time, but not at others 12.7
While I have doubts, I feel that I do believe in God 25.5
I know God really exists and I have no doubts about it 23.2
(DK) 0.2
(NA) 1.7

A 2.15 [RCLSEGOD] How close do you feel to God most of the time?

PLEASE TICK **ONE** BOX ONLY

%
Don't believe in God 11.5
Not close at all 16.4
Not very close 20.7
Somewhat close 31.8
Extremely close 8.9
Can't choose 8.8
(NA) 1.8

A 2.16 [GODBELF2] Which best describes your beliefs about God?

PLEASE TICK **ONE** BOX ONLY

%
I don't believe in God now and I never have 11.6
I don't believe in God now, but I used to 12.1
I believe in God now, but I didn't used to 5.9
I believe in God now and I always have 45.8
Can't choose 22.8
(NA) 1.8

n = 1221

**A 2.17** Do you believe in ...

*PLEASE TICK **ONE** BOX ON EACH LINE*

| | Yes, definitely | Yes, probably | No, probably not | No, definitely not | Can't choose | (NA) |
|---|---|---|---|---|---|---|
| [AFTRLIFE] <br> a. Life after death? | % 22.6 | 23.9 | 20.5 | 18.2 | 11.2 | 3.6 |
| [THEDEVIL] <br> b. The Devil? | % 10.8 | 13.5 | 20.3 | 42.3 | 8.2 | 5.0 |
| [HEAVEN] <br> c. Heaven? | % 21.1 | 25.6 | 18.6 | 21.2 | 10.1 | 3.5 |
| [HELL] <br> d. Hell? | % 10.8 | 13.7 | 23.7 | 38.4 | 8.9 | 4.6 |
| [RELGMIRC] <br> e. Religious miracles? | % 13.4 | 24.8 | 20.9 | 25.6 | 11.1 | 4.2 |

**A 2.18** [BIBLFEEL]
Which **one** of these statements comes closest to describing your feelings about the Bible?

*PLEASE TICK **ONE** BOX ONLY*

| | % |
|---|---|
| The Bible is the actual word of God and it is to be taken literally, word for word | 6.0 |
| The Bible is the inspired word of God but not everything should be taken literally, word for word | 33.8 |
| The Bible is an ancient book of fables, legends, history and moral teachings recorded by man | 43.5 |
| This does not apply to me | 7.3 |
| Can't choose | 7.1 |
| (NA) | 2.2 |

*Please continue ...*

---

n = 1221

**A 2.19** How much do you agree or disagree with each of the following?

*PLEASE TICK **ONE** BOX ON EACH LINE*

| | Strongly agree | Agree | Neither agree nor disagree | Disagree | Strongly disagree | Can't choose | (NA) |
|---|---|---|---|---|---|---|---|
| [GODCONCN] <br> a. There is a God who concerns Himself with every human being personally | % 10.8 | 21.6 | 25.3 | 17.4 | 12.6 | 8.1 | 4.4 |
| [FATALIST] <br> b. There is little that people can do to change the course of their lives | % 4.1 | 16.6 | 10.8 | 44.5 | 18.2 | 2.3 | 3.6 |
| [GODGMEAN] <br> c. To me, life is meaningful only because God exists | % 6.8 | 11.8 | 23.0 | 29.6 | 19.2 | 5.6 | 4.0 |
| [LFNOPURP] <br> d. In my opinion, life does not serve any purpose | % 1.4 | 2.6 | 8.5 | 44.6 | 34.3 | 4.2 | 4.4 |
| [LIFGODDC] <br> e. The course of our lives is decided by God | % 5.4 | 13.1 | 19.3 | 32.9 | 20.8 | 4.9 | 3.6 |
| [SLFGMEAN] <br> f. Life is only meaningful if you provide the meaning yourself | % 13.3 | 51.2 | 14.6 | 11.0 | 1.8 | 4.7 | 3.5 |
| [OWNFATE] <br> g. We each make our own fate | % 11.6 | 45.0 | 19.4 | 13.8 | 2.9 | 4.3 | 3.0 |

**A 2.20** [WITHDEAD, CLSSPRIT]
How often have you felt as though you were ...

*PLEASE TICK **ONE** BOX ON EACH LINE*

| | Never in my life | Once or twice | Several times | Often | Can't say | (NA) |
|---|---|---|---|---|---|---|
| a. Really in touch with someone who had died? | % 62.6 | 17.0 | 5.3 | 2.5 | 11.1 | 1.5 |
| b. Close to a powerful, spiritual force that seemed to lift you out of yourself? | % 61.5 | 14.6 | 5.7 | 3.2 | 12.7 | 2.3 |

9

n = 1221

A 2.21 [RELGCOMH]
Has there ever been a turning point in your life when you made a new and personal commitment to religion?

PLEASE TICK **ONE** BOX ONLY

|  | % |
|---|---|
| Yes | 16.3 |
| No | 81.6 |
| (DK) | 0.1 |
| (NA) | 2.0 |

A 2.22 [MUMRELIG]
What was your mother's religion, if any, when you were a child?

PLEASE TICK **ONE** BOX ONLY

|  | % |
|---|---|
| No religion | 3.6 |
| Christian - no denomination | 5.8 |
| Roman Catholic | 14.5 |
| Church of England/Anglican | 50.8 |
| Baptist | 2.6 |
| Methodist | 5.9 |
| Presbyterian/Church of Scotland | 8.1 |
| Free Presbyterian | 0.0 |
| Brethren | 0.1 |
| United Reform Church (URC)/Congregational | 1.4 |
| Other Protestant (*PLEASE WRITE IN WHICH*) | 1.4 |
| Other Christian (*PLEASE WRITE IN WHICH*) | 0.2 |
| Hindu | 1.1 |
| Jewish | 0.6 |
| Islam/Muslim | 0.6 |
| Sikh | 0.2 |
| Buddhist | 0.1 |
| Other non-Christian (*PLEASE WRITE IN WHICH*) | 0.2 |
| Never knew mother/does not apply | - |
| Can't say/can't remember | 1.9 |
| (NA) | 1.0 |

10

n = 1221

A 2.23 [DADRELIG]
What was your father's religion, if any, when you were a child?

PLEASE TICK **ONE** BOX ONLY

|  | % |
|---|---|
| No religion | 8.8 |
| Christian - no denomination | 5.7 |
| Roman Catholic | 13.9 |
| Church of England/Anglican | 45.0 |
| Baptist | 2.2 |
| Methodist | 5.8 |
| Presbyterian/Church of Scotland | 7.2 |
| Free Presbyterian | 0.1 |
| Brethren | 0.1 |
| United Reform Church (URC)/Congregational | 1.4 |
| Other Protestant (*PLEASE WRITE IN WHICH*) | 1.0 |
| Other Christian (*PLEASE WRITE IN WHICH*) | 0.2 |
| Hindu | 1.0 |
| Jewish | 0.8 |
| Islam/Muslim | 0.6 |
| Sikh | 0.3 |
| Buddhist | 0.1 |
| Other non-Christian (*PLEASE WRITE IN WHICH*) | 0.1 |
| Never knew father/does not apply | 1.5 |
| Can't say/can't remember | 3.7 |
| (NA) | 0.7 |

*Please continue ...*

## 11

[PRTNRRLG]
**IF YOU ARE CURRENTLY MARRIED OR LIVING AS MARRIED, PLEASE ANSWER Q2.24**

**IF YOU ARE NOT CURRENTLY MARRIED OR LIVING AS MARRIED, PLEASE GO TO Q2.25**

A.2.24 What is your husband's/wife's/partner's religion, if any?

*PLEASE TICK **ONE** BOX ONLY*

n = 831
Q.A2.24 only

| | % |
|---|---|
| No religion | 13.2 |
| Christian - no denomination | 6.7 |
| Roman Catholic | 12.5 |
| Church of England/Anglican | 47.7 |
| Baptist | 1.2 |
| Methodist | 4.3 |
| Presbyterian/Church of Scotland | 6.5 |
| Free Presbyterian | - |
| Brethren | 0.1 |
| United Reform Church (URC) Congregational | 1.6 |
| Other Protestant (*PLEASE WRITE IN WHICH*) | 1.2 |
| Other Christian (*PLEASE WRITE IN WHICH*) | 0.1 |
| Hindu | 0.7 |
| Jewish | 0.1 |
| Islam/Muslim | 0.6 |
| Sikh | 0.1 |
| Buddhist | 0.1 |
| Other non-Christian (*PLEASE WRITE IN WHICH*) | 0.5 |
| Can't say | 0.7 |
| (NA) | 1.9 |

*Please continue ...*

## 12

[MUMATTCH]
**EVERYONE PLEASE ANSWER REST OF QUESTIONNAIRE**

A.2.25 When you were a child, how often did your mother attend religious services?

*PLEASE TICK **ONE** BOX ONLY*

n = 1221
Q.A2.25 - A2.35

| | % |
|---|---|
| Never | 15.7 |
| Less than once a year | 8.4 |
| About once or twice a year | 14.2 |
| Several times a year | 14.4 |
| About once a month | 4.2 |
| 2-3 times a month | 3.9 |
| Nearly every week | 10.8 |
| Every week | 12.4 |
| Several times a week | 3.0 |
| Never knew mother/does not apply | 0.2 |
| Can't say/can't remember | 10.9 |
| (NA) | 1.9 |

[DADATTCH]
A.2.26 When you were a child, how often did your father attend religious services?

*PLEASE TICK **ONE** BOX ONLY*

| | % |
|---|---|
| Never | 26.8 |
| Less than once a year | 10.6 |
| About once or twice a year | 14.2 |
| Several times a year | 9.5 |
| About once a month | 2.7 |
| 2-3 times a month | 2.3 |
| Nearly every week | 5.6 |
| Every week | 10.5 |
| Several times a week | 2.3 |
| Never knew father/does not apply | 2.0 |
| Can't say/can't remember | 12.7 |
| (NA) | 0.6 |

13

A

A 2.27 [RllATTCH]
And what about when you were around 11 or 12, how often did you attend religious services then?

PLEASE TICK **ONE** BOX ONLY

n = 1221

|  | % |
|---|---|
| Never | 11.4 |
| Less than once a year | 4.4 |
| About once or twice a year | 7.4 |
| Several times a year | 11.0 |
| About once a month | 3.4 |
| 2-3 times a month | 6.7 |
| Nearly every week | 20.5 |
| Every week | 25.3 |
| Several times a week | 6.1 |
| Can't say/can't remember | 3.2 |
| (NA) | 0.6 |

A 2.28 [PRAYFREQ]
Now thinking about the present ...
About how often do you pray?

PLEASE TICK **ONE** BOX ONLY

|  | % |
|---|---|
| Never | 32.2 |
| Less than once a year | 5.4 |
| About once or twice a year | 8.1 |
| Several times a year | 14.4 |
| About once a month | 3.6 |
| 2-3 times a month | 3.0 |
| Nearly every week | 5.0 |
| Every week | 4.3 |
| Several times a week | 5.8 |
| Once a day | 11.8 |
| Several times a day | 4.9 |
| (DK) | 0.2 |
| (NA) | 1.3 |

Please continue ...

14

A

A 2.29 [CHRCHACT]
How often do you take part in the activities or organisations of a church or place of worship, other than attending services?

PLEASE TICK **ONE** BOX ONLY

n = 1221

|  | % |
|---|---|
| Never | 60.1 |
| Less than once a year | 8.3 |
| About once or twice a year | 10.4 |
| Several times a year | 8.6 |
| About once a month | 2.8 |
| 2-3 times a month | 1.1 |
| Nearly every week | 2.6 |
| Every week | 3.0 |
| Several times a week | 1.4 |
| (NA) | 1.7 |

A 2.30 [RELIGIUS]
Would you describe yourself as ...

PLEASE TICK **ONE** BOX ONLY

|  | % |
|---|---|
| Extremely religious | 1.1 |
| Very religious | 5.7 |
| Somewhat religious | 34.5 |
| Neither religious nor non-religious | 28.6 |
| Somewhat non-religious | 10.4 |
| Very non-religious | 8.4 |
| Extremely non-religious | 7.1 |
| Can't choose | 2.8 |
| (NA) | 1.4 |

A 2.31 [SCHPRAYR]
In your opinion, should there be daily prayers in all state schools?

PLEASE TICK **ONE** BOX ONLY

|  | % |
|---|---|
| Yes, definitely | 31.7 |
| Yes, probably | 32.3 |
| No, probably not | 17.4 |
| No, definitely not | 9.4 |
| Can't choose | 7.9 |
| (NA) | 1.4 |

A

A 2.32 How much do you agree or disagree with each of the following statements?

PLEASE TICK **ONE** BOX ON EACH LINE

n = 1221

| | Strongly agree | Agree | Neither agree nor disagree | Disagree | Strongly disagree | Can't choose | (NA) |
|---|---|---|---|---|---|---|---|
| [GODRIGHT] a. Right and wrong should be based on God's laws | % 9.0 | 24.0 | 24.4 | 23.1 | 10.3 | 4.4 | 4.7 |
| [SOCRIGHT] b. Right and wrong should be decided by society | % 11.4 | 46.4 | 19.7 | 10.5 | 1.7 | 4.8 | 5.5 |
| [OWNRIGHT] c. Right and wrong should be a matter of personal conscience | % 17.4 | 39.4 | 11.6 | 17.2 | 6.0 | 3.8 | 4.6 |

A 2.33 [BAMBLASF]
Some books or films offend people who have strong religious beliefs. Should books and films that attack religions be prohibited by law or should they be allowed?

PLEASE TICK **ONE** BOX ONLY

| | % |
|---|---|
| Definitely should be prohibited | 8.6 |
| Probably should be prohibited | 18.0 |
| Probably should be allowed | 38.0 |
| Definitely should be allowed | 23.3 |
| Can't choose | 10.2 |
| (NA) | 1.8 |

*Please continue ...*

---

A

A 2.34 [SCHATTN]
Now thinking about the present.
How often do you attend religious services?

PLEASE TICK **ONE** BOX

n = 1221

| | % |
|---|---|
| Never | 36.8 |
| Less than once a year | 14.0 |
| About once or twice a year | 20.0 |
| Several times a year | 8.7 |
| About once a month | 4.5 |
| 2-3 times a month | 1.8 |
| Nearly every week | 4.4 |
| Every week | 6.8 |
| Several times a week | 2.6 |
| (NA) | 0.4 |

A 2.35 Now please think about something different.
Please tick one box on each line below to show whether you think each statement is true or false.

PLEASE TICK **ONE** BOX ON EACH LINE

| | Definitely true | Probably true | Probably not true | Definitely not true | Can't choose | (NA) |
|---|---|---|---|---|---|---|
| [CHARMS] a. Good luck charms sometimes do bring good luck | % 2.6 | 19.4 | 36.9 | 35.1 | 4.5 | 1.5 |
| [SEERS] b. Some fortune tellers really can foresee the future | % 6.4 | 33.1 | 28.9 | 23.9 | 6.2 | 1.5 |
| [FAITHHLR] c. Some faith healers really do have God-given healing powers | % 8.4 | 36.8 | 27.6 | 17.0 | 8.8 | 0.3 |
| [ASTROLOGY] d. A person's star sign at birth, or horoscope, can affect the course of their future | % 3.2 | 24.4 | 34.6 | 28.7 | 8.0 | 1.2 |

18

**A & B**

A 2.37  In the last **two years**, have you or a close family member ...

*PLEASE TICK ONE BOX ON EACH LINE*

n = 2428

| | | Yes | No | (DK) | (NA) |
|---|---|---|---|---|---|
| [NHSDOC] ... visited an NHS GP? | % | 93.2 | 4.9 | - | 1.9 |
| [NHSOUTP] ... been an out-patient in an NHS hospital? | % | 67.2 | 29.1 | - | 3.7 |
| [NHSINP] ... been an in-patient in an NHS hospital? | % | 47.7 | 47.5 | 0.1 | 4.7 |
| [NHSVISIT] ... visited a patient in an NHS hospital? | % | 72.8 | 23.7 | - | 3.5 |
| [PRIVPAT] ... had any medical treatment as a _private_ patient? | % | 13.8 | 82.2 | - | 4.0 |

A 2.38  Please tick **one** box for **each** statement to show how much you agree or disagree with it.

*PLEASE TICK ONE BOX ON EACH LINE*

| | | Agree strongly | Agree | Neither agree nor disagree | Disagree | Disagree strongly | (DK) | (NA) |
|---|---|---|---|---|---|---|---|---|
| a. [WELFRESP] The welfare state makes people nowadays less willing to look after themselves | % | 7.0 | 25.7 | 26.2 | 32.3 | 6.9 | 0.1 | 1.8 |
| b. [WELFSTIG] People receiving social security are made to feel like second class citizens | % | 12.2 | 39.7 | 22.8 | 21.4 | 2.2 | 0.2 | 1.5 |
| c. [WELFHELP] The welfare state encourages people to stop helping each other | % | 4.6 | 22.5 | 28.5 | 37.6 | 4.9 | 0.2 | 1.8 |
| d. [MOREWELF] The government should spend more money on welfare benefits for the poor, even if it leads to higher taxes | % | 15.2 | 42.8 | 23.0 | 15.7 | 1.8 | 0.1 | 1.4 |
| e. [UNEMPJOB] Around here, most unemployed people could find a job if they really wanted one | % | 7.5 | 30.9 | 18.6 | 32.7 | 8.7 | 0.2 | 1.5 |
| f. [SOCHELP] Many people who get social security don't really deserve any help | % | 4.9 | 21.3 | 24.9 | 36.7 | 10.2 | 0.2 | 1.8 |
| g. [DOLEFIDL] Most people on the dole are fiddling in one way or another | % | 6.1 | 22.2 | 30.8 | 31.4 | 7.6 | 0.2 | 1.7 |
| h. [WELFFEET] If welfare benefits weren't so generous, people would learn to stand on their own two feet | % | 6.4 | 19.3 | 22.7 | 36.8 | 13.5 | 0.1 | 1.3 |

17

**A & B**

[HSAREA1-HSAREA17]
Now for some questions on different subjects

A 2.36  From what you know or have heard, please tick a box for **each** of the items below to show whether you think the National Health Service in your **area** is, on the whole, satisfactory or in need of improvement.

*PLEASE TICK ONE BOX ON EACH LINE*

n = 2428
Qs.A2.36-A2.39

| | | In need of a lot of improve-ment | In need of some improve-ment | Satis-factory | Very good | (DK) | (NA) |
|---|---|---|---|---|---|---|---|
| a. GPs' appointment systems | % | 11.5 | 33.0 | 42.9 | 11.5 | 0.1 | 1.1 |
| b. Amount of time GP gives to each patient | % | 9.2 | 24.7 | 52.6 | 12.3 | 0.1 | 1.2 |
| c. Being able to choose which GP to see | % | 7.6 | 18.6 | 53.6 | 18.7 | 0.1 | 1.4 |
| d. Quality of medical treatment by GPs | % | 5.7 | 19.9 | 50.3 | 22.6 | 0.1 | 1.4 |
| e. Hospital waiting lists for non-emergency operations | % | 43.7 | 41.1 | 11.9 | 1.2 | 0.5 | 1.6 |
| f. Waiting time before getting appointments with hospital consultants | % | 43.1 | 40.9 | 12.5 | 1.3 | 0.5 | 1.7 |
| g. General condition of hospital buildings | % | 20.6 | 38.1 | 32.7 | 6.8 | 0.2 | 1.6 |
| h. Hospital accident and emergency departments | % | 15.2 | 34.0 | 36.3 | 12.1 | 0.4 | 2.0 |
| i. Staffing level of nurses in hospitals | % | 28.5 | 41.4 | 24.4 | 3.4 | 0.4 | 1.8 |
| j. Staffing level of doctors in hospitals | % | 26.6 | 43.2 | 24.7 | 2.9 | 0.5 | 2.1 |
| k. Quality of medical treatment in hospitals | % | 6.9 | 25.5 | 50.2 | 15.1 | 0.3 | 2.0 |
| l. Quality of nursing care in hospitals | % | 5.1 | 19.5 | 47.8 | 25.5 | 0.3 | 1.8 |
| m. Waiting areas in accident and emergency department in hospitals | % | 19.2 | 41.0 | 33.4 | 3.4 | 0.5 | 2.5 |
| n. Waiting areas for out-patients in hospitals | % | 16.4 | 39.3 | 38.0 | 3.7 | 0.3 | 2.4 |
| o. Waiting areas at GPs' surgeries | % | 6.8 | 20.2 | 57.4 | 13.4 | 0.1 | 2.1 |
| p. Time spent waiting in out-patient departments | % | 33.6 | 46.8 | 16.4 | 1.1 | 0.4 | 1.7 |
| q. Time spent waiting in accident and emergency departments | % | 31.2 | 42.2 | 22.0 | 1.9 | 0.5 | 2.2 |

*Please continue ...*

19

**A & B**

A 2.39 [PAIDJOB]
Do you have a paid job?
PLEASE TICK ONE BOX

n = 2428

%

Yes, I have a paid job 57.2
No, I don't work for pay at the moment 42.6
(NA) 0.1

**PLEASE ANSWER Q.2.40 - Q.2.45 ABOUT YOUR MAIN JOB**

n = 1393

Qs.A2.40 - A2.45

A 2.40 [PWWKHARD]
Which of the following statements best describes your feelings about your job?
PLEASE TICK ONE BOX ONLY

%

In my job ...
... I only work as hard as I have to 7.4
... I work hard, but not so that it interferes with the rest of my life 34.0
... I make a point of doing the best work I can, even if it sometimes does interfere with the rest of my life 53.1
Can't choose 2.1
(NA) 3.4

A 2.41 [PWWKPLAN]
And which of the following statements about your work is most true?
PLEASE TICK ONE BOX ONLY

%

My job allows me to design or plan most of my daily work 41.7
My job allows me to design or plan parts of my daily work 34.1
My job does not really allow me to design or plan my daily work 19.2
(NA) 5.0

A 2.42 [PWWKSAT]
How satisfied are you in your (main) job?
PLEASE TICK ONE BOX ONLY

%

Very satisfied 28.6
Fairly satisfied 47.3
Neither satisfied nor dissatisfied 9.9
Fairly dissatisfied 6.3
Very dissatisfied 2.7
Can't choose 0.4
(NA) 4.5

*Please continue...*

---

20

**A & B**

n = 1393

A 2.43 [PWTRNSAT]
And how satisfied are you with the amount of training you get in your (main) job?
PLEASE TICK ONE BOX ONLY

%

Very satisfied 17.4
Fairly satisfied 32.3
Neither satisfied nor dissatisfied 23.1
Fairly dissatisfied 9.1
Very dissatisfied 4.1
Can't choose 8.3
(NA) 5.6

A 2.44 [PWPROSAT]
And how satisfied are you with the opportunities for promotion in your (main) job?
PLEASE TICK ONE BOX ONLY

%

Very satisfied 11.1
Fairly satisfied 25.8
Neither satisfied nor dissatisfied 24.4
Fairly dissatisfied 14.0
Very dissatisfied 7.5
Can't choose 10.9
(NA) 6.3

A 2.45 [PWLEARN]
On the whole, would you say that in your (main) job these days you learn new skills ...
PLEASE TICK ONE BOX ONLY

%

... almost all the time, 10.3
... a lot of the time, 22.5
... occasionally, 42.7
... or, hardly ever or never? 20.9
(NA) 3.7

21

**EVERYONE PLEASE ANSWER REST OF QUESTIONNAIRE**

n = 2428    Qs. A2.46-A2.49

A 2.46 Now for some questions on other subjects. Please tick one box for each statement to show how you feel about training for people in work.

PLEASE TICK ONE BOX ON EACH LINE

| | Agree strongly | Agree | Neither agree nor disagree | Disagree | Disagree strongly | (DK) | (NA) |
|---|---|---|---|---|---|---|---|
| [TRAINNG1] a. Most employers are unwilling to pay for better training for their staff | % 5.8 | 38.4 | 31.6 | 20.7 | 1.1 | 0.3 | 2.2 |
| [TRAINNG2] b. People who get training at work find their jobs more interesting | % 11.5 | 71.5 | 12.5 | 2.5 | 0.2 | 0.1 | 1.7 |
| [TRAINNG3] c. Having well-trained staff benefits employers more than workers | % 8.7 | 42.7 | 28.2 | 17.6 | 0.7 | 0.1 | 2.0 |
| [TRAINNG4] d. People who get trained at work end up with better pay | % 5.2 | 49.2 | 31.6 | 11.5 | 0.5 | 0.1 | 1.9 |
| [TRAINNG5] e. Training at work is really only for young people or people starting new jobs | % 2.3 | 12.6 | 12.8 | 58.4 | 12.0 | 0.1 | 1.8 |
| [TRAINNG6] f. The government ought to help employers pay for the training of their staff | % 9.9 | 50.3 | 19.4 | 17.2 | 1.3 | 0.1 | 1.7 |
| [TRAINNG7] g. Employers should be made to provide training for all young people starting their first real job | % 20.1 | 58.4 | 11.4 | 8.2 | 0.2 | 0.0 | 1.8 |
| [TRAINNG8] h. Employers should be made to give some sort of regular training for all staff | % 13.2 | 61.4 | 16.1 | 7.4 | 0.2 | 0.0 | 1.6 |
| [TRAINNG9] i. The government already does enough to make sure that people are trained in the skills Britain needs | % 1.3 | 8.1 | 22.0 | 52.1 | 14.6 | 0.2 | 1.8 |
| [TRAINNG0] j. Employers would benefit if they spent more time and money on training their staff | % 15.2 | 69.5 | 11.5 | 1.8 | 0.2 | 0.1 | 1.8 |
| [TRAINNGA] k. Britain's schools fail to teach the kind of skills that British industry needs | % 16.0 | 50.3 | 22.3 | 8.6 | 0.7 | 0.2 | 1.9 |
| [TRAINNGB] l. Britain's colleges and universities fail to teach the kind of skills that British industry needs | % 8.8 | 32.2 | 33.6 | 21.5 | 1.7 | 0.3 | 1.9 |

*Please continue ...*

22

[LSCHEME1 - LSCHEME4]

A 2.47 The government these days pays for a number of programmes for unemployed people.

Please tick one box to show how much you agree or disagree with each of these statements about government training programmes for school-leavers.

PLEASE TICK ONE BOX ON EACH LINE

n = 2428

| Government training programmes for school leavers ... | Agree strongly | Agree | Neither agree nor disagree | Disagree | Disagree strongly | (DK) | (NA) |
|---|---|---|---|---|---|---|---|
| a. ... are a good way of giving young people better job prospects | % 9.2 | 55.3 | 16.2 | 15.5 | 1.8 | 0.1 | 1.8 |
| b. ... benefit employers more than the young people taking part | % 11.8 | 36.2 | 28.8 | 20.4 | 0.5 | 0.2 | 2.0 |
| c. ... are a bad substitute for proper job-experience | % 10.6 | 33.7 | 28.1 | 24.5 | 0.8 | 0.1 | 2.2 |
| d. ... are a good way for young people to get training after they leave school | % 5.9 | 58.2 | 18.1 | 14.0 | 1.7 | 0.1 | 2.0 |

A 2.48 [TRAINPAY]
Thinking of young people starting their first real job. Which of these comes closest to your view?

PLEASE TICK ONE BOX ONLY

| | % |
|---|---|
| The employer should pay most of the costs of training | 25.5 |
| The government should pay most of the costs of training | 9.0 |
| The costs should be shared about equally | 60.1 |
| Can't choose | 4.4 |
| (NA) | 1.0 |

A 2.49 [TRAIN2]
Compared with other countries that compete with us, how good do you think Britain is at training employees in new skills?

PLEASE TICK ONE BOX ONLY

| | % |
|---|---|
| Better than most | 8.1 |
| Worse than most | 49.7 |
| About the same | 24.2 |
| Can't choose | 17.2 |
| (NA) | 0.9 |

Note: Qs. A2.36 - A2.49 were also asked on the B Version of the questionnaire as Qs. B2.01 - B2.02 and B2.04 - B2.15.

23

n = 1221    Qs. A2.50-A2.62

A 2.50   [BENPROFT]
Who do you think benefits **most** from the profits made by British firms?

PLEASE TICK **ONE BOX** ONLY

| | % |
|---|---|
| Mainly their owners or shareholders | 64.9 |
| Mainly their directors and managers | 25.2 |
| Mainly their employees | 3.5 |
| The public generally | 4.0 |
| (DK) | 0.5 |
| (NA) | 1.9 |

A 2.51   [BENPRFSH]
And who do you think **should** benefit most from the profits made by British firms?

PLEASE TICK **ONE BOX** ONLY

| | % |
|---|---|
| Mainly their owners or shareholders | 18.0 |
| Mainly their directors and managers | 2.9 |
| Mainly their employees | 44.0 |
| The public generally | 31.6 |
| (DK) | 0.4 |
| (NA) | 3.1 |

A 2.52   [PROTRCMX]
Some people think that better relations between Protestants and Catholics in Northern Ireland will only come about through more **mixing** of the two communities. Others think that better relations will only come about through more **separation**. Which comes closest to your views ...

PLEASE TICK **ONE BOX**

| | % |
|---|---|
| ... better relations will come about through more **mixing** | 89.1 |
| or | |
| ... better relations will come about through more **separation** | 7.4 |
| (DK) | 1.0 |
| (NA) | 2.4 |

Please continue ....

24

n = 1221

A 2.53   People feel closer to some groups than to others. For you personally, how close would you say you feel towards ...

PLEASE TICK **ONE BOX ON EACH LINE**

| | | Very close | Fairly close | A little close | Not very close | Not at all close | (DK) | (NA) |
|---|---|---|---|---|---|---|---|---|
| a. | [CLSEBORN] People born in the same area as you | 8.3 | 38.7 | 23.3 | 17.7 | 7.9 | 0.2 | 3.9 |
| b. | [CLSECLAS] People who have the same social class background as yours | 7.9 | 50.2 | 23.3 | 11.2 | 3.3 | 0.1 | 3.9 |
| c. | [CLSERELG] People who have the same religious background as yours | 6.4 | 27.8 | 25.2 | 22.4 | 12.6 | 0.1 | 5.5 |
| d. | [CLSERACE] People of the same race as you | 10.9 | 41.3 | 27.6 | 11.1 | 4.8 | – | 4.3 |
| e. | [CLSELIVE] People who live in the same area as you do now | 7.3 | 41.9 | 27.1 | 14.1 | 5.8 | – | 3.9 |
| f. | [CLSEPOL] People who have the same political beliefs as you | 4.3 | 28.2 | 29.9 | 20.7 | 12.3 | 0.2 | 4.4 |

A 2.54   [FEMJOBOP]
Would you say that job opportunities for women are, in general, better or worse than job opportunities for men with similar education and experience?

PLEASE TICK **ONE BOX** ONLY

| | % |
|---|---|
| Much better for women | 2.1 |
| Better for women | 4.7 |
| No difference | 23.0 |
| Worse for women | 54.6 |
| Much worse for women | 7.1 |
| Can't choose | 6.3 |
| (NA) | 2.2 |

## 25

**A**

**A 2.55**  *[FEMINC]*
And how about income and wages: compared with men who have similar education and jobs, are women in general paid better or worse than men?

*PLEASE TICK ONE BOX ONLY*

|  | % |
|---|---|
| Women are paid much better | 0.2 |
| Women are paid better | 1.5 |
| No difference | 23.0 |
| Women are paid worse | 60.2 |
| Women are paid much worse | 4.8 |
| Can't choose | 7.7 |
| (NA) | 2.8 |

n = 1221

**A 2.56**  For each of the jobs below, please tick a box to show whether you think the job is particularly suitable for men only, particularly suitable for women only, or suitable for both men and women equally.

*PLEASE TICK ONE BOX ON EACH LINE*

|  |  | Particularly suitable for men | Particularly suitable for women | Suitable for both equally | (NA) |
|---|---|---|---|---|---|
| *[JOBMF1]* Social worker | % | 1.1 | 14.1 | 81.6 | 3.2 |
| *[JOBMF2]* Police officer | % | 36.5 | 0.4 | 60.7 | 2.5 |
| *[JOBMF3]* Secretary | % | 0.5 | 53.6 | 43.0 | 2.9 |
| *[JOBMF4]* Car mechanic | % | 60.5 | 0.4 | 36.6 | 2.6 |
| *[JOBMF5]* Nurse | % | 0.6 | 32.4 | 64.4 | 2.6 |
| *[JOBMF8]* Bank manager | % | 21.5 | 1.3 | 74.7 | 2.5 |
| *[JOBMF9]* Family doctor/GP | % | 7.6 | 2.3 | 87.7 | 2.4 |
| *[JOBMF11]* Member of Parliament | % | 11.1 | 1.3 | 85.0 | 2.6 |
| *[JOBMF12]* Director of an international company | % | 24.6 | 0.4 | 72.2 | 2.9 |

*Please continue ...*

## 26

**A**

**A 2.57**  Please tick **one** box for **each** statement below to show how much you agree or disagree with it.

*PLEASE TICK ONE BOX ON EACH LINE*

n = 1221

|  | Strongly agree | Agree | Neither agree nor disagree | Disagree | Strongly disagree | Can't choose | (NA) |
|---|---|---|---|---|---|---|---|
| a. *[WWHAPPIR]* A woman and her family will all be happier if she goes out to work — % | 1.4 | 12.7 | 48.8 | 26.8 | 4.7 | 4.1 | 1.6 |
| b. *[WOMKKID]* Women shouldn't try to combine a career and children — % | 2.9 | 22.5 | 24.8 | 38.8 | 7.6 | 1.9 | 1.5 |
| c. *[FEMHOME]* In times of high unemployment married women should stay at home — % | 4.0 | 15.8 | 19.3 | 46.3 | 11.6 | 1.4 | 1.6 |
| d. *[WANTHOME]* A job is all right, but what most women really want is a home and children — % | 2.3 | 23.3 | 22.0 | 36.5 | 12.0 | 2.5 | 1.4 |
| e. *[WOMKGD]* If the children are well looked after, it's good for a woman to work — % | 8.6 | 58.1 | 21.0 | 7.6 | 1.3 | 1.4 | 2.0 |
| f. *[MAEXTRAS]* Most married women work only to earn money for extras, rather than because they need the money — % | 4.0 | 29.8 | 17.3 | 39.8 | 6.1 | 1.5 | 1.5 |
| g. *[WOMSUFFR]* If a women takes several years off to look after her children, it's only fair her career should suffer — % | 1.4 | 18.0 | 21.8 | 47.9 | 7.0 | 2.2 | 1.6 |
| h. *[WOMRIGHT]* Married women have a right to work if they want to, whatever their family situation — % | 16.1 | 57.4 | 12.3 | 9.6 | 1.5 | 1.4 | 1.7 |
| i. *[FEMJOB]* Having a job is the best way for a woman to be an independent person — % | 8.5 | 50.1 | 21.2 | 14.8 | 1.9 | 1.8 | 1.6 |
| j. *[WWCHDSUF]* A pre-school child is likely to suffer if his or her mother works — % | 8.2 | 36.6 | 21.3 | 25.8 | 5.0 | 1.6 | 1.4 |

27

A

n = 1221

**A 2.58** [WWCHLD1 - WWCHLD4]
Do you think that women should work outside the home **full-time**, **part-time** or **not at all** under these circumstances?

PLEASE TICK ONE BOX ON EACH LINE

| | | Work full-time | Work part-time | Stay at home | Can't choose | (NA) |
|---|---|---|---|---|---|---|
| a. | After marrying and before there are children? % | 82.3 | 7.7 | 0.9 | 7.3 | 1.8 |
| b. | When there is a child under school age? % | 5.1 | 33.2 | 52.1 | 7.6 | 2.1 |
| c. | After the youngest child starts school? % | 20.6 | 63.4 | 5.8 | 8.2 | 2.0 |
| d. | After the children leave home? % | 72.4 | 13.8 | 1.1 | 10.2 | 2.6 |

**A 2.59** Please tick one box for **each** statement to show how much you agree or disagree.

PLEASE TICK ONE BOX ON EACH LINE

| | | Agree strongly | Agree | Neither agree nor disagree | Disagree | Disagree strongly | Can't choose | (NA) |
|---|---|---|---|---|---|---|---|---|
| a. | [CHARREFSE] I can't refuse when someone comes to the door with a collecting tin % | 6.7 | 43.9 | 12.9 | 26.4 | 6.7 | 1.5 | 2.0 |
| b. | [CHARRELY] People should look after themselves and not rely on charities % | 3.6 | 24.6 | 24.8 | 36.3 | 6.8 | 2.4 | 1.5 |
| c. | [CHARRESP] It is **not** everyone's responsibility to give what they can to charities % | 5.7 | 54.7 | 18.3 | 15.2 | 2.7 | 2.0 | 1.5 |
| d. | [CHARMANY] There are so many charities that it is difficult to decide which to give to % | 11.9 | 65.4 | 10.0 | 8.3 | 1.3 | 1.5 | 1.6 |
| e. | [CHARBRIT] We should support more charities which benefit people in Britain, rather than people overseas % | 19.3 | 36.6 | 16.9 | 20.6 | 3.1 | 1.9 | 1.6 |
| f. | [CHARWAST] Most charities are wasteful in their use of funds % | 7.8 | 28.5 | 32.7 | 22.0 | 2.4 | 4.3 | 2.3 |
| g. | [CHARMORE] The government should do less for the needy and encourage charities to do more instead % | 1.1 | 5.3 | 12.2 | 51.4 | 25.9 | 2.4 | 1.8 |

*Please continue ...*

---

28

A

n = 1221

**A 2.60** Please tick **one** box for **each** statement below to show how much you agree or disagree with it.

PLEASE TICK ONE BOX ON EACH LINE

| | | Agree strongly | Agree | Neither agree nor disagree | Disagree | Disagree strongly | (DK) | (NA) |
|---|---|---|---|---|---|---|---|---|
| a. | [REDISTRB] Government should redistribute income from the better-off to those who are less well off % | 9.9 | 31.5 | 24.3 | 27.9 | 4.2 | 0.1 | 2.2 |
| b. | [PRENTBST] Private enterprise is the best way to solve economic problems % | 4.0 | 31.1 | 35.7 | 23.8 | 3.1 | 0.2 | 2.0 |
| c. | [BIGBUSNN] Big business benefits owners at the expense of workers % | 7.6 | 41.9 | 29.8 | 17.0 | 1.5 | 0.3 | 2.0 |
| d. | [LSGOVINT] The less government intervenes, the better it is for the economy % | 3.4 | 25.5 | 40.3 | 26.1 | 2.4 | 0.4 | 2.0 |
| e. | [WEALTH] Ordinary working people do not get their fair share of the nation's wealth % | 12.3 | 54.4 | 19.2 | 11.4 | 0.9 | 0.2 | 1.5 |
| f. | [PRSRVBST] Even the most important public services and industries are best run by private enterprise % | 3.2 | 23.9 | 29.6 | 34.4 | 6.4 | 0.3 | 2.3 |
| g. | [RICHLAW] There is one law for the rich and one for the poor % | 19.9 | 42.0 | 16.6 | 17.1 | 2.4 | 0.1 | 1.8 |
| h. | [GOVNOTJB] It is **not** the government's responsibility to make sure there are enough jobs for everyone % | 2.7 | 28.9 | 19.7 | 38.9 | 7.9 | 0.1 | 1.7 |
| i. | [INDUST4] Management will always try to get the better of employees if it gets the chance % | 12.4 | 45.5 | 20.8 | 18.2 | 1.0 | 0.2 | 1.8 |
| j. | [UNEMGOOD] A bit of unemployment is good because it weakens the unions % | 1.5 | 9.6 | 20.7 | 48.4 | 17.8 | 0.1 | 1.9 |

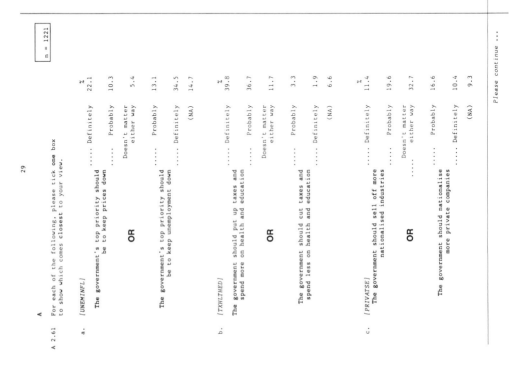

29

A

A 2.61 For each of the following, please tick **one** box to show which comes closest to your view.

n = 1221

%

a. [UNEMINFL]

| The government's top priority should be to keep prices down | ..... Definitely | 22.1 |
| | ..... Probably | 10.3 |
| | Doesn't matter either way | 5.4 |
| **OR** | | |
| The government's top priority should be to keep unemployment down | ..... Probably | 13.1 |
| | ..... Definitely | 34.5 |
| | (NA) | 14.7 |

%

b. [TXHLTHED]

| The government should put up taxes and spend more on health and education | ..... Definitely | 39.8 |
| | ..... Probably | 36.7 |
| | Doesn't matter either way | 11.7 |
| **OR** | | |
| The government should cut taxes and spend less on health and education | ..... Probably | 3.3 |
| | ..... Definitely | 1.9 |
| | (NA) | 6.6 |

%

c. [PRIVATSE]

| The government should sell off more nationalised industries | ..... Definitely | 11.4 |
| | ..... Probably | 19.6 |
| | Doesn't matter either way | 32.7 |
| **OR** | | |
| The government should nationalise more private companies | ..... Probably | 16.6 |
| | ..... Definitely | 10.4 |
| | (NA) | 9.3 |

*Please continue ...*

30

A

n = 1221

%

d. [GVINCDIF]

| The government should take steps to reduce differences in income | ..... Definitely | 33.6 |
| | ..... Probably | 31.5 |
| | Doesn't matter either way | 19.9 |
| **OR** | | |
| The government should let differences in income increase | ..... Probably | 5.6 |
| | ..... Definitely | 2.9 |
| | (NA) | 6.6 |

%

e. [CUTCRIME]

| Protecting civil rights is more important than cutting crime | ..... Definitely | 8.4 |
| | ..... Probably | 12.9 |
| | Doesn't matter either way | 17.1 |
| **OR** | | |
| Cutting crime is more important than protecting civil rights | ..... Probably | 25.3 |
| | ..... Definitely | 29.6 |
| | (NA) | 6.7 |

%

f. [GVPORHLP]

| The poor in Britain get too much help from government | ..... Definitely | 2.0 |
| | ..... Probably | 7.8 |
| | Doesn't matter either way | 10.7 |
| **OR** | | |
| The poor in Britain get too little help from government | ..... Probably | 34.6 |
| | ..... Definitely | 39.7 |
| | (NA) | 5.2 |

## 31

n = 1221

**A**

A 2.62  Please tick one box for **each** statement below to show how much you agree or disagree with it.

PLEASE TICK **ONE** BOX ON EACH LINE

| | Agree strongly | Agree | Neither agree nor disagree | Disagree | Disagree strongly | (DK) | (NA) |
|---|---|---|---|---|---|---|---|
| a. [TRADVALS] Young people today don't have enough respect for traditional British values | % 15.0 | 44.7 | 24.6 | 13.1 | 1.0 | – | 1.6 |
| b. [BANXTPTY] For a democracy to work properly, extreme political parties should be banned | % 5.0 | 27.4 | 26.3 | 33.8 | 5.4 | 0.1 | 2.0 |
| c. [STIFSENT] People who break the law should be given stiffer sentences | % 19.5 | 47.3 | 16.7 | 12.7 | 1.8 | 0.0 | 2.0 |
| d. [EQUALOPP] In a fair society, every person should have an equal opportunity to get ahead | % 33.4 | 62.5 | 2.0 | 0.7 | – | – | 1.4 |
| e. [DEATHAPP] For some crimes, the death penalty is the most appropriate sentence | % 25.1 | 33.0 | 11.7 | 16.9 | 11.8 | 0.0 | 1.5 |
| f. [NTSTRIKE] Workers in essential public services should **not** have the right to strike | % 7.6 | 28.8 | 19.9 | 35.5 | 6.4 | 0.1 | 1.7 |
| g. [OBEY] Schools should teach children to obey authority | % 23.2 | 54.9 | 13.9 | 6.0 | 0.7 | – | 1.4 |
| h. [FREESPCH] Protecting freedom of speech is more important than maintaining order in the nation | % 4.6 | 19.3 | 34.7 | 35.0 | 3.7 | 0.2 | 2.5 |
| i. [WRONGLAW] The law should always be obeyed, even if a particular law is wrong | % 4.3 | 32.8 | 24.0 | 32.3 | 4.9 | 0.1 | 1.7 |
| j. [CENSOR] Censorship of films and magazines is necessary to uphold moral standards | % 13.0 | 43.4 | 18.7 | 17.0 | 6.5 | 0.2 | 1.2 |

*Please continue ...*

## 32

n = 2428

**A & B**

A2.63a  [QTIME]
To help us plan better in future, please tell us about how long it took you to complete this questionnaire?

Also asked on Version B (Q.B2.40a,b)

PLEASE TICK **ONE** BOX ONLY

|  | % |
|---|---|
| Less than 15 minutes | 3.6 |
| Between 15 and 20 minutes | 22.6 |
| Between 21 and 30 minutes | 32.5 |
| Between 31 and 45 minutes | 22.7 |
| Between 46 and 60 minutes | 10.7 |
| Over one hour | 6.9 |
| (NA) | 1.1 |

b.  And on what date did you fill in the questionnaire?

PLEASE WRITE IN [ ] [0] 1991
DATE    MONTH

THANK YOU VERY MUCH FOR YOUR HELP

> Please keep the completed questionnaire for the interviewer if he or she has arranged to call for it. Otherwise, please post it as soon as possible in the pre-paid addressed envelope provided.

B

SCPR
SOCIAL & COMMUNITY PLANNING RESEARCH

*Head Office: 35 NORTHAMPTON SQUARE, LONDON EC1V 0AX. Telephone 071-250 1866.*

*Field and DP Office: BRENTWOOD, ESSEX*
*Northern Field Office: DARLINGTON, CO. DURHAM*

P.1135/GB

**BRITISH SOCIAL ATTITUDES 1991**

**SELF-COMPLETION QUESTIONNAIRE**

Spring 1991

| OFFICE USE ONLY: | Sampling point |
|---|---|
| Interviewer to enter: | 0 |
| | Serial No. |
| Rec. | Interviewer No. |

**To the selected respondent:**

Thank you very much for agreeing to take part in this important study - the eighth in this annual series. The study consists of this self-completion questionnaire, and the interview you have already completed. The results of the survey are published in a book each autumn; some of the questions are also being asked in twelve other countries, as part of an international survey.

*Completing the questionnaire:*

The questions inside cover a wide range of subjects, but each one can be answered simply by placing a tick (✓) in one or more of the boxes. No special knowledge is required: we are confident that everyone will be able to take part, not just those with strong views or particular viewpoints. The questionnaire should not take very long to complete, and we hope you will find it interesting and enjoyable. It should be filled in only by the person actually interviewed at your address. The answers you give will be treated as confidential and anonymous.

*Returning the questionnaire:*

Your interviewer will arrange with you the most convenient way of returning the questionnaire. If the interviewer has arranged to call back for it, please fill it in and keep it safely until then. If not, please complete it and post it back in the pre-paid, addressed envelope, AS SOON AS YOU POSSIBLY CAN.

**THANK YOU AGAIN FOR YOUR HELP.**

*Social and Community Planning Research is an independent social research institute registered as a charitable trust. Its projects are funded by government departments, local authorities, universities and foundations to provide information on social issues in Britain. The British Social Attitudes Survey series has been funded mainly by the Sainsbury Family Charitable Trusts, with contributions also from government departments, the Nuffield Foundation, universities and industry. Please contact us if you would like further information.*

**A & B**

B 2.02 In the last two years, have you or a close family member ...

PLEASE TICK ONE BOX ON EACH LINE

n = 2428
Q.B2.02 only

| | | Yes | No | (DK) | (NA) |
|---|---|---|---|---|---|
| [NHSDOC] ... visited an NHS GP? | % | 93.2 | 4.9 | - | 1.9 |
| [NHSOUTP] ... been an out-patient in an NHS hospital? | % | 67.2 | 29.1 | - | 3.7 |
| [NHSINP] ... been an in-patient in an NHS hospital? | % | 47.7 | 47.5 | 0.1 | 4.7 |
| [NHSVISIT] ... visited a patient in an NHS hospital? | % | 72.8 | 23.7 | - | 3.5 |
| [PRIVPAT] ... had any medical treatment as a private patient? | % | 13.8 | 82.2 | - | 4.0 |

**B**

B 2.03 From what you know or have heard, how would you compare NHS treatment in an NHS hospital with private treatment in a private hospital?

n = 1207
Q.B2.03 only

| | | NHS hospitals are: | | | Private hospitals are: | | | |
|---|---|---|---|---|---|---|---|---|
| | | Much better | A little better | No difference | A little better | Much better | Don't know | (NA) |
| a. [NHSWAITT] Waiting time before an operation can take place | % | 7.4 | 2.8 | 5.0 | 7.1 | 49.6 | 21.4 | 6.7 |
| b. [NHSNURSN] Quality of nursing care | % | 6.1 | 4.9 | 29.4 | 12.6 | 16.8 | 23.3 | 6.9 |
| c. [NHSMEDTR] Quality of medical treatment | % | 7.0 | 5.4 | 27.8 | 13.9 | 16.2 | 23.1 | 6.5 |
| d. [NHSINFO] The amount of information given by the doctor about the patient's condition | % | 4.5 | 4.0 | 22.2 | 13.7 | 18.2 | 30.8 | 6.5 |
| e. [NHSCOMPL] Being able to deal with unexpected medical complications | % | 13.6 | 8.2 | 26.4 | 5.5 | 8.7 | 30.6 | 7.0 |
| f. [NHSEQUIP] Having the latest medical equipment available | % | 9.1 | 7.5 | 13.9 | 14.3 | 22.0 | 26.5 | 6.7 |
| g. [NHSFOOD] Quality and choice of food | % | 6.0 | 4.1 | 7.0 | 10.9 | 42.8 | 22.4 | 6.8 |

**Note:** Q.B2.01 and B2.02 are the same as Qs. A2.36 and A2.37 on pages 17 and 18 of the A version of the questionnaire; and Qs. B2.04 - B2.15 are the same as Qs. A2.38 - A2.50 on pages 18-23 of the A version of the questionnaire.

---

**B**

B 2.16 [GVSPEND1 - GVSPEND8]

Listed below are various areas of government spending. Please show whether you would like to see more or less government spending in each area.

Remember that if you say "much more", it might require a tax increase to pay for it.

PLEASE TICK ONE BOX ON EACH LINE

n = 1207
Qs. B2.16-B2.39

| | | Spend much more | Spend more | Spend the same as now | Spend less | Spend much less | Can't choose | (NA) |
|---|---|---|---|---|---|---|---|---|
| a. The environment | % | 11.5 | 48.0 | 32.0 | 2.7 | 0.4 | 3.3 | 2.1 |
| b. Health | % | 35.7 | 53.0 | 9.0 | 0.7 | 0.1 | 0.5 | 1.1 |
| c. The police and law enforcement | % | 13.7 | 40.0 | 38.9 | 3.4 | 0.7 | 1.7 | 1.7 |
| d. Education | % | 26.8 | 54.8 | 14.6 | 1.4 | 0.2 | 0.9 | 1.4 |
| e. The military and defence | % | 3.8 | 10.1 | 38.7 | 28.6 | 14.5 | 2.1 | 2.2 |
| f. Old age pensions | % | 26.4 | 49.7 | 20.3 | 1.3 | 0.2 | 0.8 | 1.3 |
| g. Unemployment benefits | % | 8.4 | 30.8 | 43.6 | 10.0 | 2.6 | 2.8 | 1.9 |
| h. Culture and the arts | % | 2.8 | 12.4 | 35.9 | 25.7 | 15.3 | 6.1 | 1.7 |

B 2.17 [ENVIR1 - ENVIR9]

How serious an effect on our environment do you think each of these things has?

PLEASE TICK ONE BOX ON EACH LINE

| | | Very serious | Quite serious | Not very serious | Not at all serious | (DK/NA) |
|---|---|---|---|---|---|---|
| Noise from aircraft | % | 4.3 | 25.4 | 54.6 | 13.5 | 2.2 |
| Lead from petrol | % | 38.5 | 48.1 | 11.2 | 0.8 | 1.3 |
| Industrial waste in the rivers and sea | % | 69.6 | 27.6 | 1.8 | 0.2 | 0.9 |
| Waste from nuclear electricity stations | % | 57.9 | 26.5 | 12.5 | 1.6 | 1.5 |
| Industrial fumes in the air | % | 51.8 | 39.4 | 6.7 | 0.6 | 1.5 |
| Noise and dirt from traffic | % | 29.2 | 49.3 | 19.7 | 0.7 | 1.1 |
| Acid rain | % | 46.4 | 41.0 | 9.9 | 0.9 | 1.8 |
| Certain aerosol chemicals in the atmosphere | % | 42.1 | 43.3 | 11.5 | 1.1 | 1.8 |
| Cutting down tropical rainforests | % | 65.6 | 25.5 | 5.7 | 1.7 | 1.5 |

10

B

**B 2.21** [PREDICT1 - PREDICT7]
Here is a list of predictions. For each one, please say how likely or unlikely you think it is to come true **within the next ten years**?

PLEASE TICK **ONE** BOX ON EACH LINE    n = 1207

| | Very likely | Quite likely | Not very likely | Not at all likely | (DK) | (NA) |
|---|---|---|---|---|---|---|
| a. [PREDICT7] Acts of political terrorism in Britain will be common events | % 17.0 | 48.4 | 30.0 | 2.8 | 0.4 | 1.4 |
| b. Riots and civil disturbance in our cities will be common events | % 10.5 | 41.8 | 42.1 | 3.8 | 0.4 | 1.5 |
| c. There will be a world war involving Britain and Europe | % 2.5 | 14.0 | 57.0 | 24.8 | 0.3 | 1.4 |
| d. There will be a serious accident at a British nuclear power station | % 10.7 | 40.9 | 40.0 | 6.7 | 0.4 | 1.3 |
| e. The police in our cities will find it impossible to protect our personal safety on the streets | % 18.0 | 43.1 | 32.6 | 5.0 | 0.3 | 1.1 |
| f. The government in Britain will be overthrown by revolution | % 2.5 | 5.5 | 45.5 | 45.0 | 0.5 | 1.0 |
| g. A nuclear bomb will be dropped somewhere in the world | % 4.9 | 28.8 | 42.7 | 22.1 | 0.4 | 1.1 |

**B 2.22** Please tick **one** box for **each** statement below to show how much you agree or disagree with it.

PLEASE TICK **ONE** BOX ON EACH LINE

| | Agree strongly | Agree | Neither agree nor disagree | Disagree | Disagree strongly | (DK) | (NA) |
|---|---|---|---|---|---|---|---|
| a. [GOVENVIR] The government should do more to protect the environment, even if it leads to higher taxes | % 13.0 | 46.8 | 28.8 | 9.3 | 1.6 | 0.1 | 0.3 |
| b. [INDENVIR] Industry should do more to protect the environment, even if it leads to lower profits and fewer jobs | % 13.3 | 50.8 | 24.2 | 10.4 | 0.8 | - | 0.5 |
| c. [PPLENVIR] Ordinary people should do more to protect the environment, even if it means paying higher prices | % 12.6 | 55.0 | 20.5 | 10.7 | 0.7 | - | 0.6 |
| d. [CARALLOW] People should be allowed to use their cars as much as they like, even if it causes damage to the environment | % 3.3 | 15.5 | 37.7 | 34.8 | 8.0 | - | 0.7 |

---

9

B
**B2.18a** [POWER]
Which one of these three possible solutions to Britain's electricity needs would you favour most?
PLEASE TICK **ONE** BOX ONLY    n = 1207

| | % |
|---|---|
| We should make do with the power stations we have already | 53.6 |
| We should build more coal-fuelled power stations | 26.0 |
| We should build more nuclear power stations | 16.1 |
| (DK) | 0.7 |
| (NA) | 3.7 |

b. [NUCPOWER]
As far as **nuclear** power stations are concerned, which of these statements comes closest to your own feelings?
PLEASE TICK **ONE** BOX ONLY

| | % |
|---|---|
| They create very serious risks for the future | 39.8 |
| They create quite serious risks for the future | 28.9 |
| They create only slight risks for the future | 23.9 |
| They create hardly any risks for the future | 5.6 |
| (DK) | 0.5 |
| (NA) | 1.2 |

**B2.19a** [DAMAGE]
Which one of these two statements comes **closest** to your own views?
PLEASE TICK **ONE** BOX ONLY

| | % |
|---|---|
| Industry should be prevented from causing damage to the countryside, even if this sometimes leads to higher prices | 88.0 |
| OR | |
| Industry should keep prices down, even if this sometimes causes damage to the countryside | 10.4 |
| (DK) | 0.3 |
| (NA) | 1.4 |

b. [CTRYJOBS]
And which of these two statements comes **closest** to your own views?
PLEASE TICK **ONE** BOX ONLY

| | % |
|---|---|
| The countryside should be protected from development, even if this sometimes leads to fewer new jobs | 68.0 |
| OR | |
| New jobs should be created, even if this sometimes causes damage to the countryside | 28.3 |
| (DK) | 0.6 |
| (NA) | 3.1 |

**B 2.20** [COUNTRY1, COUNTRY2]
Here are two statements about the countryside. Please tick one box for **each** to show whether you agree or disagree with it.
PLEASE TICK **ONE** BOX ON EACH LINE

| | Agree strongly | Agree | Dis-agree | Disagree strongly | (DK) | (NA) |
|---|---|---|---|---|---|---|
| a. Modern methods of farming have caused damage to the countryside | % 17.2 | 53.4 | 24.3 | 1.9 | 0.4 | 2.8 |
| b. If farmers have to choose between producing more food and looking after the countryside, they should produce more food | % 6.1 | 30.6 | 49.5 | 8.6 | 0.2 | 5.0 |

Please continue ...

11

B

**B2.23a** [WRLDTEMP]
Please tick one box to show which is closest to your views about the following statement:

"Within twenty years, life on earth will be seriously damaged by a rise in the world's temperature"

PLEASE TICK ONE BOX ONLY

| | % |
|---|---|
| It is highly exaggerated | 15.2 |
| It is slightly exaggerated | 45.1 |
| It is more or less true | 38.7 |
| (DK) | 0.5 |
| (NA) | 0.4 |

b. [ENVIRDAM]
And please tick one box to show which is closest to your views about this statement:

"Within twenty years, damage to the environment will be the biggest single problem facing Europe"

PLEASE TICK ONE BOX ONLY

| | % |
|---|---|
| It is highly exaggerated | 13.1 |
| It is slightly exaggerated | 40.4 |
| It is more or less true | 45.6 |
| (DK) | 0.5 |
| (NA) | 0.3 |

**B2.24a** [TOWNTRAN]
Thinking first about towns and cities. If the government had to choose ...

PLEASE TICK ONE BOX

| | % |
|---|---|
| It should improve roads | 43.9 |
| It should improve public transport | 55.1 |
| (DK) | 0.1 |
| (NA) | 0.9 |

b. [CTRYTRAN]
And in country areas, if the government had to choose ...

PLEASE TICK ONE BOX

| | % |
|---|---|
| It should improve roads | 38.2 |
| It should improve public transport | 61.1 |
| (NA) | 0.7 |

n = 1207

---

12

B

**B 2.25** [ENVPRTCT]
On the whole, which of these statements comes closest to your own views?

PLEASE TICK ONE BOX ONLY

| | % |
|---|---|
| It's mainly up to the government to protect the environment – ordinary people can't do much on their own | 46.0 |
| OR It's mainly up to ordinary people to do what they can to protect the environment – the government can do only a limited amount | 51.8 |
| (DK) | 0.2 |
| (NA) | 2.0 |

**B 2.26** Please tick one box for **each** statement below to show how much you agree or disagree with it.

PLEASE TICK **ONE** BOX
ON EACH LINE

| | Agree strongly | Agree | Neither agree nor disagree | Disagree | Disagree strongly | (DK) | (NA) |
|---|---|---|---|---|---|---|---|
| a. [RARPLANT] Too much money is spent trying to protect rare plants and animals | % 3.4 | 13.3 | 40.4 | 35.2 | 6.7 | 0.2 | 0.7 |
| b. [SCNCSOLV] Science can solve environmental problems without any need for people to change their behaviour | % 1.8 | 9.9 | 21.2 | 53.4 | 12.2 | 0.2 | 1.3 |
| c. [CARTAXHI] For the sake of the environment, car users should pay higher taxes | % 4.1 | 21.9 | 25.7 | 39.6 | 7.4 | 0.1 | 1.2 |
| d. [HEATHOME] For the sake of the environment, people should use less heating in their homes | % 1.8 | 17.9 | 25.3 | 47.5 | 6.8 | - | 0.8 |
| e. [MOTORWAY] The government should build more motorways to reduce traffic congestion | % 6.4 | 33.1 | 22.6 | 30.2 | 6.7 | 0.1 | 0.9 |
| f. [POLUTLAW] The laws controlling industrial pollution are already strict enough | % 2.2 | 8.2 | 17.4 | 50.1 | 20.9 | 0.4 | 0.9 |

n = 1207

Please continue ...

13

B

B 2.27   Please tick one box for each statement below to show how much you agree or disagree with it.

n = 1207

PLEASE TICK ONE BOX ON EACH LINE

| | | Agree strongly | Just agree | Neither agree nor disagree | Just disagree | Disagree strongly | (DK) | (NA) |
|---|---|---|---|---|---|---|---|---|
| a. | [EXERCISE] As long as you take enough exercise you can eat whatever foods you want | % | 5.0 | 20.8 | 15.8 | 36.2 | 21.1 | - | 1.1 |
| b. | [HEARTDIS] If heart disease is in your family, there is little you can do to reduce your chances of getting it | % | 3.5 | 9.4 | 12.5 | 38.9 | 34.7 | 0.1 | 0.7 |
| c. | [FOODEXPT] The experts contradict each other over what makes a healthy diet | % | 24.7 | 45.6 | 14.5 | 12.0 | 2.2 | 0.1 | 1.0 |
| d. | [WEIGHT] People worry too much about their weight | % | 11.8 | 40.0 | 22.2 | 20.3 | 4.7 | - | 1.0 |
| e. | [HLTHLUCK] Good health is just a matter of good luck | % | 4.2 | 8.6 | 12.4 | 36.1 | 37.9 | - | 0.8 |

Please continue ...

---

14

B

B2.28   [COPAYPRF, RPAYPRF]
Suppose a large company had to choose between:
    - doing something that improves pay and conditions for its staff,
or - doing something that increases profits.

PLEASE TICK ONE BOX ON EACH LINE

| | | Improve pay and conditions for staff | Increase profits | (DK) | (NA) |
|---|---|---|---|---|---|
| a. | Which choice do you think most large companies would generally make? | % | 13.4 | 84.8 | 0.4 | 1.4 |
| b. | Which choice would you make, if it was up to you to decide? | % | 76.9 | 20.1 | 0.8 | 2.2 |

B2.29   [TUPAYSUR, RPAYSUR]
Now suppose a large trade union had to choose between:
    - doing something that improves an industry's long-term chances of survival,
or - doing something that improves the present pay and conditions of the union's members.

PLEASE TICK ONE BOX ON EACH LINE

| | | Improve long-term chance of survival | Improve present pay and conditions | (DK) | (NA) |
|---|---|---|---|---|---|
| a. | Which choice do you think most large trade unions would generally make? | % | 37.9 | 60.1 | 0.4 | 1.6 |
| b. | Which choice would you make, if it was up to you? | % | 72.8 | 25.1 | 0.4 | 1.8 |

B2.30   [HOPATDOC, RPATDOC]
And suppose a large hospital had to choose between:
    - doing something that makes life a bit easier for patients,
or - doing something that makes life a bit easier for doctors.

PLEASE TICK ONE BOX ON EACH LINE

| | | Make life easier for patients | Make life easier for doctors | (DK) | (NA) |
|---|---|---|---|---|---|
| a. | Which choice do you think most large hospitals would generally make? | % | 52.8 | 44.8 | 0.7 | 1.6 |
| b. | Which choice would you make, if it was up to you? | % | 71.3 | 25.7 | 0.4 | 2.6 |

15

**B**

B2.31 [INFLCON1 - INFLCON6]
Different institutions or groups have a lot of influence over governments; others have less.

From what you know or have heard, how much say do you think each of these groups generally has in what a Conservative government does?

PLEASE TICK ONE BOX ON EACH LINE

|  | A lot of say | Quite a bit of say | Very little say | No say at all | (DK) | (NA) |
|---|---|---|---|---|---|---|
| a. Manufacturing industry | % 15.6 | 44.3 | 33.4 | 3.5 | 0.9 | 2.3 |
| b. The 'City of London' | % 34.7 | 41.9 | 17.2 | 2.4 | 0.9 | 2.9 |
| c. The trade unions | % 6.3 | 19.8 | 51.7 | 18.6 | 0.8 | 2.8 |
| d. The police | % 7.2 | 39.3 | 44.0 | 6.2 | 0.9 | 2.3 |
| e. School-teachers | % 3.7 | 13.4 | 57.9 | 22.0 | 0.7 | 2.3 |
| f. Farmers | % 7.4 | 25.9 | 48.3 | 15.4 | 0.8 | 2.3 |

B2.32 [INFLLAB1 - INFLLAB6]
And how much say do you think each of these groups generally has in what a Labour government does?

PLEASE TICK ONE BOX ON EACH LINE

|  | A lot of say | Quite a bit of say | Very little say | No say at all | (DK) | (NA) |
|---|---|---|---|---|---|---|
| a. Manufacturing industry | % 16.1 | 45.8 | 30.0 | 3.6 | 0.8 | 3.6 |
| b. The 'City of London' | % 9.6 | 40.7 | 39.0 | 5.3 | 1.1 | 4.3 |
| c. The trade unions | % 42.4 | 40.4 | 11.1 | 1.9 | 0.8 | 3.3 |
| d. The police | % 5.3 | 37.4 | 45.6 | 7.1 | 0.8 | 3.8 |
| e. School-teachers | % 9.4 | 37.7 | 39.2 | 9.2 | 0.8 | 3.7 |
| f. Farmers | % 3.4 | 24.5 | 54.6 | 13.1 | 0.8 | 3.6 |

B2.33 [GBDMCRCY]
All in all, how well or badly do you think the system of democracy in Britain works these days?

PLEASE TICK ONE BOX ONLY

%

It works well and needs no changes  7.5
It works well and needs some changes  57.5
It does not work well and needs a lot of changes  25.9
It does not work well and needs to be completely changed  5.9
(Don't know)  0.6
(NA)  2.6

n = 1207

*Please continue ...*

---

16

**B**

B2.34 [VOTEWRTH]
Which of these statements comes closest to your views?

PLEASE TICK ONE BOX ONLY

In a general election:

%

It's not really worth voting  8.1
People should vote only if they care who wins  23.6
It is everyone's duty to vote  67.7
(NA)  0.7

B2.35 Please tick one box for each statement below to show how much you agree or disagree with it.

PLEASE TICK ONE BOX ON EACH LINE

|  | Agree strongly | Agree | Neither agree nor disagree | Disagree | Disagree strongly | (DK) | (NA) |
|---|---|---|---|---|---|---|---|
| a. [UNEMPIN2] Keeping prices, not unemployment, down should be the government's top priority | % 9.8 | 26.8 | 23.1 | 36.1 | 3.1 | - | 1.1 |
| b. [TAXSPND2] The government should put up taxes and spend more on health and education | % 10.0 | 46.5 | 23.6 | 17.1 | 1.8 | - | 1.1 |
| c. [NATNLST2] The government should sell off more nationalised industries | % 3.4 | 21.1 | 26.3 | 36.0 | 12.3 | - | 0.9 |
| d. [INCDIFF2] The government should take steps to reduce differences in income | % 15.3 | 48.2 | 17.9 | 15.0 | 1.8 | 0.2 | 1.3 |
| e. [CIVILRT2] Cutting crime is more important than protecting civil rights | % 9.8 | 33.9 | 33.1 | 19.5 | 2.2 | 0.2 | 1.3 |
| f. [POORHLP2] The poor in Britain get too little help from government | % 21.7 | 43.8 | 17.5 | 14.9 | 1.3 | - | 0.7 |

n = 1207

17

**B**

B2.36 And please tick one box for each statement to show how much you agree or disagree.

PLEASE TICK ONE BOX ON EACH LINE

n = 1207

| | Agree strongly | Agree | Neither agree nor disagree | Disagree | Disagree strongly | (DK) | (NA) |
|---|---|---|---|---|---|---|---|
| a. [TRADVAL2] It is right that young people should question traditional British values | % 9.6 | 59.8 | 20.7 | 7.6 | 1.0 | 0.1 | 1.1 |
| b. [BANXWPT2] For a democracy to work properly no political party should ever be banned | % 7.0 | 49.8 | 23.5 | 16.3 | 2.1 | 0.1 | 1.3 |
| c. [STIFSNT2] British courts generally give sentences that are too harsh | % 3.0 | 5.4 | 19.9 | 58.5 | 11.8 | 0.1 | 1.4 |
| d. [EQUALOP2] In a fair society, some people should have more opportunity than others to get ahead | % 3.0 | 17.1 | 21.0 | 47.7 | 9.6 | 0.2 | 1.3 |
| e. [DEATHAP2] The death penalty is never an appropriate sentence | % 13.2 | 23.8 | 17.4 | 33.8 | 10.3 | 0.1 | 1.3 |
| f. [NTSTRIK2] All workers, even in essential public services, should have the right to strike | % 8.7 | 42.2 | 18.5 | 26.4 | 3.4 | - | 0.8 |
| g. [OBEY2] Schools should teach children to question authority | % 4.2 | 25.5 | 27.3 | 35.6 | 6.3 | 0.1 | 1.1 |
| h. [FREESPC2] Maintaining order in the nation is more important than protecting freedom of speech | % 5.0 | 24.5 | 30.6 | 34.0 | 4.5 | 0.1 | 1.3 |
| i. [WRONGLW2] There are times when people should follow their consciences, even if it means breaking the law | % 6.6 | 37.9 | 19.2 | 31.0 | 3.9 | 0.1 | 1.4 |
| j. [CENSOR2] Censorship of films and magazines has no place in a free society | % 5.7 | 20.0 | 22.3 | 43.0 | 7.6 | 0.1 | 1.2 |

Please continue ...

18

**B**

B2.37 [COUNCIL1 - COUNCIL3] Which of the following statements do you think are generally true and which false?

PLEASE TICK ONE BOX ON EACH LINE

n = 1207

| | True | False | (DK) | (NA) |
|---|---|---|---|---|
| Council tenants pay low rents | % 41.1 | 54.3 | 0.7 | 4.0 |
| Councils give a poor standard of repairs and maintenance | % 60.4 | 36.1 | 0.5 | 3.0 |
| Council estates are generally pleasant places to live | % 31.7 | 63.4 | 0.7 | 4.2 |

B2.38 [RENTBUY] Suppose a newly-married young couple, both with steady jobs, asked your advice about whether to buy or rent a home. If they had the choice, what would you advise them to do?

PLEASE TICK ONE BOX ONLY

| | % |
|---|---|
| To buy a home as soon as possible | 59.8 |
| To wait a bit, then try to buy a home | 31.1 |
| Not to plan to buy a home at all | 2.5 |
| Can't choose | 5.4 |
| (NA) | 1.2 |

## 19

**B**

B2.39 Still thinking of what you might say to this young couple, please tick one box for each statement below to show how much you agree or disagree with it.

PLEASE TICK **ONE** BOX ON EACH LINE

n = 1207

| | Agree strongly | Just agree | Neither agree nor disagree | Just disagree | Disagree strongly | (DK) | (NA) |
|---|---|---|---|---|---|---|---|
| a. [HOMERISK] Owning your home can be a risky investment | % 10.3 | 32.2 | 15.4 | 27.4 | 12.4 | 0.1 | 2.2 |
| b. [BUYCHEAP] Over time, buying a home works out less expensive than paying rent | % 29.9 | 45.7 | 12.2 | 7.6 | 2.1 | 0.3 | 2.1 |
| c. [MOVEHOME] Owning your home makes it easier to move when you want to | % 15.9 | 38.0 | 22.2 | 17.5 | 4.1 | 0.1 | 2.3 |
| d. [MONEYTIE] Owning a home ties up money you may need urgently for other things | % 5.5 | 29.8 | 22.8 | 34.1 | 5.5 | 0.1 | 2.2 |
| e. [FREEDOM] Owning a home gives you the freedom to do what you want | % 21.8 | 54.7 | 10.1 | 9.8 | 1.6 | 0.1 | 1.9 |
| f. [FINBURDN] Owning a home is a big financial burden to repair and maintain | % 13.0 | 43.6 | 22.2 | 16.4 | 2.8 | 0.1 | 2.0 |
| g. [LEAVEFAM] Your own home will be something to leave your family | % 25.7 | 57.3 | 10.1 | 3.5 | 1.3 | 0.1 | 2.0 |
| h. [HOMERESP] Owning a home is just too much of a responsibility | % 3.8 | 6.3 | 21.0 | 43.6 | 22.9 | 0.1 | 2.2 |
| i. [RISKJOB] Owning a home is too much of a risk for couples without secure jobs | % 22.7 | 45.7 | 14.0 | 13.5 | 1.6 | 0.1 | 2.3 |
| j. [WAITFAM] Couples who buy their own homes would be wise to wait before starting a family | % 17.7 | 43.0 | 22.1 | 12.4 | 2.7 | 0.1 | 2.1 |

*Please continue ...*

## 20

**A & B**

n = 2428

Also asked on Version A (Q2.63a,b)

B2.40a [QTIME]
To help us plan better in future, please tell us about **how long** it took you to complete this questionnaire.

PLEASE TICK **ONE** BOX ONLY

| | % |
|---|---|
| Less than 15 minutes | 3.6 |
| Between 15 and 20 minutes | 22.6 |
| Between 21 and 30 minutes | 32.5 |
| Between 31 and 45 minutes | 22.7 |
| Between 46 and 60 minutes | 10.7 |
| Over one hour | 6.9 |
| (NA) | 1.1 |

b. And on what date did you fill in the questionnaire?
PLEASE WRITE IN

[ ] DATE  [ 0 ] MONTH  1991

## THANK YOU VERY MUCH FOR YOUR HELP

Please keep the completed questionnaire for the interviewer if he or she has arranged to call for it. Otherwise, please post it as soon as possible in the pre-paid addressed envelope provided.

SOCIAL & COMMUNITY
**SCPR**
PLANNING RESEARCH

Head Office: 35 NORTHAMPTON SQUARE,
LONDON EC1V 0AX Telephone 071-250 1866

Field and DP Office: BRENTWOOD, ESSEX
Northern Field Office: DARLINGTON, CO. DURHAM

Spring 1991

P1135/Northern Ireland

## NORTHERN IRELAND SOCIAL ATTITUDES:

## 1991 SURVEY

---

Serial
Number

Region   1   2

Area Number

Interviewer
Number   0

Card   02    Version   A = 1
              B = 2
              NI = 3    3

Time interview
started    24 hr clock

OUO
Batch
Code

NI

## SECTION ONE

n = 906
Qs. 1-8

**1a.** [READPAP]
Do you normally read any daily morning newspaper at least 3 times a week?

| | % |
|---|---|
| Yes | 56.4 |
| No | 43.6 |

**b.** [WHPAPER]
IF YES AT a.
Which one do you normally read?
IF MORE THAN ONE ASK: Which one do you read most frequently?
ONE CODE ONLY

| | % |
|---|---|
| (Scottish) Daily Express | 3.6 |
| Daily Mail | 2.9 |
| Daily Mirror/Record | 12.9 |
| Daily Star | 2.7 |
| The Sun | 12.1 |
| Today | 1.6 |
| Daily Telegraph | 1.5 |
| Financial Times | 0.2 |
| The Guardian | 0.5 |
| The Independent | 0.9 |
| The Times | 0.5 |
| Morning Star | - |
| The News Letter | 6.8 |
| The Irish News | 8.3 |
| The Irish Times | 0.2 |
| Other Irish/Northern Irish/Scottish regional or local daily morning paper (WRITE IN:) | 0.3 |
| Other (WRITE IN:) | - |
| More than one paper | 1.4 |

---

NI

n = 906

ASK ALL
CARD A

**2.** Here are some items of government spending. Which of them, if any, would be your highest priority for extra spending? And which next? Please read through the whole list before deciding.
ONE CODE ONLY IN EACH COLUMN

| | [SPEND1] Highest priority % | [SPEND2] Next highest % |
|---|---|---|
| Education | 20.6 | 27.9 |
| Defence | 1.5 | 2.0 |
| Health | 48.5 | 24.5 |
| Housing | 7.4 | 13.3 |
| Public transport | 1.9 | 2.4 |
| Roads | 3.5 | 5.2 |
| Police and prisons | 1.6 | 1.5 |
| Social security benefits | 10.0 | 14.2 |
| Help for industry | 4.1 | 8.0 |
| Overseas aid | 0.5 | 0.6 |
| (None of these) | 0.2 | 0.1 |
| (Don't know) | 0.2 | 0.4 |
| (NA) | - | 0.1 |

CARD B

**3.** Thinking now only of the government's spending on social benefits like those on the card. Which, if any, of these would be your highest priority for extra spending? And which next?
ONE CODE ONLY IN EACH COLUMN

| | [SOCBEN1] Highest priority % | [SOCBEN2] Next highest % |
|---|---|---|
| Retirement pensions | 38.0 | 22.6 |
| Child benefits | 18.2 | 18.7 |
| Benefits for the unemployed | 11.5 | 13.1 |
| Benefits for disabled people | 24.9 | 33.0 |
| Benefits for single parents | 6.4 | 11.4 |
| (None of these) | 0.2 | 0.4 |
| (Don't know) | 0.5 | 0.7 |
| (NA) | 0.2 | 0.1 |

NI
3

n = 906

4. [DOLE]
Opinions differ about the level of benefits for the unemployed. Which of these two statements comes closest to your own view ... READ OUT ...

|  | % |
|---|---|
| ... benefits for the unemployed are <u>too low</u> and cause hardship | 58.6 |
| OR - benefits for the unemployed are <u>too high</u> and discourage people from finding jobs? | 27.3 |
| (Neither) | 5.3 |
| Other (WRITE IN:) | - |
| (Both - some hardship, but because wages are low, no incentive) | 0.5 |
| (Both - some people benefit, others suffer) | 1.8 |
| (About right - in between the two) | 0.8 |
| (Don't know) | 5.4 |
| (NA) | 0.3 |

CARD C

5. [TAXSPEND]
Suppose the government had to choose between the three options on this card. Which do you think it should choose?

|  | % |
|---|---|
| Reduce taxes and spend <u>less</u> on health, education and social benefits | 6.3 |
| Keep taxes and spending on these services at the <u>same</u> level as now | 35.9 |
| Increase taxes and spend <u>more</u> on health, education and social benefits | 55.1 |
| (None) | 0.9 |
| (Don't know) | 1.7 |
| (NA) | 0.1 |

CARD D

6. [NHSSAT]
All in all, how satisfied or dissatisfied would you say you are with the way in which the National Health Service runs nowadays? Choose a phrase from this card.

|  | % |
|---|---|
| Very satisfied | 7.4 |
| Quite satisfied | 37.1 |
| Neither satisfied nor dissatisfied | 20.6 |
| Quite dissatisfied | 20.4 |
| Very dissatisfied | 14.4 |
| (NA) | 0.1 |

NI
4

n = 906

7. CARD D AGAIN
From your own experience, or from what you have heard, please say how satisfied or dissatisfied you are with the way in which each of these parts of the National Health Service runs nowadays.

READ OUT a.-f. BELOW AND
CODE ONE FOR EACH

| | Very satisfied | Quite satisfied | Neither satisfied nor dissatisfied | Quite satisfied dissatisfied | Very dissatisfied | (DK) | (NA) |
|---|---|---|---|---|---|---|---|
| a. [GPSAT] First, local doctors/GPs? % | 34.8 | 50.3 | 6.3 | 6.2 | 2.2 | - | 0.1 |
| b. [DENTSAT] National Health Service dentists? % | 24.8 | 50.5 | 16.2 | 5.0 | 2.6 | 0.7 | 0.2 |
| c. [HVSAT] Health visitors? % | 18.5 | 34.0 | 32.3 | 4.2 | 1.5 | 8.4 | 1.1 |
| d. [DNSAT] District nurses? % | 26.6 | 37.4 | 26.4 | 2.2 | 0.4 | 6.8 | 0.1 |
| e. [INPATSAT] Being in hospital as an inpatient? % | 31.6 | 40.5 | 14.8 | 8.7 | 2.8 | 1.5 | 0.1 |
| f. [OUTPASAT] Attending hospital as an out-patient? % | 16.9 | 41.7 | 15.4 | 17.4 | 6.7 | 1.8 | 0.1 |

8a. [PRIVMED]
Are you covered by a private health insurance scheme, that is an insurance scheme that allows you to get private medical treatment? For example: BUPA and PPP.

|  | % |
|---|---|
| Yes | 9.0 |
| No | 90.9 |
| (NA) | 0.1 |

b. [PRIVPAID]
IF YES AT a.
Does your employer (or your husband's/wife's employer) pay the majority of the cost of membership of this scheme?

|  | % |
|---|---|
| Yes | 4.6 |
| No | 4.2 |
| (Don't know) | 0.2 |
| (NA) | 0.1 |

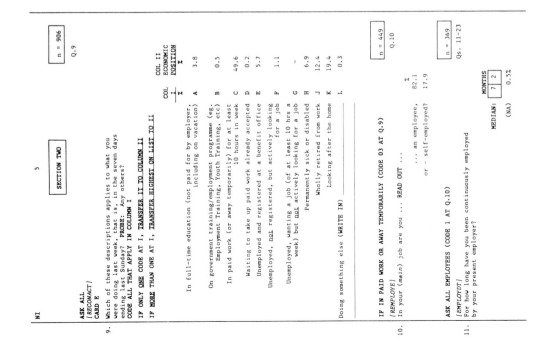

NI    6    n = 369

12. *[ESRJBTIM]*
In your present job, are you working ... READ OUT ...
RESPONDENT'S OWN
DEFINITION

| | % |
|---|---|
| ... full-time, | 82.6 |
| or – part-time? | 17.4 |

13. *[EJBHOURS]*
How many hours a week do you _normally_ work in
your (*main*) job?
(IF RESPONDENT CANNOT ANSWER,
ASK ABOUT LAST WEEK)
    MEDIAN: | 3 | 8 | HOURS

| *[EJBHRCAT]* | % |
|---|---|
| 10-15 hours a week | 2.6 |
| 16-23 hours a week | 8.0 |
| 24-29 hours a week | 4.4 |
| 30 or more hours a week | 84.7 |
| (NA) | 0.3 |

14a. *[WAGENOW]*
How would you describe the wages or salary you
are paid for the job you do – on the low side,
reasonable, or on the high side? IF LOW: Very
low or a bit low?

| | % |
|---|---|
| Very low | 10.3 |
| A bit low | 20.1 |
| Reasonable | 61.9 |
| On the high side | 7.4 |
| | – |
| (NA) | 0.3 |

Other answer (WRITE IN) _____

CARD F
b. *[PAYGAP]*
Thinking of the highest and the lowest paid
people at your place of work, how would you
describe the gap between their pay, as far
as you know? Please choose a phrase from
this card.

| | % |
|---|---|
| Much too big a gap | 17.6 |
| Too big | 28.3 |
| About right | 39.6 |
| Too small | 3.3 |
| Much too small a gap | 0.5 |
| (Don't know) | 9.1 |
| (NA) | 1.6 |

15. *[WAGEXPCT]*
If you stay in this job, would you expect
your wages or salary over the coming year
to ... READ OUT ...

| | % |
|---|---|
| ... rise by _more_ than the cost of living, | 15.1 |
| rise by the _same_ as the cost of living, | 46.7 |
| rise by _less_ than the cost of living, | 31.9 |
| or – _not_ to rise at all? | 4.2 |
| (Will not stay in job) | 0.5 |
| (Don't know) | 1.3 |
| (NA) | 0.3 |

---

NI    5

SECTION TWO    n = 906

ASK ALL
*[RECONACT]*
CARD E
9. Which of these descriptions applies to what you
were doing last week, that is, in the seven days
ending last Sunday? PROBE: Any others?
CODE ALL THAT APPLY IN COLUMN I
IF ONLY _ONE_ CODE AT I, TRANSFER IT TO COLUMN II
IF _MORE_ THAN ONE AT I, _TRANSFER HIGHEST ON LIST TO II_

Q.9

| | COL I % | COL II ECONOMIC POSITION % |
|---|---|---|
| In full-time education (not paid for by employer, including on vacation)   A | | 3.8 |
| On government training/employment programme (eg. Employment Training, Youth Training, etc)   B | | 0.5 |
| In paid work (or away temporarily) for at least 10 hours in week   C | | 49.6 |
| Waiting to take up paid work already accepted   D | | 0.2 |
| Unemployed and registered at a benefit office   E | | 5.7 |
| Unemployed, _not_ registered, but actively looking for a job   F | | 1.1 |
| Unemployed, wanting a job (of at least 10 hrs a week) but _not_ actively looking for a job   G | | – |
| Permanently sick or disabled   H | | 6.9 |
| Wholly retired from work   J | | 12.4 |
| Looking after the home   K | | 19.4 |
| Doing something else (WRITE IN)   L | | 0.3 |

IF IN PAID WORK OR AWAY TEMPORARILY (CODE 03 AT Q.9)
*[REMPLOYE]*    n = 449
10. In your (*main*) job are you ... READ OUT ...

Q.10

| | % |
|---|---|
| ... an employee, | 82.1 |
| or – self-employed? | 17.9 |

ASK ALL EMPLOYEES (CODE 1 AT Q.10)    n = 369
*[EMPLOYDT]*    Qs. 11-23
11. For how long have you been continuously employed
by your present employer?

MEDIAN: | 7 | 2 | MONTHS
    (NA)   0.5%

n = 369

n = 369

NI    7

[NUMEMP]
16. Over the coming year do you expect your workplace to be ... READ OUT ...

| | % |
|---|---|
| ... increasing its number of employees, | 17.0 |
| reducing its number of employees, | 24.0 |
| or - will the number of employees stay about the same? | 57.4 |
| Other answer (WRITE IN) | 0.3 |
| (Don't know) | 1.0 |
| (NA) | 0.3 |

[LEAVEJOB]
17a. Thinking now about your own job. How likely or unlikely is it that you will leave this employer over the next year for any reason? Is it ... READ OUT ...

| | % |
|---|---|
| ... very likely, | 7.8 |
| quite likely, | 11.2 |
| not very likely, | 32.5 |
| or - not at all likely? | 48.2 |
| (NA) | 0.3 |

IF VERY OR QUITE LIKELY AT a.
CARD G
b. Why do you think you will leave? Please choose a phrase from this card or tell me what other reason there is.
CODE ALL THAT APPLY

| | % |
|---|---|
| [WHYGO1] Firm will close down | 1.2 |
| [WHYGO2] I will be declared redundant | 2.3 |
| [WHYGO3] I will reach normal retirement age | 1.6 |
| [WHYGO4] My contract of employment will expire | 2.1 |
| [WHYGO5] I will take early retirement | 0.7 |
| [WHYGO6] I will decide to leave and work for another employer | 8.5 |
| [WHYGO7] I will decide to leave and work for myself, as self-employed | 0.7 |
| [WHYGO10] I will leave to look after home/children/relative | 1.8 |
| [WHYGO8] Other answer (WRITE IN:) | 0.8 |
| (NA) | 0.3 |

ASK ALL EMPLOYEES
[EUNEMP]
18a. During the last five years - that is since March 1986 - have you been unemployed and seeking work for any period?

| | |
|---|---|
| Yes | 18.0 |
| No | 81.7 |
| (NA) | 0.3 |

n = 369

NI    8

[EUNEMPT]
IF YES AT a.
18b. For how many months in total during the last five years?

MEDIAN: 1 1 MONTHS

(NA) 0.5%

ASK ALL EMPLOYEES
[WPUNIONS]
19a. At your place of work are there unions, staff associations, or groups of unions recognised by the management for negotiating pay and conditions of employment?

| | % |
|---|---|
| Yes | 62.1 |
| No | 37.3 |
| (Don't know) | 0.3 |
| (NA) | 0.3 |

[WPUNIONW]
IF YES AT a.
b. On the whole, do you think these unions or staff associations do their job well or not?

| | % |
|---|---|
| Yes | 31.6 |
| No | 28.9 |
| (Don't know) | 1.6 |
| (NA) | 0.7 |

[INDREL]
ASK ALL EMPLOYEES
20a. In general how would you describe relations between management and other employees at your workplace ... READ OUT ...

| | % |
|---|---|
| ... very good, | 30.9 |
| quite good, | 48.6 |
| not very good, | 14.5 |
| or - not at all good? | 5.2 |
| (NA) | 0.8 |

[WORKRUN]
b. And in general, would you say your workplace was ... READ OUT ...

| | % |
|---|---|
| ... very well managed, | 29.8 |
| quite well managed, | 53.0 |
| or - not well managed? | 17.0 |
| (NA) | 0.3 |

Now for some more general questions about your work.
[EMPEARN]
21. For some people their job is simply something they do in order to earn a living. For others it means much more than that. On balance, is your present job ... READ OUT ...

| | % |
|---|---|
| ... just a means of earning a living, | 33.6 |
| or - does it mean much more to you than that? | 66.2 |
| (NA) | 0.3 |

NI    9

**22a.** CARD H
[EWORK1 - EWORK10]
Now I'd like you to look at the statements on the card and tell me which ones best describe your own reasons for working at present. Any others? CODE ALL THAT APPLY IN COL a. IF MORE THAN ONE REASON ASK b. OTHERS GO TO Q.23

**b.** And which one of these would you say is your main reason for working? RECORD IN COL b.

n = 369

| | a. Reasons for working % | b. [EWRKMAIN] Main Reason % |
|---|---|---|
| Working is the normal thing to do | 23.5 | 6.8 |
| Need money for basic essentials such as food, rent or mortgage | 68.1 | 54.2 |
| To earn money to buy extras | 32.6 | 6.1 |
| To earn money of my own | 29.8 | 8.9 |
| For the company of other people | 21.7 | 1.3 |
| I enjoy working | 54.8 | 10.3 |
| To follow my career | 30.9 | 11.2 |
| For a change from my children or housework | 7.8 | 0.7 |
| Other (WRITE IN) | 0.3 | - |
| (Don't know/NA) | 0.3 | 0.5 |

[SAYJOB]
ASK ALL EMPLOYEES
**23a.** Suppose there was going to be some decision made at your place of work that changed the way you do your job. Do you think that you personally would have any say in the decision about the change, or not?

| | % |
|---|---|
| Yes | 42.8 |
| No | 50.5 |
| (It depends/Don't know) | 6.4 |
| (NA) | 0.3 |

[MUCHSAY]
IF YES AT a.
**b.** How much say or chance to influence the decision do you think you would have ... READ OUT ...

| | % |
|---|---|
| ... a great deal, | 8.7 |
| quite a lot, | 15.3 |
| or - just a little? | 18.0 |
| (It depends/Don't know) | 0.8 |
| (NA) | 0.3 |

[MORESAY]
ASK ALL EMPLOYEES
**c.** Do you think you should have more say in decisions affecting your work, or are you satisfied with the way things are?

| | % |
|---|---|
| Should have more say | 43.7 |
| Satisfied with way things are | 55.2 |
| (Don't know) | 0.4 |
| (NA) | 0.7 |

NI    10

n = 190    Qs. 24-25

IF RESPONDENT IS MAN, ASK Q.24
IF RESPONDENT IS WOMAN,SKIP TO Q.26

ASK MALE EMPLOYEES [EWSNEWRK]
**24.** Where you work, are there any women doing the same sort of work as you?

| | % |
|---|---|
| Yes | 40.5 |
| No | 55.8 |
| (Works alone) | - |
| (No-one else doing the same job) | 2.6 |
| (NA) | 0.5 |

[EMSEXWRK]
**25a.** Do you think of your work as ... READ OUT ...

| | % |
|---|---|
| ... mainly men's work, | 33.1 |
| mainly women's work, | - |
| or - work that either men or women do? | 66.3 |
| Other (WRITE IN) | - |
| (Don't know) | - |
| (NA) | 0.5 |

[EWWOMCLD]
IF MAINLY MEN'S WORK (CODE 1 AT a.)
**b.** Do you think that women could do the same sort of work as you?

| | % |
|---|---|
| Yes | 16.8 |
| No | 14.2 |
| (Don't know) | 2.1 |

[EWWOMWLD]
IF YES OR DON'T KNOW AT b.
**c.** Do you think that women would be willing to do the same sort of work as you?

| | % |
|---|---|
| Yes | 7.9 |
| No | 8.9 |
| (Don't know) | - |

n = 129    Qs. 26-27

[EWSMEWRK]
ASK FEMALE EMPLOYEES
**26.** Where you work, are there any men doing the same sort of work as you?

| | % |
|---|---|
| Yes | 51.9 |
| No | 46.9 |
| (Works alone) | - |
| (No-one else doing same job) | - |
| (NA) | 1.1 |

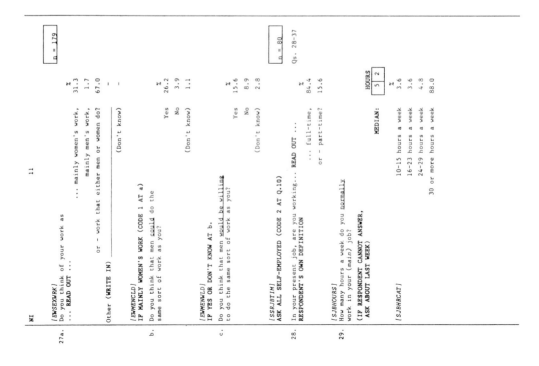

## NI    11

n = 179

**27a.** [EWSEXWRK]
Do you think of your work as
... READ OUT ...

| | % |
|---|---|
| ... mainly women's work, | 31.3 |
| mainly men's work, | 1.7 |
| or - work that either men or women do? | 67.0 |
| Other (WRITE IN) | – |
| (Don't know) | – |

**b.** [EWMENCLD]
IF MAINLY WOMEN'S WORK (CODE 1 AT a)
Do you think that men could do the
same sort of work as you?

| | % |
|---|---|
| Yes | 26.2 |
| No | 3.9 |
| (Don't know) | 1.1 |

**c.** [EWMENWLD]
IF YES OR DON'T KNOW AT b.
Do you think that men would be willing
to do the same sort of work as you?

| | % |
|---|---|
| Yes | 15.6 |
| No | 8.9 |
| (Don't know) | 2.8 |

**28.** [SSRJBTIM]
ASK ALL SELF-EMPLOYED (CODE 2 AT Q.10)    Qs. 28-37
In your present job, are you working... READ OUT ...
RESPONDENT'S OWN DEFINITION

n = 80

| | % |
|---|---|
| ... full-time, | 84.4 |
| or - part-time? | 15.6 |

**29.** [SJBHOURS]
How many hours a week do you normally
work in your (main) job?
(IF RESPONDENT CANNOT ANSWER,
ASK ABOUT LAST WEEK)

MEDIAN:   HOURS   | 5 | 2 |

[SJBHRCAT]

| | % |
|---|---|
| 10-15 hours a week | 3.6 |
| 16-23 hours a week | 3.6 |
| 24-29 hours a week | 4.8 |
| 30 or more hours a week | 88.0 |

## NI    12

n = 80

**30.** [SUNEMP]
During the last five years - that is since March
1986 - have you been unemployed and seeking work
for any period?

| | | % |
|---|---|---|
| | Yes | 11.4 |
| | No | 88.6 |

**31.** [SEMPLEE]
Have you, for any period in the last five years,
worked as an employee as your main job rather
than as self-employed?

| | | % |
|---|---|---|
| | Yes | 10.2 |
| | No | 89.8 |

**32.** [BUSIOK]
Compared with a year ago, would you say
your business is doing ... READ OUT ...

| | % |
|---|---|
| ... very well, | 4.8 |
| quite well, | 25.1 |
| about the same, | 47.3 |
| not very well, | 19.8 |
| or - not at all well? | 1.8 |
| (Business not in existence then) | 1.2 |

**33.** [BUSIFUT]
And over the coming year, do you think
your business will do ... READ OUT ...

| | % |
|---|---|
| ... better, | 27.5 |
| about the same, | 43.7 |
| or - worse than this year? | 25.7 |
| Other (WRITE IN: ) | – |
| (Don't know) | 3.0 |

**34.** [SPARTNRS]
In your work or business, do you have any
partners or other self-employed colleagues?
**NOTE: DOES NOT INCLUDE EMPLOYEES**

| | % |
|---|---|
| Yes, have partner(s) | 37.7 |
| No | 62.3 |

**35.** [SNUMEMP]
And in your work or business do you have
any employees, or not?
**NOTE: FAMILY MEMBERS MAY BE EMPLOYEES
ONLY IF THEY RECEIVE A REGULAR
WAGE OR SALARY**

| | % |
|---|---|
| Yes, has employee(s) | 41.3 |
| No | 58.7 |

NI    14

[WGUNEMP]
ASK ALL ON GOVERNMENT PROGRAMMES OR WAITING TO TAKE UP PAID WORK (CODES 02,04 AT Q.9)

n = 7
Q.39 only

39. During the last five years - that is since March 1986 - have you been unemployed and seeking work for any period?

| | No. |
|---|---|
| Yes | 5 |
| No | 1 |

[JUUNEMP]
ASK ALL UNEMPLOYED (CODES 05,06,07 AT Q.9)

n = 62
Qs. 40-43

40a. In total how many months in the last five years - that is, since March 1986 - have you been unemployed and seeking work?

MEDIAN: | 3 | 0 |  MONTHS

[CURUNEMP]
b. How long has this present period of unemployment and seeking work lasted so far?

MEDIAN: | 2 | 4 |  MONTHS

[JOBQUAL]
41. How confident are you that you will find a job to match your qualifications ... READ OUT ...

| | % |
|---|---|
| ... very confident, | 18.6 |
| quite confident, | 27.9 |
| not very confident, | 31.0 |
| or - not at all confident? | 19.4 |
| (NA) | 3.1 |

[UFINDJOB]
42a. Although it may be difficult to judge, how long from now do you think it will be before you find an acceptable job?

MEDIAN: | 0 | 3 |  MONTHS

| | % |
|---|---|
| Never | 14.7 |
| (Don't know) | 32.6 |
| (NA) | 3.1 |

[UJOBCHNC]
b. Do you think that there is a real chance nowadays that you will get a job in this area, or is there no real chance nowadays?

| | % |
|---|---|
| Real chance | 43.4 |
| No real chance | 52.7 |
| (NA) | 3.9 |

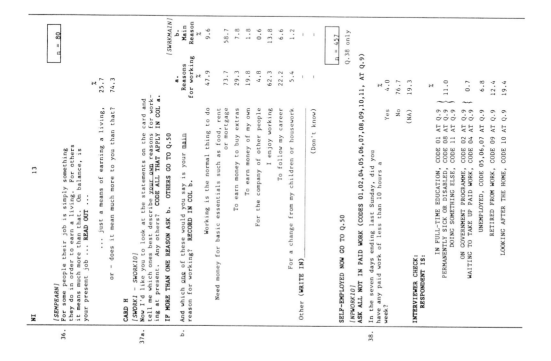

NI    13

[SEMPEARN]
36. For some people their job is simply something they do in order to earn a living. For others it means much more than that. On balance, is your present job ... READ OUT ...

n = 80

| | % |
|---|---|
| ... just a means of earning a living, | 25.7 |
| or - does it mean much more to you than that? | 74.3 |

CARD H
[SWORK1 - SWORK10]
37a. Now I'd like you to look at the statements on the card and tell me which ones best describe your own reasons for working at present. Any others? CODE ALL THAT APPLY IN COL a.
IF MORE THAN ONE REASON ASK b. OTHERS GO TO Q.50

b. And which one of these would you say is your main reason for working? RECORD IN COL b.

[SWRKMAIN]

| | a. Reasons for working % | b. Main Reason % |
|---|---|---|
| Working is the normal thing to do | 47.9 | 9.6 |
| Need money for basic essentials such as food, rent or mortgage | 73.7 | 58.7 |
| To earn money to buy extras | 29.3 | 7.8 |
| To earn money of my own | 19.8 | 1.8 |
| For the company of other people | 4.8 | 0.6 |
| I enjoy working | 62.3 | 13.8 |
| To follow my career | 22.2 | 6.6 |
| For a change from my children or housework | 5.4 | 1.2 |
| Other (WRITE IN) ___ | – | – |
| (Don't know) | – | – |

SELF-EMPLOYED NOW GO TO Q.50

n = 457
Q.38 only

[NPWORK10]
ASK ALL NOT IN PAID WORK (CODES 01,02,04,05,06,07,08,09,10,11, AT Q.9)
38. In the seven days ending last Sunday, did you have any paid work of less than 10 hours a week?

| | % |
|---|---|
| Yes | 4.0 |
| No | 76.7 |
| (NA) | 19.3 |

INTERVIEWER CHECK:
RESPONDENT IS:

| | % |
|---|---|
| IN FULL-TIME EDUCATION, CODE 01 AT Q.9 | |
| PERMANENTLY SICK OR DISABLED, CODE 08 AT Q.9 | 11.0 |
| DOING SOMETHING ELSE, CODE 11 AT Q.9 | |
| ON GOVERNMENT PROGRAMME, CODE 02 AT Q.9 | 0.7 |
| WAITING TO TAKE UP PAID WORK, CODE 04 AT Q.9 | |
| UNEMPLOYED, CODE 05,06,07 AT Q.9 | 6.8 |
| RETIRED FROM WORK, CODE 09 AT Q.9 | 12.4 |
| LOOKING AFTER THE HOME, CODE 10 AT Q.9 | 19.4 |

NI    16

**[RPENINYR]**
46b. Do you expect your state pension in a year's time to purchase more than it does now, less, or about the same?

| | % |
|---|---|
| More | 6.9 |
| Less | 61.8 |
| About the same | 17.6 |
| (Don't know) | 3.4 |
| (NA) | 2.6 |

**[RETIRAG2]**
47. ASK ALL WHOLLY RETIRED
At what age did you retire from work?

MEDIAN: 6 2   YEARS

| | % |
|---|---|
| Never worked | 5.2 |
| (DK/NA) | 2.5 |

n = 176
Qs. 48-49

**[EVERJOB]**
48. ASK ALL LOOKING AFTER HOME (CODE 10 AT Q.9)
Have you, during the last five years, ever had a full- or part-time job of 10 hours or more a week?

| | % |
|---|---|
| Yes | 26.3 |
| No | 73.4 |
| (NA) | 0.3 |

**[FTJOBSER]**
49a. IF NO AT Q.48
How seriously in the past five years have you considered getting a full-time job ... READ OUT ...

PROMPT, IF NECESSARY: FULL-TIME IS 30+ HOURS A WEEK

| | % |
|---|---|
| ... very seriously, | 3.6 |
| quite seriously, | 4.4 |
| not very seriously, | 11.2 |
| or - not at all seriously? | 54.0 |
| (NA) | 0.5 |

**[PTJOBSER]**
b. IF 'NOT VERY' OR 'NOT AT ALL SERIOUSLY' AT a.
How seriously, in the past five years, have you considered getting a part-time job ... READ OUT ...

| | % |
|---|---|
| ... very seriously, | 1.9 |
| quite seriously, | 4.9 |
| not very seriously, | 11.0 |
| or - not at all seriously? | 46.0 |
| (NA) | 1.9 |

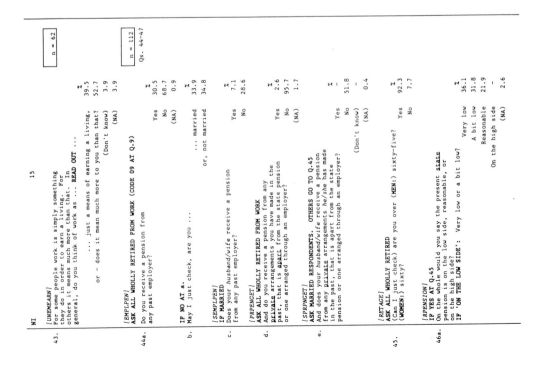

NI    15

**[UNEMEARN]**
43. For some people work is simply something they do in order to earn a living. For others it means much more than that. In general, do you think of work as ... READ OUT ...

| | % |
|---|---|
| ... just a means of earning a living, | 39.5 |
| or - does it mean much more to you than that? | 52.7 |
| (Don't know) | 3.9 |
| (NA) | 3.9 |

n = 62

**[EMPLPEN]**
44a. ASK ALL WHOLLY RETIRED FROM WORK (CODE 09 AT Q.9)
Do you receive a pension from any past employer?

| | % |
|---|---|
| Yes | 30.5 |
| No | 68.7 |
| (NA) | 0.9 |

n = 112
Qs. 44-47

IF NO AT a.
b. May I just check, are you ...

| | % |
|---|---|
| ... married | 33.9 |
| or, not married | 34.8 |

**[SEMPLPEN]**
c. IF MARRIED
Does your husband/wife receive a pension from any past employer?

| | % |
|---|---|
| Yes | 7.1 |
| No | 28.6 |

**[PRPENGET]**
d. ASK ALL WHOLLY RETIRED FROM WORK
And do you receive a pension from any private arrangements you have made in the past, that is apart from the state pension or one arranged through an employer?

| | % |
|---|---|
| Yes | 2.6 |
| No | 95.7 |
| (NA) | 1.7 |

**[SPRPNGET]**
e. ASK MARRIED RESPONDENTS. OTHERS GO TO Q.45
And does your husband/wife receive a pension from any private arrangements he/she has made in the past, that is apart from the state pension or one arranged through an employer?

| | % |
|---|---|
| Yes | - |
| No | 51.8 |
| (Don't know) | - |
| (NA) | 0.4 |

**[RETAGE]**
45. ASK ALL WHOLLY RETIRED
(Can I just check) are you over (MEN:) sixty-five? (WOMEN:) sixty?

| | % |
|---|---|
| Yes | 92.3 |
| No | 7.7 |

**[RPENSION]**
46a. IF YES AT Q.45
On the whole would you say the present state pension is on the low side, reasonable, or on the high side?
IF 'ON THE LOW SIDE': Very low or a bit low?

| | % |
|---|---|
| Very low | 36.1 |
| A bit low | 31.8 |
| Reasonable | 21.9 |
| On the high side | - |
| (NA) | 2.6 |

NI    17    n = 906    Qs. 50-63

---

**SECTION THREE**

ASK ALL
Now a few questions about the UK's relationships with other countries.

[EEC]

50. Do you think the UK should continue to be a member of the European Community or should it withdraw?

|  | % |
|---|---|
| Continue | 82.3 |
| Withdraw | 11.3 |
| (Don't know) | 6.2 |
| (NA) | 0.3 |

[ECGBCLSE]

51. As a member state, would you say that the UK's relationship with the European Community should be ... READ OUT ...

|  | % |
|---|---|
| ... closer, | 41.1 |
| less close, | 6.6 |
| or - is it about right? | 41.1 |
| (Don't know) | 11.0 |
| (NA) | 0.2 |

[ECLNKINF]

52a. Do you think that closer links with the European Community would give the UK ... READ OUT ...

|  | % |
|---|---|
| ... more influence in the world, | 38.9 |
| less influence in the world, | 8.7 |
| or - would it make no difference? | 43.2 |
| (Don't know) | 9.0 |
| (NA) | 0.2 |

b. And would closer links with the European Community make the UK ... READ OUT ...
[ECLNKSTR]

|  | % |
|---|---|
| ... stronger economically, | 50.3 |
| weaker economically, | 10.0 |
| or - would it make no difference? | 27.2 |
| (Don't know) | 12.3 |
| (NA) | 0.2 |

[NIRELAND]

53a. Do you think the long term policy for Northern Ireland should be for it ... READ OUT ...

|  | % |
|---|---|
| ... to remain part of the United Kingdom, | 70.9 |
| or - to reunify with the rest of Ireland? | 22.0 |
| Other answer (WRITE IN:) | 0.9 |
| (To become an independent state) | 0.6 |
| (Up to Irish to decide) | 0.2 |
| (Don't know) | 3.8 |
| (NA) | 1.6 |

[TROOPOUT]

53b. Some people think that government policy towards Northern Ireland should include a complete withdrawal of British troops. Would you personally support or oppose such a policy? PROBE: Strongly or a little?

|  | % |
|---|---|
| Support strongly | 13.7 |
| Support a little | 11.7 |
| Oppose strongly | 52.2 |
| Oppose a little | 15.5 |
| Other answer (WRITE IN:) | 1.1 |
| (Withdraw in the long-term) | 0.5 |
| (Don't know) | 3.6 |
| (NA) | 1.6 |

---

NI    18    n = 906

54. Now I would like to ask you about two economic problems - inflation and unemployment.
[PRICES]
First, inflation: in a year from now, do you expect prices generally to have gone up, to have stayed the same, or to have gone down?

|  | % |
|---|---|
| IF GONE UP OR GONE DOWN: To have gone up by a lot | 46.6 |
| By a lot or a little? To have gone up by a little | 38.3 |
| To have stayed the same | 6.1 |
| To have gone down by a little | 5.8 |
| To have gone down by a lot | 1.9 |
| (Don't know) | 1.1 |
| (NA) | 0.2 |

[UNEMP]

55. Second, unemployment: in a year from now, do you expect unemployment to have gone up, to have stayed the same, or to have gone down?

|  | % |
|---|---|
| IF GONE UP OR GONE DOWN: To have gone up by a lot | 39.4 |
| By a lot or a little? To have gone up by a little | 34.8 |
| To have stayed the same | 14.6 |
| To have gone down by a little | 7.9 |
| To have gone down by a lot | 1.4 |
| (Don't know) | 1.7 |
| (NA) | 0.2 |

[UNEMPINF]

56a. If the government had to choose between keeping down inflation or keeping down unemployment, to which do you think it should give highest priority?

|  | % |
|---|---|
| Keeping down inflation | 37.1 |
| Keeping down unemployment | 60.6 |
| (Both equally) | 0.9 |
| (Don't know) | 1.0 |
| (NA) | 0.5 |

[CONCERN]

b. Which do you think is of the most concern to you and your family ... READ OUT ...

|  | % |
|---|---|
| ... inflation, | 63.0 |
| or - unemployment? | 34.8 |
| Other answer (WRITE IN:) | - |
| (Both equally) | 0.7 |
| (Don't know) | 1.0 |
| (Neither) | 0.2 |
| (NA) | 0.3 |

[INDUSTRY]

57. Looking ahead over the next year, do you think the UK's general industrial performance will improve, stay much the same, or decline?

|  | % |
|---|---|
| IF IMPROVE OR DECLINE: Improve a lot | 3.3 |
| By a lot or a little? Improve a little | 15.0 |
| Stay much the same | 42.6 |
| Decline a little | 24.8 |
| Decline a lot | 8.1 |
| (Don't know) | 6.0 |
| (NA) | 0.2 |

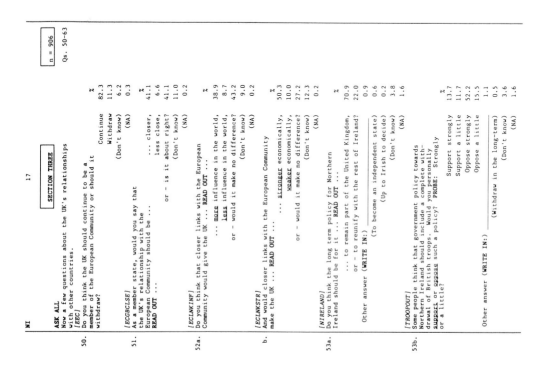

## NI — 20

n = 906

**61a.** [SRINC]
Among which group would you place yourself
... READ OUT ...

|  | % |
|---|---|
| ... high income, | 2.7 |
| middle income, | 46.4 |
| or – low income? | 50.4 |
| (Don't know) | 0.2 |
| (NA) | 0.4 |

**b.** CARD J
[HINCDIFF]
Which of the phrases on this card would you
say comes closest to your feelings about your
household's income these days?

|  | % |
|---|---|
| Living comfortably on present income | 23.0 |
| Coping on present income | 49.8 |
| Finding it difficult on present income | 18.7 |
| Finding it very difficult on present income | 8.3 |
| Other (WRITE IN:) | – |
| (Don't know) | 0.1 |
| (NA) | 0.1 |

**62.** [HINCPAST]
Looking back over the last year or so, would you
say your household's income has ... READ OUT ...

|  | % |
|---|---|
| ... fallen behind prices, | 52.8 |
| kept up with prices, | 39.1 |
| or – gone up by more than prices? | 6.2 |
| (Don't know) | 1.5 |
| (NA) | 0.4 |

**63.** [HINCXPCT]
And looking forward to the year ahead, do you
expect your household's income will ...
READ OUT ...

|  | % |
|---|---|
| ... fall behind prices, | 47.6 |
| keep up with prices, | 41.1 |
| or – go up by more than prices? | 7.3 |
| (Don't know) | 3.5 |
| (NA) | 0.4 |

## NI — 19

n = 906

**58.** Here are a number of policies which might
help the UK's economic problems. As I read
them out, will you tell me whether you would
support such a policy or oppose it?

READ OUT ITEMS a.-j. AND CODE FOR EACH

|  |  | Support | Oppose | (Don't know) | (NA) |
|---|---|---|---|---|---|
| a. | [ECOHELP1] Control of wages by law | 37.1 | 59.8 | 2.9 | 0.3 |
| b. | [ECOHELP2] Control of prices by law | 66.2 | 31.9 | 1.6 | 0.3 |
| c. | [ECOHELP3] Reducing the level of government spending on health and education | 6.7 | 92.0 | 0.5 | 0.8 |
| d. | [ECOHELPC] Government controls to cut down goods from abroad | 66.1 | 30.5 | 2.4 | 1.0 |
| e. | [ECOHELP5] Increasing government subsidies for private industry | 65.9 | 29.6 | 3.8 | 0.7 |
| f. | [ECOHELP7] Reducing government spending on defence | 54.5 | 42.7 | 2.2 | 0.5 |
| g. | [ECOHELP8] Government schemes to encourage job sharing | 79.3 | 17.6 | 2.6 | 0.5 |
| h. | [ECOHELP9] Government to set up construction projects to create more jobs | 90.2 | 8.2 | 1.2 | 0.4 |
| i. | [ECOHELPA] Government action to cut interest rates | 91.8 | 6.0 | 1.6 | 0.6 |
| j. | [ECOHELPB] Government controls on hire purchase and credit | 83.6 | 12.8 | 3.0 | 0.6 |

**59.** [INCOMGAP]
Thinking of income levels generally in the UK today,
would you say that the gap between those with high
incomes and those with low incomes is ... READ OUT ...

|  | % |
|---|---|
| ... too large, | 81.6 |
| about right, | 14.4 |
| or – too small? | 2.2 |
| (Don't know) | 1.1 |
| (NA) | 0.7 |

**60.** CARD I
Generally, how would you describe levels of taxation?

**a.** [TAXHI]
Firstly for those with high incomes? Please choose a phrase from
this card. RECORD ANSWER IN COL a. BELOW

**b.** [TAXMID]
Next for those with middle incomes? Please choose a phrase from
this card. RECORD ANSWER IN COL b. BELOW

**c.** [TAXLOW]
And lastly for those with low incomes? Please choose a phrase from
this card. RECORD ANSWER IN COL c. BELOW

|  | a. High incomes % | b. Middle incomes % | c. Low incomes % |
|---|---|---|---|
| Taxes are: Much too high | 3.7 | 4.1 | 37.0 |
| Too high | 12.0 | 31.0 | 43.4 |
| About right | 30.0 | 56.7 | 15.8 |
| Too low | 37.5 | 5.7 | 1.0 |
| Much too low | 14.0 | 0.6 | 0.9 |
| (Don't know) | 2.4 | 1.6 | 1.7 |
| (NA) | 0.3 | 0.3 | 0.3 |

NI 22

**CARD K**    n = 906

67. From this card, about how often these days do you eat ...

READ OUT a.-f. AND CODE ONE FOR EACH

| | Every day/ nearly every day | At least once a week | At least once a month | Less often | Never | (NA) |
|---|---|---|---|---|---|---|
| a. [FREQMEAT] Red meat like beef, lamb or pork | % 37.8 | 52.5 | 4.2 | 1.1 | 4.3 | 0.1 |
| b. [FREQPOUL] Poultry like chicken or turkey | % 11.9 | 65.2 | 13.9 | 5.6 | 3.2 | 0.1 |
| c. [FREQFISH] Fish of any kind | % 6.5 | 52.3 | 19.0 | 10.7 | 11.4 | 0.1 |
| d. [FREQEGGS] Eggs | % 26.8 | 46.0 | 11.2 | 6.7 | 9.3 | 0.1 |
| e. [FREQCAKE] Biscuits, pastries or cakes | % 60.0 | 22.2 | 6.1 | 6.1 | 5.6 | 0.1 |
| f. [FREQFRUT] Fresh fruit | % 62.1 | 25.4 | 6.7 | 3.7 | 2.0 | 0.1 |

68. Compared with two or three years ago, would you say you are now ...

READ OUT a.-i. AND CODE ONE FOR EACH

| | Yes | No | (Don't know) | (NA) |
|---|---|---|---|---|
| a. [SPREADS] ... using more low fat spreads or soft margarine instead of butter, or not? | % 62.8 | 37.1 | – | 0.2 |
| b. [GRILFOOD] ... eating more grilled food instead of fried food, or not? | % 64.2 | 35.6 | 0.2 | 0.1 |
| c. [FISHPOUL] ... eating more fish and poultry instead of red meat, or not? | % 42.2 | 56.9 | 0.4 | 0.5 |
| d. [SKIMMILK] ... drinking or using more semi-skimmed or skimmed milk instead of full cream milk, or not? | % 42.9 | 56.4 | 0.6 | 0.2 |
| e. [BREAD] ... eating more wholemeal bread instead of white bread, or not? | % 54.8 | 44.4 | 0.6 | 0.2 |
| f. [BAKEDPOT] ... eating more boiled or baked potatoes instead of chips or roast potatoes, or not? | % 60.6 | 39.1 | 0.2 | 0.1 |

And compared with two or three years ago, would you say you are now ...

| | Yes | No | (Don't know) | (NA) |
|---|---|---|---|---|
| g. [HIFIBRE] ... eating more high fibre foods like fresh fruit and vegetables and high fibre cereals, or not? | % 58.0 | 41.9 | 0.1 | 0.1 |
| h. [SALTFOOD] ... cutting down on salty food, or not? | % 42.3 | 57.4 | 0.3 | 0.1 |
| i. [XERCISE] ... taking more exercise, or not? | % 33.8 | 65.6 | 0.6 | 0.1 |

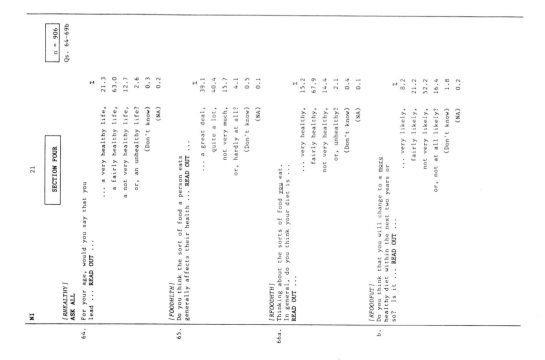

NI 21

**SECTION FOUR**    n = 906    Qs. 64-69b

64. [RHEALTHY] ASK ALL

For your age, would you say that you lead ... READ OUT ...

| | % |
|---|---|
| ... a very healthy life, | 21.3 |
| a fairly healthy life, | 63.0 |
| a not very healthy life, | 12.7 |
| or, an unhealthy life? | 2.6 |
| (Don't know) | 0.3 |
| (NA) | 0.2 |

65. [FOODHLTH]

Do you think the sort of food a person eats generally affects their health ... READ OUT ...

| | % |
|---|---|
| ... a great deal, | 39.1 |
| quite a lot, | 40.4 |
| not very much, | 15.7 |
| or, hardly at all? | 4.1 |
| (Don't know) | 0.5 |
| (NA) | 0.1 |

66a. [RFOODHTH]

Thinking about the sorts of food you eat. In general, do you think your diet is ... READ OUT ...

| | % |
|---|---|
| ... very healthy, | 15.2 |
| fairly healthy, | 67.9 |
| not very healthy, | 14.4 |
| or, unhealthy? | 2.1 |
| (Don't know) | 0.4 |
| (NA) | 0.1 |

b. [RFOODFUT]

Do you think that you will change to a more healthy diet within the next two years or so? Is it ... READ OUT ...

| | % |
|---|---|
| ... very likely, | 8.2 |
| fairly likely, | 21.2 |
| not very likely, | 52.2 |
| or, not at all likely? | 16.4 |
| (Don't know) | 1.8 |
| (NA) | 0.2 |

NI
23

[FAGSNOW]
69a. Do you smoke cigarettes at all nowadays?

n = 906
Qs. 69a.-b.

|  | % |
|---|---|
| Yes | 34.2 |
| No | 65.8 |

IF 'NO' AT a.
[PIPCGNOW]
b. Do you smoke a pipe or cigars at all nowadays?

|  | % |
|---|---|
| Yes | 3.0 |
| No | 62.7 |
| (NA) | 0.1 |

IF 'YES' AT a.
[SMOKDAY]
c. About how many cigarettes a day do you usually smoke?

n = 338
Qs. 69c.-71

MEDIAN: 0 1 5

|  | % |
|---|---|
| Less than one | 2.8 |
| Can't say | 0.2 |
| (NA) | 0.2 |

[SMOKMUCH]
ALL SMOKERS ('YES' AT a. OR b.)
d. Would you describe yourself as ... READ OUT ...

|  | % |
|---|---|
| ... a light smoker, | 32.1 |
| a moderate smoker, | 46.5 |
| a fairly heavy smoker, | 15.3 |
| or, a heavy smoker? | 5.8 |
| (Don't know) | 0.1 |
| (NA) | 0.1 |

[SMOKMORE]
70. Compared with two or three years ago, would you say you are now smoking ... READ OUT ...

|  | % |
|---|---|
| ... more, | 19.5 |
| less, | 26.8 |
| or, about the same? | 53.5 |
| (NA) | 0.1 |

[TRYSTPSM]
71. How likely is it that you will give up smoking within the next two years or so? Is it ... READ OUT ...

|  | % |
|---|---|
| ... very likely, | 17.3 |
| fairly likely, | 29.4 |
| not very likely, | 26.7 |
| or, not at all likely? | 23.8 |
| (Don't know) | 2.7 |
| (NA) | 0.1 |

NI
24

[DRINKNOW]
ASK ALL
72. On average, how often do you drink alcohol? Is it ... READ OUT ...

n = 906
Q.72 only

|  | % |
|---|---|
| ... every day or nearly every day, | 3.1 |
| several days a week, | 8.8 |
| at least once a week, | 24.5 |
| less than once a week, | 30.2 |
| or, never? | 31.2 |
| (Varies a great deal) | 2.2 |

[DRINKMCH]
ALL WHO EVER DRINK
73a. Would you describe yourself as ... READ OUT

n = 624
Q.73 only

|  | % |
|---|---|
| ... a light drinker, | 70.0 |
| a moderate drinker, | 26.5 |
| a fairly heavy drinker, | 2.2 |
| or, a heavy drinker? | 1.0 |
| (Don't know) | 0.3 |

[DRINKMOR]
b. Compared with two or three years ago, would you say you are now drinking ... READ OUT ...

|  | % |
|---|---|
| ... more, | 9.0 |
| less, | 34.9 |
| or, about the same? | 55.9 |
| (Don't know) | 0.2 |

[DRINKFUT]
c. In two or three years' time, do you think you will be drinking ... READ OUT ...

|  | % |
|---|---|
| ... more, | 1.9 |
| less, | 17.3 |
| or, about the same as now? | 79.2 |
| (Don't know) | 1.7 |

NI   25

n = 906
Qs. 74-75

[EXERHLTH]
ASK ALL
74. Do you think the amount of exercise a person takes generally affects their health ... READ OUT ...

|  | % |
|---|---|
| ... a great deal, | 43.5 |
| quite a bit, | 42.2 |
| not very much, | 9.7 |
| or, hardly at all? | 3.7 |
| (Don't know) | 0.9 |

[RACTIVE]
CARD L
75. Using this card, how physically active would you say you are, compared with people of your age?

|  | % |
|---|---|
| Much more active than most | 13.5 |
| A bit more active | 20.6 |
| About average | 45.6 |
| A bit less active | 14.5 |
| Much less active than most | 5.2 |
| (Housebound) | 0.5 |
| (Don't know) | 0.1 |

NI   26

n = 906
Qs. 76-97

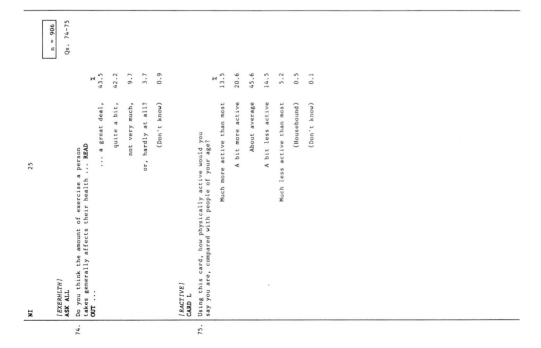

## SECTION FIVE

Now I would like to ask some questions about religious prejudice against both Catholics and Protestants in Northern Ireland.

[PREJRC]
76. First thinking of Catholics - do you think there is a lot of prejudice against them in Northern Ireland nowadays, a little, or hardly any?

|  | % |
|---|---|
| A lot | 28.4 |
| A little | 45.6 |
| Hardly any | 21.7 |
| (Don't know) | 3.0 |
| (NA) | 1.2 |

[PREJPROT]
77. And now, thinking of Protestants - do you think there is a lot of prejudice against them in Northern Ireland nowadays, a little, or hardly any?

|  | % |
|---|---|
| A lot | 18.7 |
| A little | 50.2 |
| Hardly any | 26.6 |
| (Don't know) | 3.1 |
| (NA) | 1.3 |

[SRRLPREJ]
78. How would you describe yourself ... READ OUT ...

|  | % |
|---|---|
| ... as very prejudiced against people of other religions, | 1.0 |
| a little prejudiced, | 15.7 |
| or, not prejudiced at all? | 81.8 |
| (Don't know) | 0.3 |
| (NA) | 0.1 |
| Other answer (WRITE IN) | 1.2 |

[RLRELAGO]
79a. What about relations between Protestants and Catholics? Would you say they are better than they were 5 years ago, worse, or about the same now as then?

IF 'IT DEPENDS', PROBE BEFORE CODING

|  | % |
|---|---|
| Better | 28.7 |
| Worse | 15.2 |
| About the same | 52.2 |
| (Don't know) | 0.7 |
| Other answer (WRITE IN) | 2.7 |
| (NA) | 0.6 |

## NI 27

n = 906

**79b.** [RLRELFUT]
And what about in 5 years time? Do you think relations between Protestants and Catholics will be better than now, worse than now, or about the same as now?
IF 'IT DEPENDS', PROBE BEFORE CODING

|  | % |
|---|---|
| Better than now | 33.5 |
| Worse than now | 8.3 |
| About the same | 52.1 |
| Other answer (WRITE IN) | 0.1 |
| (Don't know) | 5.5 |
| (NA) | 0.5 |

**c.** [RELGALWY]
Do you think that religion will always make a difference to the way people feel about each other in Northern Ireland?

|  | % |
|---|---|
| Yes | 82.6 |
| No | 12.2 |
| Other answer (WRITE IN) | 0.5 |
| (Don't know) | 3.5 |
| (NA) | 1.2 |

**80a.** [FRENDRLG]
CARD M
About how many of your friends would you say are the same religion as you - that is, Protestant or Catholic? Please choose an answer from this card.
PROBE AS NECESSARY: As far as you know?

|  | % |
|---|---|
| All | 15.9 |
| Most | 46.0 |
| Half | 28.9 |
| Less than half | 7.1 |
| None | 0.6 |
| (Don't know) |  |
| (NA) | 1.0 |

**b.** [RELATRLG]
CARD M AGAIN
What about your relatives, including relatives by marriage?

|  | % |
|---|---|
| All | 49.5 |
| Most | 33.1 |
| Half | 8.6 |
| Less than half | 6.8 |
| None | 0.5 |
| (Don't know) | 0.5 |
| (NA) | 1.0 |

**c.** [NEIGHRLG]
CARD M AGAIN
And what about your neighbours?
PROBE AS NECESSARY: As far as you know?

|  | % |
|---|---|
| All | 32.9 |
| Most | 30.1 |
| Half | 20.3 |
| Less than half | 9.5 |
| None | 0.9 |
| (Don't know) | 5.5 |
| (NA) | 0.7 |

## NI 28

CARD N

**81.** For each of the next questions, please use this card to say whether you think Catholics are treated better than Protestants in Northern Ireland, or whether Protestants are treated better than Catholics, or whether both are treated equally.
READ OUT a.-j. AND CODE ONE FOR EACH

n = 906

|  | Catholics treated much better | Catholics treated a bit better | Both treated equally | Protestants treated a bit better | Protestants treated much better | (It depends/ Don't know/ Can't say) | (NA) |
|---|---|---|---|---|---|---|---|
| **a.** [NHSRLGPJ] First, the National Health Service in Northern Ireland. How does it treat Catholic and Protestant patients? % | 1.6 | 2.1 | 88.9 | 1.2 | 0.4 | 4.6 | 1.2 |
| **b.** [NIHRLGPJ] What about the Northern Ireland Housing Executive - how does it treat Catholics and Protestants who apply for a home? % | 3.7 | 8.7 | 63.6 | 6.2 | 1.1 | 15.6 | 1.1 |
| **c.** [DCRLGPJ] What about your local district council - how does it treat Catholics and Protestants who apply for jobs? % | 1.6 | 5.2 | 51.0 | 17.1 | 3.2 | 20.9 | 1.1 |
| **d.** [STRRLGPJ] And what about central government in Stormont - how does it treat Catholics and Protestants who apply for jobs? % | 1.6 | 9.6 | 54.3 | 11.9 | 4.0 | 17.5 | 1.1 |
| **e.** [GSURLGPJ] What about government programmes for the unemployed - how do they treat Catholics and Protestants who apply for places? % | 1.1 | 7.8 | 70.5 | 3.2 | 0.4 | 15.7 | 1.2 |
| **f.** [RUCRLGPJ] And the RUC - how do they treat Catholic and Protestant members of the public? % | 0.3 | 1.7 | 57.0 | 19.7 | 11.6 | 8.5 | 1.2 |
| **g.** [ARMRLGPJ] What about the army - how do they treat Catholic and Protestant members of the public? % | 0.2 | 1.0 | 56.3 | 18.9 | 9.7 | 12.8 | 1.1 |
| **h.** [UDRRLGPJ] And the Ulster Defence Regiment - how do they treat Catholic and Protestant members of the public? % | 0.2 | 0.5 | 41.8 | 26.0 | 17.1 | 13.3 | 1.1 |
| **i.** [NTRRLGPJ] And the courts - how do they treat Catholics and Protestants accused of committing non-terrorist offences? % | 0.6 | 1.6 | 84.4 | 3.7 | 0.7 | 7.9 | 1.1 |
| **j.** [TERRLGPJ] And how do the courts treat Catholics and Protestants accused of committing terrorist offences? % | 1.1 | 4.7 | 69.4 | 8.1 | 6.4 | 8.8 | 1.4 |

NI    29

**82a.** [MXRLGNGH]
If you had a choice, would you prefer to live in a neighbourhood with people of only your own religion, or in a mixed-religion neighbourhood?

PROBE IF NECESSARY: Say if you were moving ...

n = 906

|  | % |
|---|---|
| Own religion only | 23.0 |
| Mixed-religion neighbourhood | 69.9 |
| (Don't know) | 6.1 |
| (NA) | 1.0 |

**b.** [MXRLGWRK]
And if you were working and had to change your job, would you prefer a workplace with people of only your own religion, or a mixed-religion workplace?

PROBE IF NECESSARY: Say if you did have a job ...

|  | % |
|---|---|
| Own religion only | 8.1 |
| Mixed-religion workplace | 86.5 |
| (Don't know) | 4.3 |
| (NA) | 1.1 |

**c.** [OWNMXSCH]
And if you were deciding where to send your children to school, would you prefer a school with children of only your own religion, or a mixed-religion school?

PROBE IF NECESSARY: Say if you did have school-age children ...

|  | % |
|---|---|
| Own religion only | 41.4 |
| Mixed-religion school | 52.2 |
| (Don't know) | 5.5 |
| (NA) | 1.0 |

**83a.** [JBRLGCH1]
On the whole, do you think the Protestants and Catholics in Northern Ireland who apply for the same jobs have the same chance of getting a job or are their chances of getting a job different?

IF 'IT DEPENDS': On the whole ...

|  | % |
|---|---|
| Same chance | 49.4 |
| Different chance | 41.1 |
| (Don't know/Can't say) | 8.5 |
| (NA) | 0.9 |

**b.** [JBRLGCH2]
IF 'DIFFERENT' OR 'DON'T KNOW' AT a.
Which group is more likely to get a job - Protestants or Catholics?

IF 'IT DEPENDS': On the whole ...

|  | % |
|---|---|
| Protestants | 28.0 |
| Catholics | 11.9 |
| (Don't know) | 7.4 |
| (NA) | 3.3 |

NI    30

n = 906

**83c.** [JOBRLGCH]
Are they much more likely or just a bit more likely to get a job?

|  |  | % |
|---|---|---|
| Protestants: | much more | 8.5 |
|  | bit more | 19.2 |
|  | (DK how much more) | 0.3 |
| Catholics: | much more | 3.6 |
|  | bit more | 7.5 |
|  | (DK how much more) | 0.8 |
|  | (Don't know) | 7.4 |
|  | (NA) | 3.3 |

**d.** [JOBRLGSH]
ASK ALL
And do you think Protestants and Catholics in Northern Ireland who apply for the same jobs should have the same chance of getting a job or should Protestants have a better chance, or should Catholics have a better chance?

|  | % |
|---|---|
| Same chance | 94.9 |
| Protestants better | 2.8 |
| Catholics better | 0.2 |
| (Don't know/Can't say) | 1.0 |
| (NA) | 1.1 |

**84.** Now I'm going to ask separately about employment chances of Protestants and Catholics.
[PROTJOB]
Some people think that many employers are more likely to give jobs to Protestants than to Catholics. Do you think this happens ... READ OUT ...

|  | % |
|---|---|
| ... a lot, | 18.8 |
| IF 'IT DEPENDS': In general, what would you say?   a little, | 50.3 |
| or, hardly at all? | 23.5 |
| (Don't know) | 5.8 |
| (NA) | 1.5 |

**85.** [RCJOB]
Some people think that many employers are more likely to give jobs to Catholics than to Protestants. Do you think this happens ... READ OUT ...

|  | % |
|---|---|
| ... a lot, | 11.6 |
| IF 'IT DEPENDS': In general, what would you say?   a little, | 54.6 |
| or, hardly at all? | 26.2 |
| (Don't know) | 6.2 |
| (NA) | 1.5 |

NI
31

n = 906

**86a.** [FREMPLAW - Q.86 a.& b.]
Do you generally support or oppose the Fair
Employment law in Northern Ireland, that is,
the law which requires employers to keep records
on the religion of their employees and make sure
there is no discrimination?

|  | % |
|---|---|
| Support | 71.7 |
| Oppose | 23.0 |
| (Don't know/Can't say) | 4.6 |
| (NA) | 0.7 |

**b.** IF SUPPORT OR OPPOSE AT a.
Do you support/oppose it strongly, or
just a bit?

|  | % |
|---|---|
| Support strongly | 45.5 |
| Support a bit | 26.0 |
| Support (unspecified) | 0.2 |
| Oppose a bit | 9.6 |
| Oppose strongly | 13.3 |
| Oppose (unspecified) | 0.1 |

[GOVMXSCH]
ASK ALL
**87.** Thinking about education ...

First, about mixed or integrated schooling - that
is, schools with fairly large numbers of both
Catholic and Protestant children: do you think
the government should encourage mixed schooling,
discourage mixed schooling or leave things as they are?

|  | % |
|---|---|
| Encourage it | 62.7 |
| Discourage it | 4.3 |
| Leave things as they are | 31.8 |
| (Don't know) | 0.4 |
| (NA) | 0.7 |

---

NI
32

n = 906

CARD O
**88.** All pupils in state secondary schools study certain subjects -
like English and maths. For each subject I read out, please
tell me whether you agree or disagree that all secondary
school pupils should have to study it ...
READ a.-g. AND CODE ONE FOR EACH

|  | Strongly agree | Agree | Neither agree nor disagree | Disagree | Strongly disagree | (Don't know) | (NA) |
|---|---|---|---|---|---|---|---|
| **a.** [NIHISTRY] ... the history of Northern Ireland? | % 24.5 | 55.8 | 8.0 | 9.7 | 0.9 | 0.6 | 0.5 |
| **b.** [BHISTORY] ... British history? | % 19.8 | 57.8 | 9.8 | 10.6 | 0.7 | 0.5 | 0.7 |
| **c.** [ERHISTRY] ...the history of the Republic of Ireland? | % 14.4 | 48.8 | 13.4 | 19.2 | 2.8 | 1.1 | 0.5 |
| **d.** [IRSHLANG] ... Irish language and culture? | % 7.4 | 27.4 | 17.8 | 36.3 | 9.5 | 1.1 | 0.5 |
| **e.** [PROTRELG] ... Protestant religious beliefs? | % 9.7 | 41.4 | 16.5 | 27.6 | 3.0 | 1.2 | 0.5 |
| **f.** [RCRELG] ... Catholic religious beliefs? | % 7.4 | 37.6 | 17.9 | 30.8 | 4.9 | 0.9 | 0.5 |
| **g.** [NONDRELG] religious beliefs in general - not specifically Catholic or Protestant? | % 11.4 | 61.6 | 10.1 | 12.2 | 3.2 | 1.1 | 0.5 |

CARD P
**89.** Do you think the government and public bodies
should or should not ...
READ OUT a. TO d.
AND CODE ONE FOR EACH

|  | Definitely should | Probably should | Probably should not | Definitely should not | (Don't know) | (NA) |
|---|---|---|---|---|---|---|
| **a.** [CHRLGRSP] Do more to teach Catholic and Protestant children greater respect for each other? | % 71.5 | 24.8 | 1.9 | 0.9 | 0.3 | 0.7 |
| **b.** [INTEGHSE] Do more to create integrated housing? | % 46.9 | 37.6 | 9.8 | 2.6 | 2.4 | 0.7 |
| **c.** [BTRCOMRL] Do more to create better community relations generally? | % 64.9 | 30.2 | 2.6 | 0.3 | 1.3 | 0.7 |
| **d.** [INTEGWRK] Do more to create integrated workplaces? | % 58.8 | 32.9 | 4.7 | 1.8 | 1.1 | 0.7 |

NI 33

CARD Q

90. For each of the following, please say how active you think each should be in trying to improve relations between the communities in Northern Ireland.

READ OUT a.-d. AND CODE ONE FOR EACH

n = 906

| | Much more active than now | A little more active than now | About the same as now | A little less active than now | Much less active than now | (Don't know) | (NA) |
|---|---|---|---|---|---|---|---|
| [GBIMPNI] a. The British government | % 47.6 | 27.6 | 19.9 | 2.8 | 0.3 | 0.5 | 1.2 |
| [IRIMPNI] b. The government of the Irish Republic | % 39.9 | 23.7 | 16.7 | 7.0 | 9.4 | 2.1 | 1.3 |
| [UIMPNI] c. Unionist politicians | % 48.8 | 27.5 | 14.8 | 4.7 | 1.0 | 2.0 | 1.2 |
| [NATIMPNI] d. Nationalist politicians | % 46.5 | 24.2 | 15.5 | 6.4 | 3.9 | 2.4 | 1.2 |

91. Now some questions about crime and the police - some about sectarian crime - by this I mean crime directly to do with the Troubles - and some about non-sectarian crime.
[RUCNTRCR]
First, from what you know or have heard, would you say the RUC do a good job or a bad job in controlling non-sectarian crime - crime not to do with the Troubles?
IF GOOD OR BAD: Very good/bad or fairly good/bad?

|  | % |
|---|---|
| Very good | 27.6 |
| Fairly good | 55.6 |
| Fairly bad | 8.9 |
| Very bad | 4.9 |
| (Don't know) | 1.7 |
| (NA) | 1.2 |

[RUCTERCR]
92. And from what you know or have heard, would you say the RUC do a good job or a bad job in controlling sectarian crime?
IF GOOD OR BAD: Very good/bad or fairly good/bad?

|  | % |
|---|---|
| Very good | 20.0 |
| Fairly good | 46.5 |
| Fairly bad | 17.4 |
| Very bad | 11.0 |
| (Don't know) | 3.8 |
| (NA) | 1.2 |

---

NI 34

n = 906

93. There are a number of different security operations in use as a result of the Troubles. I would like to ask your views about a few of them.
[VEHCHECK]
a. First, vehicle check points, where cars are stopped for random or routine search. Do you think they are used ... READ OUT ...

|  | % |
|---|---|
| ... too much, | 22.3 |
| about the right amount, | 48.4 |
| or, too little? | 24.7 |
| (Don't know) | 3.6 |
| (NA) | 1.0 |

[PEDSERCH]
b. And what about random searches of pedestrians - are they used ... READ OUT ...

|  | % |
|---|---|
| ... too much, | 20.0 |
| about the right amount, | 39.1 |
| or, too little? | 24.8 |
| (Don't know) | 15.0 |
| (NA) | 1.0 |

[HSESERCH]
c. And what about house searches - are they used ... READ OUT ...

|  | % |
|---|---|
| ... too much, | 18.0 |
| about the right amount, | 40.5 |
| or, too little? | 17.2 |
| (Don't know) | 23.3 |
| (NA) | 1.1 |

[RCMARCH]
d. And what about controls on Catholic protest marches and demonstrations - are they used ... READ OUT ...

|  | % |
|---|---|
| ... too much, | 19.3 |
| about the right amount, | 53.7 |
| or, too little? | 17.0 |
| (Don't know) | 8.9 |
| (NA) | 1.0 |

[PRTMARCH]
e. And what about controls on Protestant protest marches and demonstrations - are they used ... READ OUT ...

|  | % |
|---|---|
| ... too much, | 8.1 |
| about the right amount, | 62.3 |
| or, too little? | 19.6 |
| (Don't know) | 8.8 |
| (NA) | 1.2 |

NI    35     n = 906

94a. *[NISUPPTY]*
Generally speaking, do you think of yourself as a supporter of any one political party?

|  |  |
|---|---|
|  | % |
| Yes | 30.1 |
| No | 69.3 |
| (NA) | 0.6 |

*[NICLSPTY]*
**IF NO AT a.**
b. Do you think of yourself as a little closer to one political party than to the others?

|  |  |
|---|---|
|  | % |
| Yes | 25.1 |
| No | 43.6 |
| (NA) | 1.2 |

c. If there were a general election tomorrow, which political party do you think you would be most likely to support? **CODE ONE ONLY UNDER c & d.**

**IF YES AT a. OR b.**
d. Which one? **CODE ONE ONLY UNDER c & d.**

**IF MAINLAND PARTY NAMED AT c. OR d.**
e. If there were a general election in which only Northern Ireland parties were standing, which one do you think you would be most likely to support? **CODE ONE ONLY UNDER e.**

|  | *[NIPTYID1]* c. & d. | *[NIPTYID3]* e. |
|---|---|---|
|  | % | % |
| Conservative | 13.4 | |
| Labour | 6.8 | |
| Liberal Democrat/Liberal/SLD | 1.1 | |
| Alliance (NI) | 7.0 | 9.8 |
| DUP/Democratic Unionist Party | 5.9 | 8.2 |
| OUP/Official Unionist Party/Ulster Unionist Party | 23.4 | 29.8 |
| Other Unionist | 0.9 | 1.5 |
| Sinn Fein | 3.6 | 3.7 |
| SDLP | 13.9 | 17.8 |
| Workers Party | 0.8 | 1.5 |
| Campaign for Equal Citizenship | 0.6 | 0.8 |
| Green Party | 1.3 | 0.7 |
| Other Party (**WRITE IN**) | 0.1 | 0.2 |
| Other answer (**WRITE IN**) | 0.5 | 0.9 |
| None | 14.6 | 16.9 |
| Refused/unwilling to say | 5.2 | 5.4 |
| (Don't now/Undecided) | 0.1 | 0.5 |
| (NA) | 1.0 | 2.3 |

**MAINLAND PARTIES** (Conservative, Labour, Liberal Democrat/Liberal/SLD)

---

NI    36     n = 906

94f. *[NIIDSTRN]*
**IF ANY NORTHERN IRELAND PARTY CODED AT c. & d. OR e.**
Would you call yourself very strong ... (**QUOTE PARTY NAMED**) ... fairly strong, or not very strong?

|  |  |
|---|---|
|  | % |
| Very strong | 6.3 |
| Fairly strong | 26.0 |
| Not very strong | 41.1 |
| (Don't know) | 0.2 |
| (NA) | 4.1 |

*[NINATID]*
**ASK ALL.**
**CARD R**
95a. Which of these best describes the way you usually think of yourself?

|  |  |
|---|---|
|  | % |
| British | 43.3 |
| Irish | 24.2 |
| Ulster | 10.6 |
| Northern Irish | 18.4 |
| (Sometimes British, sometimes Irish) | 1.9 |
| Other (**WRITE IN**) _____ | 0.5 |
| (NA) | 1.0 |

*[BRTIRSDE]*
b. When there is an argument between Britain and the Republic of Ireland, do you generally find yourself on the side of the British or of the Irish government?
**IF 'IT DEPENDS', PROBE BEFORE CODING**

|  |  |
|---|---|
|  | % |
| Generally British government | 56.1 |
| Generally Irish government | 13.5 |
| It depends (**AFTER PROBE**) | 15.5 |
| (Neither) | 8.9 |
| (Don't know/Can't say) | 5.1 |
| (NA) | 1.0 |

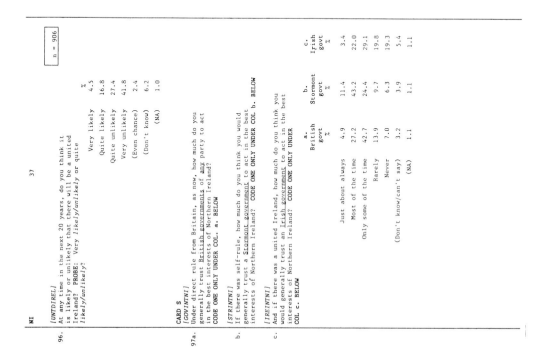

NI 38

n = 906
Qs. 98-104

## SECTION SIX

98. **[DIVORCE]**
Do you think that divorce in Northern Ireland should be ... **READ OUT** ...

|  | % |
|---|---|
| ... easier to obtain than it is now, | 14.6 |
| more difficult, | 27.0 |
| or, should things remain as they are? | 50.9 |
| (Don't know) | 7.2 |
| (NA) | 0.3 |

99. **[SEXLAW]**
There is a law in the UK against sex discrimination, that is against giving unfair preference to men - or to women - in employment, pay and so on. Do you generally support or oppose the idea of a law for this purpose?

|  | % |
|---|---|
| Support | 88.3 |
| Oppose | 10.3 |
| (Don't know) | 0.7 |
| (NA) | 0.6 |

100a. **[MARSTAT - See Q.900a]**
Can I just check your own marital status?
At present are you ... **READ OUT** ...

**CODE FIRST TO APPLY**

|  | % |
|---|---|
| ... married, | 62.8 |
| living as married, | 2.3 |
| separated or divorced, | 3.5 |
| widowed, | 7.9 |
| or, not married? | 23.5 |

b. And are there any children under 16 years old in this household?

|  | % |
|---|---|
| Yes | 66.9 |
| No | 33.1 |

---

NI 37

n = 906

96. **[UNTDIREL]**
At any time in the next 20 years, do you think it is likely or unlikely that there will be a united Ireland? PROBE: *Very likely/unlikely* or *quite likely/unlikely?*

|  | % |
|---|---|
| Very likely | 4.5 |
| Quite likely | 16.8 |
| Quite unlikely | 27.4 |
| Very unlikely | 41.8 |
| (Even chance) | 2.4 |
| (Don't know) | 6.2 |
| (NA) | 1.0 |

**CARD S**

97a. **[GOVINTNI]**
Under direct rule from Britain, as now, how much do you generally trust British governments of any party to act in the best interests of Northern Ireland? **CODE ONE ONLY UNDER COL. a. BELOW**

b. **[STRINTNI]**
If there was self-rule, how much do you think you would generally trust a Stormont government to act in the best interests of Northern Ireland? **CODE ONE ONLY UNDER COL b. BELOW**

c. **[REINTNI]**
And if there was a united Ireland, how much do you think you would generally trust an Irish government to act in the best interests of Northern Ireland? **CODE ONE ONLY UNDER COL c. BELOW**

|  | a. British govt % | b. Stormont govt % | c. Irish govt % |
|---|---|---|---|
| Just about always | 4.9 | 11.4 | 3.4 |
| Most of the time | 27.2 | 43.2 | 22.0 |
| Only some of the time | 42.7 | 24.4 | 29.1 |
| Rarely | 13.9 | 9.7 | 19.8 |
| Never | 7.0 | 6.3 | 19.3 |
| (Don't know/can't say) | 3.2 | 3.9 | 5.4 |
| (NA) | 1.1 | 1.1 | 1.1 |

NI    39    n = 906

**101. IF MARRIED OR LIVING AS MARRIED (CODES 1 OR 2 AT Q.100a.) ASK Q.101. OTHERS GO TO Q.102**
*[DOCHORE1 - DOCHORE7]*
I would like to ask about how you and your *husband/wife/partner* generally share some family jobs. Who *does* the household shopping: mainly the man, mainly the woman or is the task shared equally?
**RECORD ANSWER IN GRID BELOW AND CONTINUE WITH b.-g.**

CODE ONE FOR EACH ITEM

| | | Mainly man | Mainly woman | Shared equally | (DK) | (NA) |
|---|---|---|---|---|---|---|
| a. | Household shopping? | % 6.3 | 59.2 | 33.7 | - | 0.8 |
| b. | ... who makes the evening meal? | % 9.9 | 73.1 | 16.1 | - | 0.8 |
| c. | ... who does the evening dishes? | % 18.4 | 44.3 | 34.5 | - | 1.5 |
| d. | ... who does the household cleaning? | % 3.8 | 72.9 | 21.8 | - | 0.5 |
| e. | ... who does the washing and ironing? | % 1.9 | 89.3 | 7.4 | - | 0.6 |
| f. | ... who repairs the household equipment? | % 82.2 | 7.6 | 7.9 | 0.2 | 1.2 |
| g. | ... who organises the household money and payment of bills? | % 25.8 | 42.8 | 30.6 | - | 0.5 |

*[DOCHILD1, DOCHILD2]*
IF CHILD(REN) AT Q.100b. ASK h.-i. OTHERS GO TO Q.102

| | | Mainly man | Mainly woman | Shared equally | (DK) | (NA) |
|---|---|---|---|---|---|---|
| h. | ... who looks after the child(ren) when they are sick? | % 2.0 | 27.2 | 19.1 | - | 0.6 |
| i. | ... who teaches the child(ren) discipline? | % 4.4 | 9.5 | 34.5 | - | 0.8 |

*[SHCHORE1 - SHCHORE7]*
**ASK ALL**
**102.** (Now) I would like to ask about how you think family jobs *should generally* be shared between men and women. Who do you think *should* do the household shopping: mainly the man, mainly the woman, or should the task be shared equally?
**RECORD ANSWER IN GRID BELOW AND CONTINUE WITH b.-i.**

CODE ONE FOR EACH ITEM

| | | Mainly man | Mainly woman | Shared equally | (DK) | (NA) |
|---|---|---|---|---|---|---|
| a. | Household shopping? | % 1.0 | 37.7 | 60.2 | 0.5 | 0.6 |
| b. | ... who should make the evening meal? | % 1.8 | 46.8 | 50.1 | 0.4 | 0.9 |
| c. | ... who should do the evening dishes? | % 10.8 | 17.5 | 70.2 | 0.4 | 1.2 |
| d. | ... who should do the household cleaning? | % 0.4 | 43.3 | 55.3 | 0.3 | 0.6 |
| e. | ... who should do the washing and ironing? | % 0.3 | 68.8 | 30.0 | 0.3 | 0.6 |
| f. | ... who should repair the household equipment? | % 73.7 | 2.1 | 22.8 | 0.4 | 0.9 |
| g. | ... who should organise the household money and payment of bills? | % 16.4 | 16.7 | 65.7 | 0.6 | 0.6 |

*[SHCHILD1, SHCHILD2]*

| | | Mainly man | Mainly woman | Shared equally | (DK) | (NA) |
|---|---|---|---|---|---|---|
| h. | ... who should look after the child(ren) when they are sick? | % 0.4 | 36.1 | 62.3 | 0.3 | 0.9 |
| i. | ... who should teach the child(ren) discipline? | % 8.3 | 5.4 | 85.1 | 0.4 | 0.8 |

---

NI    40    n = 906

**103.** *[PROMOTE]*
Some people think that women are generally less likely than men to be promoted at work, even when their qualifications and experience are the same.
Do you think this happens ... READ OUT ...

| | % |
|---|---|
| ... a lot, | 40.0 |
| a little, | 42.5 |
| or, hardly at all? | 12.6 |
| (Don't know) | 4.6 |
| (NA) | 0.3 |

**104a.** CARD T
I'd like you to look at the statements on this card. In general, which ones do you think best describe the reasons why many *married women* work? Any others? CODE ALL THAT APPLY. RECORD IN COL. a.
IF MORE THAN ONE REASON MENTIONED AT a., ASK b. OTHERS GO TO Q.105

**b.** And which one of these would you say is generally the *main* reason why married women work? RECORD IN COL. b.

| | a. Reasons for working % | b. [MWWKMAIN] Main reason % |
|---|---|---|
| [MWWORK1] Working is the normal thing to do | 4.8% | 0.4 |
| [MWWORK2] Need money for basic essentials such as food, rent or mortgage | 69.6% | 56.9 |
| [MWWORK3] To earn money to buy extras | 54.3% | 19.3 |
| [MWWORK4] To earn money of their own | 43.9% | 10.0 |
| [MWWORK5] For the company of other people | 27.1% | 1.3 |
| [MWWORK6] They enjoy working | 23.5% | 1.7 |
| [MWWORK8] To follow a career | 34.2% | 5.8 |
| [MWWORK9] For a change from children or housework | 0.1% | 3.2 |
| [MWWORK7] Other (WRITE IN) | 38.4% | - |
| [MWWORK10] (Don't know/NA) | 0.7% | 1.3 |

NI

42

## CARD V

n = 906

**106.** Here are some things on which money is spent. For each one, please tell me where you think the money should come from.

READ OUT a. TO f.
AND CODE ONE FOR EACH

| | | Entirely from govern-ment | Mainly from govern-ment | Shared equally | Mainly from charities | Entirely from charities | From some-where else | (Don't know) | (NA) |
|---|---|---|---|---|---|---|---|---|---|
| a. | [KIDNEYSH] Kidney machines for NHS hospitals % | 60.3 | 31.3 | 6.2 | 1.5 | - | 0.1 | 0.4 | 0.3 |
| b. | [HOMELSSH] Housing for homeless people % | 50.0 | 38.6 | 8.2 | 1.6 | 0.1 | 0.1 | 0.8 | 0.5 |
| c. | [FODAIDSH] Food aid to poor countries % | 14.1 | 22.7 | 39.1 | 17.0 | 3.7 | 2.3 | 0.7 | 0.4 |
| d. | [DISHOLSH] Holidays for disabled people % | 13.9 | 22.7 | 34.9 | 22.6 | 3.7 | 0.9 | 0.7 | 0.5 |
| e. | [LIFEBTSH] Lifeboats % | 29.7 | 31.2 | 24.0 | 10.3 | 3.1 | 0.3 | 1.0 | 0.4 |
| f. | [RANIMLSH] Protecting rare animals % | 13.2 | 22.6 | 30.1 | 21.1 | 6.2 | 3.8 | 2.5 | 0.4 |

---

NI

41

## SECTION SEVEN

n = 906
Qs. 105-106

**ASK ALL**
**CARD U**

**105a.** On this card are ways in which people are asked to give to charity. Some people are not able to give. How about you: in which, if any, of these ways have you given money to charity in the last year? Any others? PROBE UNTIL 'No'.
CODE ALL THAT APPLY

| | Given in last year |
|---|---|
| [CHARRAFF] Buying raffle tickets | 75.2% |
| [CHARFETE] Buying goods in a sale or fete | 32.5% |
| [CHARSHOP] Buying goods in a charity shop | 22.3% |
| [CHARCAT] Buying goods from a charity catalogue | 18.6% |
| [CHARDOOR] Giving in a door-to-door collection | 78.1% |
| [CHARST] Giving in a street collection | 73.5% |
| [CHARCHCH] Giving in a church collection | 71.5% |
| [CHARTVRD] Giving to a TV or radio appeal | 18.9% |
| [CHARSPON] Sponsoring someone in a fundraising event | 75.5% |
| [CHAREVNT] Attending an event in aid of charity | 38.8% |
| [CHARNONE] (None of these) | 0.8% |
| (NA) | 0.3% |

[CHAROTHR]
**b.** And are there any other ways you have given money to charity in the last year, such as special appeals, collection tins in shops or pubs, covenants, or some other way?

| | % |
|---|---|
| No | 61.9 |
| (Yes, given in a pub collection) | 4.4 |
| (Yes, given in a shop collection) | 10.9 |
| (Yes, given in other collection/type of collection not stated) | 2.0 |
| (Yes, given by covenant) | 5.6 |
| (Yes, given by regular subscription/payment) | 1.1 |
| (Yes, given to special/direct appeals) | 5.9 |
| (Yes, other donations than those listed above) | 1.0 |
| (Yes, in more than one of these ways) | 3.9 |
| (DK/NA) | 3.2 |

NI

43

## SECTION EIGHT

n = 906
Qs. 107-109

ASK ALL

Now a few questions on housing.

*[HOMETYPE]*
107a. INTERVIEWER CODE FROM OBSERVATION AND CHECK WITH RESPONDENT
Would I be right in describing this accommodation as a ...
READ OUT ONE THAT YOU THINK APPLIES

|  | % |
|---|---|
| ... detached house or bungalow | 37.2 |
| ... semi-detached house or bungalow | 23.9 |
| ... terraced house | 32.5 |
| ... self-contained, purpose built flat/maisonette (inc. in tenement block) | 4.7 |
| ... self-contained converted flat/maisonette | 1.2 |
| ... room(s) - not self-contained | - |
| Other (WRITE IN) | 0.3 |
| (NA) | 0.2 |

*[HOMEEST]*
b. May I just check, is your home part of a housing estate?
NOTE: MAY BE PUBLIC OR PRIVATE, BUT IT IS THE RESPONDENT'S VIEW WE WANT

|  | % |
|---|---|
| Yes, part of estate | 41.4 |
| No | 56.9 |
| (NA) | 1.7 |

*[HOMEIYR]*
108a. How long have you lived in your present home ... READ OUT ...

|  | % |
|---|---|
| ... less than a year, | 5.7 |
| or, one year or more? | 94.1 |
| (NA) | 0.2 |

*[HOMEYR]*
b. IF 'ONE YEAR OR MORE' AT a.
How many years?
PROBE FOR BEST ESTIMATE

MEDIAN: | 1 | 1 |  YEARS

ASK ALL
*[TENURE]*
109. Does your household own or rent this accommodation?
PROBE AS NECESSARY
IF OWNS: Outright or on a mortgage?
IF RENTS: From whom?

|  |  | % |
|---|---|---|
| Owns: | Own (leasehold/freehold) outright | 28.3 |
|  | Buying (leasehold/freehold) on mortgage | 38.9 |
| Rents: | Housing Executive | 25.5 |
|  | Housing Association | 1.0 |
|  | Property company | 1.6 |
|  | Employer | 0.6 |
|  | Other organisation | 0.6 |
|  | Relative | 0.5 |
|  | Other individual | 2.4 |
| Rent free: | Rent free, squatting, etc. | 0.4 |
|  | (NA) | 0.2 |

NI

44

## SECTION NINE

n = 906
Q. 110-112

*[RELIGION]*
ASK ALL
110. Do you regard yourself as belonging to any particular religion? IF YES: Which?
CODE ONE ONLY - DO NOT PROMPT

|  | % |
|---|---|
| No religion | 8.2 |
| Christian - no denomination | 2.5 |
| Roman Catholic | 35.2 |
| Church of Ireland/Anglican | 18.6 |
| Baptist | 1.5 |
| Methodist | 4.0 |
| Presbyterian | 24.5 |
| Free Presbyterian | 1.0 |
| Brethren | 0.9 |
| Other Protestant (WRITE IN:) | 2.3 |
| Other Christian (WRITE IN:) |  |
| Hindu | - |
| Jewish | - |
| Muslim | 0.2 |
| Sikh | 0.1 |
| Buddhist | - |
| Other non-Christian (WRITE IN:) |  |
| Refused/unwilling to say | 0.7 |
| (NA) | 0.3 |

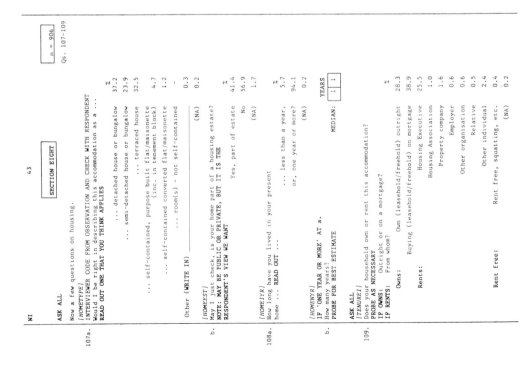

NI · 45

**111.** [FAMRELIG]
IF 'REFUSED' AT Q.110 (CODE 97), SKIP TO Q.900
ASK ALL OTHERS

In what religion, if any, were you brought up? PROBE IF NECESSARY: What was your family's religion?

CODE ONE ONLY - DO NOT PROMPT

| | % |
|---|---|
| No religion | 1.3 |
| Christian - no denomination | 1.0 |
| Roman Catholic | 36.4 |
| Church of Ireland/Anglican | 23.1 |
| Baptist | 1.2 |
| Methodist | 4.5 |
| Presbyterian | 28.0 |
| Free Presbyterian | 0.1 |
| Brethren | 1.8 |
| Other Protestant (WRITE IN:) | 1.3 |
| Other Christian (WRITE IN:) | 0.1 |
| Hindu | – |
| Jewish | – |
| Muslim | 0.2 |
| Sikh | 0.1 |
| Buddhist | – |
| Other non-Christian (WRITE IN:) | – |
| Refused/unwilling to say | 0.2 |
| (NA) | 0.2 |

**112.** [CHATTEND]
IF ANY RELIGION AT a. OR b. ASK Q.112; OTHERS SKIP TO Q.900

Apart from such special occasions as weddings, funerals and baptisms, how often nowadays do you attend services or meetings connected with your religion?

PROBE AS NECESSARY

| | % |
|---|---|
| Once a week or more | 49.8 |
| Less often but at least once in two weeks | 7.5 |
| Less often but at least once a month | 9.4 |
| Less often but at least twice a year | 10.3 |
| Less often but at least once a year | 2.4 |
| Less often | 3.7 |
| Never or practically never | 14.4 |
| Varies too much to say | 0.4 |
| Refused/unwilling to answer | – |
| (No religion) | 0.9 |
| (NA) | 1.2 |

n = 906

---

NI · 46

**SECTION TEN**

n = 906
Qs. 900-912a

**900a.** [MARSTAT]
Can I just check whether at present you are
... READ OUT ...
CODE FIRST TO APPLY

| | % |
|---|---|
| ... married, | 62.8 |
| living as married, | 2.3 |
| separated or divorced, | 3.5 |
| widowed, | 7.9 |
| or, not married? | 23.5 |

**b.** [HOUSEHLD]
Finally, a few questions about you and your household. Including yourself, how many people live here regularly as members of this household?
CHECK INTERVIEWER MANUAL FOR DEFINITION OF HOUSEHOLD IF NECESSARY.

MEDIAN: [0][3]

**901.** Now I'd like to ask for a few details about each person in your household. Starting with yourself, what was your age last birthday?
WORK DOWN COLUMNS OF GRID FOR EACH HOUSEHOLD MEMBER

| | Resp | 2 | 3 | 4 | 5 | 6 | 7 | 8 | 9 | 10 |
|---|---|---|---|---|---|---|---|---|---|---|
| | % | % | | | | | | | | |

**a.** [RSEX] [P2SEX - P10SEX]
Sex:
Male 44.3
Female 55.7

**b.** [RAGE] [P2AGE - P10AGE]
Age last birthday:

**c.** [P2REL - P10REL]
Relationship to respondent:
Spouse/partner
Son/daughter
Parent/parent-in-law
Other relative
Not related

**d.** [RRESP] [P2RESP - P10RESP]
HOUSEHOLD MEMBER WITH LEGAL RESPONSIBILITY FOR ACCOMMODATION (INC. JOINT AND SHARED)

| | % |
|---|---|
| Yes | 75.4 |
| No | 23.9 |
| (NA) | 0.7 |

CHECK THAT NUMBER OF PEOPLE IN GRID EQUALS NUMBER GIVEN AT Q.900b

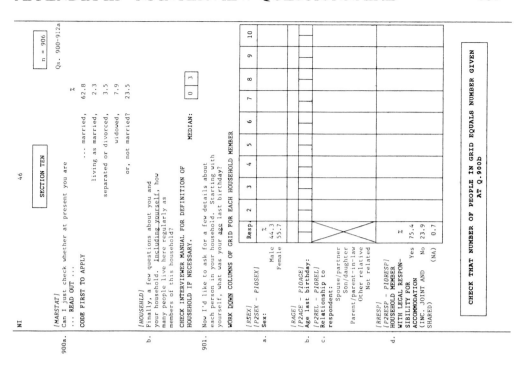

n = 906

**NI**

47

**902.** [SLFMXSCH]
Did you ever attend a mixed or integrated school, that is, a school with fairly large numbers of both Catholic and Protestant children?

IF YES: In Northern Ireland or somewhere else?

| | % |
|---|---|
| Yes, in Northern Ireland | 21.1 |
| Yes, somewhere else | 2.7 |
| No, did not | 75.4 |
| (Don't know) | 0.6 |
| (NA) | 0.2 |

**903a.** [NIRCHILD]
INTERVIEWER CHECK:
WHETHER RESPONDENT HAS CHILD(REN) AGED 5 OR OLDER IN HOUSEHOLD — SEE GRID AT Q.901

| | % |
|---|---|
| HAS | 43.8 |
| HAS NOT | 56.2 |

[CHDMXSCH]
IF CODE 1 AT a.

**b.** And have any of your children ever attended a mixed or integrated school, with fairly large numbers of both Catholics and Protestants attending?

IF YES: In Northern Ireland or somewhere else?

| | % |
|---|---|
| Yes, in Northern Ireland | 5.7 |
| Yes, somewhere else | 0.1 |
| No, have not | 28.8 |
| (Don't know) | 0.2 |
| (NA) | 8.9 |

**904a.** [SNGPERHH]
ASK ALL
INTERVIEWER: IS THIS A SINGLE PERSON HOUSEHOLD?
RESPONDENT ONLY PERSON AT Q.901 (p.46)

| | % |
|---|---|
| Yes | 9.9 |
| No | 89.4 |
| (NA) | 0.7 |

[DUTYRESP]
IF NO AT a.

**b.** Who is the person mainly responsible for general domestic duties in this household?

| | % |
|---|---|
| Respondent mainly | 37.3 |
| Someone else mainly (WRITE IN RELATIONSHIP TO RESP.) | 38.4 |
| Duties shared equally (WRITE IN BY WHOM) | 13.1 |
| (NA) | 1.3 |

(See derived variable [ELSEDUTY] for gender and relationship of persons other than the respondent)

---

n = 906

**NI**

48

**905a.** [CHLDINHH]
INTERVIEWER: IS THERE A CHILD UNDER 16 YEARS IN THE HOUSEHOLD? SEE H/H GRID, Q.901 (p.46)

| | % |
|---|---|
| Yes | 39.8 |
| No | 60.2 |

[CHLDRESP]
IF YES AT a.

**b.** Who is the person mainly responsible for the general care of the child(ren) here?

| | % |
|---|---|
| Respondent mainly | 17.4 |
| Someone else mainly (WRITE IN RELATIONSHIP TO RESP.) | 12.7 |
| Care shared equally (WRITE IN BY WHOM) | 8.7 |
| (NA) | 1.1 |

(See derived variable [ELSECHLD] for gender and relationship of persons other than the respondent)

[TEA]
ASK ALL

**906.** How old were you when you completed your continuous full-time education?
PROBE AS NECESSARY

| | % |
|---|---|
| 15 or under | 40.6 |
| 16 | 25.6 |
| 17 | 11.1 |
| 18 | 8.7 |
| 19 or over | 10.0 |
| Still at school | 0.9 |
| Still at college, polytechnic or university | 2.8 |
| Other answer (WRITE IN:) | – |
| (NA) | 0.2 |

NI 50

n = 906

909. [RECONACT]
INTERVIEWER: REFER TO ECONOMIC POSITION OF RESPONDENT Q.9 (p.5)

%
RESPONDENT IS IN PAID WORK (CODE 03) ... 49.6 ... ASK ABOUT PRESENT JOB
RESPONDENT IS WAITING TO TAKE UP PAID WORK (CODE 04) ... 0.2 ... ASK ABOUT FUTURE JOB
ALL OTHERS (CODES 01-02; 05-11) ... 50.2 ... ASK ABOUT LAST JOB

910. Now I want to ask you about your (present/future/last) job. CHANGE TENSES FOR (BRACKETED) WORDS AS APPROPRIATE.

a. What (is) your job?
PROBE AS NECESSARY: What (is) the name or title of the job?
IF 'NEVER HAD JOB', WRITE IN AND GO TO Q.911

b. What kind of work (do) you do most of the time?
IF RELEVANT: What materials/machinery (do) you use?

c. What training or qualifications (are) needed for that job?

d. [RSUPER]
(Do) you directly supervise or (are) you directly responsible for the work of any other people?
IF YES: How many? ... MEDIAN: [0][0][0][4]

%
(Yes) 27.1
No 64.3
(NA) 0.7

e. [REMPLYEE]
Can I just check: (are) you ... READ OUT ...
%
... an employee, 80.2
or, self-employed? 11.5
(NA) 0.4

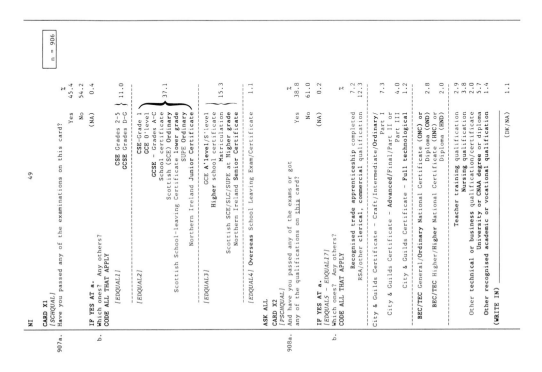

NI 49

n = 906

907a. CARD X1
[SCHQUAL]
Have you passed any of the examinations on this card?
%
Yes 45.4
No 54.2
(NA) 0.4

b. IF YES AT a. Which ones? Any others?
CODE ALL THAT APPLY
[EQUAL1]
CSE Grades 2-5 } 11.0
GCSE Grades D-G
[EQUAL2]
CSE-Grade 1
GCE O'level
GCSE - Grades A-C
School certificate } 37.1
Scottish (SCE) Ordinary
Scottish School-leaving Certificate lower grade
SUPE Ordinary
Northern Ireland Junior Certificate
[EQUAL3]
GCE A'level/S'level
Higher school certificate
Matriculation } 15.3
Scottish SCE/SLC/SUPE at Higher grade
Northern Ireland Senior Certificate
[EQUAL4] Overseas School Leaving Exam/Certificate 1.1

908a. ASK ALL
CARD X2
[PSCHQUAL]
And have you passed any of the exams or got any of the qualifications on this card?
%
Yes 38.8
No 61.0
(NA) 0.2

b. IF YES AT a. Which ones? Any others?
[EQUALS - EDQUAL7]
CODE ALL THAT APPLY
%
Recognised trade apprenticeship completed 7.2
RSA/other clerical, commercial qualification 12.3
City & Guilds Certificate - Craft/Intermediate/Ordinary/Part I 7.3
City & Guilds Certificate - Advanced/Final/Part II or Part III 4.0
City & Guilds Certificate - Full technological 1.2
BEC/TEC General/Ordinary National Certificate (ONC) or Diploma (OND) 2.8
BEC/TEC Higher/Higher National Certificate (HNC) or Diploma (HND) 2.0
Teacher training qualification 2.9
Nursing qualification 3.8
Other technical or business qualification/certificate 2.0
University or CNAA degree or diploma 5.7
Other recognised academic or vocational qualification 1.4
(WRITE IN) _____
(DK/NA) 1.1

NI     51

n = 906

**IF EMPLOYEE (CODE 1 AT e.)**
CARD X3
*[RSECTOR]*
910f. Which of the types of organisation on this
card (do) you work for?
CODE FIRST TO APPLY

|  | % |
|---|---|
| Private firm or company | 48.0 |
| Nationalised industry/public corp. | 3.2 |
| District Authority/Education and Library Board | 7.3 |
| Health Board/NHS hospital | 9.4 |
| Central Government/Civil Service | 9.1 |
| Charity or Trust | 0.6 |
| Other (WRITE IN:) | 2.1 |
| (DK) | 0.1 |
| (NA) | 0.4 |

*[PREMISES]*
g. Is where you (work) your employer's only premises, or (are)
there other premises elsewhere?

|  | % |
|---|---|
| Employer's only premises | 23.8 |
| Employer has other premises elsewhere | 52.5 |
| (Don't know) | 1.7 |
| (NA) | 2.2 |

**ASK ALL WHO HAVE EVER WORKED**
h. What (does) your employer (IF SELF-EMPLOYED: you) make
or do at the place where you usually (work)?
IF FARM, GIVE NO. OF ACRES

*[REMPWORK]*
i. Including yourself, how many people (are) employed at the
place where you usually (work) (from)?

|  | % |
|---|---|
| (No employees) | 6.4 |
| Under 10 | 22.0 |
| 10-24 | 13.0 |
| 25-99 | 21.8 |
| 100-499 | 17.3 |
| 500 or more | 10.8 |
| (Don't know) | 0.4 |
| (NA) | 0.5 |

IF SELF-EMPLOYED: (Do) you have any employees?
IF YES: How many?

*[RPARTFUL]*
j. (Is) the job...READ OUT...

|  | % |
|---|---|
| ...full-time (30+ HOURS) | 75.4 |
| or, part-time (10-29 HOURS)? | 14.6 |
| (NA) | 2.1 |

---

NI     52

n = 906

O.U.O
RESPONDENT'S OCCUPATIONAL DETAILS

*[UNION]*
ASK ALL
91la. Are you <u>now</u> a member of a trade union or
staff association?
CODE FIRST TO APPLY

|  | % |
|---|---|
| Yes, trade union | 17.2 |
| Yes, staff association | 6.3 |
| No | 76.0 |
| (NA) | 0.4 |

*[UNIONEVR]*
IF NO AT a.
b. Have you <u>ever</u> been a member of a
trade union or staff association?
CODE FIRST TO APPLY

|  | % |
|---|---|
| Yes, trade union | 25.0 |
| Yes, staff association | 2.7 |
| (No) | 48.0 |
| (NA) | 0.8 |

912a. INTERVIEWER:
RESPONDENT IS:

|  | % |
|---|---|
| Married or living as married (CODES 1 OR 2 AT Q.900) | 65.2 |
| All others | 34.8 |

NI    53

n = 590

Qs. 912b-915

**912.b** [SECONACT]
CARD X4
Which of these descriptions applied to what your (husband/wife/partner) was doing last week, that is the seven days ending last Sunday? **PROBE:** Any others?
**CODE ALL THAT APPLY IN COL. I**
IF ONLY ONE CODE AT I, TRANSFER IT TO COL. II
IF MORE THAN ONE AT I, TRANSFER HIGHEST ON LIST TO II

| | COL I | COL. II ECONOMIC POSITION |
|---|---|---|
| In full-time education (not paid for by employer, including on vacation) | A | 0.4 % |
| On government training/employment programme (eg.Employment Training, Youth Training programme etc.) | B | 0.7 |
| In paid work (or away temporarily) for at least 10 hours in week | C | 59.0 |
| Waiting to take up paid work already accepted | D | - |
| Unemployed and registered at a benefit office | E | 5.6 |
| Unemployed, not registered, but actively looking for job | F | 0.6 |
| Unemployed, wanting a job (of at least 10 hrs a week), but not actively looking for a job | G | 1.8 |
| Permanently sick or disabled | H | 4.6 |
| Wholly retired from work | J | 11.4 |
| Looking after the home | K | 15.5 |
| Doing something else (WRITE IN) | L | 0.2 |
| (NA) | | 0.2 |

IF CODES 01-02, OR 05-11 AT b.

**c.** [SLASTJOB]
How long ago did your (husband/wife/partner) last have a paid job (other than the government programme you mentioned) of at least 10 hours a week?

| | % |
|---|---|
| Within past 12 months | 5.4 |
| Over 1, up to 5 years ago | 9.1 |
| Over 5, up to 10 years ago | 9.8 |
| Over 10, up to 20 years ago | 7.7 |
| Over 20 years ago | 5.6 |
| Never had a paid job of 10+ hours a week | 3.2 |
| (NA) | 0.2 |

---

NI    54

n = 590

**913.** INTERVIEWER:
REFER TO ECONOMIC POSITION OF SPOUSE/PARTNER (Q.912b.)

| | % | |
|---|---|---|
| SPOUSE/PARTNER IS IN PAID WORK (CODE 03) | 59.0 | ASK ABOUT PRESENT JOB |
| SPOUSE/PARTNER IS WAITING TO TAKE UP PAID WORK (CODE 04) | - | ASK ABOUT FUTURE JOB |
| ALL OTHERS (CODES 01-02; 05-11) | 41.0 | ASK ABOUT LAST JOB |

**914a.** Now I want to ask you about your (husband's/wife's/partner's) (present/future/last) job.
CHANGE (BRACKETED) WORDS AS APPROPRIATE

What (is) (his/her) job?

PROBE AS NECESSARY: What (is) the name and title of that job?

IF 'NEVER HAD A JOB', WRITE IN AND GO TO Q.915

**b.** What kind of work (does) (he/she) do most of the time?
IF RELEVANT: What materials/machinery (does) (he/she) use?

**c.** What training or qualifications (are) needed for that job?

**d.** [SSUPER]
(Does) (he/she) directly supervise or (is) (he/she) directly responsible for the work of any other people?

IF YES, How many?    MEDIAN: [  ] [ 0 ] [ 5 ]

| | % |
|---|---|
| (Yes) | 28.3 |
| No | 66.3 |
| (Don't know) | 1.5 |
| (NA) | 0.7 |

**e.** [SEMPLOYE]
(Is) (he/she) ... READ OUT ...

| | % |
|---|---|
| ... an employee, | 82.9 |
| or, self-employed? | 13.7 |
| (NA) | 0.2 |

NI                                                                      56

ASK ALL

IF RESPONDENT IS MARRIED OR LIVING AS
MARRIED, ASK Q.915, ALL OTHERS GO TO Q.916

n = 590
Q.915 only

915. [RELIGSAM]
Is your (husband/wife/partner) the same religion
as you?
PROBE AS NECESSARY

| | % |
|---|---|
| Yes, same religion | 91.7 |
| No, not same religion | 6.3 |
| No religion at all | 1.5 |
| (Refused) | 0.3 |
| (NA) | 0.2 |

n = 906
Qs. 916-923

916. [CAROWN]
ASK ALL
Do you, or does anyone else in your household,
own or have the regular use of a car or a van?

| | % |
|---|---|
| Yes | 72.4 |
| No | 27.4 |
| (NA) | 0.3 |

917a. [ANYBENFT]
CARD X6
Have you or anyone in this household received
any of the state benefits on this card during
the last five years?

| | % |
|---|---|
| Yes | 89.5 |
| No | 10.4 |
| (NA) | 0.2 |

b. IF YES AT a.
Which ones? Any others?
CODE ALL THAT APPLY

| | % |
|---|---|
| [BENEFT1] Child benefit | 48.4 |
| [BENEFT2] Maternity benefit or allowance | 10.2 |
| [BENEFT3] One-parent benefit | 4.7 |
| [BENEFT4] Family credit | 4.9 |
| [BENEFT5] State retirement or widow's pension | 23.3 |
| [BENEFT6] State supplementary pension | 2.5 |
| [BENEFT15] Community Charge rebate/Poll Tax rebate or benefit | - |
| [BENEFT7] Invalidity or disabled pension or benefit | 12.5 |
| [BENEFT8] Attendance/invalid care/Mobility allowance | 4.9 |
| [BENEFT9] State Sickness or injury benefit | 12.6 |
| [BENEFT10] Unemployment benefit | 19.8 |
| [BENEFT11] Income support | 23.3 |
| [BENEFT12] Housing benefit (rate or rent rebate) | 15.9 |
| [BENEFT13] Other state benefit(s) volunteered (WRITE IN) | 0.1 |

NI                                                                      55

n = 590

914f. IF EMPLOYEE (CODE 1 AT e.)
CARD X5
[SSECTOR]
Which of the types of organisation on
this card (does) (he/she) work for?

| | % |
|---|---|
| Private firm or company | 42.1 |
| Nationalised industry/public corporation | 6.0 |
| District Authority/Education and Library Board | 10.5 |
| Health Board/NHS hospital | 8.9 |
| Central Government/Civil Service | 11.9 |
| Charity or Trust | 0.9 |
| Other (WRITE IN) | 1.9 |
| (Don't know) | 0.2 |
| (NA) | 0.7 |

g. ASK ALL WHOSE SPOUSE/PARTNER HAS EVER WORKED
What (does) the employer (IF SELF-EMPLOYED: (he/she)) make or
do at the place where (he/she) usually (works)?
IF FARM, GIVE NO. OF ACRES

h. [SEMPWORK]
Including (him/herself), roughly how many
people (are) employed at the place where
(he/she) usually (works) (from)?

| | % |
|---|---|
| Under 10 | 19.7 |
| 10-24 | 11.6 |
| 25-99 | 20.9 |
| 100-499 | 23.2 |
| 500 or more | 10.7 |
| (Don't know) | 1.9 |
| (NA) | 1.5 |

IF SELF-EMPLOYED: (Does) (he/she) have any employees?
IF YES: How many?

| | % |
|---|---|
| (No employees) | 7.3 |

i. [SPARTFUL]
(Is) the job ... READ OUT ...

| | % |
|---|---|
| ... full-time (30+ HOURS) | 78.1 |
| or, part-time (10-29 HOURS)? | 16.6 |
| (NA) | 2.1 |

0.U.0
SPOUSE'S OCCUPATIONAL DETAILS

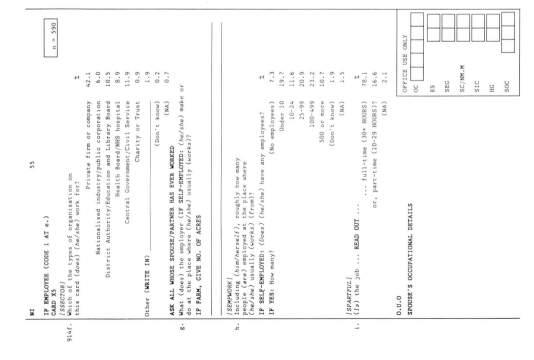

OFFICE USE ONLY
OC
ES
SEG
SC/NM.M
SIC
HG
SOC

NI  57

n = 590

## ASK ALL

**[EVRLIVGB]**

918a. Have you <u>ever</u> lived in mainland Britain for more than a year?

|  |  | % |
|---|---|---|
| | Yes | 14.9 |
| | No | 84.9 |
| | (NA) | 0.2 |

b. **[EVRLIVER]**
And have you <u>ever</u> lived in the Republic of Ireland for more than a year?

|  |  | % |
|---|---|---|
| | Yes | 4.6 |
| | No | 95.0 |
| | (NA) | 0.4 |

919a. **[UNINATID]**
Generally speaking, do you think of yourself as a unionist, a nationalist or neither?

|  |  | % |
|---|---|---|
| | Unionist | 41.4 |
| | Nationalist | 18.5 |
| | Neither | 39.3 |
| | (NA) | 0.8 |

b. **[UNINATST]**
IF UNIONIST OR NATIONALIST AT a.
Would you call yourself a very strong... (QUOTE ANSWER AT a.) ... fairly strong, or not very strong?

|  |  | % |
|---|---|---|
| | Very strong | 8.1 |
| | Fairly strong | 27.6 |
| | Not very strong | 24.1 |
| | (Don't know) | 0.1 |
| | (NA) | 0.8 |

---

NI  58

n = 590

## ASK ALL
CARD X7

**[HHINCOME]**

920a. Which of the letters on this card represents the total income of your household from <u>all</u> sources <u>before</u> tax? Please just tell me the letter.

NOTE: INCLUDES INCOME FROM BENEFITS, SAVINGS, ETC.

CODE ONE IN COLUMN a.

b. INTERVIEWER: CHECK Q.9, (P.5):

|  | % |
|---|---|
| RESPONDENT IS IN PAID WORK (CODE 03) | 49.6 |
| ALL OTHERS | 50.4 |

c. **[REARN]**
Which of the letters on this card represents your <u>own</u> gross or total <u>earnings</u>, before deduction of income tax and national insurance?

CODE ONE IN COLUMN c.

| | | | a. Household income % | c. Own earnings % |
|---|---|---|---|---|
| Less than £3,999 | Q = | | 9.2 | 5.4 |
| £4,000 - £5,999 | T = | | 13.5 | 8.8 |
| £6,000 - £7,999 | O = | | 7.5 | 7.3 |
| £8,000 - £9,999 | K = | | 7.1 | 6.3 |
| £10,000 - £11,999 | L = | | 8.5 | 4.8 |
| £12,000 - £14,999 | B = | | 8.2 | 4.5 |
| £15,000 - £17,999 | Z = | | 6.0 | 2.8 |
| £18,000 - £19,999 | M = | | 4.7 | 2.1 |
| £20,000 - £22,999 | F = | | 5.4 | 1.2 |
| £23,000 - £25,999 | J = | | 4.7 | 1.9 |
| £26,000 - £28,999 | D = | | 3.1 | 1.1 |
| £29,000 - £31,999 | H = | | 2.4 | 0.1 |
| £32,000 - £34,999 | C = | | 2.0 | 0.3 |
| £35,000 or more | G = | | 5.3 | 0.7 |
| (Refused) | | | 1.6 | 0.9 |
| (Don't know) | | | 6.6 | 0.4 |
| (NA) | | | 4.3 | 0.9 |

## ASK ALL
**[OWNSHARE]**

921. Do you (or your husband/wife/partner) own any shares quoted on the Stock Exchange, including unit trusts?

|  |  | % |
|---|---|---|
| | Yes | 15.9 |
| | No | 83.0 |
| | (Don't know) | 0.2 |
| | (NA) | 0.9 |

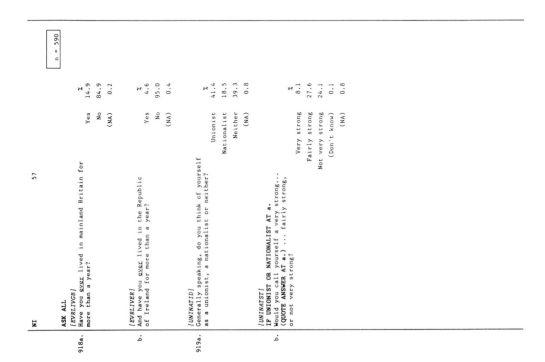

NI

60

THANK YOU

PLEASE MAKE SURE THAT THE ARF IS COMPLETELY FILLED IN, INCLUDING THE RESPONDENT'S NAME

* RETURN THE COMPLETED ARF TO PPRU IN AN A5 ENVELOPE, NOT WITH THE QUESTIONNAIRE.

* CHECK THE MAIN QUESTIONNAIRE, AND THE SELF-COMPLETION QUESTIONNAIRE (IF YOU HAVE COLLECTED IT).

* DOUBLE CHECK THAT YOU HAVE FILLED IN ALL THE IDENTIFICATION NUMBERS: ESPECIALLY THE SERIAL NUMBER AND YOUR INTERVIEW NUMBER.

* THEN RETURN BOTH QUESTIONNAIRES IN THE A4 ENVELOPE AS SOON AS YOU CAN.

---

NI

59

n = 906

SHOW ADVANCE LETTER

*[LETTERRM]*

922a. In February we sent your household a letter, giving advance notice that an interviewer would be calling to ask for an interview. The letter looked like this (SHOW).

Do you remember receiving this letter?

|  | % |
|---|---|
| Yes, remembers letter | 71.2 |
| No, does not | 27.9 |
| Other (WRITE IN) | 0.7 |
| (NA) | 0.2 |

*[LETTERPR]*

b. If you were given a choice, would you have preferred ...READ OUT...

|  | % |
|---|---|
| ...to have a letter in advance saying an interviewer would call, | 62.5 |
| or, to have an interviewer simply call round, | 2.1 |
| or, wouldn't it really matter? | 35.2 |
| (Don't know) | 0.1 |

INTERVIEWER: THANK RESPONDENT FOR HIS OR HER HELP AND COMPLETE Q.923

*[QFILLED]*

923a. THE SELF-COMPLETION QUESTIONNAIRE WAS ...

|  | % |
|---|---|
| ... filled in immediately after interview in your presence | 39.3 |
| ... left behind to be filled in later | 58.2 |
| or ... refused (WHY?) | 2.6 |

b. INTERVIEWER: COMPLETE Q.18 ON ARF ABOUT HOW YOU EXPECT SELF-COMPLETION QUESTIONNAIRE TO BE RETURNED.

c. TIME INTERVIEW COMPLETED: WRITE IN:    24 hour clock

d. *[DURATION]* TOTAL LENGTH OF INTERVIEW: (SEE FRONT COVER AND c. ABOVE)    MEDIAN: Minutes [6 5]

e. INTERVIEWER SIGNATURE:
     ... AND INTERVIEWER NUMBER:

f. DATE OF INTERVIEW:   DAY [ ]   MONTH [0]   YEAR [9 1]

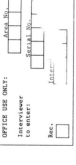

*Head Office: 35 NORTHAMPTON SQUARE*
*LONDON EC1V 0AX Telephone071-250 1866*

*Field and DP Office: BRENTWOOD, ESSEX*
*Northern Field Office: DARLINGTON, CO. DURHAM*

**P.1135/NI**

## NORTHERN IRELAND SOCIAL ATTITUDES 1991

### SELF-COMPLETION QUESTIONNAIRE

Spring 1991

OFFICE USE ONLY:

Interviewer
to enter:

Rec.

Area No.

Serial No.

Inter

**To the selected respondent:**

Thank you very much for agreeing to take part in this important study - the third in this annual series. The study consists of this self-completion questionnaire, and the interview you have already completed. The results of the survey are published in a book each autumn; some of the questions are also being asked in twelve other countries, as part of an international survey.

*Completing the questionnaire:*

The questions inside cover a wide range of subjects, but each one can be answered simply by placing a tick (✓) or a number in one or more of the boxes. No special knowledge is required: we are confident that everyone will be able to take part, not just those with strong views or particular viewpoints. The questionnaire should not take very long to complete, and we hope you will find it interesting and enjoyable. It should be filled in only by the person actually interviewed at your address. The answers you give will be treated as confidential and anonymous.

*Returning the questionnaire:*

Your interviewer will arrange with you the most convenient way of returning the questionnaire. If the interviewer has arranged to call back for it, please fill it in and keep it safely until then. If not, please complete it and post it back in the pre-paid, addressed envelope, AS SOON AS YOU POSSIBLY CAN.

### THANK YOU AGAIN FOR YOUR HELP.

*Social and Community Planning Research is an independent social research institute registered as a charitable trust. Its projects are funded by government departments, local authorities, universities and foundations to provide information on social issues in the UK. This survey series has been funded mainly by the Sainsbury Family Charitable Trusts, with contributions also from government departments, the Nuffield Foundation, universities and industry. Please contact us if you would like further information.*

## 1

n = 848

Qs. 2.01-2.23

NI

[RUHAPPY]
2.01 If you were to consider your life in general these days, how happy or unhappy would you say you are, on the whole?

PLEASE TICK ONE BOX ONLY

|  | % |
|---|---|
| Very happy | 36.0 |
| Fairly happy | 57.0 |
| Not very happy | 4.5 |
| Not at all happy | 0.9 |
| Can't choose | 0.9 |
| (NA) | 0.8 |

[GOVRESP1, GOVRESP7]
2.02 On the whole, do you think it should or should not be the government's responsibility to ...

PLEASE TICK ONE BOX ON EACH LINE

|  | Definitely should be | Probably should be | Probably should not be | Definitely should not be | Can't choose | (NA) |
|---|---|---|---|---|---|---|
| a. Provide a job for everyone who wants one? % | 36.7 | 34.3 | 13.0 | 8.5 | 5.5 | 2.0 |
| b. Reduce income differences between the rich and poor? % | 51.6 | 28.4 | 6.5 | 6.8 | 3.4 | 3.4 |

[STIFSNT3, MURDRPEN]
2.03 Here are some measures to deal with crime. Some people are in favour of them while others are against them. Do you agree or disagree that ...

PLEASE TICK ONE BOX ON EACH LINE

|  | Strongly agree | Agree | Neither agree nor disagree | Disagree | Strongly disagree | Can't choose | (NA) |
|---|---|---|---|---|---|---|---|
| a. People who break the law should be given stiffer sentences? % | 42.1 | 36.6 | 14.0 | 4.3 | 0.3 | 1.6 | 1.1 |
| b. People convicted of murder should be subject to the death penalty? % | 28.4 | 16.4 | 12.4 | 23.5 | 13.5 | 4.7 | 1.2 |

## 2

n = 848

NI

[SEX8FMAR]
2.04 Do you think it is wrong or not wrong if a man and a woman have sexual relations before marriage?

PLEASE TICK ONE BOX ONLY

|  | % |
|---|---|
| Always wrong | 30.9 |
| Almost always wrong | 9.2 |
| Wrong only sometimes | 13.4 |
| Not wrong at all | 37.4 |
| Can't choose | 8.6 |
| (NA) | 0.6 |

[ADULTERY]
2.05 What about a married person having sexual relations with someone other than his or her husband or wife, is it ...

PLEASE TICK ONE BOX ONLY

|  | % |
|---|---|
| Always wrong | 74.9 |
| Almost always wrong | 15.5 |
| Wrong only sometimes | 5.3 |
| Not wrong at all | 1.5 |
| Can't choose | 2.3 |
| (NA) | 0.5 |

[SEXHOMO]
2.06 And what about sexual relations between two adults of the same sex, is it ...

PLEASE TICK ONE BOX ONLY

|  | % |
|---|---|
| Always wrong | 71.6 |
| Almost always wrong | 8.6 |
| Wrong only sometimes | 4.1 |
| Not wrong at all | 6.8 |
| Can't choose | 8.2 |
| (NA) | 0.6 |

Please continue ...

NI

3

**2.07** [ABORLAWA, ABORLAWB] Do you think the law should or should not allow a woman to obtain a legal abortion ...

PLEASE TICK **ONE** BOX ON EACH LINE

n = 848

| | Definitely should allow it | Probably should allow it | Probably should not allow it | Definitely should not allow it | Can't choose | (NA) |
|---|---|---|---|---|---|---|
| a. If there is a strong chance of a serious defect in the baby? % | 45.4 | 25.7 | 5.5 | 16.5 | 6.3 | 0.6 |
| b. If the family has a very low income and cannot afford any more children? % | 17.7 | 17.8 | 16.5 | 36.8 | 8.4 | 2.8 |

**2.08** [ABORWRGA, ABORWRGB] Do you **personally** think it is wrong or not wrong for a woman to have an abortion ...

PLEASE TICK **ONE** BOX ON EACH LINE

| | Always wrong | Almost always wrong | Wrong only sometimes | Not wrong at all | Can't choose | (NA) |
|---|---|---|---|---|---|---|
| a. If there is a strong chance of a serious defect in the baby? % | 25.2 | 10.3 | 16.0 | 41.0 | 6.8 | 0.7 |
| b. If the family has a very low income and cannot afford any more children? % | 43.6 | 14.3 | 12.7 | 18.4 | 8.4 | 2.6 |

**2.09** [SEXROLE, WWFAMSUF] How much do you agree or disagree ...

PLEASE TICK **ONE** BOX ON EACH LINE

| | Strongly agree | Agree | Neither agree nor disagree | Disagree | Strongly disagree | Can't choose | (NA) |
|---|---|---|---|---|---|---|---|
| a. A husband's job is to earn the money; a wife's job is to look after the home and family % | 15.1 | 20.3 | 20.2 | 27.2 | 15.6 | 0.6 | 1.0 |
| b. All in all, family life suffers when the woman has a full-time job % | 11.4 | 25.7 | 16.9 | 33.2 | 9.3 | 2.3 | 1.3 |

*Please continue ...*

---

NI

4

**2.10** [TAXCHEAT, BENCHEAT] Consider the situations listed below. Do you feel it is wrong or not wrong if ...

PLEASE TICK **ONE** BOX ON EACH LINE

n = 848

| | Not wrong | A bit wrong | Wrong | Seriously wrong | Can't choose | (NA) |
|---|---|---|---|---|---|---|
| a. A taxpayer does not report all of his income in order to pay less income tax? % | 5.3 | 21.2 | 47.2 | 20.2 | 5.1 | 1.0 |
| b. A person gives the government incorrect information about himself to get government benefits that he is not entitled to? % | 2.3 | 7.6 | 50.0 | 35.6 | 3.4 | 1.1 |

**2.11** How much confidence do you have in ...

PLEASE TICK **ONE** BOX ON EACH LINE

| | Complete confidence | A great deal of confidence | Some confidence | Very little confidence | No confidence at all | Can't choose | (NA) |
|---|---|---|---|---|---|---|---|
| a. [PARLCONF] The Westminster parliament? % | 4.1 | 13.0 | 43.7 | 23.4 | 7.8 | 6.9 | 1.1 |
| b. [BUSCONF] Business and industry? % | 2.5 | 13.9 | 55.0 | 15.9 | 2.3 | 8.4 | 2.0 |
| c. [CIVSCONF] The Civil Service? % | 4.7 | 13.7 | 53.0 | 16.5 | 4.9 | 5.3 | 1.8 |
| d. [CHCHCONF] Churches and religious organisations? % | 13.2 | 26.9 | 38.2 | 11.7 | 4.4 | 4.2 | 1.4 |
| e. [CORTCONF] Courts and the legal system? % | 5.6 | 21.4 | 42.8 | 16.5 | 8.0 | 4.3 | 1.5 |
| f. [SCHLCONF] Schools and the educational system? % | 8.4 | 27.7 | 46.7 | 10.1 | 2.0 | 3.8 | 1.3 |

## NI

**2.12 How do you agree or disagree with each of the following?**

*PLEASE TICK ONE BOX ON EACH LINE*

n = 848

| | Strongly agree | Agree | Neither agree nor disagree | Disagree | Strongly disagree | Can't choose | (NA) |
|---|---|---|---|---|---|---|---|
| [POLINGOD] a. Politicians who do not believe in God are unfit for public office | % 14.6 | 12.3 | 21.2 | 30.3 | 14.8 | 5.3 | 1.4 |
| [RLGINFVT] b. Religious leaders should not try to influence how people vote in elections | % 31.1 | 37.8 | 10.7 | 12.0 | 4.5 | 2.7 | 1.2 |
| [BETRBELF] c. It would be better for Northern Ireland if more people with strong religious beliefs held public office | % 8.0 | 15.1 | 19.4 | 33.0 | 19.0 | 4.1 | 1.4 |
| [RLGINFGV] d. Religious leaders should not try to influence government decisions | % 21.6 | 36.4 | 14.9 | 17.2 | 4.0 | 4.4 | 1.5 |

[CHCHPOWR]

**2.13 Do you think that churches and religious organisations in Northern Ireland have too much power or too little power?**

*PLEASE TICK ONE BOX ONLY*

| | % |
|---|---|
| Far too much power | 11.8 |
| Too much power | 21.0 |
| About the right amount of power | 39.7 |
| Too little power | 13.9 |
| Far too little power | 1.8 |
| Can't choose | 10.6 |
| (NA) | 1.3 |

*Please continue ...*

## NI

[GODBELF1]

**2.14 Please tick one box below to show which statement comes closest to expressing what you believe about God.**

*PLEASE TICK ONE BOX ONLY*

n = 848

| | % |
|---|---|
| I don't believe in God | 1.5 |
| I don't know whether there is a God and I don't believe there is any way to find out | 4.0 |
| I don't believe in a personal God, but I do believe in a Higher Power of some kind | 3.9 |
| I find myself believing in God some of the time, but not at others | 7.2 |
| While I have doubts, I feel that I do believe in God | 21.6 |
| I know God really exists and I have no doubts about it | 60.8 |
| (NA) | 1.0 |

[RCLSEGOD]

**2.15 How close do you feel to God most of the time?**

*PLEASE TICK ONE BOX ONLY*

| | % |
|---|---|
| Don't believe in God | 1.5 |
| Not close at all | 5.5 |
| Not very close | 15.9 |
| Somewhat close | 45.5 |
| Extremely close | 25.6 |
| Can't choose | 5.2 |
| (NA) | 0.8 |

[GODBELF2]

**2.16 Which best describes your beliefs about God?**

*PLEASE TICK ONE BOX ONLY*

| | % |
|---|---|
| I don't believe in God now and I never have | 1.3 |
| I don't believe in God now, but I used to | 3.1 |
| I believe in God now, but I didn't used to | 6.1 |
| I believe in God now and I always have | 78.2 |
| Can't choose | 10.3 |
| (NA) | 1.0 |

8

NI

2.19 How much do you agree or disagree with each of the following ...

PLEASE TICK **ONE** BOX ON EACH LINE

n = 848

| | Strongly agree | Agree | Neither agree nor disagree | Disagree | Strongly disagree | Can't choose | (NA) |
|---|---|---|---|---|---|---|---|
| [GODCONCN] a. There is a God who concerns Himself with every human being personally | % 39.3 | 34.5 | 11.9 | 5.3 | 1.7 | 5.4 | 1.9 |
| [FATALIST] b. There is little that people can do to change the course of their lives | % 6.1 | 19.9 | 7.6 | 43.8 | 17.6 | 2.7 | 2.4 |
| [GODGMEAN] c. To me, life is meaningful only because God exists | % 21.9 | 26.9 | 21.4 | 15.8 | 4.7 | 6.5 | 2.8 |
| [LFNOPURP] d. In my opinion, life does not serve any purpose | % 1.5 | 3.4 | 5.5 | 46.4 | 36.0 | 4.7 | 2.6 |
| [LIFGODDC] e. The course of our lives is decided by God | % 20.4 | 29.9 | 20.6 | 16.8 | 6.1 | 4.1 | 2.1 |
| [SLFGMEAN] f. Life is only meaningful if you provide the meaning yourself | % 12.9 | 37.4 | 13.8 | 19.0 | 7.1 | 7.0 | 2.8 |
| [OWNFATE] g. We each make our own fate | % 11.6 | 35.9 | 19.4 | 19.6 | 6.0 | 4.5 | 3.0 |

2.20 [WITHDEAD, CLSSPRIT]
How often have you felt as though you were ...

PLEASE TICK **ONE** BOX ON EACH LINE

| | Never in my life | Once or twice | Several times | Often | Can't say | (NA) |
|---|---|---|---|---|---|---|
| a. Really in touch with someone who had died? | % 73.9 | 10.3 | 2.8 | 1.0 | 11.2 | 0.7 |
| b. Close to a powerful, spiritual force that seemed to lift you out of yourself? | % 65.5 | 11.3 | 7.3 | 2.2 | 12.2 | 1.5 |

---

7

NI

2.17 Do you believe in ...

PLEASE TICK **ONE** BOX ON EACH LINE

n = 848

| | Yes, definitely | Yes, probably | No, probably not | No, definitely not | Can't choose | (NA) |
|---|---|---|---|---|---|---|
| [AFTRLIFE] a. Life after death? | % 48.2 | 20.3 | 10.1 | 9.4 | 9.4 | 2.6 |
| [THEDEVIL] b. The Devil? | % 38.9 | 23.7 | 11.1 | 17.0 | 6.0 | 3.4 |
| [HEAVEN] c. Heaven? | % 59.5 | 25.2 | 4.6 | 4.6 | 4.7 | 1.4 |
| [HELL] d. Hell? | % 48.3 | 23.8 | 11.6 | 11.3 | 6.9 | 3.1 |
| [RELGMIRC] e. Religious miracles? | % 39.9 | 27.8 | 11.8 | 8.9 | 9.4 | 2.2 |

2.18 [BIBLFEEL]
Which one of these statements comes closest to describing your feelings about the Bible?

PLEASE TICK **ONE** BOX ONLY

| | % |
|---|---|
| The Bible is the actual word of God and it is to be taken literally, word for word | 30.9 |
| The Bible is the inspired word of God but not everything should be taken literally, word for word | 45.5 |
| The Bible is an ancient book of fables, legends, history and moral teachings recorded by man | 15.9 |
| This does not apply to me | 1.8 |
| Can't choose | 5.2 |
| (NA) | 0.8 |

*Please continue ...*

9

NI

**[RELGCOMM]**
2.21 Has there ever been a turning point in your life when you made a new and personal commitment to religion?

*PLEASE TICK ONE BOX ONLY*

n = 848

|  | % |
|---|---|
| Yes | 28.6 |
| No | 70.0 |
| (NA) | 1.4 |

**[MUMRELIG]**
2.22 What was your mother's religion, if any, when you were a child?

*PLEASE TICK ONE BOX ONLY*

|  | % |
|---|---|
| No religion | 0.3 |
| Christian - no denomination | 1.6 |
| Roman Catholic | 35.9 |
| Church of Ireland/Anglican | 22.4 |
| Baptist | 0.6 |
| Methodist | 4.4 |
| Presbyterian | 28.7 |
| Free Presbyterian | 0.2 |
| Brethren | 1.8 |
| Other Protestant *(PLEASE WRITE IN WHICH)* | 1.3 |
| Other Christian *(PLEASE WRITE IN WHICH)* | - |
| Hindu | - |
| Jewish | - |
| Muslim | 0.2 |
| Sikh | 0.1 |
| Buddhist | 0.1 |
| Other non-Christian *(PLEASE WRITE IN WHICH)* | 0.1 |
| Never knew mother/does not apply | 0.1 |
| Can't say/can't remember | 1.2 |
| (NA) | 0.9 |

*Please continue ...*

---

10

NI

**[DADRELIG]**
2.23 What was your father's religion, if any, when you were a child?

*PLEASE TICK ONE BOX ONLY*

n = 848

|  | % |
|---|---|
| No religion | 1.8 |
| Christian - no denomination | 1.2 |
| Roman Catholic | 35.2 |
| Church of Ireland/Anglican | 24.0 |
| Baptist | 0.5 |
| Methodist | 4.7 |
| Presbyterian | 25.9 |
| Free Presbyterian | 0.1 |
| Brethren | 2.0 |
| Other Protestant *(PLEASE WRITE IN WHICH)* | 0.8 |
| Other Christian *(PLEASE WRITE IN WHICH)* | - |
| Hindu | - |
| Jewish | - |
| Muslim | 0.2 |
| Sikh | 0.1 |
| Buddhist | 0.2 |
| Other non-Christian *(PLEASE WRITE IN WHICH)* | - |
| Never knew father/does not apply | 1.1 |
| Can't say/can't remember | 1.5 |
| (NA) | 0.8 |

12

NI
n = 848
Q. 2.25 - 2.50

[MUMATTCH]
EVERYONE PLEASE ANSWER REST OF QUESTIONNAIRE

2.25 When you were a child, how often did your mother attend religious services?

PLEASE TICK ONE BOX ONLY

|  | % |
|---|---|
| Never | 4.4 |
| Less than once a year | 2.1 |
| About once or twice a year | 4.4 |
| Several times a year | 8.4 |
| About once a month | 3.6 |
| 2-3 times a month | 4.1 |
| Nearly every week | 17.0 |
| Every week | 36.4 |
| Several times a week | 11.4 |
| Never knew mother/does not apply | 0.3 |
| Can't say/can't remember | 5.9 |
| (NA) | 1.9 |

[DADATTCH]
2.26 When you were a child, how often did your father attend religious services?

PLEASE TICK ONE BOX ONLY

|  | % |
|---|---|
| Never | 8.7 |
| Less than once a year | 3.8 |
| About once or twice a year | 6.1 |
| Several times a year | 10.3 |
| About once a month | 4.7 |
| 2-3 times a month | 4.9 |
| Nearly every week | 11.0 |
| Every week | 34.5 |
| Several times a week | 7.3 |
| Never knew father/does not apply | 1.7 |
| Can't say/can't remember | 6.4 |
| (NA) | 0.5 |

11

NI
n = 562
Q. 2.24 only

[PRTNRRLG]
IF YOU ARE CURRENTLY MARRIED OR LIVING AS MARRIED, PLEASE ANSWER Q2.24

IF YOU ARE NOT CURRENTLY MARRIED OR LIVING AS MARRIED, PLEASE GO TO Q2.25

2.24 What is your husband's/wife's/partner's religion, if any?

PLEASE TICK ONE BOX ONLY

|  | % |
|---|---|
| No religion | 2.1 |
| Christian - no denomination | 2.3 |
| Roman Catholic | 33.5 |
| Church of Ireland/Anglican | 18.7 |
| Baptist | 1.8 |
| Methodist | 4.1 |
| Presbyterian | 31.5 |
| Free Presbyterian | 0.9 |
| Brethren | 0.7 |
| Other Protestant (PLEASE WRITE IN WHICH) | - |
| Other Christian (PLEASE WRITE IN WHICH) | - |
| Hindu | - |
| Jewish | - |
| Muslim | 0.2 |
| Sikh | 0.2 |
| Buddhist | - |
| Other non-Christian (PLEASE WRITE IN WHICH) | - |
| Can't say | 0.2 |
| (NA) | 1.9 |

Please continue ...

13

NI

**2.27** [R11ATTCH]
And what about when you were around 11 or 12, how often did you attend religious services then?

PLEASE TICK *ONE* BOX ONLY

n = 848

|  | % |
|---|---|
| Never | 1.9 |
| Less than once a year | 0.9 |
| About once or twice a year | 1.1 |
| Several times a year | 2.7 |
| About once a month | 1.5 |
| 2-3 times a month | 3.5 |
| Nearly every week | 23.3 |
| Every week | 49.7 |
| Several times a week | 13.1 |
| Can't say/can't remember | 1.8 |
| (NA) | 0.6 |

**2.28** [PRAYFREQ]
Now thinking about the present ...
About how often do you pray?

PLEASE TICK *ONE* BOX ONLY

|  | % |
|---|---|
| Never | 10.0 |
| Less than once a year | 1.5 |
| About once or twice a year | 2.7 |
| Several times a year | 7.7 |
| About once a month | 2.7 |
| 2-3 times a month | 4.5 |
| Nearly every week | 5.8 |
| Every week | 10.7 |
| Several times a week | 11.0 |
| Once a day | 26.8 |
| Several times a day | 15.6 |
| (NA) | 1.0 |

Please continue ...

14

NI

**2.29** [CHRCHACT]
How often do you take part in the activities or organisations of a church or place of worship, other than attending services?

PLEASE TICK *ONE* BOX ONLY

n = 848

|  | % |
|---|---|
| Never | 42.5 |
| Less than once a year | 7.6 |
| About once or twice a year | 10.1 |
| Several times a year | 11.3 |
| About once a month | 5.6 |
| 2-3 times a month | 4.4 |
| Nearly every week | 5.6 |
| Every week | 8.7 |
| Several times a week | 3.6 |
| (NA) | 0.7 |

**2.30** [RELIGIUS]
Would you describe yourself as ...

PLEASE TICK *ONE* BOX ONLY

|  | % |
|---|---|
| Extremely religious | 2.5 |
| Very religious | 11.0 |
| Somewhat religious | 52.7 |
| Neither religious nor non-religious | 20.1 |
| Somewhat non-religious | 6.8 |
| Very non-religious | 1.9 |
| Extremely non-religious | 2.6 |
| Can't choose | 1.6 |
| (NA) | 0.7 |

**2.31** [SCHPRAYR]
In your opinion, should there be daily prayers in all state schools?

PLEASE TICK *ONE* BOX ONLY

|  | % |
|---|---|
| Yes, definitely | 53.6 |
| Yes, probably | 27.4 |
| No, probably not | 7.3 |
| No, definitely not | 4.5 |
| Can't choose | 6.8 |
| (NA) | 0.4 |

16

NI

**2.35** [SCCHATTN]
Now thinking about the present.
How often do you attend religious services?

*PLEASE TICK ONE BOX*

n = 848

| | % |
|---|---|
| Never | 12.9 |
| Less than once a year | 4.8 |
| About once or twice a year | 8.8 |
| Several times a year | 9.3 |
| About once a month | 5.5 |
| 2-3 times a month | 5.6 |
| Nearly every week | 11.4 |
| Every week | 33.8 |
| Several times a week | 7.6 |
| (NA) | 0.4 |

**2.36** Now please think about something different.
Please tick one box on each line below to show whether you think each statement is true or false.

*PLEASE TICK ONE BOX ON EACH LINE*

| | Definitely true | Probably true | Probably not true | Definitely not true | Can't choose | (NA) |
|---|---|---|---|---|---|---|
| [CHARMS] a. Good luck charms sometimes do bring good luck | % 2.7 | 17.7 | 30.5 | 41.7 | 6.1 | 1.3 |
| [SEERS] b. Some fortune tellers really can foresee the future | % 3.9 | 26.9 | 26.7 | 34.0 | 7.2 | 1.3 |
| [FAITHHLR] c. Some faith healers really do have God-given healing powers | % 18.5 | 43.7 | 16.0 | 12.3 | 8.6 | 0.9 |
| [ASTROLGY] d. A person's star sign at birth, or horoscope, can affect the course of their future | % 1.8 | 14.7 | 30.7 | 42.8 | 8.9 | 1.1 |

15

NI

**2.32** How much do you agree or disagree with each of the following statements?

*PLEASE TICK ONE BOX ON EACH LINE*

n = 848

| | Strongly agree | Agree | Neither agree nor disagree | Disagree | Strongly disagree | Can't choose | (NA) |
|---|---|---|---|---|---|---|---|
| [GODRIGHT] a. Right and wrong should be based on God's laws | % 29.0 | 36.0 | 15.7 | 9.7 | 2.4 | 4.9 | 2.2 |
| [SOCRIGHT] b. Right and wrong should be decided by society | % 7.6 | 32.7 | 19.0 | 25.5 | 5.6 | 5.7 | 3.9 |
| [OWNRIGHT] c. Right and wrong should be a matter of personal conscience | % 15.2 | 39.6 | 13.9 | 16.7 | 6.4 | 5.5 | 2.7 |

**2.33** [BANBLASF]
Some books or films offend people who have strong religious beliefs. Should books and films that attack religions be prohibited by law or should they be allowed?

*PLEASE TICK ONE BOX ONLY*

| | % |
|---|---|
| Definitely should be prohibited | 22.5 |
| Probably should be prohibited | 24.6 |
| Probably should be allowed | 27.2 |
| Definitely should be allowed | 13.0 |
| Can't choose | 11.5 |
| (NA) | 1.1 |

**2.34** [BORNAGIN]
Would you say that you have been "born again" or have had a "born again" experience - that is, a turning point in your life when you committed yourself to Christ?

*PLEASE TICK ONE BOX*

| | % |
|---|---|
| Yes | 18.1 |
| No | 65.5 |
| This does not apply to me | 14.9 |
| (NA) | 1.5 |

*Please continue ...*

17

NI

2.37 Please tick one box for each statement below to show how much you agree or disagree with it.
PLEASE TICK ONE BOX ON EACH LINE

n = 848

| | Agree strongly | Just agree | Neither agree nor disagree | Just disagree | Disagree strongly | (NA) |
|---|---|---|---|---|---|---|
| a. [EXERCISE] As long as you take enough exercise you can eat what-ever foods you want | % 7.2 | 22.4 | 18.9 | 30.9 | 19.8 | 0.8 |
| b. [HEARTDIS] If heart disease is in your family, there is little you can do to reduce your chances of getting it | % 5.6 | 15.4 | 15.0 | 32.4 | 30.4 | 1.2 |
| c. [FOODEXPT] The experts contradict each other over what makes a healthy diet | % 28.1 | 38.4 | 19.9 | 8.7 | 3.4 | 1.5 |
| d. [WEIGHT] People worry too much about their weight | % 24.8 | 40.1 | 14.2 | 14.6 | 4.9 | 1.4 |
| e. [HLTHLUCK] Good health is just a matter of good luck | % 6.2 | 8.2 | 14.5 | 30.1 | 39.9 | 1.1 |

Please continue ...

18

NI

2.38 [PROTRCMX] Some people think that better relations between Protestants and Catholics in Northern Ireland will only come about through more mixing of the two communities. Others think that better relations will only come about through more separation. Which comes closest to your views ...
PLEASE TICK ONE BOX

n = 848

%

Better relations will come about through more **mixing**    91.8

Better relations will come about through more **separation**    5.9

(Don't know)    1.4

(NA)    1.0

2.39 And are you in favour of more mixing or more separation in ...
PLEASE TICK ONE BOX ON EACH LINE

| | Much more mixing | Bit more mixing | Keep things as they are | Bit more separation | Much more separation | (DK) | (NA) |
|---|---|---|---|---|---|---|---|
| a. [MIXDPRIM] ...primary schools? | % 43.8 | 26.9 | 25.0 | 1.0 | 1.5 | 0.2 | 1.5 |
| b. [MIXDGRAM] ...secondary and grammar schools? | % 45.3 | 29.3 | 21.2 | 0.7 | 1.5 | 0.1 | 1.9 |
| c. [MIXDLIV] ...where people live? | % 38.4 | 38.1 | 19.6 | 1.3 | 0.8 | - | 1.8 |
| d. [MIXDWORK] ...where people work? | % 45.6 | 38.9 | 12.4 | 0.6 | 0.7 | - | 1.9 |
| e. [MIXDLEIS] ..people's leisure or sports activities? | % 52.0 | 33.3 | 11.8 | 0.8 | 0.4 | - | 1.8 |
| f. [MIXDMARR] ...people's marriages? | % 24.1 | 22.2 | 38.9 | 4.8 | 7.0 | 0.4 | 2.6 |

19

NI

2.40 People feel closer to some groups than to others. **For you personally,** how close would you say you feel towards ...

PLEASE TICK **ONE** BOX ON EACH LINE

n = 848

| | | Very close | Fairly close | A little close | Not very close | Not at all close | (NA) |
|---|---|---|---|---|---|---|---|
| [CLSEBORN] | | | | | | | |
| a. | People born in the same area as you | % 14.3 | 44.6 | 22.1 | 11.8 | 5.1 | 2.2 |
| [CLSECLAS] | | | | | | | |
| b. | People who have the same social class background as yours | % 10.7 | 53.4 | 23.2 | 8.4 | 2.4 | 1.9 |
| [CLSERELG] | | | | | | | |
| c. | People who have the same religious background as yours | % 15.4 | 46.9 | 23.5 | 9.7 | 2.6 | 1.9 |
| [CLSERACE] | | | | | | | |
| d. | People of the same race as you | % 14.7 | 46.1 | 25.0 | 7.4 | 3.5 | 3.2 |
| [CLSELIVE] | | | | | | | |
| e. | People who live in the same area as you do now | % 12.0 | 43.6 | 26.4 | 12.4 | 3.2 | 2.4 |
| [CLSEPOL] | | | | | | | |
| f. | People who have the same political beliefs as you | % 9.6 | 36.8 | 26.8 | 16.9 | 6.4 | 3.5 |

2.41 Please tick one box for **each** statement below to show how much you agree or disagree with it.

PLEASE TICK **ONE** BOX ON EACH LINE

| | | Agree strongly | Just Agree | Neither agree nor Disagree | Just Disagree | Disagree strongly | (DK/NA) |
|---|---|---|---|---|---|---|---|
| [PEACFLNI] | | | | | | | |
| a. | Northern Ireland is a much more peaceful place than people living in Britain think | % 54.9 | 32.8 | 6.4 | 2.1 | 2.4 | 1.3 |
| [PCARMYOF] | | | | | | | |
| b. | When the police or the army commit an offence in Northern Ireland, they usually get away with it. | % 18.4 | 15.6 | 21.8 | 18.7 | 23.9 | 1.6 |
| [RCINRUC] | | | | | | | |
| c. | It would be better for Northern Ireland if there were more Catholics in the RUC | % 32.9 | 27.0 | 25.5 | 7.0 | 5.7 | 1.8 |

*Please continue ...*

20

NI

[DSBNDUDR]

2.42 Some people say that the Ulster Defence Regiment - the UDR - should be disbanded. Others say it is necessary.

Which comes closest to your views?

PLEASE TICK **ONE** BOX ONLY

n = 848

| | % |
|---|---|
| The UDR definitely should be disbanded | 17.6 |
| The UDR probably should be disbanded | 12.3 |
| The UDR probably should **not** be disbanded | 19.9 |
| The UDR definitely should **not** be disbanded | 35.1 |
| OR It doesn't matter either way | 13.4 |
| (Don't know) | 0.2 |
| (NA) | 1.5 |

[FEMJOBOP]

2.43 Would you say that job opportunities for women are, in general, better or worse than job opportunities for men with similar education and experience?

PLEASE TICK **ONE** BOX

| | % |
|---|---|
| Much better for women | 2.7 |
| Better for women | 2.8 |
| No difference | 30.3 |
| Worse for women | 49.1 |
| Much worse for women | 7.8 |
| Can't choose | 6.4 |
| (NA) | 0.8 |

21

NI

[FEMINC]
2.44 And how about income and wages: compared with men who have similar education and jobs – are women, in general paid better or worse than men?

n = 848

PLEASE TICK ONE BOX

%

| | |
|---|---|
| Women are paid much better | 0.5 |
| Women are paid better | 0.5 |
| No difference | 26.7 |
| Women are paid worse | 57.2 |
| Women are paid much worse | 5.8 |
| Can't choose | 8.5 |
| (NA) | 1.0 |

2.45 For each of the jobs below, please tick a box to show whether you think the job is particularly suitable for men only, particularly suitable for women only, or suitable for both men and women equally.

PLEASE TICK ONE BOX ON EACH LINE

| | Particularly suitable for men | Particularly suitable for women | Suitable for both equally | (NA) |
|---|---|---|---|---|
| [JOBMF1] Social worker | % 0.7 | 19.9 | 78.4 | 1.0 |
| [JOBMF2] Police officer | % 37.5 | 0.6 | 60.1 | 1.8 |
| [JOBMF3] Secretary | % 0.5 | 54.4 | 43.9 | 1.2 |
| [JOBMF4] Car mechanic | % 69.6 | 0.9 | 28.4 | 1.2 |
| [JOBMF5] Nurse | % 0.3 | 36.9 | 61.5 | 1.3 |
| [JOBMF8] Bank manager | % 26.8 | 0.7 | 71.2 | 1.2 |
| [JOBMF9] Family doctor/GP | % 7.6 | 1.8 | 89.7 | 1.0 |
| [JOBMF11] Member of Parliament | % 14.5 | 1.4 | 82.8 | 1.3 |
| [JOBMF12] Director of an international company | % 28.1 | 0.1 | 70.5 | 1.4 |

Please continue ...

22

NI

2.46 Please tick one box for each statement below to show how much you agree or disagree with it.

n = 848

PLEASE TICK ONE BOX ON EACH LINE

| | Strongly agree | Agree | Neither agree nor disagree | Disagree | Strongly disagree | Can't choose | (NA) |
|---|---|---|---|---|---|---|---|
| a. [WWHAPPIR] A woman and her family will all be happier if she goes out to work | % 1.9 | 11.5 | 43.8 | 30.9 | 5.8 | 5.2 | 1.0 |
| b. [WOMKKID] Women shouldn't try to combine a career and children | % 4.9 | 23.2 | 19.6 | 39.4 | 8.1 | 3.8 | 1.0 |
| c. [FEMHOME] In times of high unemployment married women should stay at home | % 6.1 | 16.0 | 16.2 | 47.0 | 10.6 | 3.4 | 0.7 |
| d. [WANTHOME] A job is all right, but what most women really want is a home and children | % 6.6 | 27.4 | 17.0 | 34.8 | 10.2 | 3.4 | 0.6 |
| e. [WOMWKGD] If the children are well looked after, it's good for a woman to work | % 13.0 | 55.6 | 15.9 | 10.5 | 2.0 | 2.2 | 0.9 |
| f. [MWEXTRAS] Most married women work only to earn money for extras, rather than because they need extra money | % 6.5 | 28.6 | 14.4 | 39.4 | 7.8 | 2.4 | 0.9 |
| g. [WOMSUFFR] If a woman takes several years off to look after her children it's only fair her career should suffer | % 3.6 | 19.4 | 15.1 | 46.5 | 10.6 | 3.9 | 0.8 |
| h. [WOMRIGHT] Married women have a right to work if they want to, whatever their family situation | % 17.4 | 54.1 | 11.9 | 12.6 | 1.5 | 1.8 | 0.7 |
| i. [FEMJOB] Having a job is the best way for a woman to be an independent person | % 14.2 | 51.6 | 16.6 | 13.8 | 0.9 | 2.0 | 0.9 |
| j. [WWCHDSUF] A pre-school child is likely to suffer if his or her mother works | % 10.9 | 30.4 | 18.6 | 31.9 | 5.2 | 2.3 | 0.7 |

24

NI

2.49 Please tick **one** box for each statement below to show how much you agree or disagree with it.

PLEASE TICK **ONE** BOX ON EACH LINE

n = 848

| | Agree strongly | Agree | Neither agree nor Disagree | Disagree | Disagree strongly | (DK/NA) |
|---|---|---|---|---|---|---|
| a. [REDISTRB] Government should redistribute income from the better-off to those who are less well off | % 19.4 | 35.7 | 20.8 | 20.5 | 2.2 | 1.5 |
| b. [TRADVALS] Young people today don't have enough respect for traditional values | % 20.5 | 49.4 | 17.6 | 11.1 | 0.8 | 0.7 |
| c. [STIFSENT] People who break the law should be given stiffer sentences | % 29.6 | 48.0 | 14.9 | 6.1 | 0.6 | 0.7 |
| d. [BIGBUSNN] Big business benefits owners at the expense of workers | % 15.8 | 41.7 | 24.6 | 14.9 | 1.1 | 1.9 |
| e. [DEATHAPP] For some crimes, the death penalty is the most appropriate sentence | % 21.6 | 27.7 | 12.4 | 24.9 | 12.6 | 0.9 |
| f. [WEALTH] Ordinary working people do not get their fair share of the nation's wealth | % 18.4 | 52.7 | 17.9 | 8.9 | 0.7 | 1.4 |
| g. [OBEY] Schools should teach children to obey authority | % 30.5 | 52.7 | 11.7 | 4.3 | 0.2 | 0.6 |
| h. [RICHLAW] There is one law for the rich and one for the poor | % 18.9 | 38.5 | 21.6 | 17.6 | 2.7 | 0.7 |
| i. [INDUST4] Management will always try to get the better of employees if it gets the chance | % 19.2 | 45.0 | 17.7 | 16.4 | 0.7 | 1.0 |
| j. [WRONGLAW] The law should always be obeyed, even if a particular law is wrong | % 8.1 | 32.6 | 23.5 | 27.9 | 6.5 | 1.3 |
| k. [CENSOR] Censorship of films and magazines is necessary to uphold moral standards | % 24.1 | 41.5 | 18.0 | 12.4 | 3.0 | 1.0 |

23

NI

2.47 [WWCHLD1 - WWCHLD4] Do you think that women should work outside the home full-time, part-time or not at all under these circumstances?

PLEASE TICK **ONE** BOX ON EACH LINE

n = 848

| | Work full-time | Work part-time | Stay at home | Can't choose | (NA) |
|---|---|---|---|---|---|
| a. After marrying and before there are children? | % 84.4 | 7.4 | 2.3 | 5.0 | 0.9 |
| b. When there is a child under school age? | % 8.2 | 35.8 | 49.5 | 5.5 | 1.0 |
| c. After the youngest child starts school? | % 26.0 | 59.9 | 7.4 | 5.6 | 1.1 |
| d. After the children leave home? | % 73.8 | 16.0 | 1.6 | 7.5 | 1.1 |

2.48 Please tick **one** box for each statement to show how much you agree or disagree.

PLEASE TICK **ONE** BOX ON EACH LINE

| | Agree strongly | Agree | Neither agree nor disagree | Disagree | Disagree strongly | Can't choose | (NA) |
|---|---|---|---|---|---|---|---|
| a. [CHARRFSE] I can't refuse when someone comes to the door with a collecting tin | % 15.6 | 48.0 | 10.3 | 20.2 | 3.7 | 1.5 | 0.6 |
| b. [CHARRELY] People should look after themselves and not rely on charities | % 6.3 | 29.6 | 20.0 | 36.0 | 5.6 | 1.6 | 0.8 |
| c. [CHARRESP] It is not everyone's responsibility to give what they can to charities | % 4.7 | 42.0 | 20.2 | 25.6 | 4.0 | 2.1 | 1.4 |
| d. [CHARMANY] There are so many charities that it is difficult to decide which to give to | % 15.9 | 62.7 | 10.1 | 7.7 | 1.4 | 1.3 | 0.9 |
| e. [CHARBRIT] We should support more charities which benefit people in the UK, rather than people overseas | % 13.1 | 33.2 | 16.3 | 29.9 | 4.1 | 2.4 | 1.0 |
| f. [CHARWAST] Most charities are wasteful in their use of funds | % 8.4 | 24.7 | 27.4 | 29.1 | 3.4 | 6.3 | 0.9 |
| g. [CHARMORE] The government should do less for the needy and encourage charities to do more instead | % 2.8 | 6.1 | 12.1 | 47.2 | 28.9 | 2.2 | 0.6 |

Please continue...

25

n = 848

NI

[QTIME]
2.50a.  To help us plan better in future, please tell us
        about how long it took you to complete this
        questionnaire? .

PLEASE TICK ONE BOX

|  |  | % |
|---|---|---|
| Less than 15 minutes | | 6.6 |
| Between 15 and 20 minutes | | 27.7 |
| Between 21 and 30 minutes | | 34.5 |
| Between 31 and 45 minutes | | 19.0 |
| Between 46 and 60 minutes | | 6.4 |
| Over one hour | | 4.4 |
| (NA) | | 1.3 |

b.  And on what date did you fill in the questionnaire?

PLEASE WRITE IN

☐☐        ☐☐        1991
DATE      MONTH

## THANK YOU VERY MUCH FOR YOUR HELP

Please keep the completed questionnaire for the interviewer if he or she has
arranged to call for it. Otherwise, please post it as soon as possible in the
pre-paid addressed envelope provided.

# Subject Index

## A

Abortion 124, 127
Acid rain 6, 122, 123, 126
Advance letter experiment 227
Aerosol chemicals,
    buying environmentally friendly 8
    effect on the environment 6
Agnostics, beliefs of 66-68
Aid,
    to Asians and West Indians who
        have settled in this country
        186-187
    *also see* Food aid
AIDS 114, 123-124, 126
Analysis variables, definitions used
    228-231
Animals, use of in tests 8
Army, in Northern Ireland,
    withdrawal of 161-162
Atheists,
    beliefs of 66-68
    fitness for public office 58, 59

## B

Banning anti-religious books 58, 59
Bible, belief in as 'actual' word of God
    51, 55
Blasphemy, laws against 59

*British General Election studies* xiii-xiv
*British Social Attitudes Cumulative*
    *Sourcebook* xiv
Business,
    benefits owners at the expense of
        workers 80
    confidence in 159-160
    power of 133, 134, 149

## C

Carbonfluorochlorides: *see* Ozone
    depletion
Cars, and damage to the environment
    9, 22
Central Community Relations Unit
    (CCRU) 155
**Changes in values** 113-129
Charitable donations, types of 197-198
Charities,
    as wasteful 204-205
    number of ways given to 198
    reliance on *versus* self-sufficiency
        202-203
    responsibilities of *versus* government
        195-196, 198-202, 206
    responsibility to give to 203
    support for domestic *versus* overseas
        205
    *also see* 195-208 *passim*